Teaching Mildly and Moderately Handicapped Students

Bill R. Gearheart
University of Northern Colorado

James A. DeRuiter
University of Northern Colorado

Thomas W. Sileo
University of Alaska, Anchorage

Prentice-Hall, Inc., Englewood Cliffs, New Jersey 07632

Library of Congres Cataloging-in-Publication Data

Gearheart, Bill R. (Bill Ray) (Date)
   Teaching Mildly and Moderately Handicapped Students.

   Bibliography: p.
   Includes index.
   1. Handicapped children—Education.   2. Handicapped
children—Education—Curricula.   I. De Ruiter, James A.
II. Silio, Thomas W. (Date).   III. Title.
LC 4015.G398 1986   371.9   85-16900
ISBN 0-13-893900-4

Editorial/production supervision: Anthony Keating and Joseph O'Donnell
Cover design: Wanda Lubelska
Manufacturing buyer: Barbara Kelly Kittle

Printed in the United States of America

10 9 8 7 6 5 4 3 2 1

ISBN 0-13-893900-4   01

PRENTICE-HALL INTERNATIONAL (UK) LIMITED, *London*
PRENTICE-HALL OF AUSTRALIA PTY. LIMITED, *Sydney*
PRENTICE-HALL CANADA INC., *Toronto*
PRENTICE-HALL HISPANOAMERICANA, S.A., *Mexico*
PRENTICE-HALL OF INDIA PRIVATE LIMITED, *New Delhi*
PRENTICE-HALL OF JAPAN, INC., *Tokyo*
PRENTICE-HALL OF SOUTHEAST ASIA PTE. LTD., *Singapore*
EDITORA PRENTICE-HALL DO BRASIL, LTDA., *Rio de Janeiro*
WHITEHALL BOOKS LIMITED, *Wellington, New Zealand*

Contents

Preface

This volume was conceived and written in response to an apparent need for a basic methods book for teachers of children identified traditionally as having learning disabilities, behavior disorders, and/or below-average intellectual ability. Its primary focus is on methods and techniques—a "how-to" emphasis; however, many years in the field of special education have taught us that "how-to" by itself is not enough. For methods and techniques to be successful, we must determine *what* to teach, and we must know *why* we are teaching. This principle is especially important when we are dealing with children for whom the learning process is not proceeding smoothly and normally. Thus, we have developed a "how-to" book, with careful consideration of both "what" and "why."

This is not a non-categorical text, for we do not reject the reality of certain deviations from normal learning behavior and/or ability that have commonly recognized "labels." We have already mentioned learning disabilities, behavior disorders, and below-average intellectual ability, thereby recognizing the existence of these types of handicaps or disabilities. This *is* a *cross-categorical* text in the sense that we have presented methods and techniques that are appropriate for students to whom any of these three labels might apply. Most of these methods are applicable across all three areas of disability for both mildly and moderately handicapped students, and in some cases (with appropriate modifications), they may even apply to the more severely handicapped or disabled. *However, in all cases, we must remember to look beyond the actual methods and techniques and ask ourselves why we are teaching whatever it is that we are teaching.* Our goals and objectives must be clear, or we may make very poor use of valuable instruction time.

Traditionally, programs for mildly and moderately handicapped students have been implemented from an empiricist paradigm that provides the basis for a psychometrically oriented view of learning. This approach presumes an atomistic, sequential learning process in which the learner builds knowledge by adding new information to old in building-block fashion. From this perspective, learning depends upon the presentation of information in an appropriate sequence with adequate repetition of the material. Empiricists usually identify problems through formal and informal tests, label the problem or problem behavior, and select curriculum materials and teaching methods that are presumed to be related to the problem. Determination of the theoretical basis for the use of particular methods or materials is nearly impossible. The specific cognitive characteristics of the learner and the nature of learning itself are not used as a primary basis for instruction. The widespread use of the empiricist paradigm in special education has resulted in a large collection of psychometric tests and sequenced curriculum materials. Although these instruments and materials appear logically sound, the theoretical bases are limited when applied to the task of developing teaching methods, for they tend to ignore *how* children learn; they regard learners as essentially passive, and they emphasize a static view of processes such as attention, perception, and memory. These limitations are of particular concern when applied to analysis of—and planning for—students with learning and behavioral disorders.

In contrast, we will address the concept of and need for a constructivist approach to identifying children's educational needs and providing appropriate intervention strategies to meet these needs. From this view, learning is a constructive process based on interaction with the environment. Rather than receiving isolated sequential units of information, the learner constructs whole systems of knowledge in an organic fashion. The nature of learning and development have direct impact upon teaching. Rather than identifying a problem in an abstract way and fitting a student into a curriculum sequence, teaching depends upon direct interactions between a teacher and a student. The teacher's responsibility is to discover the internal mental structures of the students and to set up conditions so that the students can interact with the environment in a way that enables them to construct new knowledge. Historically, educators such as Dewey and Montessori have advocated approaches consistent with this paradigm. The testing and teaching processes, then, are related intimately to each other and help to identify what and how to teach children.

There are many methods texts founded on the empiricist paradigm and related to teaching children on categorical bases. The methods and techniques presented in those texts are consistent with traditional views of learning and are based on the apparent existence of quantitative differences among children. This text is founded on the belief that children exhibit more similarities than they do differences. From this perspective, education programs should be based on children's needs—i.e., qualitative differences in learning—not on their problems as manifested by categories and labels.

Discussion of this text with our colleagues resulted in questions as to whether it would be designed for resource-room teachers, for teacher-consultants, or for self-contained class teachers and whether it was for teachers who had a "mix" of handicapped students (a cross-categorical teaching assignment) or for more traditional categorical programs. They also asked about our concern with constructivist theory, and how "pure" we intended to be (pure, as opposed to pragmatic). Our responses were as follows: (a) the methods presented are those that have worked with students who have been labeled learning disabled, behavior disordered, and mentally handicapped; thus, they should be of value to all of those teachers mentioned by our colleagues, and (b) we plan to attempt to convince the reader of the value of the constructivist point of view, but in presenting time-tested methods, we will present some methods that seem to also be consistent with the empiricists' way of thinking. When it comes to assisting teachers to teach more effectively, we would undoubtedly be called pragmatists.

We will address the question of how an understanding of the principles of metacognition may be of great value in teaching mathematics, reading, and language skills. We will also provide concrete suggestions relating to the use of perceptual cueing strategies and language cueing strategies with disabled or handicapped students. Specific step-by-step examples of learning strategies instruction will be provided. In addition, we will suggest strategies that will assist in the development of social skills and abilities, an important area that is too often overlooked. We will present an overview of behavior management strategies, including a number of practical suggestions for implementing such strategies in the classroom. Though this concept—behaviorism—may be viewed as not entirely consistent with certain of our philosophical beliefs, as pragmatists we feel that behavior management techniques are a must for the teachers for whom this volume was written.

Finally, we will discuss a number of highly practical suggestions designed to assist the teacher in properly organizing for effective instruction. This will include a discussion of controlling and/or manipulating the physical aspects of the classroom and planning and organizing for the teaching/learning process. In our opinion, too many teachers who have developed good instructional techniques have not learned to organize effectively, and thus, their instructional time is used inefficiently.

Our recommendations are based on the conviction that teachers *can* develop the ability to view learning as a dynamic, ongoing process in which students interact with their environment, constructing new systems of knowledge in a very individual manner. Teaching strategies are, then, based on an understanding of this process. This does not mean throwing out all the old ways of teaching, but in most cases, it simply means looking at the teaching/learning process in a different way. We believe it also means more success for students, which is, of course, the only real purpose of special education programs. Our hope is that the years we have spent working with handicapped children and their teachers have permitted us to make this a valuable resource for all who want to know more about what and how to teach the special children for whom they are responsible. This text is dedicated to that goal.

CHAPTER ONE

Historical and Theoretical Perspectives

- How has the definition of mental retardation changed over the past twenty years? What changes in populations served and in type of service have resulted?

- What is meant by the phrase "litigation drives legislation"?

- What major criticisms have been leveled against most present definitions of learning disabilities? How do critics suggest the problem be solved?

- How do traditional learning theorists and developmental learning theorists differ with respect to their recommendations for teachers of students with handicapping conditions?

- How do "capacity deficits" and "strategy deficits" differ?

- What are executive-control strategies? Who, besides executives, needs them?

INTRODUCTION

Education in the public schools across the United States faces many critical issues over the next decade. Of prime importance is the provision of comprehensive educational opportunities to the many diverse student populations who attend our schools. Quality education for handicapped, non-English-speaking, and culturally diverse students must be provided on an equal basis with education for average and typical students. The provision of these services must be accomplished despite limited public understanding and support and the lack of a comprehensive plan for federal assistance to public education.

Federal legislation enacted during the past twenty-five years has provided the major impetus for a restructuring of public education, based on a philosophy that recognizes the dignity and worth of individual students. This change dictates the protection of individual rights and privileges and recognizes that individual differences among students are assets that contribute to societal progress and prosperity. The schools, then, must educate all students and have an ongoing commitment to the successful development of the cognitive, affective, communicative, and physical skills necessary to enable them to cope with and function within society.

The educational system attempts to provide equal educational opportunities to diverse student populations through specialized education services, thereby meeting the letter of federal and state legislation. Legislation provides direction to education as an avenue for attaining minimal standards of quality and guaranteeing appropriate educational opportunities for handicapped students. The law itself, however, does not assure significant change in the public schools nor does it promote ownership of the problems and solutions that come with change. Improvement in the quality of educational services to America's diverse school population necessitates internalization of the intent of the law. Meaningful and lasting change will not occur without internal acceptance and understanding of those values upon which legislation is predicated.

Historically, public schools attempted to serve the needs of diverse populations through programs that provided separate but equal educational opportunities. This led to the categorization and segregation of handicapped students and students with racial and ethnic differences into separate schools and self-contained classrooms. Categorical approaches to programming for the handicapped were based on norm-referenced eligibility tests, which purported to identify distinct groups of students. Such approaches, however, did not withstand the weight of litigation, especially in relation to the culturally diverse students who were too often identified inaccurately as handicapped.

Resulting civil-rights legislation challenged traditional educational structures; public schools have been desegregated legally and now must attempt to accommodate racially and culturally diverse children. Public law 94-142 served as a strong catalyst for a decentralized movement in programs for the handicapped. Handicapped children moved from more restrictive settings within the continuum of educational services, and most are now educated in less restrictive classroom settings with their nonhandi-capped peers. There is a general thrust toward dealing with handicapped children in regular classroom and building settings rather than in cen-tralized programs. The resource room as a service-delivery model is the primary vehicle through which mildly and moderately handicapped chil-dren are educated in the regular classroom while still benefiting from the specialized services of a special educator. The focus of this chapter is on the historical and theoretical perspectives related to a cross-categorical frame-work for the delivery of special education services to students identified as mentally retarded, emotionally disturbed, or learning disabled.

HISTORICAL PERSPECTIVE

Early special education efforts for the mentally retarded, the emotionally disturbed, and the learning disabled were founded in attempts to divide students into different categories based on the presence of common char-acteristics. The primary goal for categorical programs was identification of subsets of students with specific learning and behavioral characteristics and the development of appropriate educational programs to serve their needs. Special educators worked on the assumption that students identified as mentally retarded, emotionally disturbed, or learning disabled were differ-ent from each other and from other students who were not successful in school. As a result, special educators established classification systems to determine students' eligibility for special education services. The classifica-tion systems were based on inclusionary and exclusionary principles upon which definitions were written. The definitions specified characteristics to be used as a means for identifying students based on the extent to which the students exhibited those characteristics. Our discussion of the historical perspective focuses on the evolution of cross-categorical special education services for each of the populations addressed in this text.

Mental Retardation

Special education services for students identified as educable mentally retarded (EMR) have undergone a major transformation in the last decade. These changes may be attributed to definitional changes, a concomitant shift in the EMR population from mild to moderately handicapped, recog-nition of the severely handicapped as a distinct program area, and the emergence of learning disabilities as a separate categorical program.

Students who were once classified as educable mentally retarded may no longer meet the criteria for identification given in national, state, and local definitions. Changes in the definition of mental retardation offered by the American Association on Mental Deficiency (AAMD) have lowered the ceiling of derived intelligence quotients from one to two standard de-viations below the mean, as an approximate guideline (subject to profes-sional judgment) for classifying students as mentally retarded. It would appear that the EMR category is reserved currently for students with earned intelligence quotients of less than 65–69 (depending on geographical location). In addition, the current definition of mental retardation includes adaptive behavior as a primary consideration for identification purposes. This two-pronged definition, which includes both intellectual and adaptive behavior components, has decreased the potential number of individuals who can be identified as mentally retarded. The AAMD definition states that mental retardation refers to "significantly subaverage general intellectual functioning existing concurrently with deficits in adaptive behavior, and manifested during the developmental period" (Grossman 1973, 1977). Federal guidelines are similar to the AAMD definition and add that "mental retardation . . . adversely affects the child's educational performance" (section 124a.5, *Federal Register,* August 23, 1977). The inclusion of adaptive behavior in the definition of mental retardation has complicated the identification process and has contributed to the decrease in the numbers of students identified as mentally retarded. In addition, Grossman (1983) now specifies that mental retardation is a current life status and is not necessarily chronic or irreversible. It would appear then that mental retardation is placed within a conceptual framework that considers persons' intellectual status as being representative of their behavioral-functioning level at the time of assessment. Controversies over definition in the area of mental retardation have been the basis of litigation that has greatly affected the field of special education and caused a shift in the population once identified as mildly mentally retarded. That is true especially in relation to the placement of children from culturally different groups. Perhaps the two most important cases related to the issue of equal educational opportunities for Mexican American and black children, respectively, were *Diana* v. *State Board of Education* (1970) and *Larry P.* v. *Riles* (1972), both of which occurred in California.

The case of *Diana* v. *State Board of Education* challenged the use of culturally biased and discriminatory testing procedures that led to inappropriate educational placement, inadequate education, and the stigma of mental retardation. The plaintiffs sought compensatory damages and relief from existing identification and placement practices, which were based on use of intelligence scales written in English, standardized on white, native-born American children, and administered to students whose primary language was not English. The plaintiffs argued that use of the tests maintained racial segregation and violated the equal protection clause of the Fourteenth Amendment of the United States Constitution. The case, which was settled out of court, minimized the likelihood of future unfair and inappropriate testing practices and served as the foundation for similar cases. The case of *Larry P.* v. *Riles* (1972) charged inappropriate educational placement and segregation of black children into special classes for the mentally retarded. The plaintiffs charged that testing procedures failed to recognize black students' unfamiliarity with the white middle-class cultural background and ignored black students' limited language aptitude and learning experiences. The plaintiffs also argued that the use of intelligence tests as the sole basis for educational placement violated the equal-protection clause of the Constitution. It was alleged that minority students did not have the same opportunities as other students to demonstrate their true intellectual ability when examiners were unable to understand or to compensate for linguistic and cultural differences.

Larry P v. *Riles* was in the courts for an extended time period. A preliminary injunction, granted in 1972, and affirmed in 1974 by the California District Court, forbade the placement of black students in classes for the mentally retarded soley on the basis of intelligence tests.

The focus of these cases was that educational placement based on discriminatory assessment procedures had a negative effect on students' educational progress. An important result was a decrease nationally in the number of students identified and labeled as educable mentally retarded on the basis of cultural-familial factors. This approach viewed race, ethnicity, inadequate health, and nutritional status as contributing to the labeling or identification of persons as mentally retarded (Patrick and Reschly 1982). The declassification of minority-group students resulted in an overall decrease in the number of students identified as mentally retarded and eligible for special education services. There was an approximate 13 percent decline in the number of mentally retarded students, three to twenty-one years of age, served under the auspices of PL 89-313 and PL 94-142 between the 1976–77 school year and the 1980–81 school year (U.S. Department of Education, Office of Special Education, Data Analysis System 1981). This decrease reflects fundamental changes in the concept of mental retardation, and a major concern today is that some students may be shortchanged and denied an appropriate education. The courts may legislate changes in identification procedures, but students continue to have learning problems with which we must deal. The population no longer eligible for EMR programs has continued need for educational assistance based on identified cognitive, social and emotional, and academic needs beyond the regular classroom setting.

A second contributing factor in the change in composition of the EMR population is the prevention of some cases of mild retardation as a result of early intervention programs for indigent families. Garber and Heber (1981) and Ramey and Haskins (1981) report changes in the intellectual level of children identified as high risk for mental retardation and related school difficulties. The "new" EMR population has increased deficits in intellectual functioning, academic achievement, and oral language development; it is a "more patently disabled group" (MacMillan and Borthwick 1980). In addition, students with concomitant behavior disorders are more likely to be served in programs for emotionally disturbed/behavior-disordered students, and some students identified previously as educable mentally retarded are now served under the learning-disabilities umbrella. Polloway and Smith (1983) indicate concern over whether these students will continue to receive special education services based on recent efforts within the field of learning disabilities to focus on students with more specific learning disabilities to the exclusion of slow learners. Their concern is that these students may be "declassified" again and denied eligibility for special education services. One option perhaps is to label services instead of students, as proposed initially with the field of learning disabilities, and to provide programmatic services designed to meet students' identified needs. Extensive discussion of a needs-based approach may be found in chapter 2.

Emotional Disturbance

Emotional disturbance refers to a broad spectrum of conditions that range from mild and temporary conflict with the environment to severe and profound distress. The term *emotional disturbance* is one of many labels used interchangeably and sometimes in conjunction with *behavior disorders* to signify inappropriate behaviors and accompanying aberrant feelings about oneself and the environment. *Emotional disturbance* is a label that indicates the individual exhibits maladaptive behavior, whereas *behavior disorder* may describe more accurately students' socialization difficulties.

Apter and Conoley (1984) indicate that there are increasing numbers of students in modern society who experience serious emotional difficulties. Incidence figures indicate that emotionally disturbed/behavior disordered students range from 2 to 30 percent of the school-age population. Based on these figures, it may be estimated that from one to fifteen million students experience problems in attempting to cope with the stresses of everyday life and require special education services. Discrepancies in these figures are based on variations in the definition of emotional disturbance, and it would appear that the need for educational programs for emotionally disturbed/behavior disordered students may expand rapidly within the next decade. Educators must be able to assess a situation and intervene where necessary with programs for students with serious emotional and behavior problems. The determination of exact numbers of students who require special educational services related to emotional and behavior problems depends on definitional precision, yet there is very little agreement regarding an accepted definition of emotional disturbance. An official and widely accepted definition such as that offered by the AAMD for mental retardation has not been developed. Definitional problems often relate to the orientation and purposes of the examiner. For example, the same individual may be identified as mentally ill, emotionally disturbed, or behavior disordered by a psychiatrist, psychologist, or special educator, respectively. Complicating factors related to establishment of an appropriate definition include:

1. The lack of valid and reliable instruments that measure personality, adjustment, anxiety, or other relevant psychological constructs to provide a sound basis for definition
2. A variety of conceptual models that include different assumptions about students' behavior and sometimes conflicting suggestions to correct those disorders
3. The range of behaviors from mild to severe and profound exhibited by individuals who also exhibit both behavior deficiencies and excesses
4. The transitory nature of many individual behavior problems
5. The problems associated with labeling students or their behaviors and the

difficulties related to stigmatizing students and thus altering their opportunities for education, employment, and socialization

6. The difficulty in defining behavior disorders in a manner that excludes other handicapping conditions. Behavior disordered children often exhibit characteristics common to other handicapping conditions

It is apparent from these factors why numerous definitions have been offered in an attempt to describe, identify, and assess disturbance among students who have trouble "fitting" into current social-educational systems. However, despite the problems, definitions of emotional disturbance found in federal and state legislation have served as catalysts for the development and implementation of educational services for emotionally disturbed/behavior disordered students. The term *seriously emotionally disturbed* is defined as follows in PL 94-142:

> (i) The term means a condition exhibiting one or more of the following characteristics over a long period of time and to a marked degree, which adversely affects educational performance: (a) an inability to learn which cannot be explained by intellectual, sensory, or health factors; (b) an inability to build or maintain satisfactory interpersonal relationships with peers and teachers; (c) inappropriate types of behavior or feelings under normal circumstances; (d) a general pervasive mood of unhappiness or depression; or (e) a tendency to develop physical symptoms or fears associated with personal or school problems. (ii) The term includes children who are schizophrenic. The term does not include children who are socially maladjusted, unless it is determined that they are seriously emotionally disturbed. [*Federal Register* 42 (1977), 42478, as amended in *Federal Register* 46 (1981), 3866].

The definition provided in PL 94-142 is based on a definition developed by Bower (1969) and Bower and Lambert (1971) in their attempts to describe mild and moderately involved emotionally disturbed children and youths, based on characteristic behaviors exhibited *to a marked degree over a prolonged period of time.* Bower and Lambert described emotional disturbance as the involvement of a youngster in one or more of the following behavior patterns:

1. An inability to learn that cannot be traced to other factors
2. An inability to relate satisfactorily to peers or adults
3. Inappropriate reactions to normal stimuli and events
4. Pervasive unhappiness
5. The development of physical symptoms as a frequent response to stress

The definition offered by PL 94-142 has both advantages and disadvantages in facilitating the identification of emotionally disturbed students as a prerequisite for receiving educational services. This definition, like those for mental retardation and learning disabilities, is an initial step in the identification of students with learning and behavioral problems. The definition has an eclectic orientation that cuts across the various theoretical perspectives (psychodynamic, behavioral, and socioecological) and is at least minimally acceptable to professionals with different conceptual backgrounds. Disadvantages in the current definition of emotional disturbance relate to the lack of specific provisions and criteria for measuring the stated conditions, and the difficulty it presents in setting severity levels as required to make reliable and valid decisions about identification of students and subsequent intervention. In addition, there appears to be some confusion surrounding the exclusion of socially maladjusted students who, by definition, are antisocial and have difficulty relating satisfactorily to their peers and conforming to societal expectations (Apter and Conoley 1984). Grosenick and Huntze (1980) believe it is difficult to separate the socially maladjusted from students identified as emotionally disturbed. Therefore, they suggest the term *behavior disorders* as being more practical and less stigmatizing—an umbrella for behavior problems that range from mild to severe and include socially maladjusted, aggressive, withdrawn, autistic, and schizophrenic children.

The categorical descriptors related to emotional disturbance and behavior disorders have their origins in different theoretical perspectives; descriptors such as "children in conflict" and "maladjusted" also depend on the author's orientation. It would appear that we should abandon discussions related to the appropriateness of specific labels that emphasize reasons behind students' learning difficulties. Instead, our efforts should be focused on meeting students' learning and behavioral needs. Labels are an attempt to "round up" a variety of learning and behavior problems into single categories for administrative convenience. Students' behaviors, however, do not occur in isolation; they occur more often in combinations. Therefore, we should look at students' behavior as an ever-changing manifestation that varies across situations and experiences. Additional discussion on the effects of labeling and the provision of educational services based on students' identified needs is found later in this chapter.

Learning Disabilities

During the past thirty years, a variety of terms and theoretical constructs have been generated to facilitate communication among those concerned with the learning disabilities. Differences in terminology and definition have, for the most part, reflected the theoretical viewpoints of the various disciplines that have an impact on the field of learning disabilities. Physicians, for example, view a student's learning problems from a medical vantage point and attempt to obtain assessment information that might be useful in preventing or reducing causative factors. Educators, on the other hand, require a more functional definition, one that will aid in identifying, managing, and remediating a student's problems through educational intervention and classroom management. In many ways, diverse terminology is healthy; it fosters increased interdisciplinary collaboration and focuses on the need for continued research. The field of learning disabilities has become increasingly more sophisticated since its beginnings, when the primary emphasis was on the effects of brain injury on children's development and learning.

Many early researchers were concerned with the inefficient and inappropriate behaviors of students identified as brain injured. The term *brain injury*, however, was objectionable to parents and teachers. It was later replaced by the term *minimal brain dysfunction* (MBD), which implied a link between brain injury and learning problems. Minimal brain dysfunction focused on students with average or above-average intelligence and included the behavioral manifestations of motor and language disorders. Identification of the disorder was based on the presence of soft neurological signs, which were considered representative of overall learning and behavioral functioning. Soft signs include poor balance, involuntary motor movement, tremor, and general clumsiness; soft signs are erratic and may be affected by the environment.

Minimal brain dysfunction was not accepted widely because it relied on psychological and etiological variables as a basis for identification; and, it did not facilitate appropriate educational intervention. Therefore, the term *learning disabilities* was introduced in the early 1960s to refer to a large student population identified previously as brain injured, as MBD, or as having perceptual disorders; that is, students with learning difficulties who did not fit the other categories but who needed help in acquiring academic skills. In 1968, the National Advisory Committee on Handicapped Children (NACHC) developed a definition of learning disabilities, which was later incorporated into the Learning Disabilities Act of 1969, PL 91-230.

In 1977 the NACHC definition of learning disabilities was modified slightly as it applied to Public Law 94-142. The current federal definition of learning disabilities follows.

> "Specific learning disability" means a disorder in one or more of the basic psychological processes involved in understanding or in using language, spoken or written, which may manifest itself in an imperfect ability to listen, think, speak, read, write, spell, or to do mathematical calculations. The term includes such conditions as perceptual handicaps, brain injury, minimal brain dysfunction, dyslexia, and developmental aphasia. The term does not include children who have learning problems which are primarily the result of visual, hearing, or motor handicaps, of mental retardation, or emotional disturbance, or of environmental, cultural, or economic disadvantage. [USOE 1977, 65083]

The definition includes:

1. A process component that (although it lacks clarity and specific criteria for identification) focuses on perceptual motor, psycholinguistic, and cognitive processes that interfere with the understanding and use of spoken and written language
2. An academic component that includes reading, language arts, and mathematics.
3. A neurological component that considers central nervous system (CNS) dysfunction and infers the probable existence of neurological deficits in learning disabled students.

4. An exclusion component that is included to differentiate the learning disabled from those who have similar symptoms or characteristics but are also mentally retarded or have primary difficulties related to behavior disorders. Most authorities recognize that students who are mentally retarded or emotionally disturbed may have learning problems that would be called learning disabilities if they were not mentally retarded or emotionally disturbed, but this exclusion component was added to establish a new category of handicap for administrative (i.e., funding) purposes.

The learning-disabilities definition has been criticized because it does not indicate how much discrepancy must exist between a student's level of academic achievement and his or her estimated potential. However, some individual states have established "discrepancy formulas." Algozzine and Ysseldyke (1983) believe that there are large numbers of students who are not identified as learning disabled even though they would appear to be eligible, based on current discrepancy schemes.

Dissatisfaction with the current federal definition and efforts to operationalize its various components have led to the emergence of the National Joint Committee for Learning Disabilities (NJCLD), which consists of representatives from six professional organizations.* The NJCLD has developed the following definition:

> Learning disabilities is a generic term that refers to a heterogeneous group of disorders manifested by significant difficulties in the acquisition and use of listening, speaking, reading, writing, reasoning or mathematical abilities. These disorders are intrinsic to the individual and presumed to be due to central nervous system dysfunction. Even though a learning disability may occur concomitantly with other handicapping conditions (e.g., sensory impairment, mental retardation, social and emotional disturbance) or environmental influences (e.g., cultural differences, insufficient/inappropriate instruction, psychogenic factors), it is not the direct result of those conditions or influences. [Hammill, Leigh, McNutt, and Larsen 1981]

Hammill et al. (1981) indicate that the definition is not "etched in stone" and that it may be discarded in the future in light of a newer and a more improved version. The definition recognizes that learning disability is pervasive and that it affects all age levels and handicapping conditions. In addition, it eliminates the term *basic psychological processes* and focuses on learning disorders as being indigenous to the individual.

Despite the criticisms leveled against the definitions of learning disabilities, they served as the foundation for providing educational services to learning disabled students. During the 1960s and 1970s, most educational services for learning disabled students had either a psychological-processing or a behavioral orientation. The psychological-processes approach focused on discrete psychological functions that could be identified, mea-

---

*ASHA (American Speech and Hearing Association), ACALD (Association for Children and Adults with Learning Disabilities), CLD (Council for Learning Disabilities), DCCD (Division for Children with Communication Disorders), IRA (International Reading Association), and the Orton Dyslexia Society.

sured, and trained, as prerequisites for academic and social learning. The behavioral model viewed students' learning difficulties as resulting from unlearned academic and social behaviors that could be defined in observable and measurable terms. Remediation in this model is based on the application of behavioral principles and task analysis.

In the late 1970s there was a rather successful attempt to combine the two seemingly opposite approaches into a unified perspective that focuses on cognitive strategies. Current theoretical perspectives in learning disabilities (and the conceptual foundation upon which this text is predicated) consider most learning and behavior difficulties to be the result of inefficient cognitive and learning strategies. A cognitive approach views learning as an active, internal constructive process in which learners construct meaning from their experiences. It is based on the assumption that effective strategies can be defined, measured, and taught to students through the application of behavioral self-instructional and self-monitoring techniques. This trend toward cognitive approaches is discussed more extensively elsewhere (Reid and Hresko 1981; DeRuiter and Wansart 1982; Mercer 1983; and Sileo 1985), and its application is illustrated throughout this text.

Summary—Historical Perspective

Efforts to provide appropriate educational services to all students have resulted in the creation of separate systems—as implied by labels—which exist as segregated units of a total system. Systems within the public schools include regular and special education as well as special programs such as remedial reading and bilingual/bicultural education, each of which is founded upon different assumptions. The provision of special education services to students who require modified educational programs has become the responsibility of separate units within individual schools and local administrative units. In the past, little effort was made to coordinate the educational endeavors of the various units; and in some instances the services of general, special, and remedial education were in competition with each other, resulting in fractionated services to students. There was little attempt to articulate students' needs and to coordinate the total education process.

Special education often assumed the role of primary service provider in meeting the students' educational needs, with little participation from regular education. Exceptional students were referred for special education services, labeled according to characteristics they exhibited, and placed in self-contained or resource programs. Individualized education programs were then developed according to specific labels, with limited consideration of students' personal, academic, and social needs.

Attempts to identify students who did not progress academically in regular classes were based on a set of common characteristics that were attributed to sensory, motor, physical, cognitive or emotional deficits presumed to be within students. In recent years, special education programs have been based on classification systems founded on federal and state guidelines designed to encourage appropriate educational services to handicapped students. The ability to implement, monitor, enforce, and evaluate program effectiveness has been based historically on classification and identification of students (Clarizo and McCoy 1983). Each state has developed its own definition in an attempt to protect students' rights to equal educational opportunities, as specified by federal legislation. However, there are no precise, universal definitions to facilitate the identification of students as potential candidates for special education services. Craig, Kaskowitz, and Malgoire (1978) indicate a need to refine the classification system to insure better identification of students' educational needs.

Current classification practices in mental retardation, emotional disturbance, and learning disabilities appear to be plagued by both conceptual and practical problems. One solution is to move beyond the concept of categories as the basis for service delivery to programs that focus on students' identified needs. To accomplish this goal, Reynolds and Wang (1981) suggest that the federal government should no longer regulate the classification of handicapped students. Instead, the federal government should focus on innovative program development as a means of ensuring productive learning environments for all students.

CROSS-CATEGORICAL PROGRAMS: AN EMERGING TREND

There is a sizable school-age population that requires special education services to attain personal and academic goals. Reynolds (1979), Marsh, Price, and Smith (1983), and Gearheart and Weishahn (1984) indicate that many of the students categorized historically as educable mentally retarded, emotionally disturbed, and learning disabled may be served successfully in regular classrooms when they receive intensive support services based on their individual needs. As early as the mid-1970s Hallahan and Kauffman (1976, 1977) and Gajar (1979) supported the idea that students so classified exhibit similar behavioral characteristics related to etiology and environmental influences and that often their behavioral characteristics cannot be associated exclusively with any of the three categories. They believe that traditional descriptors are not functional and suggest grouping students according to behavioral characteristics in cross-categorical programs. Heller et al. (1979) state that teaching techniques for the mentally retarded, the emotionally disturbed, and the learning disabled do not differ significantly from each other. Our focus then should be on individual student needs as evidenced in their responses to specific task requirements. Educational programs for the mildly handicapped should reject the narrow focus on academic and remedial concerns in favor of broad-based instruction in personal, social, and vocational development. Educators need to be concerned with teaching students strategies for acquiring academic, social, and vocational skills.

A needs-based perspective allows educators to identify students with special needs and then to alter their learning environments to meet those needs. This approach encourages teachers to determine students' current levels of functioning and to identify their needs in the areas of compensatory training, environmental adaptation, vocational and avocational skills, physical fitness and health, home and school interaction, and transportation. Upon determination of needs, a decision can be made concerning the characteristics of the services needed by students and a program developed to meet those needs. Thus, a program may be developed to meet students' needs as opposed to fitting students to a previously conceived program within a resource or self-contained perspective. The uniqueness of this approach necessitates a shift in emphasis from one in which the student is "placed" into a program to an approach in which an individualized program is developed to meet student needs. Program services may be provided through the collaborative efforts of regular and special educators and coordinated and managed by a special educator who serves as the student's advocate. Extensive discussion of a needs-based perspective is found in chapter 2.

Proponents of a cross-categorical approach to special-education service delivery assert that the labeling process requires review and change. While it is recognized that labeling entitles schools to fiscal and personnel support needed for special services and allows schools to have individualized education programs in a least restrictive environment, they question the necessity of labeling students before help can be provided. A concomitant concern is the stereotyping that accompanies the label and the implications of stereotyped treatment rather than individual and personalized treatment based on a student's needs (Reger 1979).

A cross-categorical approach dictates that students should receive part of their education in the regular program with special educators providing consultant or resource services to a broad range of teachers and students. Such an approach requires a shift in emphasis and extends the primary responsibility for the delivery of special education services to include regular educators as well as special educators.

The wide support for a cross-categorical approach reflects a general reaction to the burgeoning number of special education programs. Recent growth in special education has been in programs for the mildly handicapped who exhibit similar characteristics and academic and social behaviors. There is continued need, however, for a categorical approach for students who are severely and profoundly handicapped, deaf, blind, and speech impaired.

In conclusion, the issue of categorical versus cross-categorical programs must be assessed in light of the incidence of exceptional students in rural and urban areas, economic factors, and differing state certification requirements. Traditionally, certification has been based on the premise that each category requires different materials and teaching methods. In a study of the national trend toward comprehensive/noncategorical teacher certification, Belch (1979) indicated that almost one-half of the states have adopted a program of cross-categorical certification or are considering a change. These results complement the Hebeler and Reynolds (1976) study, which indicated a trend in the 1970s toward a reduced number of categories for special-education teacher certification and toward educational services based on students' identified needs rather than on categories founded on quantitative differences, which may not be accurate. Categorical programs establish professional barriers and often cause regular and special educators to look for differences in students that may be nonexistent. It would appear that special educators should provide comprehensive services based on identified needs without becoming bogged down with categories and assumed differences between categories.

THEORETICAL PERSPECTIVES

Theoretical perspectives related to students' intellectual and social development and learning are found in two divergent schools of thought. Many learning theorists view learning as a product or as a permanent change in behavior due to environmental experience. This approach assumes a mechanistic view of learning in which learners are viewed as passive respondents to their environments. Their behaviors are shaped by environmental consequences. This view of development uses principles proposed by different researchers who endorsed a common set of assumptions. The principles, however, have not been combined to form a single, organized theory (Biehler 1981).

At the other end of the continuum are the developmental theorists, who view learning as an active process in which children seek relationships among their experiences and tend to perfect their capacities at each developmental stage. Developmentalists present a comprehensive theory that consists of interrelated concepts tied to specific developmental stages.

Human behavior and learning can be explained by both learning theory and a developmental approach. Therefore, it is critical that we, as educators, have a working knowledge of both perspectives and their implications for teaching students with learning and behavioral difficulties. The following discussion will include a brief overview of both perspectives; emphasis will be on a developmental approach as the foundation for a constructivist framework to educating students identified as mentally retarded, emotionally disturbed, and learning disabled.

Traditional Learning Theory

Traditional learning theory focuses almost exclusively on the quantitative aspects of how learning occurs. Traditional learning theory evolved from the work of the early behaviorists, who emphasized external environmental variables as the basis for acquiring and forming behaviors. In the seventeenth century, John Locke proposed that a child's mind is initially a blank slate, which evolves and matures through learning and experience.

Locke also emphasized the importance of making careful observations of children's behaviors. His ideas on education provided the foundation for contemporary learning theory. In the early 1900s, Pavlov went beyond Locke's ideas and established the existence of a conditioned reflex, or response, based on association. His work moved learning theory from the realm of speculation to empirically based research.

John B. Watson combined Locke's philosophy that the mind was a blank slate to be filled through experiences with Pavlov's principles of conditioning and established a theory of human development. He was confident that we could emphasize sequences of conditioned responses in order to control behavior. His work inspired a number of investigations into the role of classical conditioning in infancy. Watson failed, however, to recognize the limits of Pavlovian conditioning, restricted as it was to reflexes and innate responses. Thus it could not explain the acquisition of complex behaviors such as talking. Accordingly, learning theorists such as B. F. Skinner have developed other models of conditioning.

Skinner believes that behavior is determined by its consequences. He developed a theory of operant conditioning as a means to shape and strengthen behavior based on principles of reinforcement. Skinner chose the term *operant conditioning* to stress that an organism "operates" on the environment when it learns. Skinner feels that through the principles of operant conditioning we can control any type of behavior. The behaving organism is controlled by reinforcing experiences; those who supply reinforcements are in control of the behavior. Skinner's principles of operant conditioning are discussed in some detail in chapter 10.

Implications for Education and Assessment

Principles of learning theory have been applied to child development and education in a number of ways. Behavior modification techniques, which are based on these principles, are used extensively in classroom management, in language development, and in helping children to overcome abnormal or self-destructive forms of behavior. Skinner has made significant contributions to the education of children through the invention of teaching machines and programmed instruction, both of which embody several Skinnerian principles. According to Skinner, the best way to establish new behavior is to shape it bit by bit. Therefore, learning should proceed in small steps. Second, the learner should be involved actively in learning, since such involvement is the natural condition of the organism. Third, immediate feedback is necessary; Skinner believes that learning is rapid when reinforced promptly.

Locke, Watson, and Skinner recommend that parents and educators should be more systematic in encouraging desirable traits and in minimizing the emergence of negative behaviors. In addition, they argue that to guide children's successful development, it is critical to make careful observations of their overt behavior. According to Skinner, the only way to discover the determinants of children's behavior is through observation. The work of traditional learning theorists is the foundation for assessment of students' abilities and concomitant instruction through task analysis.

Developmental Perspectives

Developmental theorists are less concerned with how we influence students' behaviors than in how children grow and learn on their own. They believe that students have an inner need to perfect certain capacities and to seek out certain experiences at each developmental stage. Developmentalists have conceptualized theories of how children acquire cognitive, affective, and social competencies. Discussion of cognitive, affective, and social development in this text will center around the works of Piaget, Kohlberg, and Erikson, who together provide a foundation for understanding children's development and concomitant learning behaviors. The work of each theorist is founded in *stage* theory, which emphasizes that although children progress through the various developmental stages at different rates, they do so in an invariant manner; that is, they progress through each period in an established order. In addition, developmentalists consider the individual's development as a continuous process of change and refinement of global behaviors to more specific and refined activities. For example, as children get older, they refine their motor behaviors from global responses (scribbling) to more refined motor responses (writing letters). Extensive discussion of affective and social development may be found in chapter 9.

Piaget's contributions to the study of developmental psychology were based on critical exploration of the qualitative changes in individuals' cognitive functioning from birth to adolescence. Piaget's work helps teachers to understand how children perceive and interpret their worlds at specific ages and what can be expected of them at different developmental stages. Piaget was a genetic epistemologist, who studied the acquisition of knowledge. He attempted to identify those principles that underlie the development of logical reasoning. In addition, Piaget was a constructivist, interested in the transformation of cognitive structures, which change constantly as individuals interact with their worlds. According to Piagetian thought, individuals are active organisms in an active environment who continually refine their knowledge to higher and more complex levels.

Cognitive activity is an attempt to adapt to experience. Children do not adjust passively to the demands of their environments, but they impose a structure, or a scheme, on their environments to interpret environmental experiences, and they modify or change the structure when it does not coincide with significant aspects of reality. Our knowledge of the world is based on the modification and refinement of existing knowledge. Knowledge is never totally new—rather it always has a referent to prior knowledge. Also, knowledge is organized at all times; it is structured, or systematized, into coherent systems according to how individuals know their environment.

Cognitive behavior can be traced to a combination of four factors:

1. Maturation of bodily processes
2. Experiences with the environment
3. Social transmission
4. Equilibration

Physiological, or biological, maturation plays an important role in children's development because it fosters movement from one stage of cognitive development to another. For example, physiological maturation of the central nervous system is probably needed before children attain the level of concrete operations. However, to enhance development, physiological maturation must be accompanied by other factors, that is, the student's intelligence level and cultural environment.

Physical experiences or contact with the environment are important because they nourish, stimulate, and challenge students to learn about their environment and to develop new cognitive schemes that enable them to deal with their worlds.

Social transmission or social experiences come through interaction with people and include social relationships, education, language, and culture. Social interaction has a profound effect on development because it enables students to decenter or to notice more than just one property or attribute. Second, it enables them to understand varying viewpoints and perspectives and to become more flexible in their reasoning. Another factor that contributes to social experiences is formal education, which influences the rate at which students learn and determines the content of knowledge. According to Piaget, language helps students to represent their actions in images and thoughts. Although he agrees that language is essential to thought, Piaget argues that children evidence intelligent behaviors prior to speaking. Language is only one aspect of the ability to function symbolically (Gallagher and Reid 1981).

Children's environmental experiences often cause a state of internal conflict or disequilibrium, but they are immediately motivated to resolve the conflict. Equilibration is a self-regulating process in which our cognitive structures constantly seek a state of balance or equilibrium. Equilibrium is a balance between assimilation and accommodation, which are cognitive functions that work together and allow us to adapt to the environment. Assimilation is a quantitative change that occurs in our cognitive structures when we incorporate environmental events into our existing cognitive structures or knowledge base.

If the new information does not fit these existing cognitive structures, then we must change or modify those cognitive structures to conform to environmental demands. Accommodation is the mechanism by which qualitative changes occur in our mediating processes, that is, how we understand and interpret environmental information. Through accommodation, cognitive schemes and structures are modified to solve problems and to conform to environmental experiences. Eventually, these schemes represent the student's knowledge of experiences and reflect reality.

When disequilibrium occurs, students are motivated to assimilate and accommodate, that is, to seek equilibrium. Assimilation and accommodation work together to provide the balance necessary for behavior to be adaptive and for learning to occur. Cognitive structures thus develop through the process of equilibration, or self-regulation. Cognitive development may be thought of as students' increasing capacity to think about the world in new and more complex ways (Moses 1981). From this perspective, then, cognitive development is characterized by the student's cognitive con-

TABLE 1-1   Piaget's Developmental Stages

STAGE	CHILDREN'S ACTIVITIES	PARENT-TEACHER RESPONSIBILITIES
Sensorimotor Intelligence (birth to two years) Organization of physical (sensory and motor) schemes to deal with immediate environment. Initial refinement of innate reflex activities at birth to awareness of causal, temporal and spatial relationships, and problem solving.	Early discrimination among environmental objects/ events as bases for learning. Manipulate objects and develop object permanence; Sequence previous activities and imitate others' behaviors without direct referent; Integrate relationships and apply old skills in new situations. Initial use of language symbols.	Respond to and stimulate child's senses with enriched and varied environment (toys, rattles, mobiles of different nature, shapes and colors) —Hide toys as child watches, play "peek-a-boo." —Encourage imitation and provide experiences with familiar objects and toys that can be manipulated. —Provide opportunities for generalizing old skills to new situations and social interaction with peers.
Preoperational Thought (two to seven years) Children's thinking is unsystematic and illogical, translates sensory knowledge to symbolic representation (language and imagery). Thinking is based on symbols and internal images; gradual acquisition of ability to conserve and decenter toward end of stage.	Language appears and is idiosyncratic (private meaning). Imagination and egocentrism are prevalent; unable to reason using language. Thoughts based on perceptual features; cannot conserve actions/thinking.	—Provide manipulatives/ concrete objects. —Communicate at or above child's level. —Provide experiences with liquid, volume, and length and encourage decision making based on forced choices (apple or banana).
Concrete Operations (seven to eleven years) Students begin to think logically and systematically; thinking and problem solving are bound to concrete objects and experiences; unable to manipulate conditions mentally unless they are experienced.	Apply simple logic and reason inductively to arrive at conclusions. Conclusions based on facts and empirical tests. Perform simple mental operations based on observed relationships. Conserves.	—Provide opportunities to pursue interest areas. —Probe child's reasoning with questions to ascertain thought processes.
Formal Operations (eleven to adulthood) Students develop capacity to think logically and systematically at an abstract and hypothetical level; engage in mental manipulations.	Reason abstractly; employ logical thought and draw conclusions based on logical relationships. Solve problems deductively. Propositional thinking.	—Propose hypothetical problem-solving situations. —Discuss ethical/moral issues. —Encourage personal decision making and problem solving.

Adapted from J. P. Thibault and J. S. McKee, "Practical Parenting with Piaget." *Young Children* 38 (1982), 18–27.

structions, that is, how they reason about a problem and the mental activities they create to attain equilibrium. Cognitive development then is a spontaneous process in which students assimilate and accommodate new information in an attempt to resolve internal contradictions.

The information presented in table 1-1 provides a brief overview of the competencies attained at each of Piaget's developmental stages. The table also highlights activities at each developmental stage that will foster appropriate cognitive growth and development. Extended discussion of competencies attained at each stage can be found in Gallagher and Reid (1981), Crain (1981), Biehler (1981), and Miller (1983).

IMPLICATIONS FOR INTERVENTION

A constructivist approach to education encourages students' active involvement with their physical and social worlds. This approach is child centered and based on the idea that learning is a process of active discovery and problem solving that facilitates the construction of knowledge. From a constructivist viewpoint, cognition is action, and the brain is considered an active organizing and dynamic system and not just a passive receptacle manipulated by external rewards. Thus learning occurs without external rewards. Educators, therefore, should provide opportunities, such as learning and interest-center activities and small-group and individualized instruction, that allow children and youths to manipulate real things as a basis for exploration and discovery of ideas, especially if they are functioning below the stage of formal operations. Piagetians believe the cognitive structures are constructed upon earlier cognitive structures and that new developmental stages integrate and transform previous knowledge. In addition, education should be a process of social interaction in which students interact with their peers and with their teachers. This process offers opportunities for students to decenter and to deal with other perspectives and viewpoints, which challenge their own thinking. Social experiences and language help to guide students' cognition. Also, teacher-pupil interaction enables teachers to analyze students and determine their levels of cognitive development in different academic areas. Children function differently in various subject areas, and their performance may vary from task to task and day to day. If students are provided with opportunities to explain their reasoning, teachers can then arrange instruction to harmonize with students' thinking. Focus on students' level of thinking also has implications for assessment and intervention as indicated in the discussions on assessment and intervention throughout this text.

Concomitant learning principles derived from Piagetian theory and their implications for teaching are presented by Gallagher and Reid (1981), Moses (1981), and DeRuiter and Wansart (1982). These principles, which have implications for human development and learning, are as follows:

1. Learning is an internal process of construction in which students' activities determine their reactions to environmental stimuli. We must help

students to construct knowledge by guiding their educational experiences and structuring learning situations, as opposed to teaching tasks directly. This may be accomplished by providing some direction and helping students to set goals as a means of structuring and understanding learning problems. In addition, students should be encouraged to experiment and to devise solutions to meet their own needs rather than relying solely on copying information and meeting specific performance standards.

2. Learning is subordinate to development and is based on the capacity to respond to and understand new experiences (assimilation) and to modify this knowledge when it is not consistent with reality (accommodation). Students must have the necessary competencies or prerequisites to learn. They develop knowledge structures based on previous information. Therefore, not only must they have opportunities to assimilate information into their current mental structures but also their structures must be able to stabilize prior to the introduction of new information.

3. Learning occurs not only through observation but also through reorganization of knowledge to higher cognitive levels based on environmental interaction. This process of reorganization occurs via the equilibratory process and leads to advanced states of equilibrium. Students therefore should be afforded opportunities to control and to understand problematic situations as a vehicle for solving problems. We must provide manipulative and concrete experiences so that students may impose a structure on those experiences as a basis for understanding.

4. Growth in knowledge occurs through an internal feedback process that results from questions, contradictions, and consequent reorganization. Internal feedback is a process of self-correction in which children adjust initial expectations as a result of their actions. Effective learning occurs when students anticipate the results of their actions, observe those results, and compare predictions with the outcomes of their actions to verify success or failure. This process of self-evaluation helps students to recognize their errors and to accept responsibility for them and for their ultimate resolution. In essence, learning becomes self-regulated and motivated internally in contrast with external or environmental motivation, which fosters dependence. Students should enjoy their problem-solving efforts, and they should be praised for the cognitive processes used in problem solving, in contrast with praise for the attainment of a correct solution.

5. Questions, contradictions, and consequent reorganization of thought are stimulated by social interaction. Therefore students must be presented with problem-solving situations and contradictions and encouraged to derive various solutions even if they are unconventional. In essence, we want to facilitate the development of students' learning and problem-solving strategies rather than teaching solutions to problems.

6. Awareness or conscious realization is a process of reconstructing knowledge rather than having sudden insight; students' understanding often lags behind their ability to perform. In other words, students may

perform a particular task in a rote manner and not understand what they are doing. True understanding occurs when students are able to control the learning situation, to make inferences, and to reorganize their knowledge based on their environmental experiences. Students must have the opportunity to "massage," refine, and consider environmental information in light of their previous knowledge.

These principles of learning provide insight into the formal and informal assessment of children with learning and behavior problems and concomitant educational intervention. General implications for assessment indicate that educators responsible for assessment should view learners from the perspective of their mental structures rather than seeking a cause for their learning problems. Students' responses are based on their own mental structures, which indicate the cognitive levels at which they are functioning and the point at which they are ready to learn new material. Second, information concerning mental structures can be determined through observing students' behaviors and through interaction with them. We must be able to assess not just whether students know an answer, but how they think. We must look at the quality of their thinking and at their thinking deficiencies as well as at their mastery of content. Therefore, we must focus on how students arrive at specific answers. Assessment of children's thinking is the basis for providing developmentally appropriate opportunities for learning, which in turn foster discovery and progression to more complex stages of knowing. Additional discussion related to assessment of students' learning and behavioral needs from a constructivist standpoint, as a means of identifying students' learning strategies and setting appropriate instructional goals, may be found in chapter 2.

The focus of a constructivist paradigm is on students' acquisition of new knowledge and the qualitative changes that occur in their thinking as they interact with the environment. The development of cognitive behavior, from a Piagetian viewpoint, is a continuous and evolving process that includes four distinct stages, or periods, through which students "spiral" in an invariant manner but at different developmental rates. As students progress through this spiral of knowledge (see figure 1-1), new cognitive

FIGURE 1-1   Spiral of Knowledge

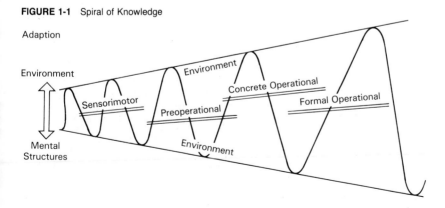

structures are integrated with, and constructed upon, previous mental structures. Each succeeding developmental stage is the summation of behaviors at the previous stage and the genesis upon which the new stage develops. Students with learning and behavior problems appear to pass through the same developmental stages as typical children do but with some delay. In addition, their learning appears to be haphazard and not integrative in nature. The resulting qualitative differences in their learning and performance may relate to the construction of an inadequate or incorrect mental framework with which to consider new environmental information. Concomitantly, students are unable to access information needed for problem solving. They seem to have difficulty in acquiring and using appropriate learning strategies as a basis for constructing new knowledge. One of our responsibilities, therefore, is to teach specific learning or study strategies to students that will enable them to be more efficient and active learners.

A cognitive-strategies approach to learning is founded on the notion that as children develop cognitively, they create strategies for learning based on their previous experiences. However, it appears that some students with learning and behavior difficulties do not produce strategies independently and that their learning is ineffective and disorganized. Teaching cognitive strategies should help students to produce additional strategies and to become more active in their learning.

Strategies are the plans, actions, steps, and processes that are designed to accomplish any learning or problem-solving task. Strategies may be specified externally, but it is intended that they become internal. The primary goal in teaching students to use strategies is to make them more responsible for their learning and to help them to "learn how to learn." The major focus is on teaching students to guide their own thinking and learning.

Strategies may be either teacher strategies or student strategies. Teacher strategies are the internal mental plans or methods that help to guide a teacher's decisions in what and how to teach. They usually include the principles upon which a strategy is based as well as the specific steps and processes in a teaching technique or method. Examples of teacher strategies are interspersed throughout this text.

Student strategies, on the other hand, are the internal mental plans that specify the thinking actions, steps, and processes that help students to construct reality, solve problems, and learn how to learn (DeRuiter 1983; Sileo 1985). Student strategies include metacognitive, executive control, and specific task strategies. Metacognitive strategies include a person's broad general awareness and knowledge of cognition (what we know) and cognitive processes (how we know). Metacognitive strategies help us to recognize when we do not understand something and how we learn best (based on cognitive style), and they are helpful in monitoring and controlling the effective use of strategies. Examples of metacognitive strategies include reflecting on a task or problem situation before acting, questioning prior to and during the performance of a task, and monitoring the response.

Executive control strategies are used to direct and control other strategies in a flexible manner as demanded by task requirements. They include the ability to choose and use specific strategies to attain a particular goal and the ability to shift to other strategies as we progress through a task or as task demands change. Study strategies and cognitive behavior modification are examples of executive control strategies. Study strategies facilitate students' acquisition of knowledge and competence. They help students to learn how to learn and how to take greater responsibility for their own learning. Sheinker and Sheinker (1983) and Alley and Deshler (1979) believe that in addition to knowing about study strategies, students should understand why, how, and when to use them effectively. Cognitive behavior modification (CBM) is an executive control strategy (closely related to metacognition) that can help students to organize and to control their thought patterns and learning behaviors through self-treatment techniques. These techniques provide a structure for organizing incoming environmental information and monitoring one's own responses. Cognitive-behavior modification is a tool that helps increase students' self-reliance and independent decision making by remediating problems at the executive level of cognitive functioning. Additional discussion of study strategies and cognitive behavior modification can be found in chapters 3, 4, and 5.

Task strategies are used with executive control strategies and are designed to accomplish specific tasks, such as skill development in reading or mathematics. Specific task strategies, for example, may include the various word-attack skills applicable to teaching reading. Additional discussion related to the development and use of task strategies in teaching reading and mathematics can be found in chapters 6 and 8, respectively.

In summary, there are two critical considerations when teaching cognitive strategies to students. First, strategies should lead to long-term acquisition of skills and knowledge. Second, students' cognitive processes and academic abilities must be considered as one for purposes of teaching.

Teaching strategies can range from general strategies (recognizing when we do not understand something) to specific strategies (learning how to regroup in addition from the one's place to the ten's place). It is recognized that in developing strategies for teaching, different strategies may be needed at various age or ability levels. Strategies must fit both the quantitative and the qualitative differences in students' cognitive and language abilities. In addition, strategies are affected by teacher style, environmental-arrangement factors, and specific content and procedures. It is also important to remember that students should participate actively in the development of strategies. We cannot just tell students the steps in developing a strategy, but rather we must *involve them actively* if strategies are to be effective and to be generalized to other situations. We cannot assume that students will transfer strategies on their own. Strategy development and transfer is a complex process; therefore, transfer of strategies must be planned by the instructor.

Finally, strategies should fit the specific task and should be detailed specifically to have meaning for students. Students should be provided with opportunities to practice the strategy in the specific area for which it is designed and in various experimental settings. The more ways we learn something, the better we know it. In conjunction with this idea, students should see the need for, and the value of, strategies used to facilitate their learning. They must be encouraged to use appropriate strategies and reinforced when they do so, in addition to being given recognition for finding the correct answer or solution to a problem. In essence, we must focus on the learning process as the most primary element in learning. We should also recognize that it is the essential means whereby the learner arrives at the traditionally prized learning product.

SUMMARY

In this chapter we have considered educational programming for students who are identified as mentally retarded, emotionally disturbed, and learning disabled. We have emphasized two perspectives—the historical and the theoretical. Both historical and theoretical considerations have had a major influence on the nature of the educational services students have received and the manner in which these services have been provided. These considerations have shaped the face of special education.

Historically, the past twenty-five to thirty years have witnessed great changes in educational programming for those students who are the major concern of this volume. During that time, services for the mentally retarded have been redefined; the population served has been reduced greatly through the lowering of the upper IQ limit recognized as appropriate for an identification of mental retardation, through the added requirement of evidence of deficits in adaptive behavior; and through recognition that educators had often inaccurately identified minority-group members as mentally retarded. During that same time period, learning disabilities became a recognized subarea of special education and the largest group of handicapped students served in the public schools. In a similar manner, the emotionally disturbed, recognized but seldom served prior to the mid-1960s, are now receiving special education services across the nation. Although recognized as separate handicapping conditions (despite various definitional ambiguities), these three conditions have come to be viewed as overlapping in many cases.

As for theoretical concerns, it is possible to highlight newer theories, which are receiving much attention presently, but we cannot say with certainty which is the "right" theory. Perhaps there are two, three, or several "right" or applicable theories. At any rate, in this chapter we have considered briefly traditional learning theories, which tend to view the quantitative aspects of how learning takes place, and developmental learning theories, which relate to how children learn on their own, as opposed to how we influence their learning through outside intervention.

The major emphasis in this theoretical discussion was on constructivist theory (for that is the major emphasis of this text). We will, however, present an overview of successful behavior management techniques in chapter 10, for those techniques have proved to be highly successful for some purposes. Our discussion of the developmental or constructivist point of view emphasized the principle that as children develop cognitively, they create "learning strategies" based on their previous experiences. According to this theoretical construct, students develop metacognitive, executive-control, and specific task strategies, all of which are internal processes related to learning how to learn, and then utilize what has been internalized. Cognitive behavior modification, a technique in which the key component is self-instructional internal dialogue, was also mentioned. The final goal is that students recognize the need for such strategies to facilitate their learning. Much of the material that will be presented in the remainder of this text is designed to assist the teacher to understand this concept and to establish conditions in which students will develop such study strategies.

REFERENCES

ALGOZZINE, B., AND J. YSSELDYKE. Learning disabilities as a subset of school failure: The over-sophistication of a concept. *Exceptional Children* 2 (1983), 242–45.

ALLEY, G., AND D. DESHLER. *Teaching the Learning Disabled Adolescent.* Denver: Love Publishing Company, 1979.

APTER, STEVEN J., AND JANE C. CONOLEY. *Childhood Behavior Disorders and Emotional Disturbance.* Englewood Cliffs, N.J.: Prentice-Hall, 1984.

BELCH, PETER J. Toward non-categorical teacher certification in special education—myth or reality? *Exceptional Children* 46 (1979), 129–31.

BIEHLER, R. *Child Development.* Boston: Houghton Mifflin Co., 1981.

BOWER, E. M. *Early Identification of Emotionally Handicapped in School,* 2d ed. Springfield, Ill.: Charles C Thomas, 1969.

———, AND N. M. LAMBERT. In-school screening of children with emotional handicaps. In N. Long, W. Morse, and R. Newman, eds., *Conflict in the Classroom.* Belmont, Calif.: Wadsworth, 1971.

BRYAN, T. H. Learning disabilities: A new stereotype. *Journal of Learning Disabilities* 5 (1974), 46–50.

CLARIZO, HARVEY F., AND GEORGE F. McCOY. *Behavior Disorders in Children.* New York: Harper & Row Publishers, 1983.

CRAIG, P., D. KASKOWITZ, AND M. MALGOIRE. Studies of handicapped students, Vol. 2, *Teacher Identification of Handicapped Pupils.* Menlo Park, Calif.: SRI International, 1978.

CRAIN, WILLIAM. *Theories of Development.* Englewood Cliffs, N.J.: Prentice-Hall, 1981.

DERUITER, JAMES A. Presentation to Denver Academy, Symposium on Learning Disabilities. Denver: February 4, 1983.

———, AND W. WANSART. *Psychology of Learning Disabilities.* Rockville, Md.: Aspen System Corporation, 1982.

GAJAR, A. Educable mentally retarded, learning disabled, emotionally disturbed: similarities and differences. *Exceptional Children* 45 (1979), 470–72.

GALLAGHER, JEANETTE, AND D. KIM REID. *Learning Theory of Piaget and Inhelder.* Monterey, Calif.: Brooks/Cole, 1981.

GARBER, H. L., AND R. HEBER. The efficacy of early intervention with family rehabilitation. In M. J. Begab, H. C. Haywood, and H. L. Garber, eds., *Psychological Influences in Retarded Performance: Strategies for Improving Competency,* vol. 2. Baltimore: University Park Press, 1981.

GEARHEART, B. R., AND M. W. WEISHAHN. *The Exceptional Student in the Regular Classroom,* 3d ed. St. Louis: C. V. Mosby, 1984.

GROSENICK, J. K., AND S. L. HUNTZE. *National Needs Analysis in Behavior Disorders: Adolescent Behavior Disorders.* Columbia: University of Missouri-Columbia, Department of Special Education, 1980.

GROSSMAN, H. J.   *Manual on Terminology and Classification in Mental Retardation.* Washington, D.C.: American Association on Mental Deficiency, special publication, no. 2, 1973, 1977.

———. *Classification in Mental Retardation.* Washington, D.C.: American Association on Mental Deficiency, 1983.

HALLAHAN, D. P., AND J. M. KAUFFMAN.   *Introduction to Learning Disabilities.* Englewood Cliffs, N.J.: Prentice-Hall, 1976.

———. Labels, Categories, Behaviors: ED, LD, and EMR Reconsidered. *Journal of Special Education* 11 (1977), 139–49.

HAMMILL, D. D., J. E. LEIGH, G. McNUTT, AND S. C. LARSEN.   A new definition of learning disabilities. *Learning Disability Quarterly* 4 (1981), 336–42.

HEBELER, J. R., AND M. C. REYNOLDS, PROJECT DIRECTORS.   *Guidelines for Personnel in the Education of Exceptional Children.* Reston, Va.: Council for Exceptional Children, 1976.

HELLER, H. W., K. McCOY, AND BETH McENTIRE.   Categorical vs. non-categorical teacher training: Group summary. *Teacher Education and Special Education* 2 (1979), 8–9.

KEELEY-STANNARD, MARGARET.   *A Comparison of Subtest and Total Scores of Normal and Learning Disabled, Emotionally Disturbed and Other Students on the Quick Neurological Screening Test.* Published doctoral dissertation, University of Northern Colorado, Greeley, 1980.

KEPHART, N., AND A. STRAUSS.   A Clinical Factor Influencing Variations in IQ. *American Journal of Orthopsychiatry,* 10 (1940), 343–50.

LAMBRIC, THOMAS M.   *Use of the Quick Neurological Screening Test to Compare Emotionally Disturbed, Learning Disabled and Normal Children.* Published doctoral dissertation, University of Northern Colorado, Greeley, 1978.

MacMILLAN, D. L., AND S. BORTHWICK.   The new educable mentally retarded population: Can they be mainstreamed? *Mental Retardation* 18 (1980), 155–58.

MARSH, G., B. PRICE, AND T. SMITH.   *Teaching Mildly Handicapped Children.* St. Louis: C. V. Mosby Co., 1983.

MERCER, CECIL D.   *Students with Learning Disabilities.* Columbus, Ohio: Charles E. Merrill Publishing Co., 1983.

MILLER, PATRICIA H.   *Theories of Developmental Psychology.* San Francisco: W. H. Freeman and Co., 1983.

MOSES, N.   Using Piagetian principles to guide instruction. *Topics in Learning and Learning Disabilities* 1 (1981), 11–19.

PATRICK, J. L., AND D. J. RESCHLEY.   Relationship of state educational criteria and demographic variables to school system prevalence of mental retardation. *American Journal of Mental Deficiency* 86 (1982), 351–60.

POLLOWAY, EDWARD A., AND J. DAVID SMITH.   Changes in mild mental retardation: Population, programs and perspectives. *Exceptional Children* 50 (1983), 149–59.

RAMEY, C. T., AND R. HASKINS.   The causes and treatment of school failures: Insights from the Carolina abecedarian project. In M. J. Begab, H. C. Haywood, and H. L. Garber, eds., *Psychosocial Influences in Retarded Performance: Strategies for Improving Competencies,* vol. 2. Baltimore: University Park Press, 1981.

REGER, ROGER.   Learning disabilities: Futile attempts at a simplistic definition. *Journal of Learning Disabilities* 2 (1979), 529–32.

REID, D. K., AND W. HRESKO.   *A Cognitive Approach to Learning Disabilities.* New York: McGraw-Hill Book Co., 1981.

REYNOLDS, MAYNARD D.   Categorical vs. non-categorical teacher training. *Teacher Education and Special Education* 2 (1979), 5–8.

Report to Congress.   Menlo Park, Calif.: SRI International, 1979.

REYNOLDS, M. C., AND M. C. WANG.   Restructuring "special" school programs: A position paper. Paper presented at the National Invitational Conference on Public Policy and the Special Education Task of the 1980's. Racine, Wis., September 1981.

RICH, H. LYNDALL.   *Disturbed Children.* Baltimore: University Park Press, 1982.

SHEINKER, J., AND A. SHEINKER.   *Study Strategies: A Metacognitive Approach.* Rock Springs, Wyo.: White Mountain Publishing Co., 1983.

SILEO, T. W.   Cognitive Approaches. In B. R. Gearheart, *Learning Disabilities: Educational Strategies.* St. Louis: C. V. Mosby, 1985.

SMITH, J. DAVID, AND EDWARD A. POLLOWAY.   Learning disabilities: Individual needs or categorical concerns. *Journal of Learning Disabilities* 2 (1979), 525–28.

STRAUSS, A. A., AND L. L. LEHTINEN.   *Psychopathology and Education of the Brain Impaired Child*, vol. 1. New York: Grune & Stratton, 1947.
THIBAULT, J. P., AND J. S. McKEE.   Practical parenting with Piaget. *Young Children* 38 (1982), 18–27.
U.S. DEPARTMENT OF EDUCATION, OFFICE OF SPECIAL EDUCATION, DATA ANALYSIS SYSTEM.   *Numbers and Changes in Number of Children Ages 3–4 Served under PL 89–313 and PL 94–142 Annually since School Year 1976–1977*, November 6, 1981.
U.S. OFFICE OF EDUCATION.   Assistance to states for education of handicapped children: Procedures for evaluating specified learning disabilities. *Federal Register* 42 (1977), 75 082-65085.
U.S. OFFICE OF EDUCATION.   *First Annual Report of National Advisory Committee on Handicapped Children*. Washington, D.C.: U.S. Department of Health, Education and Welfare, 1968.
WERNER, H., AND A. STRAUSS.   Pathology of figure-background relation in the child. *Journal of Abnormal and Social Psychology* 36 (1941), 236–48.

CHAPTER TWO

Assessment for Identification and Intervention

- How does a developmental perspective differ from a psychometric perspective? How does the focus of assessment differ in the view of advocates of these two perspectives?

- What significant differences exist between assessment for identification and assessment for intervention?

- What are the essential characteristics of the assessment-intervention model of student-program management?

- How is the concept of due process applied to assessment and intervention in special education?

- What changes has due process, as required by Public Law 94-142, required in the public schools?

- What is an IEP? Why is it felt to be such an important part of the regulations of Public Law 94-142?

- What is a mental-structures approach to assessment?

INTRODUCTION

Special-education assessment is a multifaceted and dynamic data-collection process through which educators seek to identify learning and behavior problems that interfere with students' academic functioning. It is a collaborative endeavor initiated by the members of an interdisciplinary team, who direct and organize assessment activities. These activities may include the administration of standardized norm-referenced and criterion-referenced tests, informal inventories and teacher-made tests, observations, and interviews.

The field of educational assessment has evolved from a psychometric perspective, in which tests were administered primarily to determine differences among children. This perspective was based on a behavioral approach to development and learning, which viewed learning as the acquisition of incremental units of information. This viewpoint was inherent in the work of the early experimental psychologists, who attempted to assess distinct functions *within* individuals (using norm-referenced tests) and to quantify differences *among* individuals based on the analysis of these discrete and separate functions.

A developmental approach to education, in contrast, views human beings as totally functioning individuals, who cannot be analyzed and reduced to separate components. From this perspective, discrete behaviors do not exist in isolation (except in the sensory systems, where sensory stimuli are transmitted along modal specific pathways from the point of sensation to a specific location within the brain for initial processing).

If we follow a developmental perspective, then assessment should not focus on differences in test performance, which purportedly indicate students' strengths and weaknesses. Instead, our focus should be on the qualitative changes in students' thinking.

Assessment is much broader than test administration and the quantitative aspects of obtaining test scores that are based on children's responses to previously determined questions or on their performance of tasks under specific conditions. Tests are but one component of the assessment process; and as such, they should be used to benefit students in their pursuit of educational opportunities. However, we should remember that tests measure only a small sample of behavior (under controlled conditions), which may or may not be representative of a larger constellation of behaviors.

Tests, then, should not be the sole basis for educational decision making. Rather, they should be viewed as tools that *may* help us to answer questions about children. Tests are part of the larger process of assessment, which is concerned with students' problem-solving skills and abilities, how they perform on tasks in different settings, the meaning of any particularly unique test performance, and the reasons why they perform in a certain manner.

Special education assessment is not an end in itself and does not result in a score; rather, assessment focuses on gathering systematic, valid, reliable, and relevant information as the basis for appropriate educational decision making. Assessment is an ongoing and active process that incorporates data from a variety of disciplines. It encompasses two major perspectives—assessment for identification of students' learning skills and abilities and assessment for intervention (program planning). We recognize that these assessment components overlap significantly, yet common sense and legal considerations that arise in this area suggest that they be presented and discussed separately.

The topics presented in this chapter include the purposes of assessment; a systematic needs-based assessment-intervention model of student-program management which illustrates the obligations of regular and special educators in identifying and providing services to students with learning and behavior disorders; and a discussion of a holistic approach to assessment as a means of identifying how students think and learn.

PURPOSES OF ASSESSMENT

A comprehensive assessment-intervention model acknowledges that students are active participants in the teaching-learning process. It also recognizes that we need a flexible data-collection system to gather important information concerning students' interactions with peers, instructional staff, and parents, which cannot be obtained solely from formal tests. This information is readily available through observation, interviews, and other informal assessment tools that allow educators to make appropriate decisions about educational programming. Assessment is not static; rather it is a continuous process, which considers that the conditions surrounding students are ever changing and that all decisions concerning programming and educational placement are tentative and subject to review and periodic comprehensive reassessment.

The primary purpose of assessment is to gather information related to decision making that will enhance a student's educational opportunities. This decision-making process allows us to make choices among possible alternatives that affect student progress. Part of that process is identifying the need for individual program change and concomitant program goals and objectives. Historically, assessment in public schools has been for the purposes of both identification and intervention, and these two factors comprise a comprehensive assessment-intervention model.

We agree on the twofold perspective of assessment for identification and intervention. However, the idea that assessment for identification must, in nearly all cases, lead to classification and labeling of a handicapping condition is false. Currently, too many students are classified and labeled as a result of assessment data that *suggest characteristics* related to a specific handicapping condition. The educational system has devised a way to identify learning and behavior problems, based on symptoms manifested by students. At present, many educators operate under an assessment paradigm that seeks to identify students according to certain characteristics that distinguish them from their peers. Classification and placement decisions are based on data collected from a number of different sources and compared to criteria for known handicapping conditions. We often identify and label students according to textbook characteristics, cut-off scores, and profile analyses alone. We seek to prove that the students with whom we are working exhibit certain characteristics and behaviors similar to an identified group, and therefore we can conclude that they belong to that group.

This practice can be illustrated by the following:

Learning disabled children exhibit distractible behaviors;
Carrie is easily distracted;
Therefore, Carrie is learning disabled.

If we accept this type of reasoning, then the characteristic behaviors exhibited by students must be both universal and specific. In other words, the characteristics must be present in all individuals with a given specific disorder and must not occur in students who do not have the disorder. The extent to which universal and specific characteristics exist in students who fail in school and who need special or remedial education services is marginal.

Students who are assessed and classified according to different categorical labels often display similar psychoeducational profiles. The characteristics that they exhibit are not universal, nor are they specific. There is considerable overlap among characteristics that are used to differentiate within and among individuals classified in remedial and special education. Many students do not manifest a substantial number of behavioral characteristics that have been used to define the category into which they are placed. Some students demonstrate deviant behaviors that have been used to define different categories; other students demonstrate behaviors that do not fit any category.

Identification and classification based on the presence of certain characteristics and on inferential observation of behavioral trends indicated by current norm-referenced tests seems to be circular reasoning. Decisions based on such reasoning may result in an inappropriate educational placement and restriction of educational opportunities. Simply because a student's performance on a test is similar to the typical performance of members of a particular disability group, that student does not necessarily belong to that group.

The purpose of assessment for identification as postulated in this text refers to the determination of students' learning and behavioral needs as a basis for understanding their interactions within their daily environments. Assessment of a student's needs serves to delineate further assessment goals, objectives, and complementary teaching strategies.

In essence, this model for assessment ignores labels and translates directly into improved educational programming. Differences in performance are acceptable under the premise that individuals work at their own level of accomplishment and at their own pace. Students should receive educational services based on their individual needs rather than on abstract labels. The emphasis in assessment, therefore, is on a functional approach that insures adequate programming. We do, however, recognize that "labeling" is necessary, in most states, to the process of providing appropriate intervention. We would hope that in educational planning we might provide for student needs based on broad-range, multidisciplinary assessment. Such an approach attempts to reduce the bias in educational programming and placement. We are not predetermining that a child is emotionally disturbed, learning disabled, or mentally retarded by giving a specific test battery and looking for patterns. To accomplish the reduction in bias, we must use all the available data to make educational decisions that result in changing a student's learning environment to something other than the regular classroom.

Assessment for Identification of Learning and Behavioral Needs

Determination of students' learning and behavioral needs recognizes that assessment is an inquiry process upon which we develop individualized instructional programs.

Assessment for identification is part of the data-collection process that helps to describe the student with whom we are working and to suggest other factors that may influence educational-programming decisions. A great deal of attention must be given to this step of the identification process, but our sole concern should not be with which tests to administer; that is a common oversimplification of the assessment process. A majority of the most pertinent data may be gathered through questionnaires, interviews, and observations. The type of information required to meet the assessment needs of a given student must relate specifically to the student under consideration.

Assessment for Intervention

Assessment for intervention aids in individualizing instruction to meet a student's identified educational needs revealed in the first phase of assessment. It relies on informal inventories and teacher-made tests, interviews, observations, hypothesis teaching and testing, task analysis, and criterion-referenced tests. This phase of assessment includes continual analysis and appraisal of a student's performance and is the base upon which decisions are made for any needed changes in instructional programs.

Assessment for intervention also includes evaluation of pupil progress and program effectiveness. It allows us to combine the teaching and learning processes. Through assessment for intervention, educators are able to determine qualitative differences in the way students think and they can use that information to decide what to teach and how to teach.

These decisions can be made only when the teaching-learning process is monitored closely. Assessment for intervention relies on a holistic approach. Holistic assessment of learning disabled, emotionally disturbed, and educable mentally retarded students is consistent with the presentation of teaching methods and strategies offered in this text. Further discussion of holistic assessment may be found later in this chapter.

NEEDS-BASED
ASSESSMENT-INTERVENTION MODEL

It is imperative that our educational systems respond to the diverse needs of students identified as having learning and behavior difficulties. Attainment of this goal requires an understanding on the part of both regular and special educators that the assessment-intervention process rests with the total educational system and NOT solely with special education. All students are the responsibility of regular education. The special educator's role is to assist in providing services to students who cannot benefit from regular education without adaptation or modification because of a handicapping condition.

We believe that *students* must be the focus of the assessment-intervention process. Schools, therefore, should respond to a student's unique needs rather than requiring students to conform to the school's needs. Educators, then, must identify students' needs and the appropriate characteristics of services to meet those needs. Therefore, assessment should be a comprehensive process that determines how students function physically, psychologically, communicatively, educationally, and socially. To accomplish this goal, educators need to conduct a total assessment in each of these areas. We must not look at students from a limited perspective, nor should we look at discrete abilities and functioning levels.

The assessment-intervention model of student-program management presented in this text emphasizes an inquiry process that dictates comprehensive individual assessment and recognizes that assessment must be a multifaceted effort. Assessment includes the efforts of parents, teachers, administrators and any other professionals who provide data about the student through formal and informal testing, observation, interviews, and consultation. It is not necessary to give each student a specific battery of tests. Such an approach only serves as a means of predetermining students' problems and labeling them. The assessment process, then, asks the question, "What are the students' needs?" and it is conducted specifically to determine those needs. The resulting program is tailored specifically for the student. In essence, we are fitting the program to the students, rather than fitting the student to a predetermined program.

The model requires that several persons participate in the responsibility for decision making about a student; it integrates the services of regular and special education. Educational programming and intervention become a shared responsibility. The special education teacher is no longer the "rescuer" of the school; and no longer will there be a "magic time" in which special educators "cure" students.

FIGURE 2-1 Needs-Based - Assessment - Intervention Model

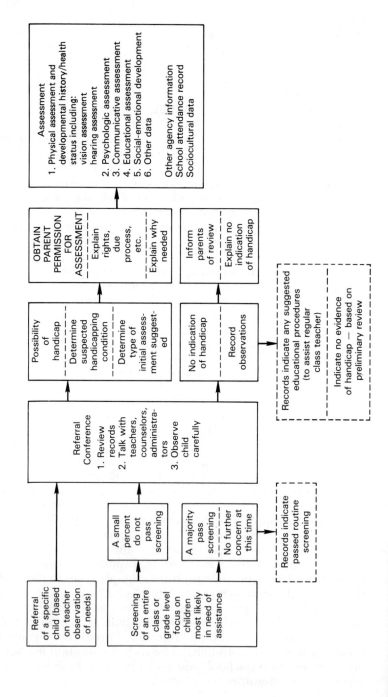

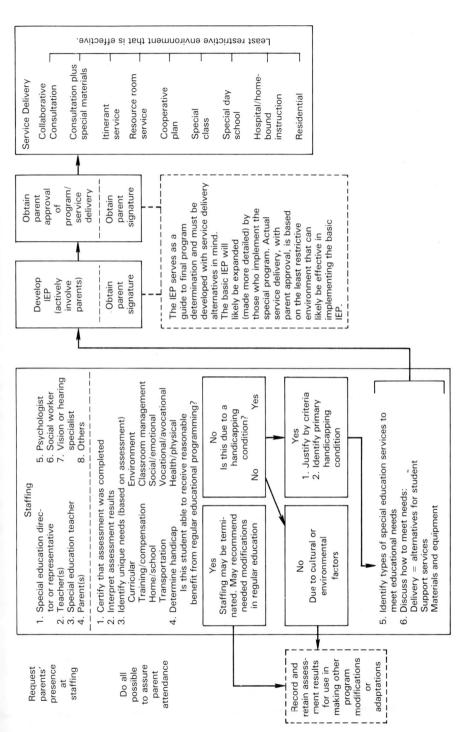

Adapted from Gearheart, *Learning Disabilities: Educational Strategies.* St. Louis: C. V. Mosby, 1985.

A comprehensive process for assessment and intervention includes six steps that will facilitate delivery of the appropriate educational services. They include:

1. Screening
2. Referral
3. Assessment
4. Staffing
5. Service Delivery
6. Review

Figure 2-1 is a graphic illustration of the processes involved in this model.

Screening

Screening is a process that occurs throughout the total educational system. It helps to identify students who may have different needs from those of the general school population. The screening process helps to determine if there are any unusual concerns about a student's functioning and may address a student's health and physical state, psychological, communicative, educational, and social and emotional development. This approach provides an overall perspective of a student's impairments and aids in identifying students who may require additional assessment or alternative educational strategies. It should be noted that parental permission is not required for the screening process when screening is applied to all students. Parental involvement, however, at the information-sharing level is a good educational practice. If as a result of screening there are concerns, the student enters the next phase of the process—a referral conference.

Referral

The referral process falls within the jurisdiction of regular education and may be initiated by classroom teachers, administrators, parents, or community members. Referral may be made when a student experiences learning or behavior difficulties in the regular classroom setting or is viewed as handicapped or requiring special services. Referral and screening are complementary processes that enable us to focus additional attention on students who may require special assistance. Many school districts provide general guidelines to assist teachers in determining whether a referral should be made. These guidelines may include a description of the referral process and actual referral forms. The forms help teachers to objectify their observations (Gearheart 1985).

A referral conference or preliminary review is conducted as part of the referral process to determine if regular education can meet the needs of the student about whom there is concern or if additional assessment considerations are necessary. It is a review of the available information (cumulative records, observations, interviews) in which questions are generated concerning the student's current educational status. The conference participants include those persons who are involved directly with the student and who can provide insight concerning the student's total functioning. Most often referral conferences include school administrators, regular and special education teachers, and parents. Since referral is part of general education's responsibilities, parent permission is not required; however, it is important to keep parents informed. Parents must know that concerns were expressed about their children's current educational status, the possible need for special education assistance, and the resolution of the concerns that were expressed.

The referral conference should be considered a problem-solving activity to determine if the student can benefit from a regular education setting and to explore alternatives and modifications to the student's present educational program. Consultation assistance should be provided to the regular classroom teacher to assist in making instructional modifications.

If there are indications of a possible handicap and that the student should receive special education services, the student is referred for special education assessment. Questions are then generated concerning the student's functioning in the five areas to be assessed: health and physical state, and psychological, communicative, educational, and social and emotional development.

It is at this phase of the assessment-intervention process that the student enters the area that is more directly the responsibility of special education and in which procedural safeguards must be initiated. Parents must be notified that their child is being referred for special education consideration based on the possibility of a handicapping condition. In addition, they must be notified, in their native language, of their rights according to due process, and they should be apprised of the type of assessment to be conducted in each of the five areas. Finally, written parent permission must be obtained prior to initiating formal assessment procedures. See the box below for a brief review of due-process guidelines.

It is also at this point that a case manager is appointed to oversee and coordinate the functions of the assessment team. The case manager should be a person who is aware of the difficulties being experienced by the student and may be one of the following: regular classroom teacher, special educator, administrator, or psychologist. The case manager is not necessarily the same person for each and every assessment that occurs within a particular school.

DUE PROCESS

Due-process provisions related to educational assessment and intervention protect the rights of parents and their children in all procedures related to the identification, evaluation, and program placement and the provisions of an appropriate education for students in the least restrictive and most appropriate environment. They also provide for the opportunity to protect educational decisions made by school personnel. Special education due-process procedures are found in a variety of forms. While there is some flexibility in construction and administration of such a process, there are basic ingredients guaranteed by federal legislation. These ingredients include:

1. Written notice in the parents' primary language prior to any change in the student's educational status.
2. Access by parents to all educational records related to the identification, evaluation, and placement of their children.
3. The opportunity for parents to express concerns related to educational services received by the student, to obtain an independent assessment of their child, and to present this information to the school for consideration.
4. An impartial due-process hearing where parents and the school cannot agree on identification, evaluation, and program placement for the child. The law specifies rights available to parents at such hearings to ensure fairness and impartiality.
5. Adequate appeals procedures if parents are not satisfied with results of the due-process hearing. Parents have the right to appeal to the state department of education and ultimately the state and federal courts. The decision of the courts is binding.

During the hearing and appeals procedure, the student has the right to remain in the educational placement in effect at the time the hearing was initiated unless otherwise mutually agreed upon by the parents and school officials. These procedural safeguards were specified in PL 93-380—*The Education Amendments of 1974*. They were refined and their scope substantially enlarged in PL 94-142—*The Education for All Handicapped Children Act.*

Assessment

As indicated earlier, the assessment process must be multifaceted in order to provide a total picture of the student's integrities. This is accomplished by assessing the student's physical, psychological, communicative, educational, and social status through formal evaluation, classroom observation, hypothesis teaching, interview, and consultation. It is critical that each of the five areas be assessed *to the extent necessary* to provide a comprehensive picture of the student's functioning. In addition, no one facet of the assessment should be considered to be more important than another.

The primary goal of the assessment process is to gather sufficient information to provide a basis for decisions about the student's educational program and alternative remediation approaches. This includes a determination of possible learning and/or behavior disorders, the degree and severity of such disorders, and the existence of related environmental factors. As such, the assessment should be process oriented rather than instrument or test-score oriented. In other words, the professionals' judgment is critically more important to the decision-making process than isolated data. The assessment should be a collaborative effort that involves the active participation of all team members to determine the student's educational status and the impact of the suspected handicapping condition on the student's overall functioning. It is imperative that team members maintain open lines of communication.

Assessment of students with suspected learning disabilities, emotional and/or behavioral disorders, or mental retardation varies from state to state. The requirements of PL 94-142, however, have led to many similarities in assessment procedures in various areas of our country.

Staffing. The major purposes of the special education staffing are to determine the existence of an identifiable handicapping condition and to develop an appropriate educational-programming alternative for the student. The members of the assessment team, then, should be represented at the staffing and include at least the following:

1. The local school principal who has basic responsibility for all students in the building.
2. The classroom teacher(s) and/or counselor(s) who provides services to the student.
3. The special educator(s) who helps to interpret educational-assessment data.
4. The school psychologist and/or social worker who assists in the interpretation of assessment data related to the cognitive and social-emotional aspects of assessment.
5. The special education director or representative who serves as an advisor on appropriate procedural safeguards.
6. The parents, who can provide insight concerning their child's needs and levels of functioning outside the academic environment. They may assist in formulating the annual goals of the individual education program (IEP). If the parents choose not to attend the staffing, documented evidence must be maintained to verify the school's attempts to involve them in the assessment-intervention process.
7. Any other specialists who can help to interpret and discuss information about the child (vision and hearing specialists or speech and language pathologists, as appropriate).

The primary functions of the staffing committee should be accomplished through the following sequential activities.

First, the committee should certify that the particular student was assessed in each of the five areas and that the necessary reports were written.

Second, assessment results should be interpreted to determine the student's present functioning levels and to answer questions posed at the referral conference to identify the student's unique needs. Interpretation of assessment results should be a collaborative effort to provide a complete picture of a student's functioning and to determine specific needs. Special education intervention based on students' needs, in contrast with program placement, is gaining popularity throughout the nation. Ysseldyke (1983) suggests that "referrals require interventions at many levels, from instructional changes within the regular classroom to intensive self-contained special education programming." He advocates further "a change *from* referral-to-placement *to* referral-to-intervention" (1983, p. 232). We would second this recommendation strongly and note that assessment must not be viewed as a vehicle for "proving that a student is either learning disabled, emotionally disturbed or mentally retarded." Assessment should help us gain additional insight into each student's unique educational needs. Determination of these needs is accomplished through a brainstorming process in which all members of the staffing committee participate. The process should be based on the assessment results and not be affected by the availability of services or by whether specific services are the school's responsibility. Determination of the student's needs can be identified by asking the following questions:

1. Does the student need any curricular or academic changes, adaptation, or modification to function within the regular program including method and rate of presentation, level of materials, or type of equipment or materials used?

2. Does the student need any specific adaptive, developmental, or compensatory training because of a handicap? This may include training in the use of residual vision or hearing, orientation and mobility training, and gross and fine motor-skill development.

3. Does the student have any social or emotional needs related to self-concept, peer relationships, or knowledge and acceptance of a handicap or disability?

4. Does the student need adaptations or changes to the physical environment related to noise level, visual stimulation, seating, lighting, and physical accessibility?

5. Does the student need alternative styles of classroom management related to the amount of structure, level of activity or stress, group versus individual instruction, or adaptive teaching techniques unique to vision or hearing handicaps?

6. Does the student have any needs related to home-school interaction, that is, with family or parents, that have to do with consistency or reinforcement of training or educational concepts?

7. Does the student have any unique prevocational, vocational, or avocational needs related to awareness of economic and career problems (establishing realistic occupational goals, employability skills) or to problems with recreational and leisure-time activities?

8. Does the student have any unique transportation needs?

9. Does the student have any special health and physical needs?

Third, the staffing committee must decide whether it can certify the presence of a handicapping condition. It is important to understand the underlying conditions that cause the student's needs; however, it is equally important, perhaps more important, to identify the student's unique needs and the characteristics of services required to meet those needs. Therefore, the initial question to be asked is whether the student can profit from regular educational programming with appropriate modifications and without direct special education intervention. If the response to this question is yes, and no special educational intervention is needed, the student exits the assessment-intervention process. Recommendations and consultation assistance for individualized program modifications to be made within the regular class setting are provided to the classroom teacher.

If it is determined that the student cannot receive reasonable benefits from regular education, the question to be answered is whether the need for specialized programming other than that implemented within regular education is due to a handicapping condition. If it is determined that the student's needs are not due to a handicapping condition, then a statement related to the likely cause is needed. If the cause relates to cultural or environmental factors, the student should be referred for further consideration to programs established for that purpose.

If the committee determines that there appears to be a handicapping condition that underlies the student's identified needs, then determination of the student's primary handicapping condition is made for data collection and reimbursement purposes, since state and federal funding is determined at the present time on categorical bases. Labels should not be used outside the context of data collection and reimbursement. The student's program should be based on unique needs rather than on some abstract inexact label. Annual program goals should be developed in a manner consistent with the philosophy of meeting the student's needs.

The fourth step in the staffing process is to identify the characteristics of instructional and related services to meet established goals. It is important that these characteristics flow directly from the student's needs and describe specifically the services required to allow the student to function and learn. The entire process should be student centered and focus on the student rather than on trying to find an appropriate placement or assignment to a room. An example of an appropriate description of service characteristics is "a structured and consistent small-group learning situation."

In conjunction with determining the characteristics of services to be delivered, the staffing committee also recommends service providers, the initiation date and expected duration of services, and the percent of time the student should spend in the regular education program. The steps completed to this point are preliminary and lead to the development of an individualized education program (IEP). (see the box below.)

CONTENT OF THE INDIVIDUALIZED EDUCATIONAL PROGRAM (IEP)*

    I. *Identification and background information*
       Student's name, parents' names, address, telephone number, birth date, sex, age, date of referral, primary language, and similar information.
    II. *Participants in IEP conference*
       Names and titles and/or identification of all participants.

*A composite of the essential content of many different forms.

III. *Assessment information*

Summaries of all assessment information used in any manner in staffing and development of the IEP.; definitive statement of the student's present level of academic functioning plus functioning in any nonacademic area that may be pertinent to and/or a target of program efforts. Assessed abilities and present levels of performance should reflect current status in each area assessed as the basis for determining student's needs.

IV. *Other information*

Medical, sociocultural, or other pertinent information.

V. *Statement of annual goals*

A description of educational performance to be achieved by the close of the school year, based on student's determined needs, including evaluative criteria.

VI. *Statement of short-term objectives*

More specific objectives (than annual goals), indicated on a monthly or quarterly basis; statements include (1) who will provide specific services, (2) where service will be provided, (3) materials or media required, and (4) such information as effective reinforcers and behavioral strengths. Objectives should further clarify student's needs.

VII. *Specific educational services provided*

For example, individualized instruction free from distraction and speech pathology services.

VIII. *Service-delivery recommendations*

Specific type of service delivery, time to be spent in various settings, participation in regular education, rationale for service delivery, and primary service provider.

IX. *Significant time frame*

Dates such as (1) initiation of service, (2) duration of service, (3) approximate dates for evaluation, additional conferences.

X. *Signatures*

All conference participants plus specific parent signature indicating program approval.

Adapted from Gearheart, *Learning Disabilities: Educational Strategies.* St. Louis: C. V. Mosby, 1985.

The format, specific content, and complexity of IEPs vary throughout the nation. However, all must meet the content requirements indicated in the box.

The final step in the staffing process is completion of the IEP, which is an action plan that provides essential guidelines for program implementation and a means of determining the extent to which educational goals are being met. The IEP is developed jointly by the parents and other members of the staffing committee. Depending on the administrative design of the local school, short-term objectives may or may not be developed at the time of the staffing. The basic IEP may be expanded by those who deliver the program services to include more detail. Parents must approve of the IEP and provide written consent for the services to be provided.

Service Delivery

The provision of special education and related services is a coordinated effort that may involve community services as well as more traditional in-school programs. Services must be appropriate to the student's learning and behavior needs and be provided in the least restrictive/most productive environment by appropriately qualified personnel. Therefore, we should attempt to keep students who have been identified as learning disabled, emotionally disturbed, and mentally retarded in the regular classroom when feasible. However, if more extensive, segregated service is required, it must be provided. PL 94-142 requires that we provide a continuum of educational services and that we utilize the least restrictive service delivery for students based on their special education needs. A continuum of possible educational services for students with learning disabilities, emotional and/or behavior disorders, and mental retardation is illustrated in figure 2-2. In addition, these services to students should include transportation, nonacademic and extracurricular activities, and facilities comparable to those afforded to, and used by, nonhandicapped students.

Review

The review process and revision of the IEP should occur at least annually and appropriate changes made in the annual goals, short-term objectives, and service delivery. Changes should be consistent with individual academic growth and should reflect new needs based on the notion that the student is an active learner in an ever-changing environment. Annual review usually occurs within a given twelve-month calendar year. In some districts the review occurs at the end of the school year, whereas in other districts it may occur on the student's birthday or anniversary date of

FIGURE 2-2   A Continuum of Alternative Educational Services

Regular class plus collaborative consultation	Least
Regular class plus special education resource services	restrictive
Cooperative plan—regular class plus	
special class (approximately half time each)	↑
Special class in regular school	
Special class in separate day school	↓
Home or hospital programs (usually temporary measures)	Most
Residential schools	restrictive

the initial IEP. Reassessment of the student's total functioning in all areas should occur every three years or more frequently if warranted or if requested by the student's parents or teachers.

In conclusion, current assessment practices in the United States are similar to those outlined in this chapter. Similarities are undoubtedly due to federal and state legislative mandates, which require procedural due process, the importance of providing services in the least restrictive environment, and requirements for the individualized education program (IEP).

The comprehensive assessment-intervention model of student-program management recognizes that assessment is an active decision-making process based on data collected through formal and informal measurement. Appropriate program choices are made from a number of alternatives, and the decision will directly affect a student's education. In addition, the model is designed to provide insight into the student's total functioning. It is also a needs-based model, which requires a shift in focus from "appropriate placement into a specific program" to "identification of the student's needs and assignment of appropriate service deliverers to meet those needs." Determination of needs is critical to the decision-making process.

HOLISTIC ASSESSMENT

The foundation for a holistic approach to assessment is a developmental perspective on learning, which considers the functional relationship among the parts within a whole, rather than an atomistic perspective, which is concerned with discrete behaviors. Holistic assessment is concerned with the integrative and reciprocal relationships among cognitive processes. To provide a total picture of the students, assessment should consider more than just a comparison of children to norms that identify differences in discrete functions within and among individuals. Traditionally, assessment specialists attempted to measure students' psychological processes, determining differences in relationship to the external norms or standards on which a test had been developed. However, in some cases the intra-individual weaknesses identified by a test may not be a problem for a student in the performance of daily activities. For example, if a student is identified on a particular test as having a visual-perception problem, we might expect that problem to manifest itself in the student's daily functioning. Yet the student may appear to function in tasks that require visual-perceptual abilities with no difficulties. The differences exist only in relationship to a norm. A major concern with the more traditional approach to assessment (which relies heavily on norm-referenced tests) is that we may not be able to measure accurately those functions or abilities we presume to assess because they do not exist separately. Rather, they share a complementary relationship with other cognitive processes. Therefore, we cannot look at the measurement of discrete skills as indicative of a total cognitive construct. We cannot assess a student's total memory ability by using a digit span activity. Memory is much more complex than auditory sequential memory alone. Memory shares a reciprocal relationship with the cognitive processes of attention, perception, cognition, and encoding. The question we must ask is, How can we measure a student's total functioning as an integrated whole?

Holistic assessment attempts to consider students from a developmental perspective in which we evaluate the effect of health and physical integrities and sociocultural factors on their cognitive and affective development. Such assessment leads to a deemphasis of the empiricist paradigm of learning and assessment, which presumes an atomistic view of learning (built on a sequential learning process) in which students add new knowledge to previously acquired knowledge in an incremental fashion.

Assessment assumes a different meaning if we view learning as an extension of cognitive development, that is, as a continuous process of refinement or reconstruction of knowledge based on our environmental interactions. Teaching and assessment are two major elements of an integrated process that depends on direct interaction between the teachers and students to determine how students learn. Therefore, we should capitalize on students' active participation in the learning process and attempt to discover the qualitative differences in their mental structures, that is, how they think. Once we learn that, the teaching process becomes one of arranging environmental conditions to facilitate students' construction and refinement of knowledge (DeRuiter and Wansart 1982).

A holistic approach to assessment emphasizes effective teaching based on how children think as they acquire new knowledge. We believe that holistic assessment is an integration of teaching and assessment in which we attempt to understand the complexities of students' mental structures. DeRuiter and Wansart (1982) indicate that "holistic assessment is both systematic and intuitive . . . hierarchical and heterarchical . . . particular and general. . . . The pairs . . . do not reflect a continuum or a dichotomy, but an integrative set."

Systematic and *intuitive* assessment requires that examiners be knowledgeable about curricular and environmental demands and the nature of learning. This knowledge provides a systematic base for an intuitive mode of operation in which we analyze students' mental structures to determine how they think, form hypotheses about their thinking, and integrate teaching and testing.

The terms *hierarchical* and *heterarchical* concern the relationships that exist among students' mental structures, which are arranged in a hierarchical sequence from simple to complex. Each succeeding level integrates and is constructed upon the preceding level. At the same time, our mental structures are heterarchical because of their reciprocal interrelationship. The terms *particular* and *general* refer to the mental structures that enable us to process external environmental information. Particular mental structures relate to how we process information; that is, the cognitive processes of attention, perception, memory, cognition, and encoding. General structures relate to the higher-level executive function, which is a control mechanism that is goal directed and helps to coordinate the cognitive processes needed to experience our environment. This concept is explained more fully in chapter 3.

If we understand how students think, we have a basis for forming hypotheses as the foundation for instruction. These hypotheses are not static; they change as students interact with the learning environment and construct new knowledge. Hypotheses change as we acquire new evidence about the qualitative changes in students' thinking.

From this perspective, assessment is the study of students' mental structures and their transformation. It is an ongoing and changing process of analysis and appraisal that is inextricably linked to teaching. Assessment is concerned with asking questions of students with learning and behavior problems to determine how they are thinking and the qualitative differences in their mental structures. Our concern is with students' *thinking processes* and not solely with the *products* of thinking.

A mental-structures approach to assessment (DeRuiter and Wansart 1982) attempts to identify students' thinking and their level of response while they perform particular tasks. This is accomplished by analyzing the students' mental structures in relation to the task performance and the information processing abilities and specific strategies applied to that performance. The primary focus of assessment is on the relationship among students' mental structures and how they affect students' performance. This approach is illustrated throughout this text in chapters related to specific instructional strategies.

DeRuiter and Wansart propose three major components in the assessment of students' mental structures: task selection, observation of responses, and making inferences about mental structures. *Task selection* requires general knowledge of internal mental structures and human learning, assessment tasks, and environmental demands placed on the student. Task selection depends on the kind of thinking needed to perform in the individual's environment. Tasks should be relevant and allow for a variety of responses that enable us to understand a student's thought processes. Tasks are selected that require explanation by the student. After an explanation has been provided, the examiner uses a form of Piaget's critical interview to probe the individual's thinking (through alternative explanations) until the student's thinking is apparent.

Observation occurs as the student prepares to perform the task and during task performance. It is important not only to observe and record correct responses and products but to consider students' errors and error patterns as indicators of inappropriate mental structures.

Inferences about mental structures enable teachers to decide how and what to teach. They are based on observations and lead to hypotheses about students' internal mental structures. The primary goal of making inferences is to determine the student's current thinking in relation to important tasks and to decide on the nature and direction of necessary changes in that thinking.

In summary, task selection, observations, and inferences are related very closely and are crucial to the teaching-assessment process. Task selection is the basis for observations, which lead to interpretations (inferences) that are expressed as tentative hypotheses about how the students think. The hypotheses are the basis for the selection of additional tasks that help to evaluate and further clarify students' thinking. The process is critical; it is at this point that teaching and assessment become an integrated process.

DeRuiter and Wansart suggest that the following four types of analysis help to isolate the level at which an individual is performing a specific task:

1. An individual's specific knowledge structures or plans that relate to particular academic skills
2. Control structures that include intellectual capacity and motivation and their effect on learning and performance
3. Mental structures related to responding and to strategy selection
4. Control structures that involve the use of specific strategies and processes

The mental-structures model helps teachers identify areas for instructional interaction and appropriate teaching strategies needed for remediation. The model facilitates our assessment of students' learning behavior and also facilitates decision making about teaching those students. The reader is referred to DeRuiter and Wansart for a more extensive discussion of a mental-structures approach to assessment.

Holistic assessment is based on students' integrities and how they think. It does not penalize them for exhibiting differences but recognizes that their responses are based on their current mental structures. Determination of qualitative differences in students' thinking and subsequent learning needs necessitates that students be assessed from both a developmental and environmental perspective. This approach is necessary if we recognize that students' cognitive and affective development occur simultaneously. Therefore, we must also determine how the students' interactions at home and in the community impinge on their learning and academic progress. Students' primary needs must be met before they can learn; learning is secondary to their overall development. The home and community environments must be secure if students are to progress in school. Assessment of students' total functioning allows us to determine qualitative differences in their learning abilities and how to arrange environmental conditions to help them learn.

SUMMARY

Assessment in special education is designed to gather information that will assist educators to make decisions about various possible educational alternatives and interventions. Under various state regulations, assessment is also required for classification before local education agencies can become eligible to receive special education reimbursement, but the most essential purpose of assessment is to provide a basis for educational planning. It should be considered an active, ongoing process and might be characterized as assessment for intervention.

In this chapter we have reviewed the needs-based assessment model, which may include six steps: screening, referral, assessment, staffing, service delivery, and review. Within this model, we find the requirements for parent involvement, team efforts at staffing conferences, development of the IEP, and consideration of various placement alternatives. Public Law 94-142 has led to an increasing similarity in the manner in which assessment takes place and, overall, has led to more effective assessment processes throughout the nation.

Holistic assessment was featured as a preferred approach to assessment of students who may be handicapped or disabled. Holistic assessment is based on a developmental perspective of learning, which recognizes a functional relationship between parts within a whole, rather than a view that focuses on discrete behaviors. Utilizing this point of view, we emphasize teaching based on how children think (as they acquire new knowledge) and consider teaching and assessment as major elements of a process that depends on direct interaction between teachers and students to determine how students learn. From this perspective, assessment is the study of students' mental structures and their transformation; it involves continual analysis and appraisal, linked to the teaching process.

Assessment is a complex process, a team process, and an ongoing process; and to be effective it must be inextricably interwoven with the teaching process. The ideas expressed in this chapter reflect what we believe to be elements of generally accepted practice plus elements of what might be called futuristic thinking about assessment. As with the conditions that are the subject of this text (learning disabilities, mental retardation, behavior disorders), there is a great deal to be learned about assessment; but understanding of the concepts expressed in this chapter should place the reader a significant distance down the path to effective utilization of assessment procedures.

REFERENCES

DeRuiter, James A., and William L. Wansart. *Psychology of Learning Disabilities.* Rockville, Md.: Aspen Systems Corp., 1982.

Gearheart, Bill R. *Learning Disabilities, Educational Strategies.* St. Louis: C. V. Mosby, 1985.

Leviton, H. The resource room: An alternative (1). *Academic Therapy* 13 (1978a), 405–13.

———. The resource room: An alternative (2). *Academic Therapy* 13 (1978b), 589–99.

Marsh, G., B. R. Gearheart, and C. Gearheart. *The Learning Disabled Adolescent.* St. Louis: C. V. Mosby, 1978.

Salvia, John, and James Ysseldyke. *Assessment in Special and Remedial Education.* Boston: Houghton Mifflin Co., 1981.

Strauss, A., and L. Lehtinen. *Psychopathology and Education of the Brain-Injured Child.* New York: Grune & Stratton, 1947.

Strother, C. R. Minimal cerebral dysfunction: A historical overview. In F. dela Cruz, B. H. Fox, and R. H. Roberts, eds., *Annals of the New York Academy of Sciences: Minimal Brain Dysfunction,* vol. 205, 6–17, 1973.

———. Psychological aspects of learning disabilities. In S. A. Kirk and J. McCarthy, eds., *Learning Disabilities: Selected ACLD Papers,* 86–92. Boston: Houghton Mifflin Co., 1975.

SWANSON, H. LEE, AND B. WATSON. *Educational and Psychological Assessment of Exceptional Children.* St. Louis: C. V. Mosby, 1982.

WIEDERHOLT, J. L., D. HAMMILL, AND V. BROWN. *The Resource Teacher.* Austin, Tex.: Pro-Ed Publisher, 1983.

YSSELDYKE, JAMES. Current practices in making psychoeducational decisions about learning disabled students. *Journal of Learning Disabilities* 16 (1983), 226–33.

CHAPTER THREE

Learning-Strategy Instruction

- What interacting factors guide the determination of which strategy will be most effective?

- What are the major differences between the "tell-them" method, the "model-it" method, and the "develop-it" method?

- What are the differences between a student strategy and a teacher strategy? To what extent may they overlap?

- Why is disequilibrium so important in the "develop it" method?

- How do countersuggestions differ from suggestions? Why are they of value?

- What are the major sources for countersuggestions?

- Why can disequilibrium not be accomplished directly? Given this fact, how does the teacher encourage disequilibrium?

INTRODUCTION

Although our understanding of learning-strategy instruction is obviously incomplete, we believe that learning strategies have merit if used appropriately. At our present stage of development of methods for use with handicapped students, such approaches certainly deserve serious consideration. An important facet of human intelligence is to be able to determine what kinds of strategies are needed for which purposes. When can learning tasks be accomplished without a specified strategy? When can we use strategies that are not consciously applied? When can deliberate, conscious strategies be dropped after they are learned? When are strategy approaches more efficient than nonstrategy approaches? Do strategies change significantly with age? How can they be taught, transferred, and generalized effectively? These and other questions are only beginning to be answered. In this chapter, we will explore an approach to learning-strategy instruction that has evolved out of our own work with handicapped children. Perhaps these suggestions will encourage teachers to create their own effective approaches and to seek answers to some of the above questions.

We will describe three approaches to teaching strategies: the "tell-them" method, the "model-it" method, and the "develop-it" method. They can be used separately or in combination.

THE TELL-THEM METHOD

Telling students about a strategy has the advantage of requiring less time than the other two methods. Also, some students may lack the knowledge or skills that are required for developing a strategy with the teacher, especially with more difficult tasks.

A disadvantage of the tell-them method is that self-regulated thinking may not occur. Students may regard the strategy as something the teacher wants them to learn, not something that has personal benefits. Learning a strategy may then become just another difficult, meaningless task. Students must recognize the need for the strategy and realize that it will help them reach their goals. A degree of "disequilibrium" must be present. That is, students must realize that the way they are now doing a task is not adequate, that their current strategy does not fit the task demands. This disequilibrium is often more difficult to achieve if students are simply told about a strategy.

A second disadvantage of the tell-them method is that it may place too little emphasis on the way students are currently thinking about the task. Students may already be using some steps in the strategy, so these steps do not need to be presented (Schumaker et al. 1982). In addition, teachers might present a strategy that is too complex for the students if they are not aware of the students' current thinking. Since the tell-them method often requires careful, detailed planning by the teacher of the exact steps in the strategy, there is the danger of overlooking the current thinking of the students.

These pitfalls may be avoided, however, by paying close attention to *when, how,* and *what* students are told as a strategy is taught. We suggest the following rules of thumb for the tell-them method:

1. *When* to tell students about the strategy
   - After the teacher understands the students' current way of approaching the task
   - After the students know the inadequacies of their current strategy
2. *How* to tell students about the strategy
   - Present information enthusiastically
   - Use language they understand
   - Respect their current way of thinking and tie new information to this thinking
   - Use specific tasks and examples
   - Use discussion and feedback from the students
   - Require direct practice of the strategy with each task for which it is useful
   - Follow up by observing students' self-regulated use of the strategy in several settings
3. *What* to tell students about the strategy
   - The purposes, values, and uses of the strategy in relation to needs they perceive as personally relevant
   - The specific ways their current strategies will be improved
   - The specific steps in the student strategy
   - The specific way to use each step
   - The tasks for which, and the settings in which, the strategy should be used
   - The importance of self-regulated use of the strategy
   - The specific ways to use the strategy in a self-regulated manner
   - The expectation that they will use the strategy as needed
   - The follow-up techniques that will be used to see if the strategy is being used

Perhaps these lists of when, how, and what appear impossibly long. Each item is important, however, if strategy teaching is to be effective. In total, they imply an entire approach to teaching. Teaching and learning are regarded as an interaction between teacher and student through which students use strategies to actively construct their internal mental structures. To make this approach a part of students' mental structures, teachers must remember these five basic rules about strategy teaching:

1. Make strategies clear and explicit.
2. Build new strategies on old strategies.
3. Apply strategies directly to tasks.
4. Emphasize transfer and generalization.
5. Emphasize self-regulation through strategy use.

Specific steps for teachers to follow with the tell-them method are:

1. Analyze current thinking and performance of the students.
2. Generate disequilibrium. Be sure students know the old strategy is inadequate.

3. State the steps in the strategy. Tell them *what* they need to know to use the strategy.
4. Tell them *how* to use the strategy.
5. Require practice with the strategy.
6. Require transfer to other tasks and settings.
7. Follow up to assure strategy use.

THE MODEL-IT METHOD

The "model-it" method requires more than just telling students about a strategy. It involves direct demonstration of a method to the learners. This method can be incorporated with little difficulty into either the tell-them or the develop-it methods as a substep.

This method is perhaps more efficient than the develop-it method, but may take more time than the tell-them method. It has the advantage of direct demonstration, which provides one of the most effective ways to learn, that of imitating a model. If used appropriately, it has the additional advantage of providing directly for student self-regulation.

On the other hand, the model-it method may fall prey to the same disadvantages as the tell-them method. That is, if the strategy to be modeled is developed by the teacher alone and is imposed on the students, the personal meaningfulness to the students may be lessened, and the currrent thinking of the students may be overlooked. *When, how,* and *what,* as explained for the tell-them method, apply here too.

The model-it method is explained by Finch and Spirito (1980), Meichenbaum (1977), and others who emphasize the use of cognitive-behavior modification. Research by these writers indicates that some individuals can learn to modify their behavior by using verbal self-instruction. The steps in the method as presented by Meichenbaum are:

1. *Cognitive modeling:* The model (teacher) performs the task while talking out loud about how he or she is thinking, as the student observes.
2. *Overt guidance:* The student performs the task under the teacher's guidance, instructing himself or herself by talking out loud in imitation of the teacher.
3. *Overt self-guidance:* The student performs the task without teacher guidance, instructing himself or herself by talking out loud.
4. *Faded overt self-guidance:* The student performs the task while whispering the instructions.
5. *Covert self-guidance:* The student performs the task using private speech ("saying" the instructions in his or her head).

Four general types of verbalizations are used by the teacher and the student (Finch and Spirito 1980; Meichenbaum 1977). First, *problem-definition statements* are used. These verbalizations could, for example, include general self-questioning statements such as:

○ What do I have to do?
○ What do I already know about this problem?
○ Which strategy should I use?

During use of the strategy, answers to these questions are verbalized too. The teacher and then the student might, for example, say:

○ This looks like some of those long-division problems.
○ I guess I will need to read the paragraph and answer the questions at the end.
○ I think I'd better use a rehearsal strategy to learn these spelling words.
○ It looks as if this story problem requires the use of subtraction and multiplication.

A second type of verbalization serves to *focus attention* and *provide response guidance*. Typical self-guidance statements are:

○ I must concentrate and solve this problem.
○ Let's see. I remember how to do long division by thinking about dad, mom, sister, cousin, brother. The first letter in these words goes with the first letter in the steps for long division—*d*ivide, *m*ultiply, *s*ubtract, *c*ompare, *b*ring down.
○ Since this is the first question in the list, the answer is probably in the first couple of paragraphs.

Note that general attending statements, specific items on which to concentrate, and specific steps in completing the task are included in this category of verbalizations.

Self-evaluation, error correcting, or *coping* statements are a third type of verbalization. These include:

○ Even if I did it wrong, I can try again.
○ I think I worked too fast and got it wrong.
○ This answer doesn't seem to make sense because the answer says the car is going six hundred miles per hour. That's too fast for a car.
○ Did I miss any important steps?
○ Whoops, I forgot to check my work.

Again, both general and specific statements are used to provide self-guidance.

Finally, *self-reinforcement* statements may be used throughout the task. For example:

○ Good! I finished the first step without any problems.
○ Great! I solved the whole problem.

The model-it method appears useful for learning new strategies, for using strategies that are already known, and for transferring strategies to appropriate settings. Emphasis is placed on self-guidance rather than depending on the teacher. Thus, a *student* strategy, not just a teaching method, is built in.

THE DEVELOP-IT METHOD

The "develop-it" method uses a dialogue between the teacher and the student to create a strategy. The dialogue is guided carefully by the teacher so that an effective strategy is devised cooperatively. Frequently, more than one strategy is suggested during the discussion. Alternative strategies can be tried out and modified and the most effective one selected. The develop-it method can be used with a single student or with a group. If several strategies are developed with a group, each student can choose one based on individual preferences and abilities.

Develop-it has the advantages of direct student involvement and close ties to individual student characteristics. Both advantages fit very well with the goal of increasing students' responsibility for their own learning. The method does demand much of the teacher. Especially important is teacher skill in guiding the dialogue. The method is also very time consuming. The time is well spent, though, if it results in longer-lasting learning and better strategy use.

For some students, developing a strategy for themselves may be more effective than having a strategy imposed on them, but this has not been researched extensively. Evidence exists that some learning disabled students do not use a strategy that is imposed on them (DeRuiter and Wansart 1981). A study with normal adults (Petelle and Maybee 1974) found that self-generated cues resulted in more learning than imposed cueing systems. Wittrock (1974) conducted a study with fifth- and sixth-grade below-average and above-average readers in which self-generated sentences about the meaning of the paragraph were used. In this study, the teacher provided one or two word organizers for two groups, but only one group was told to generate sentences. A third group was given no guidance. The sentence-generating group remembered the content of the passage best. This study suggests that a combination of teacher suggestions and self-generated cues may be effective. More research is needed on which method or combination of methods works best for strategy teaching.

We suggest five major steps for using the develop-it method. Each step is explained in more detail in the remainder of this section. The steps and substeps are:

1. *Assessment:* Present a task for the student to complete.
   a. Observe and record the strategies the student uses.
   b. Present strategy-awareness, strategy-control, and strategy-use questions.
   c. Present suggestions.
   d. Present countersuggestions.
   e. Outline the student's strategy.
   f. Determine what the student needs to learn.

2. *Disequilibrium:* Guide the student in recognizing why and how his or her current strategy is ineffective.
   a. Present strategy-awareness, strategy-control, and strategy-use questions.
   b. Present examples.
   c. Present suggestions.
   d. Present countersuggestions.
3. *Alternatives:* Guide the student in developing a strategy or strategies for successfully doing the task.
   a. Present strategy-awareness, strategy-control, and strategy-use questions.
   b. Present examples.
   c. Present suggestions.
   d. Present countersuggestions.
   e. Specify steps for the strategy selected.
4. *Practice:* Provide direct practice of the new strategy with relevant tasks.
   a. Help the student understand the selected strategy.
   b. Help the student apply the strategy to the task.
   c. Evaluate strategy effectiveness.
   d. Modify the strategy.
   e. Repeat steps as needed.
5. *Transfer:* Use the strategy in other settings and with other tasks.
   a. Select other tasks and settings.
   b. Help the student use cues to remember the strategy.
   c. Help the student apply the strategy.
   d. Observe strategy use.
   e. Discuss results of strategy use.

The acronym for the develop-it method is ADAPT, which is derived from the first letter of the key word for each major step.

Assessment Step

The first step, *assessment,* requires analysis of the current strategies used by the student. Before this step is started, the teacher decides the general area upon which to concentrate. Referral information or observation as the student does a task usually helps the teacher identify areas of difficulty for the student.

The tasks selected should be designed to provide a helpful way to analyze the student's thinking. Simple yes and no answers are not very helpful, so the teacher designs tasks that pose a problem for the student. The problem can be very simple with the expectation that the student will solve it easily. It can be so difficult that the teacher expects that the correct answer (by adult standards) will *not* be given by the student. Bovet (1981) says that children of different ages may be given the same problems.

Notice that this is different from starting with easy questions and gradually giving harder ones. Strategy assessment involves deciding *how* the problem will be solved and how the student will think about the problem. A grade-level score or an error score are much less important. Whether the student is right or wrong is of secondary value and is useful primarily for deciding what to teach, not how to teach.

The focus is on what an error or a correct response reveals about how the student thinks. Therefore, any task that helps show the student's thinking and strategy use could be selected for the assessment step. Perhaps the only restriction is that the task should relate in some way to the demands of the student's environment. The task could be chosen from any area: spoken language, readiness skills, physical movement, music, sports, peer relationships, self-concept, reading, writing, mathematics, and so on.

Direct teaching is not emphasized in this step, although interaction with the student as the task is carried out is helpful. Immediate correction of errors is usually avoided. Instead, the teacher asks questions about what the student is doing and why and provides praise for the efforts and thinking of the student. Feedback about correct responses and errors is not provided except to the degree that it helps clarify the student's thinking. An example of a teacher doing assessment is presented in figure 3-1. Parenthetical statements in the figure refer to the type of question or comment the teacher makes. These are explained in the section below on strategy questions.

Figure 3-1   Example of the Assessment step of the ADAPT Method: Questioning, Suggestions, and Countersuggestions

---

Task and situation: The student is asked to complete this story problem:

Tim, Bob, and Jill have 5 apples that they want to share, with each person receiving an equal amount. They are all hungry, so they plan to eat all of the apples. How can they divide the apples so they all get an equal share? How much will each person receive?

The conversation below follows.

STUDENT: They could make applesauce.
TEACHER: Great! That would really be an interesting way to solve the problem. But if they don't make applesauce, how many apples will each receive?
STUDENT: Let's see. They would each get 1 apple, so that's 3 apples. Then if Tim and Bob each got 1 more, that would be all the apples.
TEACHER: What about Jill? Will she have as much as the others?
STUDENT: No, but maybe she is younger, so she doesn't need as much.
TEACHER: That could be, but the problem says that each of them is supposed to receive an equal share. (Presents a *strategy-control* question.) What are the steps for giving each of them an equal amount?
STUDENT: Well, if you didn't make applesauce, you could just cut the apples and give each of them their parts.
TEACHER: How big, exactly, would each part be?
STUDENT: Let's see. If you cut the 2 remaining apples in half, there would be 4 halves. If each person is given a half, ½ is left. Then if you cut that half in 3 equal pieces, and give 1 piece to each of them, they would all have the same amount.

TEACHER: That sounds like a good solution. Can you tell me exactly how much each person has by putting the answer in a fraction?

STUDENT: Each person has a whole apple and $\frac{1}{2}$ of an apple and $\frac{1}{3}$ of a half of an apple.

TEACHER: That sounds pretty good. Can you put the amount that each person has into a mixed number?

STUDENT: I think so. (Student stops to think, then writes $1 + \frac{1}{2} + \frac{1}{3} = 1\frac{2}{6}$.) Each of them has 1 and $\frac{1}{3}$ apples. I reduced the fraction.

TEACHER: I see. Each of them has 1 and $\frac{1}{3}$ apples. But something isn't clear to me. If I add up the 3 one-thirds, I get 1 apple. When I add that to the whole apple that each of them received, I get a total of 4 apples. What happened to the fifth apple?

STUDENT: Oh! They each get 1 and $\frac{2}{3}$ of an apple!

TEACHER: That takes care of all 5 apples! (Presents a *strategy-control* question.) But how did you get that answer? Can you tell me how you figured that out?

STUDENT: I don't know. I just knew, I guess.

TEACHER: (Since the student is unable to respond, a *suggestion* is presented.) Maybe since you knew there was 1 extra apple, you just imagined the apple cut into 3 equal pieces and added $\frac{1}{3}$ to each person's total.

STUDENT: I guess so, but I don't see why I went wrong when I figured it out on paper.

TEACHER: Let's take a look. (Points to the student's written problem and presents a *strategy-control* statement.) Tell me what you did here.

STUDENT: Well, I added $1 + \frac{1}{2} + \frac{1}{3}$ and got 1 and $\frac{2}{6}$, or 1 and $\frac{1}{3}$. To do the fraction, I added the top numbers and $1 + 1$ is 2. On the bottom, I multiplied 2×3, which is 6. Reduced down, $\frac{2}{6}$ is $\frac{1}{3}$.

TEACHER: OK, that's clear. (Presents a *strategy-use* question.) But why did you add the top numbers of the fractions and multiply the bottom numbers? The sign says plus.

STUDENT: You can't add fractions with different denominators. You have to multiply.

TEACHER: That's right! You can't add fractions with different denominators. (Presents a *strategy-use* question.) But is it correct to multiply? You said something went wrong when you did it on paper. (Presents a *strategy-control* question.) Can you explain what went wrong now? What are the alternatives?

STUDENT: Well, maybe I could multiply both the top and the bottom numbers. But 1×1 is 1, so I'd get the same answer.

TEACHER: (Presents a *countersuggestion.*) Could you find a common denominator and add the denominators?

STUDENT: That's it! I have to change both denominators to 6. Then I have to change the numerators too, by multiplying by the same number that I used to change the denominator. That makes it . . . (figures on paper) . . . $\frac{3}{6} + \frac{2}{6}$, which is $\frac{5}{6}$. They each got

1 and ⅚ apples. You don't add the denominators when you add fractions.

TEACHER: Hmm! I thought you told me they each got 1 and ⅔ apples before. (Presents a *strategy-control* question.) What did you do differently in the two strategies?

STUDENT: Maybe I *was* supposed to add the denominators after I found the common denominator. But that makes it ⁵⁄₁₂, which isn't right either. I'm stuck!

TEACHER: (Presents a *countersuggestion*.) Maybe we used the wrong numbers for the fractions. Remember, we cut the fourth and fifth apples in half, gave each person ½, then cut the last half in thirds. Maybe we have to do something with that last half. Is it ⅓ of a whole? (The last part of the countersuggestion is in question form.)

STUDENT: Oh, that's right! It's only ⅙ of an apple, because it's one-third of a half. So I just change the first ½ to ³⁄₆, then add the fractions, as I did before. That's ⁴⁄₆, which reduces to ⅔. They each got 1 and ⅔ apples!

TEACHER: (Presents a *strategy-control* question.) Do you know any other ways to figure out this problem?

STUDENT: I guess since we are dividing the apples, we could just divide. The 3 could be divided by 5.

TEACHER : (Presents a *countersuggestion*.) Wait a minute! Are we supposed to divide 3 people into 5 apples, or 5 apples among 3 people?

STUDENT: Oh, yeah! It's 5 apples and 3 people, so I need to divide 3 into 5. (Figures on paper, and arrives at the answer.) That comes out. They each get 1 and ⅔ apples.

TEACHER: Looks as though we have two ways to do it. (Presents a *strategy control question*.) Which way do you think is best?

STUDENT: Probably the second way, since it's faster. I wouldn't be quite as sure that my answer is right, though. I could check it the other way if I wasn't sure.

TEACHER: I see. (Presents a *strategy-use* question.) Could you tell me the exact steps you used in solving the problem with your second strategy?

STUDENT: Well, I figured out that we had to divide 5 apples among 3 people, so I know that they will all get more than 1 apple. I will have to divide the larger number, the 5 apples, by the smaller one, 3 people, otherwise my answer will be less than 1. Then I divide and get an answer of 1 with a remainder of 2. The denominator is 3, so I have 1 and ⅔ apples for each person.

TEACHER: That seems to work. (Presents a *countersuggestion* taken from an earlier explanation of the student.) But wouldn't it be simpler to just give each of them 1 apple, cut the remaining apples in half, and then give them each ½?

STUDENT: Not really, because you still have half of an apple, and if you needed to know the exact answer, it's slower to figure out the fractions. Maybe if you were *really* doing it, it would be OK since you could count the pieces. You still might not know the exact answer. You could just cut the two remaining apples in thirds and give them each 2 pieces.

TEACHER: Now we have 3 alternatives! That's great. (Presents a *strategy-control* question.) Which way is best, do you think?

STUDENT: If I wanted the math answer, I like the way of dividing 5 by 3. It's faster and should always be right if you know how to divide.

TEACHER: OK, they all sound like possible strategies, but that one sounds best to you if you need a math answer. I think I understand your thinking now. (Presents a *strategy-awareness* question.) What would you say a person needs to know in order to be good at problems like this?

STUDENT: You need to know how to divide, and it helps to understand fractions. Mostly, you need to know how to figure out what the problem is asking for.

Comments: Notice that some questions presented by the teacher are simply focusing questions that do not examine strategies directly (e.g., "But how much would each of them receive?"). The teacher gradually gains increasing knowledge about the student's thinking and strategy use. A small amount of teaching and error correction are included, but the emphasis is on how the student actually does the task, right or wrong, and how much the student knows about the needed strategies and alternatives. The assessment step reveals, in this case, that the student's understanding of the problem, its prerequisites, and the strategies is basically adequate. Additional learning and strategy development appear unnecessary, although the student's understanding may become more stable if some practice with similar problems is required.

Observe and record. Several substeps are suggested for the assessment step. First, the teacher concentrates on observing and recording the student's strategies. If the strategies used are not obvious, the student is asked to describe what he or she is doing as the task is completed. An effort is made to record exactly what the student did in completing the task.

Ask strategy questions. During and after task completion, the teacher asks questions about how the student did the task and why he or she did it that way. Three general kinds of questions can be asked: strategy-awareness, strategy-control, and strategy-use questions. Each type of question is illustrated in figure 3-1.

Strategy-awareness questions explore what students know about their own thinking and learning. Examples of the questions that are asked include:

○ What does a person need to know to be good at problems like this?

○ If you did not know how to do this problem, what would you do to find out?

○ Do you think there is more than one way to find the answer to this problem?

○ If someone was really good at problems like this, do you think he or she would try to solve it the same way you did? How would that person try to solve it?

Many similar questions could be asked to explore the learners' understanding of their own thinking. Swanson and Watson (1982) present several additional examples that are helpful under the heading "metacognition" (p. 165).

Strategy-control questions relate more directly to the way the student actually solved the problem. They include questions such as:

○ What is the first step you need to take to solve this problem?

○ Can you tell me all of the steps that are needed to solve this problem?

○ Can you change the order of any of the steps in this problem and still get the correct answer?

○ What are the alternative ways you can think of to solve this problem?

○ If you got stuck on one of the steps of this problem, what would you do next?

○ What is the best way to solve this problem?

Notice that some of these questions are similar to those of strategy awareness. Careful distinctions are perhaps not important, although strategy-control questions focus more on the specific strategy the student used to solve the problem. The third type of question is even more specific. The responses and ideas that the student has as the problem is solved are probed by asking questions such as:

○ How did you know you needed to subtract before you multiplied?

○ What are the steps in long division that you used in this problem?

○ How could you tell that the word you selected to fill in the blank in this sentence was the correct one?

○ Is there another word that could fit in the blank? Is this word as good as the first one you chose? Why?

○ What information would help you solve this problem faster?

These questions are examples, not specific questions that should always be asked. The important point is to ask questions that provide insight into how much the student understands about his or her thinking and problem solving. The questions should be adjusted to fit the task and the student's approach, as shown in figure 3-1. The distinctions between strategy-awareness, strategy-control, and strategy-use questions need not be carefully evaluated during the questioning process itself. Each type is important to ask, however, because of the different kinds of information they yield about the students' thinking.

  Present suggestions and countersuggestions.   The next two substeps in the ADAPT strategy are to present suggestions and countersuggestions. These steps are carried out at the same time as the questions. Suggestions are comments made by the teacher about how the problem on which the student is working could be solved. Suggestions are especially helpful when students do not present their own explanations. That is, if the teacher asks a strategy-awareness, control, or use question, and the student says, "I don't know," the teacher suggests a reasonable answer to the question. A "reasonable" answer is not necessarily a correct answer, however. The reason for giving a suggestion is *not* to solve the problem itself. Rather, the suggestion is designed to help the teacher decide how the student solved the problem and the student's degree of strategy awareness and control. Therefore, suggestions are not just answers to the problem, but explanations of *how* an answer was derived. The teacher does not say, "I think 2 + 3 is 5" but, "I think you knew 2 + 3 is 5 because you counted 2 and then 3 more on your fingers." In this example the student would have just told the teacher that 2 + 3 is 5 but would not have given a helpful answer to the teacher's strategy-use question, "How did you solve that problem?" The suggestion meets two criteria—it is closely related to a recent response of the student, and it is closely related to the unanswered question the teacher has just asked. See figure 3-1 for more examples.

  Figure 3-1 also includes examples of the use of countersuggestions. Countersuggestions differ from suggestions in that they always follow an explanation that has already been given by the student. A countersuggestion is an alternative explanation given by the teacher of how to think about or solve a problem or complete a task. However, countersuggestions are not just any alternative that may occur to the teacher. They are, instead, specific suggestions that *conflict* with the student's explanation. The objective is to test the exact nature of the student's understanding and to determine stability of the understanding. Countersuggestions are a very helpful tool in both assessment and teaching. They provide a direct alternative to giving the student a series of questions that increase in difficulty (Bovet 1981). Countersuggestions yield a much clearer idea of exactly how the student is thinking about the task than would otherwise be available.

  Countersuggestions can be drawn from two major sources, teacher knowledge and student explanation. Through study and experience, teachers gain knowledge about how children usually respond when they are asked strategy questions. This knowledge is a good source for selecting a countersuggestion that challenges a student's thinking. Usually, the teacher selects a countersuggestion that is slightly "higher" or "lower" than the explanation the student has just given. Countersuggestions that are slightly lower help the teacher decide if a student's understanding is stable, or whether the explanation the student has presented is only partly understood. If a student accepts a countersuggestion as valid (when it actually conflicts with what he or she just said), the teacher has evidence that the student may have less understanding than was at first indicated by the response. Higher-level countersuggestions, if accepted by the student, may show that the next level of understanding is about ready to be developed. Careful interpretation is needed in this case, however, because at earlier levels students are often willing to accept any number of explanations even if the explanations are in conflict. Additional probing and countersuggestions help clarify whether the learner recognizes the conflict between the explanations. Students who do not recognize the conflict are usually not ready for higher-level explanations.

A second major source for countersuggestions is the student's own earlier explanations. These countersuggestions often take the form of "You told me before that. . . . Isn't that a better way to do it? Which explanation is the best?" Again, the teacher is trying to determine whether the new understanding the student has just shown is stable and clear to the learner.

Outline the strategy and determine learning needs.   The next substep in the ADAPT strategy—and still a part of the major step of assessment—is to outline the strategy the student has used in the task. Notice that this step is *not* primarily a matter of determining whether or not the learner accomplishes the task correctly. Rather, the teacher outlines and analyzes the student's strategy to determine whether it is adequate for the task, whether prerequisites are missing, and whether new learnings are needed.

One way to outline a student strategy is illustrated in figure 3-2. The figure first reports a conversation between a teacher and student, then shows how the teacher analyzed the strategy of the student. The analysis has six sections that will help the teacher focus on the strategy (nature of the problem as reported, important statements about the problem, student strategy, and so on). Teachers may find it useful to use a similar form.

Figure 3-2   Example of assessment step of ADAPT method: Outlining student's strategy and determining what needs to be learned

Situation and task: The teacher and student have just started work on answering a set of questions from a social studies text. The student is required to read a chapter section and write answers to the questions. (The numbers on the left are used for later reference.)

(1) STUDENT: I hate social studies!
(2) TEACHER: Really? Why?
(3) STUDENT: 'Cause I can't do it.
(4) TEACHER: (Strategy-awareness question.) What makes it hard?
(5) STUDENT: The reading and the hard questions.
(6) TEACHER: (Knows from previous information that the student is capable of the reading and has until recently been answering the questions without difficulty. Strategy-awareness question.) Is it something about the way you are doing the questions that is causing you problems?

(7) STUDENT:	I don't know. I'm just tired of social studies. All the kids laugh at me.
(8) TEACHER:	What do you mean, they laugh at you?
(9) STUDENT:	Whenever I give an answer in class, they make faces, or sorta laugh.
(10) TEACHER:	Why do you think they do that?
(11) STUDENT:	'Cause they hate me. Everybody hates me.
(12) TEACHER:	Do they hate you because of your answers (suggestion), or is it something else?
(13) STUDENT:	They're just mean. All of them are mean.
(14) TEACHER:	(Countersuggestion from student's earlier explanation.) So you hate social studies because the reading and questions are hard, is that right?
(15) STUDENT:	No, I hate it because of the other kids.
(16) TEACHER:	OK, the other kids hate you because they're mean and none of them likes you. (Strategy-awareness question.) What have you tried or can you try to do about it?
(17) STUDENT:	Nothing! There's nothing I can do, because they're just mean.
(18) TEACHER:	(Strategy-use question.) What do you do when they laugh at you?
(19) STUDENT:	I fight back. I cuss at them and sometimes I fight after school.
(20) TEACHER:	I see. I suppose that doesn't help all that much, does it? Do you fight with all the kids, or just some of them?
(21) STUDENT:	Just some of them, but it's getting worse.
(22) TEACHER:	Hmm! I wonder what we can do about it?

Comments: The conversation continues, with the teacher moving to the next step of the ADAPT method—disequilibrium. The teacher believes she has identified the problem and can outline the student's strategy as shown.

Nature of problem as reported: Hates social studies.

Important statements about problem: Statements (1), (5), (7), (11), (13), (17).

Student strategy:

Steps	Evidence	Possible alternatives
1. Swearing	Statement (19)	Not replying
		Sarcasm
		Kind words
2. Fighting after school	Statement (19)	Ignoring, going home
		Talk to them

Summary of problem and strategy: The real problem seems to be that he thinks he can do nothing about the "meanness" of the other kids. His current strategy is essentially just to fight back, which is only making the problem worse.

Strategy to work on: Follow through with ADAPT method. Develop a student strategy that will help him *do* something about the reactions of his peers. This

will probably involve a change in his behavior, perhaps starting with one or two kids who are likely to be the most positive about his approach. *He needs to think that he can do something about the problem.*
Comments: At first, I thought the problem was with social studies. Since I know that he often blames others for his problems and feels helpless when he faces problems, it seems much more important to do something about this, given his explanation of the problem.

Notice in figure 3-2 how the teacher changes emphasis in her questioning as the student explains the problem. Through her questions, suggestions, and countersuggestions, she decides that the major problem is not social studies or the meanness of others but the student's concept that he can do nothing about the problem except fight back. A different direction could have been taken during the assessment. For example, at response 9, the teacher could have explored what the social studies teacher has done about the problem and how the student thought that strategy worked. The figure illustrates how the teacher stays "on track" as much as she can. She asks questions that pinpoint the student's thinking in the area that she hypothesizes is most important at this time. Her assessment could be wrong, of course, but that is another issue. She must be willing to change directions in the future if the hypothesis and the strategy that results from it do not work.

Figure 3-2 also shows the last substep in the assessment process. The teacher has decided what the student needs to learn—he needs to think that he can do something about the problem. She does not develop a specific strategy (if she had, she would be using either the tell-them or model-it method) because she plans to do this cooperatively with the student. She is ready to move to the next step.

Stating the student's problem in a "This student thinks . . ." form helps the teacher pinpoint what needs to be changed for the student. The parallel statement "This student needs to think . . ." gives additional direction to the remaining steps in the ADAPT method. The "thinking" statements are based on what the student does and says but are different from these observable behaviors. "This student thinks . . ." and "This student needs to think . . ." statements capture the essence of what strategy-based teaching is all about—the analysis of the concepts and strategies of the student and active construction of new concepts and strategies by the student.

Disequilibrium Step

Encouraging *disequilibrium* is the second major step in the ADAPT method. The assumption here is that students will not develop new ideas unless they clearly recognize that their old ideas are ineffective or incomplete. The term *disequilibrium* means that the student understands that his or her current concepts and strategies do not match with current experience. Notice the close interaction between the learner and the environment. It is as if the student says to himself or herself, "I know what I *thought* was true about this thing (idea, event), but from what just happened I can tell my idea was wrong." Disequilibrium does not occur unless the student understands this. It does not imply that the learner knows exactly what is wrong. It is awareness of a mismatch combined with a desire to correct the problem. Notice how important disequilibrium is for learning. If one believes that one's way of thinking and problem solving matches reality, if no conflict between one's ideas and experiences is recognized, motivation to change and learn is minimal. The teacher's task is to challenge as directly as possible the thinking of the student who needs to change and develop (Alley and Deshler 1979; Bovet 1981; Moses 1981).

The creation of disequilibrium cannot be done directly because disequilibrium is internal, but a teacher can encourage it. DeRuiter and Wansart (1982) explain in some detail how a teacher can encourage constructive disequilibrium. The major substeps in the process of increasing disequilibrium are similar to those in the assessment step. Strategy-awareness, strategy-control, and strategy-use questions are presented, and suggestions and countersuggestions are used. In addition, numerous examples with which the student's strategy can be tried are usually helpful. As these substeps are carried out, DeRuiter and Wansart (1982) recommend the use of a teacher strategy they call the Columbo method. Fans of 1970s television may recognize the name from the show "Columbo." Peter Falk played the role of a detective who, on the surface, appeared rather inept but in fact used this as a facade for trapping criminals. Columbo feigns ignorance, seeks help from the criminal, cites "irrelevant" facts, acts confused, presents fallacies, supports the criminal, takes the criminal's explanations to logical but eventually absurd conclusions, and so on, to ensnare the criminal (DeRuiter and Wansart 1982). Our objectives as teachers are quite different, of course, but some of the techniques are applicable. An important point is that if students are simply told they are doing something wrong, or if they are simply told how to do something, they may not experience disequilibrium. In fact, *telling* students often creates the very opposite of thinking for themselves—it stops self-regulated thinking because the teacher is doing the thinking for the student. The Columbo method, on the other hand, continuously questions and probes and requires the student to explain, apply, and transfer problems.

Figure 3-3 is an example of the use of the Columbo method to encourage disequilibrium. In figure 3-3, the illustration is carried only to the point where the student recognizes a mismatch between his thinking and his current experience. Subsequent steps are illustrated in figure 3-4. Notice how the teacher supports the student's thinking, even when he is not entirely correct. This support shows a respect for the student's thinking that enables the teacher to learn more about the extent to which the student understands the task. It also places emphasis on the student's thinking for himself, rather than depending on the teacher. DeRuiter and Wansart (1982) call this support "going with the resistance" (p. 180).

Figure 3-3   Encouraging Disequilibrium: The Columbo Method

Situation: Assessment of the student's understanding of the word *average* indicates that he has a partial and inaccurate grasp of the term and of how to calculate an average.

The teacher has formed two "He thinks . . ." hypotheses from the assessment step:

1. He thinks *average* refers to a summed total of measurements taken from several sources.
   Example: When asked "What is the average height of the males in this room?" he estimated the heights to be 5'7", 5'8", 6'1", 5'10", and 5'11". He added these together and concluded that the average height was 26'1".

2. He thinks *average* means a measurement that several objects have in common.
   Example: When asked to illustrate a use of the concept, he told about a friend who went to a tire store to buy four new tires ($82.99 each), four mag wheels ($65.00 each), and five chrome lug nuts for each wheel ($5.85 for a set of five). The friend asked the salesman for the total cost and "the average cost per tire." When the student was asked what *average cost* meant in this case, he replied, "The cost of one tire, one wheel, and one set of chrome lug nuts added together," and gave the correct answer for this sum—$153.84.

   The teacher decides he wants the student to think that an average is calculated by adding the measurements from a set and dividing the sum by the number of measurements that have been added.

   For the disequilibrium step, the teacher's task is to help the student recognize that his concept of *average* does not match the actual meaning of the term.

(1) TEACHER: (Strategy-control question.) How did you get your answer for the wheels and height questions?
(2) STUDENT: I added.
(3) TEACHER: (Strategy-control question.) Can you tell me the specific steps?
(4) STUDENT: For the wheels, I added together the cost of a tire, a wheel, and a set of lug nuts.
(5) TEACHER: (Strategy-use question.) All four tires, wheels, and sets of nuts were added together?
(6) STUDENT: No, just one of each.
(7) TEACHER: OK. How did you do the average heights?
(8) STUDENT: I added your height and my height and John's height and Scott's height and Mr. B's height.

(9) TEACHER:	I see. (Strategy-awareness question.) Would you say you did exactly the same thing in both cases?
(10) STUDENT:	I think so.
(11) TEACHER:	(Suggestion.) So the fact that you added everything together—all the males—for the height problem doesn't really make your strategy different than for the wheels problem, even though with the wheels you only added one of each, not all of the items, is that it?
(12) STUDENT:	I don't know. I added with both problems.
(13) TEACHER:	(Providing support.) Right! You added both times. (Suggestion.) But I'm wondering whether the strategy might have changed in any important way. (Seeking help through a strategy-awareness question.) Can you help me figure out the rule that could be used to find averages?
(14) STUDENT:	I think you always have to add something together. You have to add the numbers of the average you are trying to find.
(15) TEACHER:	(Seeking more help, feigning ignorance, and giving an example.) Hmmm! I'm not sure I would always know exactly which numbers I need to add. Let's try another problem. What is the average cost of an apple that costs 35¢, a peach that costs 47¢, and a pomegranate that costs 83¢? Is this a problem like the wheels problem or one like the height problem?
(16) STUDENT:	I guess I would add the prices together. Let's see . . . (writes out the problem and adds). I get $1.65.
(17) TEACHER:	(Providing support.) Good. That's the total cost. (Feigning ignorance.) I still don't quite understand, though. With the wheels problem, you didn't figure total cost but cost per set of items. (Suggestion.) I guess this must be a different kind of problem, right?
(18) STUDENT:	I guess so. I'm not sure what the difference is, though (indication of disequilibrium).
(19) TEACHER:	Well, we have two different ways to calculate averages. (Suggestion.) Maybe there are several ways to do it and it doesn't really matter which one you use.
(20) STUDENT:	Maybe. (Thinks.) But usually, in math, if you don't do it exactly right, the answer comes out wrong.
(21) TEACHER:	Hmmm. You're probably right. That's what we usually find when we work on math, isn't it? (Acts confused.) I guess there just isn't any way for us to figure this out.

It is important to focus disequilibrium on the precise point that the student does not understand. The goal of disequilibrium is not a general feeling of discomfort or frustration for the student. In figure 3-3, for example, encouraging the student to think about whether his friend who bought the tires knew what an average was would be of little help. If the teacher had asked about this, the student might have experienced disequilibrium about his friend's knowledge, but this experience would not directly address his own misunderstanding. Usually the assessment step provides the teacher with one or more hypotheses about what the student does not understand. Sometimes the teacher will focus on the wrong problem, of course, but this can usually be corrected as the dialogue continues, if the teacher is listening carefully to the student and knows the material under consideration along with some good strategies to use with it.

Alternatives Step

The *alternatives* step in the ADAPT method involves developing and exploring a variety of possible strategies for learning or problem solving. Again, dialogue between teacher and student provides the essence of the interaction. Questions, examples, suggestions, and countersuggestions are used cooperatively to develop learning strategies. The final substep here is to specify steps for the strategies that have been developed. Figure 3-4 is a continuation of the "averages" problem (figure 3-3) and illustrates the alternatives step.

Figure 3-4   Developing Alternatives

Situation: The student needs to learn how to calculate averages (continued from figure 3-3). The teacher wants the student to think as follows:

An average is calculated by adding the measurements from a set and dividing the sum by the number of measurements that have been added.

(1) TEACHER: (Strategy-awareness question.) Can you think of any way we can figure this out—how we go about calculating averages?

(2) STUDENT: You probably know. Or we could look it up in my math book.

(3) TEACHER: (Switches roles.) You're right! I do know how to do it. Instead of just telling you, though, I want to see if you can figure it out. I'll give you some examples and we'll see if you can figure out what happened. Let's see . . . (presents example). I read in the newspaper that the average Miss America contest winner has measurements of 36-24-35. What does average mean here?

(4) STUDENT: She has a great figure!

(5) TEACHER: I agree. But what is meant by the *average* Miss America? Which Miss America are they talking about?

(6) STUDENT: It doesn't mean any particular one, just that the winner usually has those measurements.

(7) TEACHER: (Going with the explanation.) OK, but how would that be calculated? (Suggestion.) Would they just guess, or what?

(8) STUDENT: I don't think so. They would measure and find out how many were 36-24-35. Most of them must have those measurements.

(9) TEACHER:	Aha! So the measurements that are found most frequently are the average. Is that it?
(10) STUDENT:	I guess so. But that doesn't work sometimes because everything in the group is different, like different prices for fruit.
(11) TEACHER:	You're right! (Switches roles.) What you just described, the measurement that is found most often, is not an average. It's another measurement called a mode. So we need to find a better alternative. (Suggestion.) Remember, you said before that you add things up to find an average. If you did that with our example, what would you add?
(12) STUDENT:	Let's see. It wouldn't help to add the three measurements for each person because we'd just say their measurements were 100 or something. I guess you'd need to add the measurements for the different people together. Like one person's waist measurement added to the next person's and so on.
(13) TEACHER:	I see. Like we did with the heights for the males in this room. Is that all we need to do? What would be the result of that addition?
(14) STUDENT:	Whoops! That wouldn't work. If we had 10 winners who each had waists of 24 inches, the average would be 240 inches.
(15) TEACHER:	(Switches roles.) OK, but now let me give you some help. You have the correct *first* step. The problem is that there is a second step needed to calculate averages. What do you think it might be?
(16) STUDENT:	I have no idea.
(17) TEACHER:	(Suggestion.) OK, I'll tell you. You have to divide. What do you have to divide, do you suppose? Let's look again at the example you just gave. If 10 winners add up to 240 inches at the waist, what will you need to divide to find the average if the average is 24?
(18) STUDENT:	Divide 240 by 10, which is 24.
(19) TEACHER:	Right! Notice that we used the number 10 before in the problem. Do you remember where?
(20) STUDENT:	Oh! It's the number of winners. We added up 10 peoples' waist sizes.
(21) TEACHER:	OK, so we had two steps in the process. What were they?
(22) STUDENT:	First we added, then we divided.
(23) TEACHER:	What was added and divided? Where did the numbers come from?
(24) STUDENT:	Well, you add up all the numbers of the things you need to find the average of. Then you divide by the number of things you added.
(25) TEACHER:	I think you've figured out the steps! Let's write them down so we don't forget. You did a great job of thinking it through and deciding on the steps in your strategy!

The teacher attempts to use the student's suggestions and under-standings as much as possible as an appropriate strategy is designed. In this case, only one specific strategy is developed because the task doesn't de-mand alternative strategies. For many learning tasks, more than one strat-egy can be developed. For example, one of our sixth-grade students sug-gested three strategies for learning spelling words that are not phonetic—writing them out ten times each, learning them in word-family groups, and spelling them out loud while riding her horse. She also suggested, for the last strategy, that if the horse nodded his head she would know the word was spelled correctly, but the teacher suspected she said this to encourage disequilibrium in the teacher. The student was told some additional alter-natives, such as visualizing the words and writing them in the air. From among these alternatives the student selected a combination of grouping similar words, spelling aloud, and visualizing (all done on horseback) as a strategy to use.

The alternatives step appears to be an especially appropriate place to help students become more aware of strategies and their use in a more general sense. The teacher tries to help students recognize that alternatives are available, that a strategies approach is useful, that they have good ideas that can be used in a strategy, that they can learn to control and use strategies, and so on. Learning to be aware of strategies and to control and apply them is a central part of the method and is integrated into the method as it is carried out. Many questions, suggestions, countersugges-tions and examples are directed toward this general level of strategy learn-ing in the context of a specific task.

Response 2 in figure 3-4 shows that this student has probably worked with this teacher before. The student recognizes that the teacher's igno-rance is not real. Sometimes students object to this and insist that the teacher tell how the task is to be done. When this happens, the teacher can make the students aware that thinking for themselves is usually more help-ful to their learning. Either a facetious (Would I keep it from you if I knew?) or a serious (I *do* know, but you'll remember it better if you figure it out yourself.) remark usually takes care of the problem. Most students enjoy the interaction, the demands on their thinking, and the gamelike aspects of the dialogues, especially if the emphasis is on thinking the task through rather than on being right.

Notice in responses 3, 11, and 15 that the teacher switches roles in the Columbo method. The switch is from the typical Columbo attitude to one of the "teacher" role. The teacher directly tells the student something when the disequilibrium is just right—when the teacher senses that the student is ready to learn it. This kind of switching from "Columbo" to "teacher" captures much of the essence of the alternatives step and the ADAPT method. The entire process is one of dialogue between teacher and stu-dent, of playfulness but with serious attention to the concepts and strat-egies, of interacting with one another, of exploration of ideas and alter-natives without fear of being wrong.

The dialogue in figure 3-4 focuses mostly on the lowest level of strat-egies, that of strategy use. In many situations teachers will want to spend more time on the levels of strategy awareness and strategy control because these levels may help with generalization, transfer, and general-strategy use in other settings. Response 25 illustrates one way to emphasize strategy awareness and control. The teacher praises the student for thinking and specifying steps. Notice also in this response that the precise steps for the strategy the student is learning are written down. If several possible strategies are developed in this step, all of them might be written down, and one would be selected for the next ADAPT step.

Practice Step

Application of a strategy follows strategy selection. This *practice* step involves learning the strategy that has been selected and applying it to relevant tasks. Evaluation of the effectiveness of the strategy and modification of it are subsequent steps. Finally, more practice with the modified strategy takes place as needed. The practice step often takes considerable time. If the strategy is a broadly applicable one, such as a reading-comprehension strategy, it may take several weeks to learn. This is not surprising because the student is not attempting to learn a few isolated facts but is learning how to learn. The results are worth the time if a strategy with lifelong applications is learned.

The first substep in practicing the selected strategy is to help the student understand the strategy. This may involve memorizing the steps in the strategy, discussing the steps with the teacher, trying out the steps one at a time, and so on. We know of no "best" way to do this because effectiveness depends on the nature of the strategy and the knowledge of the student. Generally, it helps to apply the strategy to examples as it is being learned. All or part of the strategy may be modeled by the teacher. (See the description of the model-it method.) The dialogue that was characteristic of the earlier steps can be continued, with suggestions and countersuggestions being made as the strategy is learned and applied. DeRuiter and Wansart (1982) encourage "playing with the concept" (p. 185)—trying it out, having the teacher do the problem, sometimes incorrectly, and so on—and having the student teach the teacher as part of the teaching method here.

Two important ideas are that the strategy should be very explicit, and it should be learned in context. To make the strategy explicit, write it down and talk about it openly. Discuss with the student what its usefulness may be and what its weaknesses may be. Talk about trying it out, evaluating it, and changing it. Discuss the steps and probe the student's understanding of them. The student should be as aware as possible of what is happening and of the nature of the task. Next, or as a part of the foregoing, the strategy is applied to meaningful tasks for which it is designed. The teacher should let the student choose the tasks as much as possible.

Transfer Step

Students with learning problems frequently have difficulty in applying what they have learned to other, similar situations. Dansereau and his colleagues (1979) suggest that even with normal learners, applications may need to be made to *all* of the tasks for which the strategy is useful if transfer is to occur. Explicit discussion of how and where to transfer the strategy is probably essential.

A major transfer technique is to teach students to use self-cueing to help them remember a strategy and when to use it. These techniques are described in the chapters on perceptual and language cueing techniques. The central idea is to enable the learner to take responsibility for his or her own strategy selection and use. The remaining substeps are (1) try out the strategy with the transfer tasks, (2) observe strategy use, and (3) discuss the results. Observations of strategy use refer especially to the teacher's observing the student as the strategy is applied across tasks and settings. A student might be observed on the playground, for example, to see if a strategy for avoiding playground fights is used. Regular classroom teachers are often excellent sources of information about whether strategies are being used in other settings.

A final dialogue, with the use of examples, suggestions, and counter-suggestions, concludes the transfer step. Of course, some modifications of the strategy for use with particular tasks may result. Also, the transfer step never really ends if the strategy has continuing usefulness. Many handicapped learners may need to be observed, reminded, and encouraged for a long time if they are to continue using a strategy. For broadly applicable strategies, a period of a year or more may be needed, from start to finish, in using the ADAPT method.

SUMMARY

The three approaches we have described for helping students learn strategies are designed to build a repertoire of strategies that continue to be useful to the learner. Each of them provides a means for the teacher to interact with the student in a productive way. They should not be regarded as more than general guidelines for the interaction between teachers and students. The nature of this interaction is probably much more important than the precise method of teaching. Every method works with some students, and every handicapped person is capable of learning. The teacher's task is to understand the learner, the nature of learning, and the curriculum and then to use methods that enable learners to construct their own version of reality. Flexible, integrated use of the three approaches is essential. None of these approaches provide directly for learning. They only provide a framework that teachers can use to help students learn and become responsible for continued learning and application of what they know. Each of these teaching approaches will be misapplied seriously if it is considered to be a way to "force" children to learn.

REFERENCES

ALLEY, G., AND D. D. DESHLER,   *Teaching the Learning Disabled Adolescent: Strategies and Methods.* Denver: Love Publishing Co., 1979.

BOVET, M. C.   Learning research within Piagetian lines. *Topics in Learning and Learning Disabilities,* 1 (1981), 1–9.

DANSEREAU, D. F., B. A. McDONALD, K. W. COLLINS, J. GARLAND, C. E. HOLLEY, G. M. DIEKHOFF, AND S. H. EVANS. Evaluation of a learning strategy system. In H. F. O'Neil, Jr., and C. D. Spielberger, eds., *Cognitive and Affective Learning Strategies.* New York: Academic Press, 1979.

DeRUITER, J. A., AND W. L. WANSART. Problem-solving strategies and cognitive training in learning disabled and normal adolescents. Unpublished research report. University of Northern Colorado Research Bureau, Greeley, Colo., 1981.

————. *Psychology of Learning Disabilities: Applications and Educational Practice.* Rockville, Md.: Aspen Systems Corp.: 1982.

FINCH, JR., A. J., AND A. SPIRITO. Use of cognitive training to change cognitive processes. *Exceptional Education Quarterly* 1 (1980), 31–39.

MEICHENBAUM, D. *Cognitive-Behavior Modification.* New York: Plenum Press, 1977.

MOSES, N. Using Piagetian principles to guide instruction of the learning disabled. *Topics in Learning and Learning Disabilities* 1 (1981), 11–19.

PETELLE, J. L., AND R. MAYBEE. Items of information retrieved as a function of cue system and topical area. Paper presented at the Annual Meeting of the International Communication Association. New Orleans, April 17–20, 1974.

SCHUMAKER, J. B., D. D. DESHLER, G. R. ALLEY, M. M. WARNER, AND P. H. DENTON. Multipass: A learning strategy for improving reading comprehension. *Learning Disability Quarterly* 5 (1982), 295–304.

SWANSON, H. L., AND B. L. WATSON. *Educational and Psychological Assessment of Exceptional Children.* St. Louis: C. V. Mosby, 1982.

WITTROCK, M. C. Learning as a generative process. *Educational Psychologist* 11 (1974), 87–95.

CHAPTER FOUR

Perceptual Cueing Strategies

- What is the difference between perceptual cueing strategies and language cueing strategies?

- How can we determine whether cueing strategies are needed?

- What types of perceptual cueing strategies are available for use?

- How can students learn to develop and use their own visual cueing strategies?

- What motor-performance cueing techniques have been found to be most valuable?

- What are the essential features of mnemonics?

- In which of the traditionally recognized academic and skill areas have cueing strategies been most successfully applied?

The central idea of this chapter is that perceptual cueing strategies can be used to guide learning. Cueing strategies, as we use the term, are essentially plans that are designed to help students develop their awareness of how to learn, solve problems, and carry out tasks. Cueing strategies are extended in the next chapter to applications with language cues. The following sections on theoretical and assessment perspectives apply to both this chapter and the next.

THEORETICAL PERSPECTIVES

Underlying the concept of cueing strategies is the assumption that students must learn to control their own learning and problem solving. This idea is consistent with our view that learning is an active, constructive process. We are not saying that handicapped students are inactive *learners*. In fact, we regard the words *inactive* and *learners* as mutually exclusive. If someone is learning, he or she is, by definition, active. Recent research indicates, however, that handicapped students may fail to learn what they are capable of learning, and that this failure may require more emphasis on helping these students through a metacognitive approach (Reid and Hresko 1981). Possibly these students do not use the self-regulated strategies they must use, although a direct cause-effect relationship between metacognition and performance has not been satisfactorily established.

The strategies outlined are both *student* strategies and *teacher* strategies. Teachers are involved in helping students develop strategies and improve them. The goal, however, is to enable students to guide their own thinking and behavior. Simply telling students about a strategy and how to use it is not enough. They should be actively involved in strategy development and should eventually internalize the strategies and use them independently.

The cueing strategies an individual can learn to use to guide thinking and behavior have been divided into two major types: perceptual and language. Perceptual cueing strategies typically involve presenting visual signs or symbols to remind students to use a strategy or the steps in a strategy (DeRuiter and Wansart 1982). Language cueing strategies, as explained in chapter 5, use verbal and written language cues to accomplish the same purposes. External cues are important at first but will, in most cases, be unnecessary as the students develop internal cueing systems to replace external cues. The only important distinction between these two types of strategies is that a different symbol system is used. Nonverbal symbols are called perceptual cues; language symbols are called language cues. Both strategies operate in essentially the same way, and they are frequently used together.

Three concepts emphasized in using perceptual and language cueing strategies are (1) learner control of learning is important; (2) learner competence is important; and (3) long-term learning is important. Each of these concepts is explained below.

First, cueing strategies emphasize student control of learning rather than teacher control. Reid and Hresko (1981) state that "until recently nearly all responsibility for executive functions in learning settings has been assumed by the teacher. . . . Teachers have assumed the role of the omniscient" (p. 48). A student's awareness of his or her own cognitive processes (Torgesen 1977) and sense of control over learning and performance (Henker, Whalen, and Hinshaw 1980) are significant variables to which teachers may fail to attend when they play the traditional teacher role. In addition, Powers (1973) emphasizes that "change demands consciousness from the point of view that needs changing" (p. 201). The intent of perceptual and language cueing strategies and of a strategies approach in general is to place control of learning and responsibility for learning with the learner.

An emphasis on learner control and responsibility is not intended to diminish the role of the teacher or to place the blame on students if they fail to learn. However, it does significantly change the teacher's role. Instead of imparting knowledge for the students to absorb, the teacher takes responsibility for arranging experiences for the students so that learning can occur (Reid and Hresko 1981). This concept also accounts for the active role students must take in learning. Notice here a distinction between teaching and learning. Teachers teach and learners learn. A teacher cannot simply present information and assume that learning has taken place. Additionally, when students fail to learn, teachers must seek better ways to provide the experiences that will activate the learning process.

The second concept is that learner competence is important. The distinction here is between *competence* and *performance*. Probably most teachers support the idea that students not only must be able to do a task but must be able to do it when it needs doing and with understanding. As Bovet (1981) points out, it is possible to push students into "performance without construction" (p. 6). That is, the student produces a response that is not based on understanding and the most important type of learning is not taking place. Perceptual and language cueing strategies are designed to help students learn what to do, when to do it, and why.

The third concept that is emphasized with perceptual and language-cueing strategies is that long-term learning is important. Perhaps this concept is obvious but, because the issues involved are so important, we will attempt to make it more explicit. Teaching techniques that focus on rote memorization of isolated facts are not unusual. Much of what is "learned" in schools is quickly forgotten. Obviously, this problem is not solved by telling teachers to teach that which is important and easy to remember. Disagreements about what is important and lack of information about what is easy to remember make this solution too simplistic.

Cueing strategies do not provide a complete solution to this problem. They do provide a helpful approach when they are part of a perspective that deliberately emphasizes long-term retention and competence. Brown and Palincsar (1982) state that "evidence is accumulating to suggest that an ideal training package would consist of . . . practice in the use of task-appropriate strategies, instruction concerning the significance of those activities, and instruction concerning the monitoring and control of strategy use" (p. 7). Cueing strategies are designed to provide the specific task strategies and the conscious control to which Brown and Palincsar refer. If these strategies are developed appropriately, transfer and generalization to a variety of thinking, learning, and problem-solving tasks may be possible. Ideally, these strategies may be a basis for learning new strategies that have broader and more significant applications. This point of view suggests that long-term learning is not just the recollection of facts but the use and development of strategies in appropriate contexts. Teaching of a strategy, by itself, is not enough. Imposing a strategy designed by the teacher is not enough. Students must be involved in strategy development. They must be consciously aware that they are using a strategy to do a task, of the steps in the strategy, of the value of the strategy, and of when to use it. This is what learner control and responsibility are all about. Notice that much time must be given to these aspects of learning if a strategies approach is to be successful. Underlying these three general concepts about cueing strategies is the assumption that strategies are not valuable in isolation. Rather, cueing strategies are a means to help students reach the goal of learning in school.

ASSESSMENT PERSPECTIVES

Two important decisions related to assessment are required if cueing strategies are to be used. First, teachers must decide if a strategy is needed. Second, they must determine whether the student will be able to use a cueing strategy.

Is a Cueing Strategy Needed?

We assume that handicapped students in general need to use cueing strategies in the sense that they must be active participants in learning. However, not all learning-handicapped students necessarily fail to use strategies appropriately (Torgesen 1982). Therefore, teachers need to discriminate instances in which cueing strategies are already used appropriately from instances in which a student needs assistance in their use. Although much remains to be learned about this area, Bovet (1981), DeRuiter and Wansart (1982), and Swanson and Watson (1982), among others, provide helpful suggestions regarding assessment procedures.

Assessment to determine whether a cueing strategy is needed is essentially the same as assessment of strategy use as explained in earlier chapters. Students who demonstrate that they do not have a strategy for the task, that they use an inappropriate strategy, or that they apply a useful strategy incorrectly are good candidates for cueing strategies. Especially when adequate opportunity to learn the necessary strategies has not resulted in strategy use, the student may need the assistance that cueing provides.

Essentially, teachers can decide whether a cueing strategy is needed by examining which strategies a student uses with a task, making a reasonable and practical decision about whether it appears that a cueing strategy is needed, and then trying out that strategy with the student. If more efficient, longer-lasting learning occurs, the decision to use a cueing strategy has all the support it needs. Of course, the teacher must keep records of student learning and judge whether the desired learning is occurring, but these are always part of teachers' responsibilities.

Can the Student Use a Cueing Strategy?

Evidence is rapidly accumulating that handicapped learners can use strategies when taught to do so (Reid and Hresko 1981). Much less certain are the specific relationships between strategy use and learner characteristics. Knowing which cues help with a particular task is probably a result of learning and development. Gordon and Flavell (1977) conclude from a study of children's intuitive knowledge of cognitive cues in a memory task that three-year-olds have only a rudimentary understanding of which cues are good and that the ability to know which cues help probably develops in middle childhood. Therefore, in deciding whether a particular student can use a cueing strategy, teachers should keep in mind that younger children will be less responsive to this technique. Language cueing strategies may require more language ability than perceptual cueing strategies (Osler, Draxl, and Madden 1977), and older students will probably be more capable of using strategies that require logical thinking than younger students. Other than these general guidelines, the best way to decide whether a student can use a cueing strategy is to try it out.

Suggested Assessment Procedures

To decide whether a cueing strategy is needed and which specific strategy is appropriate, we suggest use of the process presented in chapter 3 as part of the develop-it method. The assessment steps of the ADAPT strategy provide guidelines for selecting a task and evaluating students' strategy use as they carry it out. As a part of the last two substeps (outlining the student's strategy and deciding what the student need to learn), the teacher can also form a hypothesis about whether a cueing strategy is needed and what it should be. On the basis of the thinking of the student and the nature of the task, the teacher decides on a general or specific cueing strategy. Strategies may be selected from those presented later in this chapter or may be developed by the teacher, preferably in cooperation with the student.

Now the teacher and student are ready to try out the cueing strategy. This is a part of ongoing assessment rather than initial assessment, perhaps, but it is an essential part of the teaching/testing process. The usefulness of the strategy is evaluated, modifications are made, and the process is repeated as necessary.

PERCEPTUAL CUEING
STRATEGIES

In this section, we present some specific perceptual cueing strategies that may be useful for handicapped students. In each case, the strategy involves the use of nonverbal perceptual cues that are intended to help guide the thinking, learning, and responding of the learner. These strategies emphasize nonverbal cues, but they often include or can be aided by some use of verbal explanations as students learn to use them. These strategies are a set of suggestions, not a final answer to all of the cueing-strategy needs of handicapped students. More research on these strategies is needed, and not all possible strategies are described.

Cueing strategies range from simple attention-getting cues to complex flow charts for understanding concepts. We will present strategies in five categories in this sequence: attention, perception, motor performance, memory, and comprehension. Some overlap exists between categories.

Cueing for Attention

Students who are hyperactive sometimes fail to focus on the important stimuli that will enable them to accomplish a task (DeRuiter and Wansart 1982). Blackwell, McIntyre, and Murray (1978) concluded that the problem is not just that these children are very active but that they do not organize and plan how to attack a task. When hyperactive children are provided with attention-getting visual cues, they sometimes perform better (Sykes et al. 1973). These cues provide a way to both focus and organize attention.

Pick and Pick (1970) present a general guideline for using visual cues when they suggest that stimuli may be made more complex and more sharply contrasted. That is, a teacher can somehow change the important stimuli so that they are obviously different from other stimuli. Increasing the size of stimuli or adding color are good examples. Sometimes additional visual markers also help. For example, arrows or pointers in the margin may cue a student that an important concept is in that line of a paragraph.

Specific teacher strategies that have been found effective for focusing attention include using arrows or pointers (Rosonke 1975), marking lightly through important parts of a stimulus (Blackwell et al. 1978), and underlining (Schnell and Rocchio 1974; Glover et al. 1980). The last mentioned will be discussed later because it has been used primarily with comprehension tasks. Notice, however, that it can also be applied to focusing attention.

Rosonke (1975) showed line drawings to normal first and fourth graders to see if drawings with visual attention-directing devices (arrows and pointers) helped them identify parts of the drawings. With fourth graders, visual cues did not increase performance over using auditory cues alone; however, first graders' performance was significantly increased by the use of visual cues. This method is worth considering for use with handicapped students because of the attending problems they often show. One application might be the use of arrows pointing toward important words or lines of print. More research is needed to determine whether visual cues of this sort would also help students attend for longer time periods.

Hyperactive learning disabled, nonhyperactive learning disabled, and control groups of children were compared on a task that required locating a target letter in a random set of letters by Blackwell, McIntyre, and Murray (1978). In some trials, small groups of letters that contained the target letter were lightly marked to see if performance improved. Without visual cues the hyperactive learning disabled students did not show the organized search pattern of the other two groups and did not perform as well. Although the learning disabled students did not do as well as the controls when visual cues were used, the hyperactive group did as well as the non-hyperactive group when visual cues were used. Highlighting important sections of a stimulus may be helpful for students who do not seem to have an organized search pattern.

Using arrows and highlighting are both rather simple techniques. These teacher strategies, as well as other visual cues such as pointing to the place to start, circling an important word or letter, using bright colors, and underlining, are already frequently used by some teachers. More important, however, is the question: How can we teach students to develop and use their own visual cueing strategies for attention? Very little research is available on this topic. Ritter (1978) concluded that preschoolers did not use perceptual cues spontaneously but that third graders did when they were asked if there was a way to find which of six inverted cups covered a piece of candy. The children had watched as the candy was put under a cup and then the cups were moved around. A marker was available so that the children could mark the cup that covered the candy if they wished. The third graders marked the cup, but the preschoolers did not until after they had been given a series of questions that provided more and more cues about how to remember which cup covered the candy. Ritter believed that efficient strategy production depended on the children's understanding of the relationship between the cue and the task. Preschoolers apparently did not understand this relationship unless they were given guidance. Notice, however, that with guidance the strategy *was* used.

One technique that has helped students focus attention is to present an easy task first and then a more difficult task. Spiker (1959) contrasted preschoolers' ability to discriminate between very similar levels of brightness when they were given different kinds of training. One group was given forty-eight trials on the difficult discrimination. The other group was provided with twenty-four trials on an easy brightness-discrimination task followed by twenty-four trials on the difficult discrimination task. The second group was significantly more successful on the difficult discrimination even though the children had had less direct practice with this part of the task.

The studies cited above provide two suggestions related to the question of whether students can learn to develop and use their own visual-cueing strategies for attention. First, teachers should provide assistance to students who need it to develop and use these strategies. Second, teachers should use stimuli that are very different from one another, especially in early stages of learning.

Any time a teacher wants a student to attend to particular stimuli, for instance, vowel sounds, letter shapes or names, arithmetic problems, concepts in material that is being read, or some other area, stimuli that are easy to distinguish may be helpful at first. This guideline is similar to that of Pick and Pick (1970), who suggest that attending behavior may be increased by making the important stimuli more complex and more sharply contrasted. We have already suggested using color, highlighting, underlining, and pointers to attract attention. Important stimuli can also be made larger, boxes or circles can be drawn around them, or they may be embellished in other ways.

Teachers must be inventive about helping students develop their own strategies for perceptual cueing for attention. Perhaps students can learn to provide themselves with attention-getting cues. This is the goal of strategy teaching but probably cannot be achieved without involving more complex levels of strategies. That is, in order to know which stimuli are important and how to use color cues, pointers, and so on, an individual must comprehend the material and have prior control of attention. Thus, language cueing strategies may be required before perceptual cueing strategies if students do not use the latter spontaneously. If students have learned to control their own strategies, they can perhaps use perceptual cues such as cue cards to remind them to sit down and begin work. Timers may provide a visual cue to stay on task until the time runs out. In the current context, the important point is that students explicitly learn to give themselves the perceptual cues that help maintain attention and focus on important stimuli.

Cueing for Perception

Cueing for perception is very similar to cueing for attention, except that the emphasis is on discriminating between stimuli rather than on simply attending to them. Perceptual learning is regarded by some as "pulling out," or abstracting, the features that distinguish one stimulus from another (Gibson and Levin 1975). In this view, the techniques that enable perceptual learning to occur are the same as for cueing for attention: drawing attention to the feature by increasing the contrast with other features (e.g., by color coding), providing clear examples of the parts of features that do not vary, and starting with maximum contrast and progressing to minimum contrast (Gibson and Levin 1975).

Hagan and Kail (1975) noted that with normal children redundant cues may speed discrimination learning. For example, if a letter to be discriminated is made both larger and red, it may be learned faster. They note, however, that the use of more than two redundant cues may not help very much and that it may even hinder learning. Hagen and Kail also caution that some children may prefer one type of cue over another, and that young children were sometimes hindered or prevented from learning a discrimination problem when nonpreferred color, size, or shape cues were used. Generally, as age increases students need fewer cues and make better use of the cues that are available (Elkind 1978). Teachers must select cues carefully so that they match the preferences and abilities of the students as well as the task, and cues that seem important to adults may not be the most effective for children (Reese 1976).

Students may be able to develop and use their own cueing strategies to aid perception in a wide variety of tasks. Consider, for example, a worksheet task with mixed addition, subtraction, and multiplication problems. Assume that a student has had difficulty noting which operation is required. The student could provide her own visual cues by marking the addition, subtraction, and multiplication signs in red, blue, and green, respectively, before doing the problems. For some students, the teacher may need to provide a verbal reminder to do this kind of thing until they learn to recognize for themselves that such cueing strategies are helpful.

Cueing for Motor Performance

Two kinds of visual cues may be used to aid students with motor performances. One is to model the performance directly so the student can imitate the movements. The other is to provide a picture or drawing that shows the type or sequence of movements that should be performed. Many types of motor performance are required in schools, varying from large motor movements, such as somersaults done in physical-education classes, to combinations of large and fine motor movements, such as may be required in carrying out a science experiment, to fine motor movements, such as those used in handwriting. For many of these tasks, the best teacher strategy is to model the performance a time or two and then provide guided practice. For example, Zane, Walls, and Thvedt (1981) researched the best way to teach moderately and severely retarded adults to assemble complex objects. Whole-task modeling before the subjects did the task was more successful than such techniques as providing one-word prompts— "good," "no"—or allowing the subjects to make errors and then correcting them. Certainly, students will not learn most motor performances by using visual cues unless they practice the movements directly.

Visual cues may provide a helpful guide for some students, however, as they carry out motor tasks. Hayes (1982) found that visual cues, when combined with verbal cues and subject verbalization, were helpful to kindergarten and third-grade students in learning to reproduce letterlike forms. Students who practiced copying these forms without cues did no better on a letterlike-form reproduction test than a control group that did not practice. The visual cues Hayes used were visual demonstrations of the stroke sequence needed to produce the forms. Notice that visual cues by themselves were not sufficient to produce better performance. Visual cues may need to be combined with verbal cues to be effective.

The teacher strategies described above, providing a model, a stimulus to trace, or arrows showing the movements needed to form a letter, all illustrate how to use visual cues to guide motor performance. Can we help students learn to use similar techniques on their own so that the techniques become student strategies? Perhaps with teacher help in the early stages, students could learn to design their own drawings of letters with arrows that show the sequence and direction of motor movements needed. Or if students need to remember the steps in a science experiment, they may be able to learn to make drawings that show the movements and steps necessary for the task. Especially for students who do not have good written-language skills, drawings may provide a useful alternative.

Cueing for Memory

Research studies have frequently examined the strategies people use to remember. Although many of the tasks used in this research were very different from school tasks, the results show that young children may be able to use visual cues to aid memory and recall. One of the most typical ways of using perceptual cues to aid memory has been the use of visual imagery. The use of visual imagery is but one of many memory, or mnemonic, devices that have been suggested and used for centuries. Klatzky (1975) defines a mnemonic device as "a rule or system of rules that has been developed to improve our ability to recall items" (p. 120).

Visual images may be thought about as perceptual cues that are internal rather than external; that is, the cues are in the mind, although one could draw a picture of what is seen in the mind's eye. Using internal cues fits very well with the goal of helping students control their own learning by internalizing learning strategies. To call these internal images perceptual, however, changes the meaning of the term somewhat and indicates a difference between this strategy and the perceptual cueing strategies explained above.

Two recognized writers on the topic of visual imagery, Harry Lorayne and Jerry Lucas (1974), suggest that the basics of using their techniques are quite natural to humans. These basics are to picture things in the mind and to associate one thing with another. Even if these mental activities are natural to us, we probably must learn a "system" if we are to use imagery and association efficiently. Learning (or inventing) a system requires some logical thinking and some verbal instructions. Thus we see that visual imagery is clearly not just a perceptual cueing strategy. Not only is it internal, but also it relies on rather advanced cognitive and language abilities. Still, the most powerful component in this strategy is the visual image itself, and using visual images seems to be more like perceptual strategies than language strategies.

Mnemonics such as visual imagery can be used effectively with people of different ages and with a variety of tasks (Higbee 1976) but it may not work for everyone. The techniques suggested here should be used with caution and be evaluated carefully.

Two major types of mnemonics, organizing mnemonics and encoding mnemonics, are suggested by Bellezza (1981) in a summary article. Organizing operations are techniques for associating or relating items that at first appear unrelated so that they can be remembered. A typical organizing mnemonic is first-letter recoding, which uses the first letter of words to form an acronym, for instance, HOMES to remember the names of the

Great Lakes. Rhymes ("Thirty days hath September . . .") and story mnemonics, in which several items to be remembered are woven together into a story, are other organizing mnemonics. Although these techniques do not necessarily include visualizing, the words, rhymes, or stories can be pictured or combined with other techniques that include visualizing. The acronym HOMES, for example, could be used in combination with the technique called concrete word encoding that is explained in the next paragraph. An example of using a story mnemonic to remember the nines times table is presented in figure 4-1. After telling this story, the teacher can lead a discussion about the relationships between the arithmetic problems, and students can use the story to remember the arithmetic facts. This story could also be visualized, of course.

FIGURE 4-1   A Story Mnemonic for the Nines Times Table.

A man who could barely read, could not write, and could do only very simple arithmetic problems once went to apply for a job. He was told that he must pass a test before he could apply for the job. The test was to complete a sheet of arithmetic problems and to divide a square into four equal triangles using only two straight lines. The sheet looked like this:

$1 \times 9 =$	$6 \times 9 =$
$2 \times 9 =$	$7 \times 9 =$
$3 \times 9 =$	$8 \times 9 =$
$4 \times 9 =$	$9 \times 9 =$
$5 \times 9 =$	$10 \times 9 =$

"Oh, no!" the man thought. "I can't do any of this." Upon looking more closely, however, he realized that he did know the answers to two of the problems. "Everyone knows that 1×9 is 9 and 10×9 is 90," he mumbled to himself as he carefully wrote these answers next to the problems. "Well, I guess that's all I can do. Rats! I wonder how many problems I missed." He began to count the unanswered problems, writing the numbers where the answers would go as he counted so he would not become confused. He wasn't very good at counting if he wasn't careful. He counted slowly and carefully, "one, two, three, four . . . ," starting with 2×9 until each problem had a number next to it, like this:

$1 \times 9 = 9$	$6 \times 9 = 5$
$2 \times 9 = 1$	$7 \times 9 = 6$
$3 \times 9 = 2$	$8 \times 9 = 7$
$4 \times 9 = 3$	$9 \times 9 = 8$
$5 \times 9 = 4$	$10 \times 9 = 90$

"Did I really miss eight problems?" he thought. "Maybe I should count again to be sure." Again he counted, writing in the numbers next to those already there. This time, however, he started with 9 × 9 and worked his way back to 2 × 9. "I guess I did miss eight problems," he said when he had finished. "This is hopeless." Having concluded this, he signed his name in the box the only way he knew how to write it, with an X, and left the room. Of course, when he had finished, the page looked like this:

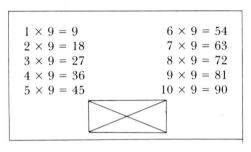

Encoding operations include concrete word encoding, which involves visualizing the object the word represents. For example, if the word to be remembered is *tree*, a tree is visualized. Abstract word encoding is another technique of this type. Words can be encoded abstractly based on meaning, or semantically, by picturing an object that has a similar meaning. For example, the word *origin* could be associated with a visual image of an egg. Abstract word encoding can also involve an association based on sound similarities, which is called phonetic encoding. Here the word *origin* might be associated with a visual picture of an orange. Another encoding system, number encoding, is used to remember numbers by associating each digit with a specific consonant and forming words from the consonants. Since this system is probably too complex for most handicapped learners, it will not be explained further here. Bellezza (1981) and Lorayne and Lucas (1974) describe each of these techniques in more detail, for interested readers.

Bellezza suggests that a mnemonic will generally work better if it is generated by the learner than if it is imposed by someone else. However, the learner must have adequate knowledge of the mnemonic system and must be able to easily invent the specific mnemonic associations for the techniques to be especially effective.

Let us look more closely at two additional applications of mnemonic techniques to school tasks. One is suggested by Forrest (1981), apparently on the basis of clinical experience with the technique. Forrest believes that visual imagery can be used for many school tasks, especially if the students have auditory-verbal processing problems. Of course, the students must have the ability to use imagery if these techniques are to be successful. For spelling, Forrest presents the following steps:

1. The student is told to mentally picture something to write on or in (a chalkboard, paper, soft cement, or the like).
2. The student is told to visualize himself or herself with eyes closed, writing the letters of a word (e.g., on the chalkboard) as the teacher says the letters.
3. The student is told to retain the image of the word but to report if it fades.
4. If the letters fade, the steps are repeated.
5. If the letters do not fade, the student is asked to say the letters in reverse quickly.
6. At intervals during the day, the student is instructed to say the letters forward and backward while picturing the word. Steps 1 to 5 are repeated as necessary. A new word is added the next day.

In Forrest's strategy, students picture themselves in action. This may be an important aid for some students because it adds meaning and more student control of thinking and strategy use. These steps may be useful for learning other information in addition to spelling. For example, students could substitute arithmetic facts, reading sight-word vocabulary, or letter sounds. Some modifications in the procedure may be needed because saying the visualized item backward (e.g., when saying letter sounds in a word) may be confusing or difficult. To convert Forrest's teacher method to a student strategy that could be used independently, the following steps and substeps may be helpful:

1. *Choose* the item (spelling word, arithmetic fact, reading word, and so on) to be learned.
2. *Activate* a mental picture.
   a. Picture a scene.
   b. Picture yourself in the scene.
3. *Practice* the task in your picture.
   a. Picture yourself in action (tracing, writing, speaking backward and forward).
   b. Repeat the action frequently.
4. *Evaluate* the learning.
   a. Is the picture helping you learn?
   b. Do you remember the item?
   c. Do you need more practice?

After the steps have been learned and applied to tasks, the first word of each step can be written on a card as a reminder to use it. By using the first letter of these words, the strategy gains a name—the CAPE strategy. Notice how a chain of associations is deliberately constructed. Each association is designed to make the use of the strategy easier and more automatic. Eventually, the students need only to provide themselves with the reminder that "I need to use the CAPE strategy," and the use of the strategy follows without a lot of effort and attention on *how* to use it. Because the strategy has become a typical procedure for learning, the student can concentrate on *what* is being learned. As before, we suggest that the actual strategy be developed cooperatively with the students, which may result in some changes in the CAPE strategy.

Another visual mnemonic technique is called *keyword*. It was developed by Atkinson (1975) for learning second languages and has been applied and tested by Jones and Hall (1982) and by Levin and his colleagues (Levin 1981; Levin et al. 1982; Shriberg et al. 1982). Keyword mnemonics "involves physically transforming to-be-learned materials into a form that makes them easier to learn and remember" (Levin 1981, p. 65). Two major steps form the teacher strategy. First, an association is made between the word or concept to be learned and a similar sounding word (the keyword) that is already familiar to the students. Second, the keyword is used as a basis for drawing a picture that illustrates both the keyword and the new word or concept with which it is associated.

Jones and Hall (1982) compared two groups of normal eighth-grade students, using keyword with one group. The other group learned a strategy for outlining sentences in two-dimensional tables, then using the tables to organize the paragraph structure of an essay. Teaching was carried out under typical classroom conditions with typical classroom material. The students studied English vocabulary and facts from social studies. In this study, the students produced their own images to associate with the items to be learned. Jones and Hall found that the keyword group was able to generate images and use the method spontaneously. Four tests were used. Two were designed to be easier for keyword subjects if they used the method for the test, and two were designed to favor the other group. As expected, the groups scored higher on the tests that favored their learning method, indicating that both groups probably used the method they had been taught. Since the study showed a match between method of teaching and method of testing, we can perhaps conclude that the keyword method (as well as the other method) can be effective when the conditions of testing are appropriate. These methods may not be effective for all types of materials and tests, of course.

Levin and his colleagues have used keyword methods with such tasks as learning vocabulary, comprehending oral languages, and learning social studies and science concepts. Results indicate that the keyword strategy is effective with a variety of materials, that images imposed by the instructor generally work better than those that are generated by the students, and that the pictures must be directly related to the content that is being learned (Shriberg et al. 1982). The keyword strategy was especially effective with material that was hard to visualize in the Shriberg et al. study. It made less difference with concrete content that was easy to visualize. More detail in the pictures was found to be helpful, at least for experienced users of the method.

Two specific illustrations of the keyword method as used by Levin and his associates are presented below. Both are taken from Levin (1981).

To teach English vocabulary to English-speaking children, the students were presented with a line drawing of two characters engaged in a conversation. One of the characters uses the keyword (a word similar in sound to the vocabulary word to be learned) in a sentence that fits the scene. The other character uses the new vocabulary word in a responding sentence that fits the situation. For example, for the vocabulary word *persuade*, the characters are looking at a table that holds several purses. The first character says, "Oh, Martha, you should buy that *purse!*" Martha replies, "I think you could *persuade* me to buy it." Below the picture the definition is written: Persuade (Purse)—When you talk someone into doing something. Levin has found that vivid images of this sort, especially when the vocabulary word is explicitly used by the second character, work even better for learning vocabulary than what he calls "experiential context" methods (1981).

The second example uses a dual keyword approach. It was successfully applied in teaching fourth- and fifth-grade students the fifty states and their state capitals. First, a state and its associated keyword were presented (e.g., Maryland—marry), then the capital was presented with its keyword (Annapolis—apple). Then the two were put together in a picture (a preacher marrying two apples) with the keywords written above the picture.

Students can probably learn to use the keyword strategy on their own. The steps in the strategy might be:

1. *Select* the item to be learned.
2. *Associate* a familiar word (keyword) that sounds similar to the item to be learned.
3. *Illustrate* the association between the keyword and the item to be learned, including as much meaning as possible.
4. *Learn* the meanings by rehearsing and reviewing the illustrations.

Students can design ridiculous and action-filled pictures that include as many associations as they can generate with the SAIL strategy, as long as the picture helps them learn and remember. It is probably important that the students become very familiar with the technique and are able to generate associations easily if they are to use this strategy on their own. Groups of students can work together to generate associations, and teacher assistance can be given as needed.

We encourage teachers to use mnemonics like these and to develop other applications with their students. Sometimes mnemonics are thought to be useful mostly for learning rote information. As Levin (1981) points out, they are really more versatile than this. Meaningful concepts and events can be visualized and associated, too, and for most of us, visualizing and associating are very powerful ways to remember.

Cueing for Comprehension

Nearly all school tasks that require comprehension involve verbal concepts, not just perceptual experiences. The techniques in this section emphasize perceptual cues that help the learner select, understand, and remember ideas. Language cues and language learning are also involved in these complex tasks. Three strategies will be described: underlining, mapping, and picture symbols.

Underlining.   Underlining strategies have been tested with college students (Glover et al. 1980) and high-school students (Schnell and Rocchio 1974). In both studies, underlining was used in reading-comprehension tasks, and ways to teach effective underlining were examined.

Apparently students learn to underline more effectively if they are taught how to do it. Glover et al. found that college students were able to organize and remember material better after they received training in how to underline. The subjects also transferred this strategy to standardized comprehension tests. The teaching method used by these researchers was rather simple. They selected eight-hundred-word passages and told the students to underline the minimum number of words that expressed the main idea of each five-line unit. Next, the students compared their underlining with an "ideal" example previously completed by the researchers. One group received points for matching the example, and the other group received only feedback about how close they were. The use of points did not have a significant effect compared to feedback. Although this technique has not been researched with handicapped students, it may be useful for students who already have some skills in picking out main ideas but need assistance in organizing and remembering them. The teacher model may improve skills in deciding which ideas are important, especially if the teacher discusses why some ideas and not others were chosen. The technique has the advantage of being adaptable to any length reading passage, all content areas, and a variety of reading levels. It appears to use sound principles of modeling and feedback.

Schnell and Rocchio, in their study with high-school students, found that underlining could result in improvement in comprehension. Active participation by the students in underlining worked better than having the instructor provide passages with the underlining already completed. Students did better if they were taught how to underline than if they were told to do it but were not told how. Schnell and Rocchio apparently used a lecture method to explain the strategy to the students. They devised four steps, or rules, for student underlining. We have adapted these steps to form the student strategy suggested below:

1. *Read* the passage through and underline a few main words.
2. *Decide* which ideas are the main ones, rereading as necessary.
3. *Plan* the underlining to include the main ideas and underline the words as planned.
4. *Evaluate* underlining for smoothness and completeness by rereading just the underlined parts.

Students are told not to underline whole sentences. Steps may be repeated as necessary so that the final underlined selections include all of the main ideas and read smoothly. This strategy requires considerable ability on the part of the students, who must be able to select main ideas and evaluate smoothness and completeness. Again, modeling by the teacher and discussions about how to select main ideas may be useful if the students have difficulty with some of the steps. Some students may need language development, concept development, or reading-skill development lessons for this strategy to be maximally effective.

Mapping.   The next perceptual cueing system we will explain is called *mapping* (Driskell 1977) or *brain patterns* (Buzan 1976). Buzan suggests that this technique encourages use of the holistic, associative patterns that are natural to human thinking. The major idea is that instead of trying to remember things in a logical, linear sequence, a mind picture is built up of the entire thought structure. These mind pictures can be drawn on paper to provide a set of perceptual cues. Using the content from the chapter you are reading, figure 4-2 shows a map of the idea of using perceptual cues.

Notice that the central idea, perceptual cueing strategies, is placed in the center of the map. Major subtopics radiate from the central idea, although the angle, direction, and order of the branches are not logically sequenced. A random arrangement is adequate because sequence is not essential in this material. Different backgrounds are shown to indicate color coding, which can provide an additional perceptual cue. Branches vary in size depending on the number of associations that are connected with them.

Driskell suggests a somewhat more organized mapping procedure than figure 4-2 illustrates. For note taking, a two-column division is suggested, with the topic in the left column and details in the right column. Boxes, circles, arrows, and so forth, are used to show relationships. Notice that techniques such as Driskell's and the illustration in figure 4-2, which is similar to the mind patterns suggested by Buzan (1976), provide perceptual patterns that may be helpful for tasks such as taking notes from a book or lecture, studying for a test, and planning an essay. With a little imagination, teachers can help students apply the technique in a wide variety of ways. Possibly, handicapped students who have difficulty with the logical, linear, and verbal approaches that are so typical in school will respond especially well with this strategy. Perhaps, as Buzan suggests, the technique calls on right-brain abilities. For handicapped students, these abilities may be stronger than the more logical, verbal abilities typically associated with the left brain. Experimental evidence of the effectiveness of this technique is not currently available, although clinical evidence indicates that it helps some handicapped students and that students enjoy learning and using this strategy.

Picture symbols.   The last strategy in this section is called *picture symbols*. Although we can find no references in the literature about this technique, we have found it helpful for some students. Essentially, it is a strategy for associating a perceptual cue with each step in another strategy the student is using. To illustrate the technique, let's assume that a student is learning to use a reading-comprehension strategy with the following steps:

1. *Review* the questions at the end of the passage.
2. *Answer* the questions you already know.
3. *Read* the passage carefully.
4. *Express* your answers to the remaining questions.

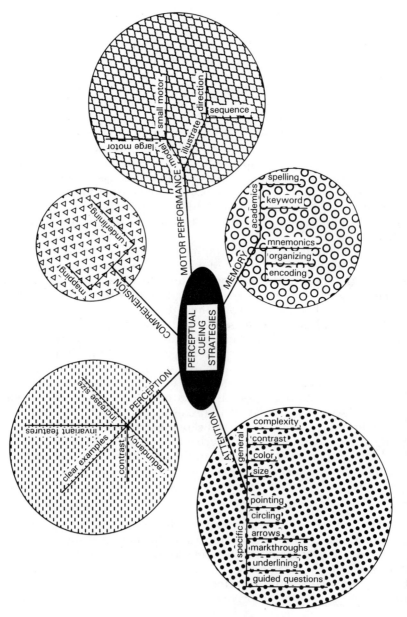

FIGURE 4-2 A Map of Perceptual-Cueing Strategies

One way for the student to remember the steps in the strategy is to use the acronym RARE. A shape-symbol strategy can be used as an additional reminder. Each step is assigned a specific symbol that is associated in some way with the step. Specifically, the *review* step could have *revolver* as a picture symbol, the *answer* step could have an *ant*, the *read* step could have a *rear-view mirror*, and the *express* step could have an *expressway*. Notice in this case that the picture symbols are associated on the basis of similar sounds and spellings. Picture symbols could also be associated on the basis of meaning. For example, the *?* symbol could be used for the *review* step, *!* could be used for *answer*, a picture of a book could be used for *read*, and a picture of a pencil could be used for *express*. Symbols that are not associated with the specific label for the step could be used too. That is, a star, a square, a circle, and a diamond could stand for the four steps in the strategy above. Each symbol should initially be associated with the appropriate step as shown in figure 4-3.

Next, the pictures are placed on a card or at the top of the student's paper with the associated words removed. Eventually, the student learns to associate the pictures with the steps without actually seeing the pictures. The student strategy steps, then, are as follows:

1. *Choose* a strategy for the task.
2. *Associate* a picture symbol with each step in the strategy.
3. *Draw* the picture next to the step on a card. Practice the strategy with the card in view.
4. *Use* the pictures alone on a card. Practice the strategy.
5. *Practice* the strategy with the picture card removed. When you can't think of the next step, think of the picture that goes with it, then associate the picture with the step.

Strategies such as this take some time to develop and may provide more structure than some students need. Obviously, they should be used only when they are helpful. Perceptual cueing techniques may help students become more aware of strategies and of their ability to control their

FIGURE 4-3

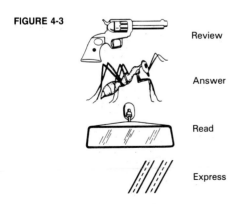

Review

Answer

Read

Express

own learning. Often, the elaborate associative networks involved in these strategies help students remember, probably because of added meaningfulness. That is, even though more learning is required, the targeted learning is actually easier because it is more meaningful.

The perceptual cueing strategies suggested rely primarily on the use of visual stimuli, not auditory, tactile, kinesthetic, or other sensory stimuli. Verbal language is sometimes included, thus involving auditory stimuli, but little study has been made of the use of nonlanguage perceptual cues with sensory systems other than the visual. Could perceptual cueing strategies that involve hearing or touch be helpful to handicapped learners? Practical classroom research may provide the answer.

It seems obvious that touching someone will usually attract that person's attention. Auditory cues, such as snapping one's fingers or clapping one's hands, may serve the same purpose. Auditory stimuli such as a buzzer or a bell could be used to cue students about when to start or stop a task. Tapping out the rhythm of letters in a word (e.g., three taps in one group, then a pause, then three more taps for a two-syllable word) as the letters are named may help students learn to spell. Blau and Loveless (1982) suggest that feeling the outline of cut-out letters may teach students to spell better.

Although each of these may be useful cues, they have not been adequately developed and researched. Also, they are not directed at teaching students to control and take responsibility for their own learning. Therefore, we will not elaborate on these potential strategies. Teachers may want to use auditory, tactile, or other sensory cues if such cues appear beneficial to their students. Careful evaluation of whether they really make a difference is especially important because these strategies are relatively untested.

REFERENCES

ATKINSON, R. C. Mnemotechnics in second-language learning. *American Psychologist* 30 (1975), 821–28.

BELLEZZA, F. S. Mnemonic devices: Classification, characteristics, and criteria. *Review of Educational Research* 51 (1981), 247–75.

BLACKWELL, S. L., C. W. McINTYRE, AND M. E. MURRAY. Hyperactivity and cueing responsivity in learning disabled boys. Paper presented at the Southwest Society for Research and Human Development. Dallas, March 17, 1978.

BLAU, H., AND E. J. LOVELESS. Specific hemispheric-routing—TAK/v to teach spelling to dyslexics: VAK and VAKT challenged. *Journal of Learning Disabilities* 15 (1982), 461–66.

BOVET, M. C. Learning research within Piagetian lines. *Topics in Learning and Learning Disabilities* 1 (1981), 1–9.

BROWN, A. L., AND A. S. PALINCSAR. Inducing strategic learning from texts by means of informed, self-control training. *Topics in Learning and Learning Disabilities* 2 (1982), 1–17.

BUZAN, T. *Use Both Sides of Your Brain.* New York: E. P. Dutton, 1976.

DeRUITER, J. A., AND W. L. WANSART. *Psychology of Learning Disabilities: Applications and Educational Practice.* Rockville, Md.: Aspen Systems Corp., 1982.

DRISKELL, J.   Mapping the idea: A notetaking system. Paper presented at the 10th Annual Meeting of the Western College Reading Association, Denver, March 31–April 2, 1977.

ELKIND, D.   *The Child's Reality: Three Developmental Themes.* Hillsdale, N.J.: Lawrence Erlbaum Associates, 1978.

FORREST, E. B.   Visual imagery as an information processing strategy. *Journal of Learning Disabilities* 14 (1981), 584–86.

GIBSON, E. J., AND H. LEVIN.   *The Psychology of Reading.* Cambridge, Mass.: MIT Press, 1975.

GLOVER, J. A., J. W. ZIMMER, R. W. FILBECK, AND B. S. PLAKE.   Effects of training students to identify the semantic base of prose materials. *Journal of Applied Behavior Analysis* 13 (1980), 655–67.

GORDON, F. R., AND J. H. FLAVELL.   The development of intuitions about cognitive cueing. *Child Development* 48 (1977), 1027–33.

HAGEN, J. W., AND R. V. KAIL.   The role of attention in perceptual and cognitive development. In W. M. Cruickshank and D. P. Hallahan, eds., *Perceptual and Learning Disabilities in Children,* vol. 2, *Research and Theory.* Syracuse, N.Y.: Syracuse University Press, 1975, 165–92.

HAYES, D.   Handwriting practice: The effects of perceptual prompts. *Journal of Educational Research* 75 (1982), 169–72.

HENKER, B., C. K. WHALEN, AND S. P. HINSHAW.   The attributional contexts of cognitive intervention strategies. *Exceptional Education Quarterly* 1 (1980), 17–30.

JONES, B. F., AND J. W. HALL.   School applications of the mnemonic keyword method as a study strategy by eighth graders. *Journal of Educational Psychology* 74 (1982), 230–37.

KLATZKY, R. L.   *Human memory: Structures and processes.* 2d ed. San Francisco: W. H. Freeman and Co., 1975.

LEVIN, J. R.   The mnemonic '80s: Keywords in the classroom. *Educational Psychologist* 16 (1981), 65–82.

————, C. B. MCCORMICK, G. E. MILLER, J. K. BERRY, AND M. PRESSLEY.   Mnemonic versus nonmnemonic vocabulary-learning strategies for children. *American Educational Research Journal* 19 (1982), 121–36.

LORAYNE, H., AND J. LUCAS.   *The Memory Book.* New York: Ballantine Books, 1974.

OSLER, S. F., M. DRAXL, AND J. MADDEN.   The utilization of verbal and perceptual cues by preschool children in concept identification problems. *Child Development* 48 (1977), 1071–74.

PICK, H. L., AND A. D. PICK.   Sensory and perceptual development. In P. H. Mussen, ed., *Carmichael's Manual of Child Psychology,* vol. 1. New York: John Wiley and Sons, 1970.

POWERS, W. T.   *Behavior: The Control of Perception.* Chicago: Aldine, 1973.

REESE, H. W.   *Basic Learning Processes in Childhood.* New York: Holt, Rinehart & Winston, 1976.

REID, D. K., AND W. P. HRESKO.   *A Cognitive Approach to Learning Disabilities.* New York: McGraw-Hill Book Co., 1981.

RITTER, K.   The development of knowledge of an external retrieval cue strategy. *Child Development* 49 (1978), 1227–30.

ROSONKE, R. J.   A study of the effectiveness of three visual attention-directing devices on the recall of relevant information from line drawings. Paper presented at the Association for Educational Communications and Technology Annual Meeting. Dallas, April 13–17, 1975.

SCHNELL, T. R., AND D. J. ROCCHIO.   A study of the relative effectiveness of various underlining strategies on reading comprehension. Paper presented at the 18th Annual Meeting of the College Reading Association. Bethesda, Md., Oct. 31–Nov. 2, 1974.

SHRIBERG, L. K., J. R. LEVIN, C. B. MCCORMICK, AND M. PRESSLEY.   Learning about "famous" people via the keyword method. *Journal of Educational Psychology* 74 (1982), 238–47.

SPIKER, C. C.   Performance on a difficult discrimination following pretraining with distinctive stimuli. *Child Development* 30 (1959), 513–21.

SWANSON, H. L., AND B. L. WATSON.   *Educational and Psychological Assessment of Exceptional Children.* St. Louis: C. V. Mosby, 1982.

SYKES, D., V. DOUGLAS, AND G. MORGENSTERN.   Sustained attention in hyperactive children. *Journal of Child Psychology and Psychiatry* 14 (1973), 213–20.

Torgesen, J. K.   The learning disabled child as an inactive learner: Educational implications. *Topics in Learning and Learning Disabilities* 2 (1982), 45–52.

————.   The rule of nonspecific factors in the task performance of learning disabled children: A theoretical assessment. *Journal of Learning Disabilities* 10 (1977), 27–34.

Zane, T., R. T. Walls, and J. E. Thvedt.   Prompting and fading guidance procedures: Their effect on chaining and whole task teaching strategies. *Education and Training of the Mentally Retarded* 16 (1981), 125–35.

CHAPTER FIVE

Language Cueing Strategies

- Why are both "knowing how" and "knowing why" so important?

- In what manner may emotionally disturbed students be different from nonhandicapped students with respect to contradictions?

- How are language cueing strategies different from perceptual cueing strategies?

- In what cases may the STOP strategy be of particular value?

- How may perceptual and language cueing be used in combination to assist students to control their own behavior?

- In what manner are all language cueing strategies actually problem-solving strategies?

- How can "blockages" assist in the process of problem solving?

- How may closed-search approaches to problem solving be particularly applicable to academic tasks?

- How is a closed search different from an open search?

Language and thinking are closely related and interact (perhaps in a variety of ways) with one another. Of course, differences between language and thinking are also important; all thoughts are not in language, and spoken and written language do not always reflect the complexities of thought. The specific relationships between language and thinking are frequently debated, and disagreements exist about how they develop and how they interact (Sigel 1983).

In this section we will put aside this debate and assume that language cues provide a potential means of organizing and regulating thought (Luria 1969). Teachers can use language cues to help students select and apply learning strategies, and students can learn to use their own language cues to guide perception (Miller and Rohr 1980; Sabatino 1976), behavior (Bornstein and Quevillon 1979; Meichenbaum 1977), and other aspects of thinking (Abikoff 1979; Meichenbaum 1977; Weithorn and Kagen 1979).

Many of the strategies described in this text include applications of the idea that language can serve as a cue or guide for thinking. After any part of language is known, an individual may be able to use it for new learning, problem solving, and interacting with the environment. As language knowledge increases, more uses are potentially available; however, cognitive knowledge is also critical, and the use of language cueing strategies probably depends as much or more on cognitive development as on language abilities (Keogh and Glover 1980). Younger children appear less aware of the need for strategies and may be less capable of using them (Loper 1980; Reid and Hresko 1981). Efforts to help students learn to activate their own language cueing strategies must be carried out in the context of understanding both the students' language and their cognitive abilities.

THEORETICAL PERSPECTIVES

In this section, the theoretical concepts expressed in the previous chapter are extended to language cueing strategies. The use of language cueing strategies makes more apparent the importance of a distinction made by Inhelder and Piaget (1980). These authors describe the bipolar, or interdependent, characteristics of procedures and structures, of knowing how and knowing why, of knowing when to reuse something already known and knowing when a new construction is needed.

Procedures are the specific, sequential aims and means necessary to do a task or reach a goal. The results of using a procedure are the major focus of the subject, and the goal is to succeed. Procedures are often changed if the results indicate that you aren't having any success. Procedures are closely related to knowing *how*. Knowing how plays a role both in developing and carrying out procedures. An individual may know how to carry out a variety of procedures to solve a problem.

Structures involve an understanding of a problem. Structures link things together and draw out connections. The goal is a general understanding of the system. Structures require both knowing *how* and knowing *why* for their construction and use. Notice that procedures and structures are closely related: "Every structure is the result of a procedural construction, and every procedure makes use of some of the aspects of structures" (Inhelder and Piaget 1980). A similar bipolarity is found between knowing when to reuse a procedure or when a new procedure or structure needs to be constructed. According to Inhelder and Piaget, "Clearly these two types of processes . . . always have to be combined and depend on each other" (p. 21). Handicapped learners may have difficulty with the activation and regulation of both processes.

Studies have been conducted using Piagetian research tasks that demonstrate how handicapped children regulate their thoughts. Frequently these children are found to have difficulty with either knowing how or knowing why. Schmidt-Kitsikis (1976) found that mentally retarded children directed their activities adequately but showed low levels of deductive ability. Perhaps they were more able to proceed adequately (the *how* aspect), although to a limited level, but did not really understand the task (the *why* aspect). Thus they achieve, as Reid (1981) notes, stable but low-level constructions. Reid examined severely emotionally disturbed and learning-disabled children and found important differences. The emotionally disturbed often did not try to adapt to task demands and showed erratic and egocentric behaviors. Whether they could not or would not give adequate explanations was unclear to the researchers. In either case, the findings indicate difficulty with both knowing how and knowing why. Learning disabled children had difficulty in both areas, too, but their greatest difficulty was more often with knowing why. They could give correct responses but could not offer explanations except for those they had heard someone else give. The learning disabled adequately perceived actions and states of objects, but the links between the actions and states were not noticed. Reid notes that they showed resistance to thinking about their activity as they did the tasks.

These problems are not likely to be easily overcome. Reid says that emotionally disturbed children did not notice contradictions even though they observed the contradictions taking place. She says learning disabled children did not construct negations, which is another way of saying that they did not recognize the relationship between an object before and after it was transformed. We assume that noticing contradictions and constructing relationships are crucial for learning. Language cueing strategies may help handicapped children observe more carefully, attend to their own actions, recognize contradictions, and construct negations. Thus although language cues probably do not directly guide and develop thought, they may stimulate interaction between actions, language, and thinking. In addition, they may provide a framework within which the learner can do a task (understand "how") and also understand "why." Verbal explanations result in better definition of structures, and learning can thus progress (Renner et al. 1976).

Assessment procedures for language cueing strategies were addressed in the previous chapter. The remainder of this chapter describes some general considerations about preparing to use language cueing and more specific strategies for using language cues to guide perception, behavior, and problem solving.

PREPARING TO USE
LANGUAGE CUEING

The readiness of the student is a major component of preparing to use language cues. From the student's perspective, getting ready to use strategies requires developing a reflective style and imposing a structure on the task (Lloyd 1980; Reid and Hresko 1981; Torgesen 1982). A reflective style is one that encourages a "stop-and-think" time before a task is begun. Students can be taught to organize themselves through a language cueing strategy with four steps. Appropriately, the acronym for this strategy is STOP:

1. *Stop* before you act.
2. *Think* about the nature of the task.
3. *Organize* the steps.
4. *Proceed* with the steps.

The first step provides a language cue to delay responding. The second consists of self-questioning about what the task requires—where to begin, the operations needed, the end results expected. Sometimes a specific previously learned strategy will be selected in this step. Alternatively, a new strategy may be required, and the student constructs it, alone or with assistance. In step 3 the specific steps are reflected upon and placed in an appropriate sequence. Finally, the steps are carried out according to plan.

Steps 2 and 3 are often the most difficult because they require some understanding of the task and the ability to impose a structure on it. If the student does not know what is important in the task, pointing out the aspects upon which to focus (Maier 1980) and providing specific category rules (Hall 1977) may help. Numerous strategies for thinking about and organizing academic tasks are explained in other chapters.

In the next three sections, we will consider the use of language cueing in three parts: guiding perception, guiding behavior, and guiding problem solving. Regarded theoretically, these areas probably should not be separated because they are closely related and may be only different ways of talking about the same thing. In practical terms, however, applications of the concept of language cueing are somewhat distinct.

GUIDING PERCEPTION
THROUGH LANGUAGE

Using language to guide perception is different from traditional perceptual training, which usually involves direct practice with perceptual tasks that gradually increase in difficulty. Language cueing emphasizes accurate and rapid perception, which results from recognizing perceptual characteristics that are explained in words. For example, when the written letters *b* and *d* are seen for the first time, they may be remembered better if someone verbally describes their visual similarities and differences; e.g., they both have a ball and stem, but the *b* has the stem on the left and the *d* has the stem on the right. The verbal cue immediately identifies what is important about the letters and provides some useful information that relates to previous information. Notice, however, that the student must have structural knowledge about the task to be able to "see" what is verbally explained. The learner must be able to recognize the correspondence in the transformation from *b* to *d*. The words alone are not enough to bring about new constructions, even when the words themselves are understood (e.g., words such as *same* and *different,* or *left* and *right*). In such cases, problem posing at an earlier level becomes necessary.

Using language cues to guide perception has potential for use at many levels (Miller and Rohr 1980), although specific research is lacking. One level, perhaps the simplest, is the recognition of specific characteristics of a single, simple object, such as a ball, or a single symbol, such as the letter *b*. More complex levels involve the recognition of word patterns, comparative movements of objects, patterns in complex charts, and so on. Both simple and complex perceptions that use other senses may be guided through language as well; for example, the difference between voiced and unvoiced sounds, between two complex bird songs, or between the bouquet of two wines can be described verbally. In each case, the learner may be better able to recognize and remember the verbally described distinctions than would be likely without the language information.

Problem posing is the first step in using language to guide perception. The problem posed provides the framework within which the hoped-for mental action of the learner can take place. Equilibration, the internal, self-regulated process that is essential for learning, is best activated by posing problems that are *just different enough.* A problem is "just different enough" when it demands a new structuring of a student's understanding at a level only very slightly above the current level. To pose problems appropriately, the teacher must understand the nature of the student's thinking and the nature of the task. Examples of using language to guide perception are presented below. Each example is intended to be illustrative of the numerous ways this idea can be creatively applied.

In the first example, language is used to guide a student's perception of motor movements in a game of basketball. Assume that our student is a rather tall and reasonably talented center who has been assigned to the low post position, to the left side and slightly to center court of the basket. Her task is to take the pass from the left forward, turn around, and shoot. A difficulty has arisen, however, in that the forward very seldom throws the ball to the center. A quick investigation by the coach during a time-out reveals that the opposing center, who is just as tall as her opponent, places her hand just behind the upstretched hand of our center. The forward hesitates to pass the ball in because an interception seems likely. Time is too short to permit practice of a set of new moves, but a quick verbal exploration is possible. The coach poses a problem to the center: What can be done to separate her hand from her opponent's so she will get the pass? Two suggestions are made by the center, both illustrating her current thinking. She suggests moving around more or trying to stretch her hand higher.

The coach knows that these suggestions have real disadvantages. Moving around more is not really the problem, puts the center out of her best shooting position, and doesn't necessarily eliminate the opponent's hand. Stretching will probably result in stretching by the opponent. Rather than extending herself, as would be typical where height is usually an advantage, the center must make herself *shorter* by bending slightly at the waist, leaning her upper body forward, and raising her arms at the angle of her upper body. The result—her hand is about eighteen inches away from her opponent's.

How can the coach communicate all of this when time is not available for demonstration and practice? (Or how could she even if time were available?) By verbally describing the moves and asking the center to notice the difference in distance between the hands, of course. If the language does guide perception (of the movements and positions), the center may construct a new procedure and a new structure. The procedure is a new set of "how to" moves. The structure may include a new understanding that includes "shorter is sometimes better." If, as is hoped, this new idea is integrated into a total new understanding of the "why" of the game, the coach may see the center using it in a variety of situations where it will be useful. Notice that a new understanding is the broader and more important goal of using language. Using language to guide perception is a subgoal.

The strategy that the coach wants the center to construct can be specified as follows:

1. Note the body and hand positions of your opponent.
2. Evaluate whether your movements, position, or posture should be changed.
3. Decide which new movements, positions, or postures may help.
4. Try out the new movements, positions, or postures.
5. Evaluate the effectiveness of the changes.

In the first stage of learning, the coach used a language cue to guide the center's awareness. If later the center uses the entire language-guided strategy, it becomes the basis for several perceptions and actions, and the process is self-regulated. Of course, some practice may be needed, and it may help to make the steps in the strategy explicit.

A second example of using language to guide perception (adapted from DeRuiter and Wansart 1982) applies this concept to recognizing similarities in words. The teacher discovers that the student takes as much time to read words with very similar spellings as he takes to read words that are dissimilar. Apparently, he does not recognize the similarities in spelling and pronunciation and therefore treats each word as entirely new. The teacher decides she wants the student to learn about word families. Specifically, the perception that she wants to guide through language is rapid, accurate recognition of words with similar spelling and pronunciation. The behavioral outcome, the teacher hopes, will be more rapid, accurate reading. This outcome depends on the student's construction of a new understanding of word patterns.

DeRuiter and Wansart suggest the following teaching steps (adapted from 1982, pp. 193–94):

1. The teacher writes several words from a word family (e.g., fight, might, right, tight), reads them aloud, and asks the student to repeat.
2. The teacher asks the student to describe how the words are similar.
3. The spelling and sound similarities are identified by the student and/or the teacher.
4. The teacher tells the student that these words are members of the "—ight" family.

These are the basic steps of using language as a guide for word patterns, but more applications usually are necessary to develop a new understanding. The teacher should probably repeat the process with several word families and should specifically emphasize the idea that recognizing spelling similarities will foster more rapid reading. A simple language-guided strategy for the student may evolve, having just one self-regulated step that can be used each time a word is not immediately recognized. The student learns to ask, "Does this word belong to a word family?"

Language cueing can also be applied to complex perceptual analyses such as chart reading. Although the specifics may vary depending on the type of chart, possible steps in a student strategy are:

1. Identify the topic of the chart.
2. Identify the recording method (dots, lines, bars, and the like).
3. Identify what is measured on the abscissa and ordinate.
4. Identify the size and type of the units of measurement.
5. Identify the range and direction (Do numbers go up or down?) of the units of measurement.
6. Identify special cues, such as color.
7. Identify relative size or positions of data recorded on the chart.

These steps obviously do not provide for full interpretation, which would require knowledge of the topic of the chart. They do present a procedural starting point that, through discussion and application, may lead students to an increased understanding of charts and how to read them.

These examples of using language to guide perception are only a beginning. We encourage teachers to create applications to other tasks, although we urge very careful evaluation of the effectiveness of applying this idea because of the lack of research. Integration of language cueing for perception with techniques for guiding behavior and problem solving (explained in the next two sections) may also be helpful.

GUIDING BEHAVIOR THROUGH
LANGUAGE CUES

Cognitive behavior modification approaches (see chapter 3) have frequently used language to help children and adults learn to control their behaviors. Studies of verbally regulated self-control of hyperactive, impulsive, aggressive, and disruptive behaviors of many specific types have been conducted (for reviews, see Finch and Spirito 1980; Hallahan and Sapona 1983; Kneedler 1980; Keogh and Glover 1980; Meichenbaum 1977). Much remains to be learned, but enough promise has been shown to indicate that these methods are potentially useful. Most research studies in this area use some variation of the model-it method described in chapter 3.

Finch and Spirito suggest the following for controlling impulsive behavior:

1. Ignore impulsive responding, and praise or reward reflective behavior.
2. Set firm limits on impulsive behavior, and establish consequences or "costs" for it.
3. Reduce response uncertainty by providing clear rules, specific, ordered steps for assignments, and cue cards to remind the student of alternative responses.
4. Use a cognitive training program that uses a self-instructional approach.

Clearly, the first three steps address conditions that the teacher sets up and controls. Step 4 is designed to enable students to learn to control their own behavior. Hallahan and Sapona used cognitive behavior modification techniques to teach inattentive children to monitor their on- and off-task behavior as they worked on academic tasks. They combined a perceptual cueing system with language cueing in the following way:

1. A tape recorder was placed near the student. On the tape was a periodic tone. When it sounded, the students were instructed to ask themselves the question, "Was I paying attention?" The answer to the question was self-recorded on a sheet.
2. The teacher told the students what was meant by on- and off-task behavior (e.g., eyes on the worksheet), and told them how to mark the recording sheet.
3. The teacher modeled what was to be done with the recorded tones and recording sheet.
4. The teacher asked the students to repeat the definitions and instructions.

The students were given these instructions in the context of tasks that they were already capable of doing. The results indicated that self-monitoring led to increases in attentional behavior and in academic productivity, and the improvements lasted up to 2½ months (the longest duration they tested). In addition, although the tone and self-recording were necessary in the procedure, the students could be weaned from them and begin to use verbal statements such as, "Yes, I was paying attention," or "No, I'd better start paying attention," whenever they thought to ask themselves whether they were paying attention.

Brown and Alford (1984) used a three-step strategy to study the effects of cognitive behavior modification techniques on the control of attention and academic performance. Students were told to (a) stop and define the problem and the steps in it, (b) consider and evaluate solutions before acting on any one, and (c) verbalize the strategy throughout the training. The subjects were taught several tasks with the emphasis on strategies that involved paying close attention to details. Compared to a control group (ten subjects per group, twelve years of age) with similar attention disorders, the trained group was significantly higher in several measures of attention and academic performance. The results generalized to some aspects of reading that were not directly taught and lasted at least three months. The researchers suggest that "training children to attend selectively in a more skillful way to relevant attributes of a stimulus will result in improved reading performance" (Brown and Alford 1984, p. 23).

These studies illustrate how perceptual and language cueing may be used in combination to help students control their own behavior. Importantly, both studies also found improved academic performance.

An application of using language to guide behavior in a much more complex way is suggested by DeRuiter and Wansart (1982). They present a strategy for helping students to use language: (a) to monitor and control their behavior and (b) as a response system that replaces responses such as hitting, crying, or running away. The major steps in the strategy are:

1. The teacher writes a short vignette of a typical conflict situation (e.g., a conflict between a student and a teacher resulting from an assignment that is not done).
2. The students participate as actors in a videotape of the scene.
3. The students view the tape with the teacher.
4. The teacher guides a discussion about the scene.
5. Students participate in writing, taping, and discussing additional scenes (De Ruiter and Wansart 1982, p. 194).

In step 4 the application of language cues as a guide for behavior is emphasized. For example, the scene may show the student destroying her test paper because the teacher has criticized her for not completing all of the problems. The discussion led by the teacher in step 4 may focus on what the student could have told herself so that she controlled this behavior. This, of course, is a means of language-mediated behavior control and can vary from simple techniques such as counting to ten before acting to complex verbal self-reinforcement (e.g., "I know I did my best, so I should not get angry when my teacher doesn't accept it."). Second, the teacher directs the discussion toward possible language responses that the student could use in place of destroying the paper. The student could explain her problem, ask for help, or request more time, for example. Through this guided discussion, the students can be explicitly taught a strategy that has these essentials:

1. Stop before you act when you are in conflict.
2. Tell yourself how to control your response.

3. Evaluate whether a language response may work.
4. Talk it over if possible.

A specific strategy may be developed cooperatively for many situations within this general framework. Along the way, the students can be actively involved in many learning tasks as they write scripts, edit them, videotape them, and so on.

Notice that with each of the techniques described in this section behavior is self-controlled through gaining a better understanding of the task or situation and through using self-directed language as a guide. Self-control of external behavior is the goal, but reaching this goal depends on changing the way the student thinks. In this sense all language-cueing strategies are problem-solving strategies. The next section extends language cueing strategies directly to problem-solving tasks.

GUIDING PROBLEM SOLVING
THROUGH LANGUAGE CUES

The emphasis in this section is on problem solving in a variety of rather general ways, not on specific academic tasks such as reading, writing, and arithmetic. Academic applications for the idea are encouraged, and some are presented in the chapters on academic areas.

In this section we will suggest a framework that is similar for all problem solving. Many different tasks and learners with wide variations in abilities can be fitted within this framework. The components of the framework are (1) problem awareness, (2) organizing the task, (3) learning new information, and (4) applying a solution strategy. These are similar to the four stages of study suggested by Towle (1982).

Problem Awareness

The problem-awareness component focuses on discovering what the task requires. Problems for a student to solve are usually made available in one of three major ways: by teachers, by environmental situations, or by the individuals themselves. With problems other than those that are self-posed, however, a major difficulty may arise: The student does not recognize that a problem exists. In such cases, the teacher may want to use techniques for helping students create disequilibrium as described in chapter 3. Some students will, of course, lack the specific understandings and abilities necessary for them to become aware of what the problem requires.

Problem awareness may require careful observation (e.g., through reading, listening, or watching). One way to help students learn to observe more carefully is to provide them with many different kinds of guided experiences (Alley and Deshler 1979). Hayes (1981) suggests two strategies that may help students observe more carefully. The first is a structuring strategy in which categories, hierarchies, networks, or other types of structure in the material are noted. For some tasks, the students may be guided to note important features such as size, shape, color, movement, and so on (see the section on using language to guide perception). Teachers can ask probing questions that guide students to look for the structure in the material. Other strategies that may also be helpful for structuring the material are summarizing, notetaking, underlining, paraphrasing, and comparing likenesses and differences. Many of these are explained in other chapters.

Hayes's (1981) second strategy is called a context strategy. The learner searches for relations between the material and things that are known before. If a student does not recognize these relationships, teacher guidance can be provided.

Observation should be followed by description of the content of the problem. The student may want to write or say (aloud or silently) the major components of the problem. Sometimes the description takes the form of brainstorming—saying everything that is remembered about the problem. Usually an organized description of the problem is better, however. That is, the problem is described in terms of its structure and important parts. Teacher guidance may be needed here for some students.

To summarize, the first major step for problem solving is to become aware of the nature of the problem. Following are the substeps, written in a self-questioning format:

1. Have I observed carefully?
   a. Can I use a structuring strategy?
   b. Can I use a context strategy?
2. Can I describe the problem?
   a. Do I need to brainstorm the content of the problem?
   b. Can I describe the structure and important parts of the problem?

These substeps provide a strategy for the student that can be taught explicitly, memorized, or written down so they can be practiced each time a new problem is presented. Specific questions (e.g., about whether the problem has categories or a hierarchy) can be added at each substep. The goal is to help students learn to follow the substeps and ask themselves the questions without teacher guidance. Writing the strategy on a cue card often serves this purpose.

Organizing the Task

Organizing the task builds directly on the problem-awareness step. It involves two main subcomponents—representing the problem and planning a solution (Hayes 1981). Representing the problem refers to forming and specifying an understanding of the whole problem. Hayes believes that four problem parts must be identified to represent a problem: the goal, the initial state, the operators, and the restrictions on the operators. This thinking may be adapted to provide a four-step self-questioning strategy for representing a problem:

1. What is the goal?
2. What are the starting conditions?

3. What are some possible actions that change the conditions?
4. What are the restrictions (rules of the problem)?

This provides a construct or framework that can be used to represent nearly any type of problem. For example, Piaget (1976) describes a problem-solving game called the Hanoi Tower (see figure 5-1) in which three vertical posts are attached to a baseboard and a set of disks is placed on one of the posts. The disks are graduated in size, with the largest on the bottom and successively smaller disks placed in order on top. The task requires that the disks be moved to one of the other posts (the goal post) in the fewest possible moves. The third post may be used for storage. The rules are that only one disk may be moved at a time, a larger disk may not be placed on a smaller one, and disks may not be held or laid on the table when another one is moved.

The parts of this problem, following the framework above, are:

1. Goal—move disks to post III, with the largest ending on the bottom and the smallest on top.
2. Starting conditions—disks are on post I.
3. Possible actions—move top disk to post II or post III. (Additional steps can be similarly stated.)
4. Restrictions—complete task in the fewest possible moves. Only one disk may be moved at a time. Larger disks may not be placed on smaller ones. Disks may not be held or laid down while another is moved.

In problems like the Hanoi Tower the parts of the problem are rather obvious. In contrast, parts of the problem are not always obvious in many

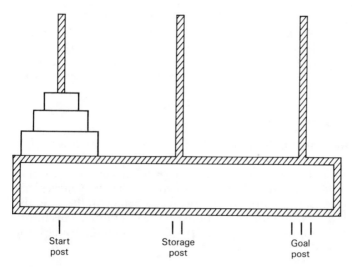

FIGURE 5-1 The Hanoi Tower Problem

school tasks. For example, if a teacher says, "Finish your homework on time," the goal is clear, but the conditions, possible actions, and restrictions are not given. The strategy above may be useful in such a case, even though at first it does not appear to be a "problem" in the sense that the Hanoi Tower is.

A reading passage followed by questions that are intended to test the student's knowledge of the passage provides an example. A student could follow the strategy and specify the following problem parts:

1. Goal—answer the questions correctly.
2. Starting conditions—one unread reading passage of four paragraphs. Six questions at the end.
3. Possible actions—read the whole passage and answer the questions from memory. Read the questions first, then search for the answers in the passage. (Many more could be specified.)
4. Restrictions—the answers must come from the passage.

For students who have difficulty representing the nature of the problem, the strategy provides a starting point and a means of organizing their activity.

Representing the problem provides for the first component, organizing the task, but often more needs to be done. The specific solution needs to be planned. In the Hanoi Tower example, the representation of the problem suggests some possible moves (in step 3), but which specific move to make remains unknown. Should the first disk be moved to the goal post or the storage post? A deeper representation of the problem is needed to provide an answer. The distinction between knowing how and knowing why (Inhelder and Piaget 1980) is important here. With some problems, students will have neither procedural knowledge (knowing how) nor structural knowledge (knowing why). In others, one or the other may be lacking.

With practical problems like the Hanoi Tower, children seem initially to be led by the stimulus and their own actions. They move the first disk to one of the empty posts and then the next disk to the other empty post (unless they break one of the rules, as frequently happens with younger children) without having specific procedural or structural understanding of the task. Over several trials, however, they appear to switch back and forth between procedural and structural knowledge as they increasingly construct their understanding of the task. Eventually, most students construct a procedural understanding—they know how to build the tower on the goal post in the minimum number of seven moves (Wansart 1984). Sometimes, however, they are unable to do the task in seven moves when the goal is changed to post II, which may show that they do not have a structural understanding of the task.

This example is very instructive about how teaching of problem solving should perhaps proceed. It shows some of the relationships between knowing how and knowing why and indicates the importance of constructing an understanding of the problem through interaction with it. Opportunities for reflecting on the problem are probably essential for understanding. Reflection may be encouraged both by providing time for it and by building blockages (e.g., restrictions or conditions that stop the problem-solving action in some way) into the problem (Blanchet 1983). Frequently, blockages must be posed directly by the teacher, although ideally students should learn to recognize for themselves when the problem is not being solved successfully. In arithmetic problems, for example, a student who does not recognize that her answer is wildly unlikely (e.g., $72 + 48 = 1,110$—student did not "carry" with $2 + 8$) may initially require teacher guidance, such as a probing question or a reminder to check her work. Later, a checking or monitoring strategy could be developed cooperatively to help enable self-regulated problem solving.

Given that appropriate problems are posed and care is taken to provide opportunities for interaction with the task, two main approaches to planning a solution can be identified. Both involve the implicit "theories" that the student has about the problem (Karmiloff-Smith and Inhelder 1975), but the first relies less on knowledge of previously learned specific strategies. We will call the first approach *open search* and the second *closed search*.

Open search is used when the problem solver is uncertain about how to proceed in planning a solution strategy. Since a solution plan is not known, the individual tries out possible strategies, based on what is known about the problem, and modifies the strategy (or starts over) if unsuccessful. Even at this general level, however, language cues can be used to make the search more systematic. The following self-questioning strategies (based on suggestions made by Hayes 1981) may be helpful. They are intended to be used after the students have gathered adequate information about the problem and have formed a representation of it but are not certain of the exact steps required to solve the problem.

Strategy 1. Can I use trial and error?
    a. What is a reasonable first step?
    b. Have I tried out the first step?
    c. Am I closer to my goal?
    d. Do I need to recycle with step *a*, step *b*, etc.?
Strategy 2. Can I break the problem into subgoals?
    a. Can I set subgoals either by starting at the beginning and going forward or by starting at the goal and working backward?
    b. Can I select a subgoal from those available and take action to meet it?
    c. Can I set a new subgoal and act on it? (Repeat until the final goal is reached.)

Trial-and-error strategies are perhaps most useful when information about which path to follow is not available and the problem is relatively small. For example, if the task is to fill in a crossword puzzle, trial and error might be efficient if the problem solver knows two words that may fit. One of the two could be tried, then checked for a match with vertical words. If the vertical words do not fit, the second word could be tried. On the other hand, if possible words are not known (or many options are known), another strategy might work better. In this case, trial and error of all possible words would result in a nearly endless search. Looking for word meanings in a dictionary might be more appropriate.

Breaking the problem into subgoals helps solve complex problems with several parts. Tasks that may appear overwhelming at first are far less intimidating when they are thought about as involving one step or part at a time. Teachers often encourage students to look for a subgoal by asking, "What must you do first?" An arithmetic problem in which more than one operation is required provides a simple example. Perhaps one difference between the current state and the goal in the problem is that some numbers must be added together. Another difference is that the resulting sum must be divided by another number. The action required for the first difference is to add; for the second, to divide. Two subgoals are obvious.

Closed-search approaches to problem solving are frequently important in academic tasks because the learner already knows the strategies that are required to do the task but needs to select a strategy from among those that are known. The essential question the student must ask is, "Which strategy will work best to solve this problem?" Loper (1982) suggests two general approaches to strategy training, which she calls mechanical and elaborative. Mechanical strategies are those related to automatic, routine performance. A student might be told to ask himself, "Am I paying attention?" every time a signal is given by the teacher, for example. Such strategies have limited uses, however, because they are mostly teacher controlled. The idea of mechanical strategies can be extended to include applications to such school tasks as spelling, arithmetic, and reading (De-Ruiter and Wansart 1982). Children have often learned entire sets of procedures (e.g., all of the acts required to read a story) and can simply select and use these strategies when they are needed.

Elaborative approaches include strategies such as self-questioning with open-ended questions, drawing inferences, or providing self-generated examples. In other chapters of this text several strategies of this type are presented, so none will be given here. As with mechanical strategies, after a student has learned these strategies, they can be used in closed searches. As soon as a problem is known, a mechanical or elaborative strategy can be put into action if it will lead to a problem solution. The greatest problem for some students may be to control the process of closed search for themselves. Essentially, this is the problem of developing a reflective style, for which we earlier suggested the STOP strategy.

Learning New Information

In some cases, the problem solver must learn new information before a problem can be solved. In broad terms, this could involve new learning that ranges from very simple to very complex. In some problems, all that might be missing is a single fact (e.g., How many home runs did Babe Ruth hit in 1927?). In others, the student must learn how to read before the problem can be solved. In this section, we will concentrate on a somewhat narrow range of problems in which the prerequisite skills are known, basic information about the problem has been gathered, and the task has been organized. However, the problem still cannot be solved, because of missing information. This is a common problem encountered in everyday situations. It comes up when someone attempts to balance his checkbook and finds a check missing, or when a child is able to solve a story problem in arithmetic except that she doesn't know the answer to $7 \times 8 =$.

Identifying missing information probably requires both the ability to carefully analyze the information that is available related to the problem and a structural (knowing why) understanding of the problem. Three general questions that students can ask themselves to help identify missing information are:

1. What do I already know about the problem?
2. What new information do I need to know?
3. Where and how can I search for the information needed?

The second question is often difficult to answer. Sometimes the missing information is obvious. The problem solver may know what he or she doesn't know—a specific fact such as $7 \times 8 =$, for example. In other cases, the student may be uncertain about what is needed, and "brainstorming" about what is missing may help identify several possibilities. The most likely possibility can be selected as a hypothesis to check. Remaining hypotheses from the brainstorming can be tried later if the first one does not lead to a solution.

A search for the needed information begins when a hypothesis about what is missing has been formed. Open or closed searches, described earlier, can be applied. Searches of many types are possible—asking a teacher, looking up information in an encyclopedia, completing a set of calculations that are prerequisites for solving the problem, memorizing some information from a book, and so on. Specific strategies for conducting each kind of search can be developed, learned, and applied. The search for new information is, in many ways, a matter of starting over with the components of problem solving because the missing information poses a new problem.

Applying a Solution Strategy

The last major component of our problem-solving framework is to apply the solution strategy. This component is really not separate from the first three because many strategy "tryouts" have already been mentioned, especially as a part of organizing the task and learning new information. The integrated, holistic nature of problem solving should be apparent from the overlap between the components. On the other hand, we sometimes find that handicapped students do not use solution strategies even when they are capable of doing so. Some of this failure to "activate" a solution strategy may result from lack of interest in the problem. More than interest or motivation is involved, however. Exceptional children are often convinced that they are poor problem solvers. Others do not make the connection between the problems they are trying to solve and the solutions that are available.

On the surface, a solution to the problem is to simply tell students to apply the strategies that they know. Our response to this solution, however, is that it inadequately addresses the need of students to regulate their own learning and problem solving. Enabling students to regulate their own solution strategies implies the entire approach to teaching that we hope this book will communicate.

Chapter 3 detailed various ways to help students learn to apply solution strategies. Close attention should be given to *when, how,* and *what* to tell students about strategies, as explained in that chapter. In addition, the tell-them, model-it, and develop-it methods in chapter 3 provide the teacher with details about strategy teaching that are directly applicable to the task of applying a solution strategy.

SUMMARY

In this chapter, we have presented ideas for using language as a mediator in three major areas—as a guide for perception, for behavior, and for problem solving. As a guide for perception, language cueing strategies enable the learner to more quickly and accurately recognize the specific characteristics and patterns in a set of stimuli. Using language in this way may help teachers avoid an overemphasis on direct perceptual training. Instead of isolated "perceptual" practice, with discrimination tapes or balance beams, for example, students learn to use cognitive and language abilities that enable them to note the important differences and similarities in stimuli. The language cues may increase perceptual analysis enough to make perceptual training unnecessary, thus allowing the student to concentrate on understanding the task rather than focusing on the perceptual demands.

Similarly, language may be used as a guide for behavior. Many of the impulsive, inattentive, aggressive, or passive responses of exceptional children can potentially be brought under the child's control by using language to regulate behavioral responses. Additionally, children can learn to replace unwanted behaviors such as hitting or crying with language, i.e., by talking about the problem.

Finally, a broad framework and several approaches to using language as a guide for problem solving were explained. Emphasis is placed on learning to consciously and deliberately use language-guided strategies for becoming aware of the nature of the problem, organizing the problem, learning new information that is required to solve the problem, and applying a solution strategy.

REFERENCES

ABIKOFF, H.   Cognitive training interventions in children: Review of a new approach. *Journal of Learning Disabilities* 12 (1979), 123–35.

ALLEY, G., AND D. DESHLER.   *Teaching the Learning Disabled Adolescent: Strategies and Methods.* Denver: Love Publishing Co., 1979.

BLANCHET, A. Reflective abstraction and problem solving. Paper presented at the 13th Annual Symposium of the Jean Piaget Society, Philadelphia, Pa., June 3, 1983.

BORNSTEIN, P. H., AND R. P. QUEVILLON. The effects of a self-instructional package on overactive preschool boys. In B. B. Lahey, *Behavior Therapy with Hyperactive and Learning Disabled Children.* New York: Oxford University Press, 1979.

BROWN, R. T., AND N. ALFORD. Ameliorating attentional deficits and concomitant academic deficiencies in learning disabled children through cognitive training. *Journal of Learning Disabilities* 17 (1984), 20–26.

DeRUITER, J. A., AND W. L. WANSART. *Psychology of Learning Disabilities: Applications and Educational Practice.* Rockville, Md.: Aspen Systems Corp., 1982.

DESHLER, D. D., W. R. FERRELL, AND C. E. KASS. Error monitoring of schoolwork by learning disabled adolescents. *Journal of Learning Disabilities* 11 (1978), 401–12.

FINCH, JR., A. J., AND A. SPIRITO. Use of cognitive training to change cognitive processes. *Exceptional Education Quarterly* 1 (1980), 31–39.

HALL, J. W. Children's use of category information as a discriminative cue for memory. Paper presented at the Biennial Meeting of the Society for Research in Child Development, New Orleans, March 17–20, 1977.

HALLAHAN, D. P., AND R. SAPONA. Self-monitoring of attention with learning-disabled children: Past research and current issues. *Journal of Learning Disabilities* 16 (1983), 616–20.

HAYES, J. R. *The Complete Problem Solver.* Philadelphia: Franklin Institute Press, 1981.

INHELDER, B., AND J. PIAGET. Procedures and structures. In D. Olson, ed., *The Social Foundations of Language and Thought.* New York: W. W. Norton, 1980.

KARMILOFF-SMITH, A., AND B. INHELDER. If you want to get ahead, get a theory. *Cognition* 3 (1975), 195–212.

KEOGH, B. K., AND A. T. GLOVER. The generality and durability of cognitive training effects. *Exceptional Education Quarterly* 1 (1980), 75–82.

KNEEDLER, R. D. The use of cognitive training to change social behaviors. *Exceptional Education Quarterly* 1 (1980), 65–73.

LLOYD, J. Academic instruction and cognitive behavior modification: The need for attack strategy training. *Exceptional Education Quarterly* 1 (1980), 53–63.

LOPER, A. B. Metacognitive development: Implications for cognitive training. *Exceptional Education Quarterly* 1 (1980), 1–8.

———. Metacognitive training to correct academic deficiency. *Topics in Learning and Learning Disabilities* 2 (1982), 61–68.

LURIA, A. R. Speech development and the formation of mental processes. In M. Cole and I. Maltzman, *A Handbook of Contemporary Soviet Psychology.* New York: Basic Books, 1969.

MAIER, A. S. The effect of focusing on the cognitive processes of learning disabled children. *Journal of Learning Disabilities* 13 (1980), 143–47.

MEICHENBAUM, D. *Cognitive-Behavior Modification.* New York: Plenum Press, 1977.

MILLER, M., AND M. E. ROHR. Verbal mediation for perceptual deficits in learning disabilities: A review and suggestions. *Journal of Learning Disabilities* 13 (1980), 319–21.

PIAGET, J. *The Grasp of Consciousness: Action and Concept in the Young Child.* Cambridge, Mass.: Harvard University Press, 1976.

REID, D. K. Learning and development from a Piagetian perspective: The exceptional child. In I. E. Sigel, D. M. Brodzinsky, and R. M. Golinkoff, *New Directions in Piagetian Theory and Practice.* Hillsdale, N.J.: Lawrence Erlbaum Associates, 1981.

———, AND W. P. HRESKO. *A Cognitive Approach to Learning Disabilities.* New York: McGraw-Hill Book Co., 1981.

RENNER, J. W., D. G. STAFFORD, A. E. LAWSON, J. W. McKINNON, F. E. FRIOT, AND D. H. KELLOGG. *Research, Teaching, and Learning with the Piaget Model.* Norman: University of Oklahoma Press, 1976.

SABATINO, D. A., ED. *Learning Disabilities Handbook: A Technical Guide to Program Development.* DeKalb: Northern Illinois University Press, 1976.

SCHMIDT-KITSIKIS, E. The cognitive mechanisms underlying problem-solving in psychotic and mentally retarded children. In B. Inhelder and H. H. Chipman, eds., *Piaget and His School: A Reader in Developmental Psychology.* New York: Springer-Verlag, 1976.

SIGEL, I. E. Is the concept of the concept still elusive or what do we know about concept development? In E. K. Scholnick, ed., *New Trends in Conceptual Representation: Challenges to Piaget's Theory?* Hillsdale, N.J.: Lawrence Erlbaum Associates, 1983.

TORGESEN, J. K.   The learning disabled child as an inactive learner: Educational implications. *Topics in Learning and Learning Disabilities*, 2 (1982), 45–52.

TOWLE, M.   Learning how to be a student when you have a learning disability. *Journal of Learning Disabilities* 15 (1982), 90–93.

WANSART, W. L.   A microanalysis of the construction of solution strategies by learning disabled and normally achieving children for the tower of hanoi. Published doctoral dissertation. Greeley: University of Northern Colorado, 1984.

WEITHORN, C. J., AND E. KAGEN.   Training first graders of high-activity level to improve performance through verbal self-direction. *Journal of Learning Disabilities* 12 (1979), 82–88.

CHAPTER SIX

Reading Strategies

- In what way may we accurately say that learning to read is easy?
- What are the major false assumptions about learning to read? What alternative assumptions are proposed by the authors?
- What is wrong with the "grade-equivalent" reading-level approach to assessment of reading?
- For which students is the "reading-to-students" approach the most valuable? What are its strengths; its shortcomings?
- Why is it so important to be concerned about reading *process,* as opposed to reading *product?*
- How are the neurological-impress method, the repeated-readings method, and the assisted-readings method similar?
- Why is it so important for teachers to understand the use of question-answer relationships (QARs) when teaching reading?

Learning to read is easy. A major difficulty with learning to read is inadequate reading instruction. These two ideas underlie our approach to reading as presented in this chapter. They are directly opposite to much of what is taught about the nature of reading and reading instruction. In the first section, we will consider theoretical concepts behind these two assertions and explain our view of reading and reading instruction. In the rest of the chapter, the theoretical ideas are translated into assessment and teaching practices.

THEORETICAL PERSPECTIVES

Why do we say that learning to read is easy when so much time and effort are involved in learning to read? We believe reading is easy in the sense that it is both typical and natural to learn to read. Nearly everyone learns to read, given the motivation and opportunity to do so. Learning to read does take time and effort, of course, but that is true for all learning. Reading, however, *is* different from other learning in some ways. It involves, for instance, working with symbols of symbols (written symbols of spoken symbols). A marvelous reality of being human, however, is that symbols and abstractions are easy, typical, and natural to learn and use. Reading is primarily a natural extension of learning about the unity and order of the world.

Why, then, do some individuals not learn to read? We suggest that many reading problems result from inadequate or inappropriate reading instruction. Reading instruction is inadequate because it frequently ignores the nature of learning and the nature of reading. This assertion raises two questions. First, why do so many children learn to read if reading instruction is inadequate? Second, precisely how is reading instruction inadequate?

The answer to the first question is that many students learn to read in spite of the method used. Reading is a natural process, and many of the roadblocks that methods for teaching reading may place in the way are overcome. The methods may be inefficient and may slow down the learning, but learning is hard to stop. Additionally, all methods of teaching reading probably work, at least to some degree, because they contain major elements that are necessary for learning to read. Our point is that many methods of teaching reading significantly interfere with the process, and reading problems frequently result from this interference, not from children's inability to learn. Some children may lack the basic human abilities required, but this is rarely the case even among the moderately handicapped youngsters who are the focus of this book.

In reference to the second question, we have already noted that reading instruction is often inadequate because it ignores the nature of learning and the nature of reading. Two mistaken assumptions about learning and reading are:

1. Learning results from sequential additions of one bit of knowledge to another.
2. Reading is a matter of decoding words to sound.

These and related assumptions are discussed in DeRuiter and Wansart (1982) and Smith (1978) and will not be fully elaborated on here. We do offer, in concert with those authors, two alternative assumptions:

1. Learning results from active construction of new understanding.
2. Reading is a matter of constructing new understandings through interaction between the learner and the material that is read.

Most traditional reading methods deemphasize meaning, break reading into small bits, and stress phonics and isolated sight word drills. In contrast, the alternative assumptions result in methods that emphasize meaning, whole language, and structural understandings. The following section details the implications of this view for assessment of reading.

ASSESSMENT OF READING STRATEGIES

An analysis of students' understanding of reading tasks in both a procedural and a structural sense is helpful for reading instruction. Procedural knowledge, or knowing *how,* can be analyzed in terms of how the student uses the actual letters, words, and sentence, paragraph, and story structure in the material to carry out the reading task. We will not emphasize detailed, highly specific analysis of this sort, for reasons explained later in this section. Understanding *why,* or structural knowledge, refers to understanding the system. In reading, a student's structural understanding of the phonetic system, of the language system, of story structure, and of the links between these systems may be of interest.

The significance of many approaches to reading assessment becomes more clear when reading is viewed in procedural and structural terms. Four common elements in reading assessment are knowledge of letters, knowledge of phonics, knowledge of words, and reading grade level. Obviously, these have some relationship to assessment and reading instruction, but they are frequently regarded as separate parts of the reading process. In addition, the goal of constructing meanings, which we regard as primary, is sometimes not sufficiently emphasized in reading assessment. The construction of meaning is regarded as entirely dependent on the student's knowledge of words, letters, or sentences, rather than on the total interaction of the reader with the text.

Smith (1978) says that "reading directly for meaning. . . becomes the best strategy for reading" (p. 123). He regards this as an alternative to, not a consequence of, reading words and letters. In a reading context, letters and words by themselves do not provide adequate meaning. Identifying individual letters is no more helpful in reading than is identifying individual sounds when we hear someone talk. Similarly, we can construct the appropriate meaning of individual words only in context. We can identify some of the possible meanings of a word in isolation. Words have so many meanings and connotations, however, that exact meanings are impossible out of context.

Further, Smith presents a convincing argument that comprehension must precede the identification of individual words (and letters). Phonics systems are extremely inconsistent (Smith cites the research finding that in 6,000 of the most common words, 211 different correspondences were found between letters and sounds) and some words cannot even be named until their meaning is comprehended. Smith uses *lead* (lēēd or lĕd?) as an example. Fortunately, Smith argues, letters and word identification are not needed for obtaining meaning. The opposite, using meaning to identify letters and words, more accurately represents the reading process, to the degree that letters and words are identified by readers. Much of Smith's book is devoted to detailed information about the relative unimportance of letter, sound, and word analysis in reading and the necessity of reading directly for meaning. We refer you to his work for a full treatment of this topic.

For our purposes, note that assessment of isolated letters, sounds, and words is deemphasized from this perspective. We suggest assessing, first of all, not whether the reader correctly identifies all the letters, sounds, or words but whether meaning was constructed and the nature of that meaning. Some may regard this approach as inadequate, but this view may be due to misconceptions about learning and reading, as we explained earlier.

Reading may also be inhibited by attending excessively to reading grade levels. This emphasis places the focus on curriculum, not on the reader's understanding. In addition, reading grade levels are contrived from adult misunderstandings of what reading is. They are a result of the way we *teach* reading more than of the *nature* of reading.

What does it really mean, for example, when we say that a reader's independent, instructional, and frustrational reading grade levels are 2-1 (i.e., second grade, first month), 2-8, and 3-3, respectively? The 2-1 grade score is assumed to mean that if the child is given a book to read independently the book should be at the second grade, first month reading level. In instructional settings, where the teacher and student are working together, the material should be at the second grade, eighth month. If the student were to be given instruction at the frustrational level little learning would be expected because the material would be too difficult. Several problems arise with this type of analysis, however. The first is a problem of measurement. Grade-level scores are usually derived from tests that measure word calling and simple literal recall. Many aspects of reading are not measured, and the total understanding or cognitive abilities of the student remain relatively unknown.

A second closely related problem is that the grade levels are set primarily on the basis of comparisons to other students, again overlooking major aspects of an individual student's understanding. These comparisons say more about how and when reading is taught in school than about reading itself. Reading grade levels would obviously change if reading were not taught until the fourth grade.

Then there is the problem of what actually makes up the words, sentences, and meanings of a particular grade level. Are "short" words easier to read and therefore accessible at an earlier grade level? Should frequently used words be placed at earlier grade levels? Are words with clear or few meanings easier? These questions are difficult to answer. Important questions such as these are often overlooked, and decisions about grade levels are based on what typical readers in each grade do. Little attention is paid to the nature of reading and the reader. We regard this "solution" as inadequate and the information obtained from this approach as insufficient.

Perhaps the most significant problem with the reading-grade-level concept is that it may lead to an emphasis on *materials* rather than *methods*. Curriculum sequence may be regarded as more important than the learner and the learner's understanding. Notice that knowing a child's grade-level score says nothing about *how* to teach. We suggest, as an alternative, that first the student's procedural and structural understanding must be broadly examined, then a method of teaching that fits those understandings should be determined. Finally, materials appropriate for the method should be selected.

We suggest, then, a much more general look at the reading process than is typical in most reading assessment. It is certainly possible to specify in detail the letters, sounds, words, and other components of reading that a reader does or does not respond to correctly. Sometimes this information may provide some help to a teacher who is trying to decide how and what to teach. Scant evidence exists, however, about exactly how methods of teaching reading are related to the specific reading performance of the learner. Knowing many details about the letter- and word-skill level of the learner will *not* inform a teacher about *how* to teach.

To illustrate, suppose we know that a child can name all of the letters of the alphabet, the most common sounds of all consonants except *x* and *q*, at least two common sounds for each vowel, and 326 common sight words. How should this child be taught more about reading? We suggest that the teacher would have just as much information about how to teach this child if she had simply asked the child to read a short passage and had no details about letter and word knowledge. In fact, a very thorough, detailed analysis that includes whether the child reads word by word, which words he sounds out correctly and which he does not, the type of errors he makes in word identification (e.g., whether words that are similar in meaning or in spelling are substituted for one another), and the specific facts he remembers from a passage he has just read still does not tell us *how* to teach. The method chosen depends, we suggest, on general knowledge of how children approach the reading task (procedural knowledge) and how they understand reading in a broad structural sense. Beyond this, and perhaps even more significant, is the teacher's understanding of reading and learning. Essentially, this is only another way of saying that the teacher's theory about reading and learning is the primary basis for deciding which method to use.

The assessment process outlined in chapter 3 as part of the develop-it method may be useful in the assessment process. As they carry out the steps, teachers may find the following questions helpful:

1. Does the student understand that the reading process is primarily a matter of constructing meaning from print?
2. Does the student read with adequate fluency so that it is possible to construct meaning?
3. What is the nature of the student's overall understanding of written materials?
4. Does the student approach different types of reading materials appropriately?

We suggest starting assessment by reading to the student or by asking him or her to read. Generally, we regard the latter as preferable if the student can read. Excellent alternatives to this starting point are numerous. Instead of reading, the teacher could tell the student a story (or describe an event or object), the student could be asked to complete a picture-sequencing task, to tell a story, to describe an event, to "read" a wordless picture story, or to talk to the teacher about what reading is and how it works. A dialogue about the student's interests and motivation to read is also helpful. The dialogue and participation in some of the reading tasks should enable the teacher to determine how the student approaches reading, whether necessary cognitive and language skills appear to be present, and how to begin the next phase of reading instruction. Translating this information into specific methods of teaching reading is the topic of the next section.

STRATEGIES FOR TEACHING READING

Smith suggests that in order to learn to read, children must be totally immersed in print. We agree that the way to learn to read is by reading—and reading and reading. Essentially, the way to teach children to read is to develop an environment in which reading is encouraged and where it is meaningful and rewarding. In this view, the best method of teaching reading is to read to the child, to read with the child, and to permit the child to read.

The assessment process described in the preceding section is intended to help the teacher decide the balance between the three parts of this method. The decision is not difficult and is based on three simple rules:

1. Read to students who do not know how to read.
2. Read with students who know how to read but lack necessary procedural or structural understanding.
3. Let students read who know how to read adequately on their own.

This approach to reading instruction is specifically designed to emphasize the holistic, constructive nature of learning to read. Learning to read is regarded as similar to learning anything. A close parallel may be found in the way children first learn language. As they learn language, children are not expected to formally learn rules, to perform flawlessly, to learn isolated or unconnected parts, or to learn every aspect of each word before moving on to other words. Similarly, Smith says that reading instruction should *not* emphasize rule mastery, phonic skills, isolated words or letters, word-perfect reading, or related skills such as spelling and writing. Instead, the beginning reader is exposed to written language by being read to and read with and by reading. Reading for meaning is emphasized, errors are often ignored, and reading is made as easy and enjoyable as possible.

This is not to say that no attention is paid to learning specific information about words, letters, sounds, or other skills related to reading. Learning these specifics does take a distant second place to reading for meaning, however, and these aspects of reading are always taught in a broad context. They are learned as reading is being carried out and as a natural part of learning to read for meaning.

In the rest of this chapter, the above method of teaching reading is discussed in four sections. First, we address the selection of reading materials. The remaining three sections contain strategies for reading categorized in relation to the three rules of reading instruction—reading to students, reading with students, and letting students read on their own.

Selecting Reading Materials

If reading for meaning is the goal, the materials that students read must be meaningful. Some materials that are intended for reading instruction have very little emphasis on meaning. Work sheets that separate reading into isolated small pieces are perhaps the worst offenders.

Sometimes linguistic and basal readers also are not very meaningful. We believe that much more attention should be paid to the meaningfulness of the material; meaningfulness should take precedence over such considerations as word regularity and repetition, and the meanings in the material should be closely related to the cognitive and language abilities of the reader. Meaningfulness refers to the reader's interests and abilities. If basal readers are highly meaningful and interesting to a particular child, they may be used.

How can a teacher be sure that reading materials are meaningful to the students? By knowing the interests and characteristics of the students, by involving them in selecting what to read, and perhaps by having the students read their own written or dictated material. Experience quickly reveals which books, stories, and reading activities children enjoy. Explore the library, ask the librarian, and ask the children. Finding meaningful reading material is relatively easy because there is a variety of such material, and it is readily available.

Reading to Students

Reading to students is a method that teaches the most about reading to those who do not yet read or are just beginning. Good readers often enjoy being read to as well, and we encourage it, especially if it increases the children's desire to read. What good readers learn from being read to, however, is different from what nonreaders learn. The former learn about the content of the material; the latter learn that and much more. They learn that books are meaningful and interesting, that little black marks on a page are distinguishable from one another, that these marks form letters and words, and that they represent sounds and language. Although much of this is not specifically taught, the learning is crucial.

What can a teacher do to help children learn this essential information about reading? First, seek and use every opportunity to read to children. The world is full of signs and symbols that can be used in a natural way. Little more than naming the words, phrases, or sentences, perhaps in association with a comment that ties the words to actions or meaning, is needed for most children. If you say, "S-T-O-P spells stop. See the sign? We stop the car at the stop sign," to a two-year-old as you approach a sign, you have created an environment where much can be learned about reading. Even more can be learned when stories or books are read to children.

Second, precede, intersperse, and follow reading with dialogue. Dialogue between the teacher and the students should be directed toward the interests, needs, and understandings of the children. Topics for discussion include the content of the passage, opinion about, evaluation of, extension of, and application of the content and discussion of aspects of the nature of reading. The teacher should use her knowledge of the children's ability to understand to decide about topics for discussion. A natural exchange, with high meaningfulness to the children, is essential. Right and wrong answers are not the focus. How the children think about reading and about the concepts in the stories should be emphasized. The *process*, not the *products*, are the concern.

Introductory dialogue may consist of simple comments such as, "I'm going to read a story from this book," followed by a question such as, "What do you think the story is about?" as the cover picture is shown. More extended dialogue, should it seem desirable, may ensue from teacher comments about specific parts of a story or book, with questions about how these parts are related to the student's experiences. Through the introductory dialogue, the teacher attempts to guide the attention and stimulate the interest of the students. Dialogue interspersed with reading or following it is much the same. The teacher makes comments, asks probing questions, explores, and encourages thinking about the story, provides opportunities for the students to ask questions and make comments, and talks with them about how the content relates to other topics and interests.

We envision a classroom, in either regular or special education, that is loaded with books and reading materials. Large amounts of time are spent in reading activities, although most are unlike those of typical reading instruction. In the early stage of teaching reading (which is the focus of this section), much time is spent looking at books, listening, and sometimes following along as the teacher reads, and perhaps listening to stories on tapes, with or without an accompanying book. "Reading" wordless picture books, drawing or sequencing pictures that tell a story, and playing with shapes and letters may all be valuable. Each of these activities should be more directed at an enjoyable interaction with reading-related activities than at learning the specific, sequenced "facts" that are often regarded as prerequisites for reading. We urge much emphasis on student choice of activity and on making reading enjoyable. Time spent in reading should provide opportunities to discover, to learn, and to develop new ideas. Ditto sheets should be eliminated and tests of isolated bits of information discarded, and testing in general should take the form of an exchange of information, a dialogue, between teacher and student. Students should feel very little pressure to perform in teacher-prescribed ways (e.g., name these sounds or answer these questions) but should enjoy many opportunities to talk about reading and the content of what the teacher reads, should they want to talk. Exploring concepts and language should become a major part of the process of learning to read. When the students seem ready to construct new understandings, probing questions that challenge and extend their thinking are appropriate.

Most older readers, even very poor readers, are beyond this early stage of reading instruction, and instruction for them would begin with the next stage—reading *with* the children. For older students who are nonreaders, however, it may help to move back to this stage, at least for a short time. Some of the activities, such as picture sequencing, are probably not appropriate for these older students. With all of the activities at this stage, care must be taken to assure that the students understand why the activity is being carried out and that they do not regard the activity as too simple or inappropriate for someone their age.

What is appropriate at older ages is an emphasis on dialogue about the nature and process of reading and an exploration of the individual student's attitude toward reading. These dialogues will help the teacher analyze the language and the conceptual knowledge of the student. The four questions in the assessment section earlier in this chapter can be used as a guide for these dialogues.

Especially important for older nonreaders is an effort to change their attitudes about reading. Since they usually regard reading as difficult and as something they cannot do, it frequently takes considerable time to change these attitudes. Simply telling older nonreaders that reading is easy is not enough. Very likely, two important events will precede attitude changes: the teacher's approach to reading and reading instruction must be perceived as different from the previous experience of the student; and the student must experience success in reading tasks. These points were stressed by Grace Fernald (1943) and other remedial-reading authorities over forty years ago.

To help students recognize that a new reading approach will be used, the teacher must first explore the past experiences of the student. Then the teacher should change several aspects of the instruction process in order to be perceived as having a new approach. Essentially, these changes involve approaching reading as we have suggested. The student needs to learn concepts such as:

1. Reading involves the construction of meaning.
2. Specific sounds, letters, and words are not the focus of reading.
3. Reading is not answering comprehension questions.
4. Fluency is more important than exact word-for-word accuracy.
5. "Educated" guesses from the context help with reading.

Students will be aided in learning these and similar concepts, we believe, if teachers attend to the following items:

1. Respect and show genuine interest in the student's understanding of reading and of concepts.
2. Give away the power.
3. Increase the meaningfulness of the materials.
4. Read to the student.
5. Study specifics about reading only in context.
6. Increase dialogue.

Instead of emphasizing a right and wrong way of reading, the teacher must attempt to understand the student's approach. Genuine respect for and interest in how a student thinks, how he or she approaches the reading and comprehending process, go a long way toward convincing the student that this teacher's approach is different. Giving away the power also helps with this. Power is given away by giving the student choices about what to read, when to read—in fact, even about *whether* to read at all. Avoiding power struggles and working cooperatively are often the only way to develop the older student's interest in reading.

The meaningfulness of materials may be increased by involving the student in the choice of materials and by using material that fits the conceptual development of the student. Since we are discussing nonreaders here, the student would not be able to read these materials alone. The material can be read to the student, however, and even older students will probably regard this as appropriate if the emphasis is on meaning, and the teacher has explained the reasons for this activity. Specifically, the teacher may need to tell the student that the reasons for reading to her are to work on understanding the process of reading (e.g., constructing meaning through fluent, holistic, context-based activity) and to help with understanding of the content without worrying about past reading difficulties. The teacher models good reading. Often, a tie to the academic interests and needs of the student can be addressed at the same time by reading from textbooks selected from classes the student is taking.

Finally, dialogue is again emphasized and replaces the giving of reading-skill and comprehension tests and other artificial means of finding out whether the student understood what was read. Through dialogue, the student begins to experience the second event that is important for changing attitudes—success with a reading task. Students will begin to feel more successful if they discover that they can construct the meaning from what is read (even if someone else does the actual reading). They must understand, of course, that constructing the meaning is the most essential aspect of reading. Reading begins to be regarded as something that *can* be done, since the most important skills that are required are already known. Once this initial hurdle is cleared, students are much better prepared to go on to more successes in the next reading stage.

Clearly, this approach to early reading instruction appears less sequenced and structured than traditional approaches. It is not based on the concept of reading as a matter of learning specific, sequenced letters, sounds, or words. Instead, it focuses on getting the gist of what reading is all about and on developing meanings. One specific method that fits with early reading instruction is the language-experience approach (Allen 1976; Allen and Allen 1970; Lee and Allen 1963). In addition to its uses at later stages of reading, a language-experience approach may help children construct the most essential prerequisites of reading at the earliest stages—the understanding that meaning can be written down and that the marks on the page have identifiable meanings. An explanation of the major parts of the entire approach, including its uses in later stages, follows.

In the language-experience approach all aspects of language are regarded as parts of the same process. Reading is but one aspect of learning language, and listening, speaking, writing and spelling are integrated with reading. When the approach is applied to the first stage of reading (under discussion here) we usually suggest that the major integration is between speaking (the children dictate stories, events, descriptions of objects, and so on) and listening to reading by the teacher. That is, the teacher writes what the children dictate and then reads the dictated material to the children.

In broader applications, the understandings that language experience seeks to present to children are:

1. What I am thinking, I can talk about.
2. What I talk about, I can write (or someone else can write).
3. What is written, I can read, and so can others.
4. I can read what I have written and what others have written for me to read. (Aukerman 1971)

These understandings can be translated into a student strategy by designating steps in the process as follows:

1. Decide on an interesting idea or story, based on something I have done or know about.
2. Discuss my ideas about the topic.
3. Write (or tell someone who can write for me) what I talked about.
4. Read what I have written (or have someone read it to me).

In early stages, of course, the teacher plays a major role in helping children learn to apply this strategy. In fact, the teacher usually continues to be involved in the process (perhaps providing experiences to write about, talking about the experiences with the students, and so on) even after the students know the strategy, because this approach is designed to be interactive.

Language experience, as its name suggests, begins with meaningful experiences for the children. The role of the teacher is to arrange for these experiences or to take advantage of the previous experiences of children. The specific type of experience is less important than that it be meaningful to the children. Students' interests can be directed to many activities, including experiences with art work, stories that are told or read to them, films, field trips, plants, animals, insects, and daily events from within or outside the classroom. The teacher's strategy can be clearly stated:

1. Provide or select a meaningful experience.
2. Discuss the experience with the students.
3. Ask the students to dictate (the teacher writes) or write about the experience.
4. Read what has been written.

Discussion about the experience can be unstructured or structured, depending on the thinking and language abilities of the students. Sometimes, for example, the teacher may want the children to focus on sequential reporting of events. At other times, careful observation and description, perhaps including new descriptive adjectives, can be emphasized. Creative story telling, developing a plot, going beyond the experience (e.g., What could happen next?), analyzing why something happened, specifying relationships to other experiences, exploring motives, and so on, can all be structured into a discussion as appropriate. This discussion provides a basis for the next step, writing about the experience.

What children dictate or write depends directly on their language ability and on the meanings they have constructed from experience. Emphasis should probably *not* be placed on error-free use of language in step three. Getting the meanings in the children's terms is more important. If the teacher is writing what is dictated, correct punctuation and spelling are used, but the grammar and semantics can be written as dictated. When the students are ready to write their own material, even the mechanical aspects (spelling, punctuation) may initially be filled with errors. If correctness (by adult standards) is discussed at all, it should be in reference to the accuracy of meanings. Even then, care should be taken to focus on that which is meaningful *to the students.*

After the material is written down, the teacher reads it to the children, perhaps with the children following along on their own copy. In later stages of reading instruction the children read their own material, with the teacher providing as much assistance as necessary. We suggest a gradual and natural transition to later stages, as soon as the students are ready. Without pressure to do so, most children will soon indicate that they are ready to do some reading of their material.

Stories can be reread as frequently as seems appropriate. In general, if the students remain interested and seem to be learning from the rereading, it can be continued indefinitely. Children may want to hear or read one another's stories, too, and that provides a large set of materials for the teacher or the students to read. Stories can also be taped so the students can listen and follow a printed copy independently.

A useful technique for many children is to make a booklet of the stories they have written or dictated. The children may want to illustrate the book. Some may want to have their stories typed. Of course, a group of students could cooperatively write stories and put them in a book, and stories from several individual children can be placed in the same book.

A final word about more advanced uses of the language-experience approach is appropriate. In later stages of reading, children usually become increasingly interested in accuracy and in correcting errors. Again the teacher must decide when to begin teaching about correct spelling, punctuation, sentence construction, and the semantic aspects of written and read language. Two rules of thumb may help: (1) teach this information when the children are ready, and (2) teach this information in meaningful context. With much reading practice, most specific aspects of reading will naturally fall into place.

In summary, the language-experience approach may provide a very productive source of written material for all stages of the reading process. We suggest that it may be an excellent part of the early stages of learning to read. Language experience can be easily combined with our more general approach of interacting with reading materials, frequent reading to the students, and discussions about reading and reading materials. This approach, we believe, prepares children for the next stage of reading, when the teacher reads *with* them.

Reading with Students

Reading *with* students provides the stage in which most direct reading instruction occurs. Specific information about words and sounds may be presented at this stage. However, primary emphasis remains on reading for meaning. Words and sounds are attended to only if they improve reading for meaning. We caution teachers that it is easy to place far too much emphasis on details and to lose sight of more important goals in this area.

Not all the instructional strategies presented here are entirely consistent with our theoretical stance. On the other hand, they do provide helpful ideas about how to approach important specific aspects of the reading process. We encourage modifications of these approaches so that active construction of meaning becomes a focus of instruction. We will describe a number of approaches as they were originally formulated and then discuss how they may be modified.

The Fernald method (Fernald 1943) is an approach that combines language experience with multisensory procedures (Kirk, Kliebhan, and Lerner 1978). Considerable emphasis is placed on teaching words as whole units, a method that reflects a sight-word approach as distinguished from phonetic decoding. The method was developed for students with severe reading difficulties, and "positive reconditioning" is considered essential before direct reading instruction takes place. That is, considerable effort is directed toward increasing the confidence of the learner that reading is something he or she can do effectively. A major prerequisite for reading instruction, then, is high motivation on the part of the student. The words to be learned are selected by the student. Four stages in the instructional process are outlined below.

Stage 1: The teacher writes a student-selected word on paper or a card with the writing large enough so it can be traced.

1. The student selects five words to learn.
2. The teacher writes the words on three-by-five-inch cards.
3. The student and teacher discuss the meaning of each word, with only the word under discussion in view.
4. All five cards are placed in full view and the teacher pronounces one word, which the student identifies by pointing to it.
   (a) Praise is given for each word correctly identified, and the teacher collects the card.
   (b) If one word is confused with another, the teacher points to each word and says it.
   (d) After errors occur, the words are shuffled, and the first two parts of this step are repeated.
   (c) No comments are made about parts of the word.
5. The cards are laid out again, and the student is asked to read each word. Errors are corrected as necessary. Cards are shuffled after errors are corrected.
6. Cards are laid out one at a time, and the student is given about two seconds to pronounce the word. If it is not correctly identified in the time limit, the teacher says it and returns the card to the pack. Only one word at a time is visible.
   (a) The student traces the word with a finger, saying each word part as it is traced.
   (b) The student traces the word until looking at the copy is no longer necessary, then writes the word from memory.
   (c) The student writes the word in an experience story.
   (d) The story is typed (usually not by the student) and read by the student.

Stage 2: The teacher writes a student-selected word and the student reads the word without tracing. The word is written, typed, and read as in stage 1.

Stage 3: Students look at the word and say it, after being told what the word is, if necessary.

(a) Reading from books begins.
(b) When a reading selection is completed, new words are reviewed, written from memory, and checked.

Stage 4: Students recognize new words from their similarities to previously learned words.

(a) Similarities are pointed out by the teacher if necessary.
(b) Students use a variety of reading materials.

Reading mastery at each stage is regarded as important in this method. Modifications of the Fernald approach have been suggested by Brown (1982), who has found success with the following strategy:

7. The student tells a story using the five words. The teacher writes the story.
8. The student reads the story, with immediate assistance as needed. The five words are underlined in color. Words that caused difficulty may be underlined in another color. The story is given a title, the student's name is placed on it as author, and the story is set aside.
9. In the next session the five words from the previous day are placed on the table, and steps four and five are repeated with all the cards left on the table. At this point, tracing of the words may be carried out if the student has considerable difficulty. The number of tracings is reduced as soon as possible. Unique aspects of words such as a silent *e* may be pointed out, although letter names and phonics rules are not discussed.
10. Stories may be bound, and records should be kept of tracings needed, all of which may encourage the learner's efforts to read.

The Fernald method and Brown's modifications place considerable emphasis on making the reading process meaningful for the students. However, we suggest that meaningfulness may be increased by always selecting from *context* the words to be traced or read. That is, if the student is reading a story (language experience or from a book), words that present extreme and continuing difficulty may be briefly worked on using the Fernald method or Brown's modification. Often, however, simply continuing to read may be more effective. That is, as the student reads, words that are unknown are said immediately by the teacher, and the emphasis is on constructing the meanings of the story. Usually if words are not read accurately, they are corrected only if the meaning is strongly affected, or if the student is not able to construct meaning from the passage. We suggest "in-context" use of the Fernald method only for cases where students are having severe problems with the aspects of reading that are the focus of the method. Frequently, a method of this intensity is simply not needed. Similarly, there may be times in the reading process when extreme difficulty with sounds requires a brief period of concentration on phonics. Individual sounds may be discussed and practiced with methods much like those suggested by Fernald.

If a *student* strategy were to be identified with these methods, it would perhaps consist of the following steps in the early parts of the Fernald method:

1. Select a word to learn from a story you are reading.
2. Trace the word as you look at it and say it. (Ask the teacher for help as needed.)
3. Repeat step 2 until you can write the word without looking at a copy.
4. Write the word in a sentence or story.
5. Read the story.

With teacher guidance, some students may find this to be a useful strategy for learning new words. Essentially, the student is learning that rehearsal is sometimes helpful. We are concerned, however, that students may also begin to think that learning new words is more important than reading for meaning.

A second method at this stage of reading instruction is the neurological-impress method (Heckelman 1969). It provides a direct means of working on fluent reading for disabled readers. The method may be criticized for being excessively teacher directed, for being based on notions about neurology that are questionable, and for placing insufficient emphasis on reading for meaning. Nevertheless, the results of using neurological impress may be relatively unaffected by these weaknesses because of the direct way it provides for reading with students.

As Heckelman (1969) has found, neurological impress may be especially useful with students who have had considerable reading instruction but are still reading very poorly. In clinical settings, we have found the method helpful for students over nine years of age who know some words by sight (at least twenty-five words or so), have some knowledge of phonics but make inefficient use of them, and read word by word in a very halting fashion. The method may also be effective with beginning readers. Although Heckelman suggests not emphasizing reading comprehension, the effect of the method may be to increase readers' ability to read for meaning because the material is read in a fluent, sustained fashion. Heckelman did find average increases of 1.9 years in reading comprehension after 7¼ hours of instruction, although he does not report how this evaluation was made.

The neurological-impress method has the following steps:

1. Select reading material, with students participating in the selection. Students are encouraged to begin with simpler material.
2. Place the reader slightly in front of the teacher and hold the book jointly. Spend a few minutes introducing the method's purposes and procedures.
3. Read the material in unison. The teacher's voice is directed into the student's ear at close range. The teacher reads slightly faster and louder than the student.
4. Repeat the same sentences/paragraphs until a fluent reading pattern is established. Drop repetition as soon as possible (after the first few minutes of a session and after a few sessions have been completed).
5. The teacher moves a finger under the words being read in a smooth, continuous flow. Later the student does this, with assistance as needed. The student is encouraged to read smoothly (sliding across the words like sliding on ice) and to not stop or back up. Students are told not to think about the words.
6. The teacher lowers his or her voice and lags just behind the student. If the student falters, the teacher increases loudness and speed. The student and teacher may alternate leading and following.
7. No interrogation of content or comprehension is carried out, although the content may be discussed if the student wants.

8. Cover as much material as possible, attending to fluency, not word accuracy. Give positive comments about fluency. Watch for signs of fatigue and give time to recover.

9. Encourage students to read at home, by themselves or with others. Do not place emphasis on sounds or word recognition.

Perhaps a better name for the neurological-impress method is the "reading-together" method. The elementary name, suggested by Heckelman, should not distract from the value of the technique. The method provides a good model and direct experience in reading. These are the most important components of the method in our experience. Less significant are Heckelman's specifications of directing the voice into the student's ear; starting with easier material; pointing in a smooth, continuous flow; and quickly reducing the number of repetitions of the material. Our experience indicates that these four recommendations can be disregarded with no loss in effectiveness. The teacher and student can sit side by side, with no particular attention paid to where the teacher's voice is directed. Some teachers use a tape recorder, which the student controls, instead of reading with the student directly. Material with content that roughly matches the student's mental age, if it is interesting to the student, is just as effective as "easier" material. Pointing may not be necessary, may be done with pauses between phrases, and may lead the voice slightly. Repetitions may be helpful whenever the student stumbles, especially if the flow seems to be affected. We also suggest adding frequent short discussions of the meaning of the material because it helps accomplish two important purposes: placing more emphasis on meaning and enabling the teacher to understand how and what the student constructs related to meaning. The method should be used flexibly, with variations introduced based on the apparent needs of the student. The main idea is simply to include large doses of fluent reading, with reading together as the main technique.

Two methods that are similar to neurological impress are repeated readings (Samuels 1979) and assisted reading (Hoskisson 1975). In repeated readings, the primary technique is to reread a short, meaningful passage several times until a fluency of about eighty-five words per minute is reached. Assisted reading starts with our stage 1, reading simple books to children. Students gradually learn to repeat the words, phrases, and sentences as the teacher reads, and eventually they do most of the reading, with teacher assistance as needed. Bos (1982) suggests a combination of neurological impress and repeated/assisted reading that she terms "repeated choral reading." Bos reports on a case study in which reading gains were demonstrated by using the following steps:

1. The student selects a book from which the teacher reads a short section (fifteen to thirty words) at the beginning of the book. The teacher points to the words as they are read, and the student watches.

2. The section is repeatedly reread together, with the teacher pointing at the words, until the student is comfortable reading it alone.

3. The student reads the passage alone. The teacher provides unknown words or occasionally asks the student to supply a word that makes sense. Words that cause difficulty are noted.

4. If there is a natural break in the information, the passage is discussed and is related to other information known by the subject.

5. The above steps are repeated until the book is completed.

6. Words that presented consistent difficulty are written on cards, their meaning is discussed, and they are located in the text. They may be studied in a "cloze" format (student fills in the word in a sentence) or listened to on a language master.

The modifications suggested by Bos are generally consistent with those we have found helpful. The construction of meaning through fluent reading delineates the major value of the neurological-impress and similar methods. During the reading-with-students stage, the teacher should be especially sensitive to the students' understanding of the task. Appropriate teaching requires extensive awareness of the structural and procedural understandings of the students. The teacher can decide when to ask probing questions about the reading process, when to directly provide new information, and when to develop new reading strategies with the student, with each decision based on an analysis of the student's understanding of the task.

The overall pattern of instruction at the reading-with-children stage involves a great amount of reading together from a wide variety of reading material. The difficulty level of the material is adjusted to the procedural and structural understandings of the student and the particular reading method that is used. Reading material may be selected by the students or by the teacher if the interests and abilities of the students are known. If the material is too easy or too difficult, the obvious and simple solution is to select another book. Through analysis of the student's procedures and structures, specific components of the reading process may be selected for additional emphasis. Throughout the process, primary emphasis is placed on constructing an understanding of the reading process and an understanding of the meaning of what is read. The following steps specify the essence of the teacher's strategy.

1. Select reading material that corresponds with the student's current understanding of reading. Adjust the difficulty level as necessary.

2. Read the material with the student, providing as much help as necessary.

3. Analyze the procedural and structural understandings of the student related to the material.

4. Set up conditions that explore and extend the student's understandings.

Although we have already discussed much of this process, a few words of explanation about the last two steps are needed. Notice, first of all, that the conditions referred to in step 4 are directly dependent on the analysis in step 3. Students' procedural and structural understandings will vary widely, thereby affecting which understandings are explored and extended.

Components that may potentially be the focus of reading instruction in step 4 include at least these:

—Overall meaning of the passage.

—Meaning of specific events or facts in the passage.

—Sequence of events or facts in the passage.

—Implications of the content related to the passage or to events and situations outside the passage.

—Using context to determine meanings of words, sentences, paragraphs, or the total passage.

—Overall meaning of the reading process.

—Specific procedural or structural understandings of the reading process, including aspects related to letters, sounds, spelling and spelling patterns, syllables, phonics rules, sounding out words, word meanings, and the structure of language at the sentence, paragraph, and passage levels.

The items in this list can be evaluated in step 3 in order to help the teacher understand the procedures and structures of the students. In step 4, the teacher sets up conditions that concentrate on the components that are judged most important as a result of the evaluation.

We assume that learning evolves from relatively global, undifferentiated understandings to more differentiated levels. Therefore, in early stages of reading instruction, concentration on the more global items from the list may be appropriate. These items include especially the overall meaning of the passage and the overall meaning of the reading process. They can be focused upon in a dialogue between the teacher and student in which the meaning of the passage is discussed.

More advanced readers may be ready to learn about important details of reading for meaning and the reading process. Again, the teacher decides on the type and extent of instructional emphasis to apply, based on the current understandings of the students and their apparent readiness to learn about these details. The more specific items in the list of components (e.g., aspects of letters, sounds, spelling, language structure) may be addressed at this point, depending on the teacher's analysis of how important they are for helping the student become a better reader. Some readers may construct all of the procedural and structural understandings they need with little specific instruction about letters, sounds, spelling patterns, or other components. Others may benefit from instruction and techniques such as those included in the Fernald method.

Care must be taken not to detract from the real purposes of reading in this stage. Such things as the meaning and sequence of events, the implications of the meanings, and context may be more important than sounds, spelling, and other details. Dialogue replaces comprehension testing as a means of extending and understanding what the students have learned from their reading. Approaches to helping students with reading comprehension are discussed in the following section.

Letting Students Read on Their Own

The title of this section may seem to indicate that all that remains in teaching reading is to leave the students to their own devices. In one sense, this notion has some merit. Much of the reading that we do as adults is carried out for its own sake. That is, we read what we want to read at our own pace and for our own purposes. We may or may not discuss the meanings with others, and whether we make direct or obvious use of what we read is a matter of individual choice. Perhaps children need more freedom to do the same thing.

On the other hand, there are two major reasons for involving teachers in reading instruction at this stage. First, in school most children will be expected to do more than just read material independently. They will, for example, be asked to take tests on what they read. Second, intellectual growth may be aided through teacher-student interaction about what is read. To state these reasons in a slightly different way—without assistance at this stage, many students will have difficulty with school tasks related to reading, and they will not attain the full benefits of reading.

We have emphasized that all stages of reading should focus on constructing meanings, but we have not detailed how teachers can help students with this task. The focus of this section is on strategies related to the process of constructing meaning, or "reading comprehension," as it is commonly called. We do not regard these strategies as separate from what is done in earlier reading stages. Rather, reading should be regarded as a continuous process of constructing and reconstructing new meanings at increasingly higher levels. The major components of reading remain the same throughout—the emphasis is on meaning, a massive amount of reading takes place, and dialogue about reading processes and content is frequent.

A strong emphasis on the so-called basics of reading has frequently resulted in a corresponding lack of attention to the processes by which students *understand* what they read. Specific strategies for comprehension may be ignored. Students are expected to understand without being instructed about what and how to understand. In fact, most instruction about reading comprehension is not instruction at all. Instead, students are only *tested* to determine their comprehension. They are told to read a passage and answer comprehension questions. If they perform poorly, they are given an "easier" passage and tested again.

We urge a focus on reading comprehension as a language process that involves constructing meanings related to the author's intended communication. Teaching students to construct meanings is a difficult task. In a sense, it is impossible; we can "teach" all we want, but learning does not necessarily result. The nature of understanding and how understanding develops is not clear. The effects that teaching has on the development of understanding need much more analysis. Nevertheless, we will forge ahead with some teaching suggestions, with the caution that these ideas should be regarded as only a beginning.

In recent years, increasing emphasis has been placed on helping students learn specific strategies that are intended to aid comprehension and cognitive growth, particularly for older students (Alley and Deshler 1979; Deshler, Schumaker, and Lenz 1984; Deshler, Schumaker, Lenz, and Ellis 1984; Schumaker, Deshler, Alley, Warner, and Denton 1982; Swanson 1982; Wong 1982). To this emphasis we add two themes that are found throughout this book. First, teachers must understand the cognitive structures of students (DeRuiter and Wansart 1982). Second, the teaching strategies must involve an understanding of learning as an active constructive process. In combination, these concepts provide a starting place for teaching reading comprehension.

In the earlier chapter on perceptual cueing strategies we presented reading comprehension strategies that used underlining, mapping, and picture symbols. In this chapter, we will add approaches that aim directly at helping students use a strategic understanding of the structure of ideas as expressed in written language. Emphasis will be placed on strategies that are closely related to the comprehension tasks that students typically are asked to undertake.

A major component of reading comprehension strategies is that of questioning. Questioning involves complex processes that require considerable language and cognitive understanding. Gavelek and Raphael (1982) point out three fundamental kinds of knowledge that students must have to be able to answer questions successfully. First, they must understand what questions are—that they request information. Second, students must understand that a question may or may not be potentially answerable. Third, if the question is answerable, students require some understanding of whether they already know an adequate answer or whether other sources must be sought. These authors also say that students must learn to recognize that some answers are partial and that often several sources of information can or should be integrated to provide an answer.

Gavelek and Raphael found that both average and low-ability students were capable of learning many important aspects of using questions by being trained to recognize question-answer relationships. A three-category taxonomy of questions was used to determine students' ability to use question-answering strategies. The taxonomy included questions that were termed *text explicit, text implicit,* and *script implicit.* As an example, Gavelek and Raphael use a question that asks about three causes for civil war. Text-explicit questions would be those for which three causes are specifically listed in the text. *Text implicit* refers to a situation where, for example, the answer must be drawn out of an article about civil war in which four pages are devoted to each of three causes. *Script implicit* means that no specific references are made to the topic in the article. That is, the article may be about the causes of war, but civil war is not directly mentioned.

Gavelek and Raphael used the following five steps to teach students about questions:

1. Introduce the students to question-answer relationships (QARs).
2. Give the students questions and corresponding answers from different texts with examples from each of the QAR categories.

3. Ask the students to explain orally how each QAR category applied and what strategy was used to get the answer.
4. The teacher provides feedback immediately on the accuracy of the student's responses in step 3.
5. Gradually lead the students to provide independent responses to questions and to explain the QAR category and strategy used.

Although this strategy is somewhat vague (note the unexplained use of words such as *introduce, provides feedback,* and *gradually lead*), it does provide a potentially helpful framework within which students can better understand question-answer relationships. From such training, students and teachers may be able to devise specific strategies that the students can use in many reading-comprehension contexts. For example, a student strategy drawn from the foregoing for a reading assignment that has questions to answer could be as follows:

1. Read the question.
2. Read the passage.
3. Reread the question and identify the apparent QAR category of the question.
4. Decide whether the answer is known or whether it can be answered from the passage.
5. If necessary, search the passage for the answer.

Of course, some students may need assistance in knowing how to search the passage, especially for text-implicit and script-implicit questions. During step 4 (feedback) of Gavelek and Raphael's method, specific reading comprehension strategies may be a focus of discussion so that students learn more about how to search for answers.

The Gavelek and Raphael framework may also help students learn more about how to formulate their own questions about a passage, a technique recommended in many reading comprehension strategies. That is, students may learn to formulate varied levels and types of questions through an increased understanding of question-answer relationships. Different types of questions may have important effects on comprehension and recall. Friedman and Rickards (1981) conclude, for example, that when questions requiring inferences (similar to script-implicit questions) were inserted following a passage, all types of recall were improved for college students. These authors also found apparent benefits from a read-question-reread format in which the subjects first read the passage, then answered an inserted question, then reread the passage.

Capelli and Markman (1982) found that younger children (third and sixth graders) who were taught to answer questions as they read were better able to detect inconsistencies in stories than untrained students. In this study, the students were asked to predict cause-effect, evaluate whether the predictions or inferences made sense after reading, present themselves with problems and possible explanations, and evaluate the adequacy of the explanations. Emphasis was placed on initial teacher modeling of the question/problem-posing (and answering) process and on teacher feedback to the students when they carried out the process themselves. Capelli and Markman state that questions about inferences, forming hypotheses, and tying information together are the most effective. They taught students about this process by using four steps:

1. The students read a series of short stories, one sentence at a time, and after each sentence answered a set of questions such as:
   (a) Who are the characters?
   (b) What is going on?
   (c) Why did the characters do what they did?
   (d) When and where did the story take place?
2. The experimenter modeled the questions and answers.
3. The students answered the questions, and the experimenter modeled the story the students had just read.
4. The explicitness of the questions was gradually diminished until the students were simply describing their current interpretations as completely as possible while keeping the questions in mind.

Again, although the steps are not explained in detail, they provide a framework for constructing a better understanding of how to ask and answer questions. The specific questions in step 1 provide a basis for a rather simple strategy that students could use to guide their own problem posing about stories. The overall student strategy that can be drawn from these steps contains two main components. First, the students learn that posing questions or problems as they read may be helpful. Second, they learn to formulate, think about, and evaluate through further reading the possible answers. For some students, these understandings may be even more effective if those two concepts and their importance for reading comprehension are discussed in a dialogue between the student and the teacher.

Brown and Palincsar (1982) have suggested a teaching approach for conducting a dialogue in reading tasks that is outlined below.

1. Both teacher and student read a partial or whole passage.
2. A dialogue leader (either teacher or student) is selected to
   (a) paraphrase the main idea,
   (b) discuss how pieces of information might be grouped or classified,
   (c) predict questions that might be asked about the passage,
   (d) hypothesize about the content of the remainder of the passage,
   (e) comment on any confusions and how they might be resolved, and
   (f) ask the other person a question about the passage.
3. The role of dialogue leader is switched.

The size of the passage can be adjusted as necessary with this approach, and slight adaptations can be made to include discussion of the type of structure used in the passage or of other aspects of reading comprehension. Brown and Palincsar report that seventh graders increased performance from 15 percent correct to 80–90 percent correct on assessment passages after working on this procedure. The strategy apparently was transferred to independent work.

Brown and Palincsar had preceded this strategy training with a corrective feedback technique in which the students carefully and silently read a passage (asking for help with words and meanings as needed), after which the teacher asked ten comprehension questions, praised correct responses, and provided corrective feedback for errors. The corrective feedback consisted of guiding the student to the paragraph that contained the answer, pointing out the specific lines containing the information if necessary, and prompting to find the answer.

Students who are able to pose questions as they read are likely to improve their ability to effectively use strategies such as those suggested by Clark et al. (1984). These authors used a self-questioning strategy that was comprised of three simple steps. First, the students read the passage as they asked themselves who, what, where, when, and why questions. Then they answered the questions as they read. Finally, they marked the answers with symbols that corresponded to each type of question. Clark et al. also used a five-step visual-imagery strategy with the same students. Both strategies were found effective with five of six students. Learning disabled students with reading difficulties learned to apply the strategies with grade-level materials, thereby attaining higher comprehension scores.

Many reading comprehension strategies are modeled on, or at least have components similar to, a method called SQ3R, which was presented by Robinson (1946). SQ3R has five steps, as follows:

1. *S—survey* a chapter quickly.
2. *Q*—convert the subtitles to *questions*.
3. *R*—*read* to locate the answer to one of the questions.
4. *R*—*recite* and make notes of the answer.
5. *R*—*review* the material.

Schumaker et al. (1982) review studies that have used SQ3R and report on the results of using an adapted version of it. Much research remains to be done on the effectiveness of the method and variations of it, although the results of its use to date provide some evidence that it is useful. Teachers are encouraged to carefully read and evaluate the evidence and references cited by Schumaker et al. if they plan to use this strategy.

Schumaker et al. developed and tested a version of SQ3R that was termed *multipass*. Three substrategies (passes) termed *survey, size-up,* and *sort-out* are the major components of the approach. These were taught to students, one at a time, by trained teachers who followed a six-step instructional procedure. Essentially, these six steps involved (1) initial assessment, (2) description of the substrategy, (3) modeling (by the teacher) of the strategy, (4) learning (memorizing) the steps in the strategy, (5) practice with the strategy, and (6) feedback (positive and corrective) to the student. Students were then tested on ability level and on understanding of grade-level materials to determine whether they used the strategies in combination. If necessary, subjects were given more practice in grade level materials, followed by feedback and a final test.

The survey, size-up, and sort-out substrategies are intended to be used in sequence as a passage is read. Each has several steps that are adaptations or expansions of SQ3R. The survey pass involved reading, in sequence, the chapter title, introductory paragraph, table of contents, major chapter subtitles, captions of illustrations (after looking at the illustrations), and the summary paragraph. Reading of the table of contents was done to provide a review of the chapter's relationship to other chapters. Subtitles were read with the goal of noting how the chapter was organized. As a final part of survey, all information gained was paraphrased.

In the size-up pass, students were instructed to search for textual cues such as bold-face print, a subtitle, colored print, and italics. When found, the cue was converted into a question, surrounding text was skimmed to answer the question, and the answer was paraphrased without looking at the book. Finally, all information gained by using size-up on the chapter was paraphrased.

The sort-out pass began by having the student read and answer the questions at the end of a chapter. Questions that could be answered were checked off. For unanswered questions, the students were asked to think where the answer might be found, to skim the section for the answer, and to repeat this process until the answer was found.

Schumaker et al. found that learning disabled students learned how to use this complex strategy effectively and improved their reading-comprehension performance. Instructional time for learning the strategy varied from $4\frac{1}{2}$ to $11\frac{1}{2}$ hours. They express concern about the amount of time required and also note the need to compare the method with other alternatives and to examine the relationship between reading-ability levels and the effects of the method.

Multipass incorporates aspects of teaching that we have previously emphasized, such as assessing the strategy skills of the student prior to instruction, modeling, and having a dialogue about results of strategy use. The substrategies can be directly specified as student strategies. Modifications that the teacher may wish to try and to evaluate are (1) develop the substrategies cooperatively with students, (2) decrease or increase the number of substrategies or the number of steps in a substrategy, and (3) substitute an interactive dialogue (with practice trials) for memorization of the substrategy steps. Students may require additional substrategies prior to, or as a part of, multipass. For example, students who have difficulty with forming questions about textual cues may be assisted through a study of question-answer relationships as described earlier in this chapter.

Learning about the structure of written language and learning how to pose and answer questions are recurring themes in this section. If students are to construct meanings from their reading, these two elements are perhaps the most essential. We assume that a structured understanding of written language and of comprehension strategies will assist students with many reading tasks. Obviously, students will need considerable time and much interaction with teachers to construct these understandings.

We believe two additional ideas must be emphasized related to reading-comprehension strategies. First, these strategies should be regarded as ways of *interacting* with written language so that students can construct meanings. We do not see these strategies as static entities that can be "funneled into" the students' heads, where they can be pulled out as needed. Rather, strategies are constructed by the students as ways of interacting when interaction is advantageous.

Second, these strategies may not be the best reflection of the actual processes most readers use. In fact, long-term use of these strategies may not even be desirable. They may make reading too complex, too slow, too fragmented, and too laborious. Perhaps they should be used only temporarily, until the handicapped learner is able to construct meanings without them. From the start, they probably should be simplified as much as possible as long as the desired learning is taking place. As with the earlier stages of reading, the best way to learn to comprehend what is read may be to read and read and read.

SUMMARY

Learning to read has been presented in this chapter as essentially a natural process that will take place primarily through the act of reading itself. Three major stages of reading instruction are presented: reading to students, reading with students, and letting students read on their own. Each stage emphasizes an overall rule of thumb: The most important aspects of learning to read are learned by participating in the process of reading. The teacher's major roles are to provide for as much reading as possible and provide interactive dialogue about the reading process and content. Specific strategies are regarded as supplements to the reading process. They should be used primarily as a support system for those students who apparently cannot progress without this specific type of assistance.

REFERENCES

ALLEN, R. V. *Language Experiences in Communication.* Boston: Houghton Mifflin Co., 1976.
————, AND C. ALLEN. *Language Experiences in Reading.* Chicago: Encyclopedia Britannica, 1970.
ALLEY, G., AND D. D. DESHLER. *Teaching the Learning Disabled Adolescent: Strategies and Methods.* Denver: Love Publishing Co., 1979.
AUKERMAN, R. *Approaches to Beginning Reading.* New York: John Wiley and Sons, 1971.
BARTLETT, B. J. Top-level structure as an organizational strategy for recall of classroom text. Unpublished doctoral dissertation. Tempe: Arizona State University, 1978.
BOS, C. S. Getting past decoding: Assisted and repeated readings as remedial methods for learning disabled students. *Topics in Learning and Learning Disabilities* 1 (1982), 51–57.
BROWN, A. L., AND A. S. PALINCSAR. Inducing strategic learning from texts by means of informed, self-control training. *Topics in Learning and Learning Disabilities* 2 (1982), 1–17.
BROWN, D. *Reading Diagnosis and Remediation.* Englewood Cliffs, N.J.: Prentice-Hall, 1982.
CAPELLI, C. A., AND E. M. MARKMAN. Suggestions for training comprehension monitoring. *Topics in Learning and Learning Disabilities* 2 (1982), 87–96.
CLARK, F. L., D. D. DESHLER, J. B. SCHUMAKER, G. R. ALLEY, AND M. M. WARNER. Visual imagery and self-questioning: Strategies to improve comprehension of written material. *Journal of Learning Disabilities* 17 (1984), 145–49.
DANSEREAU, D. F., B. A. MCDONALD, K. W. COLLINS, J. GARLAND, C. E. HOLLEY, G. M DIEKHOFF, AND S. H. EVANS. Evaluation of a learning strategy system. In H. F

O'Neil, Jr., and C. D. Spielberger, eds., *Cognitive and Affective Learning Strategies.* New York: Academic Press, 1979.

DeRuiter, J. A., and W. L. Wansart. *Psychology of Learning Disabilities: Applications and Educational Practice.* Rockville, Md.: Aspen Systems Corp., 1982.

Deshler, D. D., J. B. Schumaker, and B. K. Lenz. Academic and cognitive interventions for LD adolescents: Part I. *Journal of Learning Disabilities* 17 (1984), 108–17.

————, and Ellis, E. Academic and cognitive interventions for LD adolescents: Part II. *Journal of Learning Disabilities* 17 (1984), 170–79.

Fernald, G. *Remedial Techniques in Basic School Subjects.* New York: McGraw-Hill Book Co., 1943.

Friedman, F., and J. P. Rickards. Effect of level, review, and sequence of inserted questions on text processing. *Journal of Educational Psychology* 73 (1981), 427–36.

Gavelek, J. R., and T. E. Raphael. Instructing metacognitive awareness of question-answer relationships: Implications for the learning disabled. *Topics in Learning and Learning Disabilities* 2 (1982), 69–77.

Heckelman, R. G. A neurological-impress method of remedial-reading instruction. *Academic Therapy* 4 (1969), 277–82.

Hoskisson, K. The many facets of assisted reading. *Elementary English* 52 (1975), 312–15.

Kirk, S. A., J. M. Kliebhan, and J. W. Lerner. *Teaching Reading to Slow and Disabled Learners.* Boston: Houghton Mifflin Co., 1978.

Kohl, H. *Reading, How to.* New York: Bantam Books, 1974.

Lee, D. M., and R. V. Allen. *Learning to Read through Experience.* 2d ed. New York: Appleton-Century-Crofts, 1963.

Meyer, B. J. F., and R. Freedle. *The Effects of Different Discourse Types on Recall.* Princeton, N.J.: Educational Testing Service, 1978.

Postman, N., and C. Weingartner. *The School Book.* New York: Delacorte Press, 1973.

Robinson, F. P. *Effective Study.* New York: Harper and Brothers, 1946.

Samuels, S. J. The method of repeated readings. *Reading Teacher* 32 (1979), 403–08.

Schumaker, J. B., D. D. Deshler, G. R. Alley, M. M. Warner, and P. H. Denton. Multipass: A learning strategy for improving reading comprehension. *Learning Disability Quarterly* 5 (1982), 295–304.

Smith, F. *Reading without Nonsense.* New York: Teachers College Press, 1978.

Swanson, H. L., ed. Controversy: Strategy or capacity deficit. *Topics in Learning and Learning Disabilities* 2 (1982).

Wong, B. Y. L., ed. Metacognition and learning disabilities. *Topics in Learning and Learning Disabilities* 2 (1982).

CHAPTER SEVEN

Written Language Strategies

by Judith S. Gilbert

- How do the mechanics of writing differ from composition and expression of thought? How do differences in emphasis (on the part of teachers) influence initial teaching methods in assisting handicapped students to improve written language?

- Of what value is journal writing in promoting more effective written language? At what ages may it begin, and how does it vary across various age/grade levels?

- Why are prewriting skills so important to handicapped students? How can they be promoted most effectively?

- What are the major differences in the purposes of functional and expressive writing?

- What are the major strengths of the technique called sentence combining?

- How do rewriting and proofreading contribute to the development of written language skills?

INTRODUCTION

Written expression is a complex process in which the writer determines not only what to say but also how to say it; the subject must be expressed in a way that fits the purpose of the writing, the writer's style, and the intended audience. Written expression may be considered as a continuous and constructive process of exploration, rehearsal, drafting, and revision (Daigon 1982). It is similar to the Piagetian conceptualization of how individuals construct and refine their knowledge to higher levels of complexity through continuous interaction with the environment.

Instruction in written expression often has focused on the mechanics of writing: punctuation, capitalization, spelling, and handwriting, in contrast to the aspects of composition through which students express their thoughts. The mechanics of writing exist primarily to aid with the composing process and make the written product more accessible to its audience. Therefore, it seems logical to emphasize composition and the expression of thought first and mechanics second. The emphasis on written expression in regular classrooms has shifted recently from focusing on mechanics to focusing on composition. Unfortunately, many language-arts programs for mildly and moderately handicapped students continue to emphasize the mechanical aspects of writing. In addition, there has been greater concern in special education programs with instruction in reading and mathematics than with writing. Neither regular nor special education curricula have met adequately the needs of exceptional students in the area of written language. Drill in, and "mastery" of, the mechanical skills does not necessarily produce students who can write functionally. Rather, these skills may be viewed by students as laborious and isolated tasks that have little meaning or value for them. Drill in mechanical skills does not communicate to students that writing, like spoken language, is an act of communication. Some students, therefore, may never transfer or integrate these skills and learn to write adequately for practical daily living situations. This may be particularly true for students identified as mildly and moderately handicapped.

The purpose of this chapter is to present an approach to teaching written language that is based on a holistic, or "whole language," model. The basic premise is that written language instruction should center on the composing process, i.e., the effective communication of the writer's ideas to a reader. Mechanics will be discussed in terms of their role as conventions used to help in the transmission of the writer's message. According to Daigon, "Attention to the demands of the composing process and what teachers and peers can do to make it work is at the center of a revolution in the way writing is perceived and taught" (p. 243).

A strategy-based teaching and learning approach will be presented. Both teacher and student strategies are intended to help students to become more independent in their writing and more aware of the elements involved in becoming a writer. Use of the assessment procedures described in chapters 2 and 3 will often be helpful in guiding the teacher to a clearer understanding of a child's current functioning as a writer. Basically, this process involves analysis of how the student thinks about writing, where this thinking needs to be modified, and what the current thinking of the student indicates about the strategies he or she uses. From this information a much clearer picture of the strategies that the student can and should learn is likely to emerge.

Finally, this chapter reflects the influence of "developmental" models of language acquisition, which suggest that children develop listening, speaking, reading, and writing knowledge simultaneously rather than sequentially (Chomsky 1971; Clay 1975; Poplin 1983). Such models indicate that it may be more helpful to the teacher to view listening, speaking, reading, and writing as complementary abilities and to foster growth in all of these areas concurrently rather than wait for the child first to develop adequate listening skills and then adequate speaking and reading skills before addressing written language in the classroom curriculum.

INTERVENTION STRATEGIES
FOR WRITTEN LANGUAGE

Creating Writers

Paradoxical as it may seem, students should already *be* "writers" before traditional formal instruction in writing begins. Since it is the goal of instruction to help children come "to know" and then to construct bridges from what is known to the unknown, the teacher's first task is to help students who do not write spontaneously to become writers. Rhodes and Shannon (1982) describe one teacher's efforts to help her young students to become writers; i.e., to engage freely in meaningful written communication by providing opportunities for them to learn about written language and then to construct from that knowledge to become creators of written language. Shannon was teaching twenty first- through third-grade children in her learning disabilities resource room. She describes them all as exhibiting significant delays in written-language development and many as also exhibiting oral-language delays. Shannon began the school year by filling her classroom with all kinds of printed material: environmental signs and labels (e.g., signs that say One Way, Exit, Stop; magazine ads), poetry and songs copied onto charts, and, of course, children's books of all kinds. She found that most of her students simply ignored the material at first and even resisted listening to stories she read to them. As she persisted, however, the children gradually became interested in hearing the stories and requested that favorites be reread frequently. Student participation was encouraged as the children began to read along, filling in missing parts when the teacher paused and predicting events in a story. Many of the children were nonreaders, but they began, in time, to choose to read books on their own or in the fashion of younger children who use pictures instead of print to help them retell or "read" the story in their own language.

Most of the books in the classroom were of the predictable type that feature repetitive and rhythmic language patterns, such as *Brown Bear, Brown Bear, What do You See?* (Martin 1970):

> Brown bear, brown bear,
> what do you see?

I see a yellow duck
looking at me.

Yellow duck, yellow duck
what do you see?

Because it is so important for children to attend to print and respond to it if they are to learn more about reading and writing, Rhodes and Shannon suggest that teachers provide a variety of activities based on these "predictable" books to extend students' print interactions. These include:

1. Print the sentences in the story on separate strips that children can order for themselves or match with copies of the illustrations.
2. Print the stories and illustrations on separate ditto sheets and have children match them and color figures as described.
3. Reproduce the story with some predictable key words omitted for children to provide orally or in writing (a sort of beginning cloze procedure). The result is that each child has his or her own copy of the book to reread at will.
4. Have children work with the teacher in a group to create a new story similar to the predictable book pattern.

Clearly, the value of the preceding approach is that children are led gradually and naturally through experiences designed to help them build understanding of, and knowledge about, writing.

Another way to promote writing behavior (intended to help young students become "writers") is to make journal writing a daily part of the classroom routine. One might ask, "If children can't or don't write, how can they keep journals?" A way to start is just to have the children write whatever they can but to make it clear they must write something. We have had a variety of personal experiences with the usefulness of this procedure. For example, a first-grade boy in a resource program was being given a daily copying assignment that required transcribing to his own paper a teacher-produced language-experience story. He was unable to read the stories and obviously disliked the tedious copying task. The other children who were in the resource room at the same time were all writing in their journals, and we suggested that this boy be allowed to do the same thing. The teacher was reluctant to do this because she felt the boy was unable to write, but he was really only unable to write "correctly." He participated quite happily once he was assured that he could write whatever he wanted to in his own way and realized he could easily tell the others what was on his mind by writing about it. In the manner of younger children, he combined drawings and print to communicate his message and, in fact, had a great deal to say once he was encouraged to do so at his own level of understanding.

Shannon's students (Rhodes and Shannon 1982) started with five minutes of daily journal writing (later extended to more time). At first, many could write only their names, random letters and numbers, or lists of isolated words they had already learned to spell (*no, cat*, and so on) or draw pictures. They were given group experience in producing invented spellings in which the teacher made it clear that it was communication she was after and not correct spelling. Once students saw that they could write (even if they couldn't spell correctly) and that the teacher and other students were able to understand their messages, writing production increased greatly. Only when this ability to communicate had reached what was considered to be adequate fluency were rewriting and editing steps introduced.

A similar approach was used by Alvarez (1983) with junior high school students. Using a modification of a procedure described by Holt (1969), Alvarez sought to create self-confidence about writing and to increase the written production of his students. The objective, as explained to the students, was to write as many words as possible in a given period of time (initially six minutes) either on a topic of their choice or just random thoughts if this was all they were able to produce on any given day. Students were instructed just to write their names over and over again if they couldn't think of anything else; but once a thought did come, to proceed with that idea. For scoring purposes, only words included in sentence form were to be counted unless the student was considered to be at an earlier developmental level. Some students can be encouraged to start with drawings that they label or to change single words in repetitive sentence patterns. Student scores were kept only for intrapersonal comparisons and errors in spelling, syntax, and such were not counted because emphasis here was on production. The procedure can be expanded to writing on various teacher- or student-selected topics as development indicates readiness. Rewriting and revision activities can also be added when it appears that writing as a communicative process is well established in the students' understanding. Jochum (1982) also developed a writing program in which she emphasized daily journal writing in a "Dear Diary" letter form.

Perhaps the greatest value of journal writing is that it soon provides a comfortable and familiar vehicle for written communication. As with many other basic skills, writing ability develops only if you *do* it. We recommend at least five to ten minutes a day of journal writing for students of all ages in addition to frequent writing assignments of other kinds.

The emphasis should always be on the clear communication of information. Teachers can respond directly to information or ideas contained in the journal either through short individual conferences or in written responses right on the journal page. To many teachers, once-a-week scanning of the journal and giving *meaning-based* feedback to students seems adequate, although more frequent responses may be desirable with younger children. The key here is to keep children engaged in meaningful written discourse.

Journal entries can also be shared with other class members by reading them aloud. Children should decide for themselves which parts they are willing to share with others, as journals are usually considered private. However, the idea of writing for an audience can be fostered through this procedure. It gives children an introduction to deciding what is for private and what for public consumption. Hearing each other's writing also helps stimulate new ideas and creates a basis for discussion. This, in turn, leads to more writing. Writing begins to become an ongoing process of idea generation and written communication of those ideas.

Some very concrete suggestions for initial efforts can be made by teachers such as:

○ Write what you had for breakfast.
○ Tell what you are wearing.
○ Tell what your bedroom looks like.
○ Write a telephone message from your grandmother.
○ Make a shopping list of things you would like to get from the grocery store.
○ Tell me three things you would wish for.

Remember, the main point is not to produce Shakespeare II, but to have students writing in order to communicate and to keep them writing.

FORMAL WRITING INSTRUCTION

Writing can perhaps best be considered as a process involving the composing of a message, the transcription (the actual writing down) of the message, and the evaluation (modification) of what one has written. Formal instruction in writing may be viewed, then, as consisting of three major components—prewriting, writing, and postwriting—(Daigon 1982; Polloway, Patton, and Cohen 1981). Each of these components requires careful planning and instruction to insure student success.

Prewriting Strategies

Prewriting activities aid in the exploration of a topic. They include providing a positive and safe environment in which students can write, motivating students to write, determining a purpose for writing, and determining who the audience will be. A safe writing environment is one in which students recognize that grammatical and mechanical errors can be made without fear of teacher criticism. Second, it is an environment that includes continuous practice by the students and reinforcement and constructive suggestions from the teacher.

Motivating students to write includes helping them to develop a need to communicate and to share their thoughts and feelings with others. Motivation is related closely to the provision of a safe writing environment and must capitalize on students' interests and experiences. Therefore, writing should be functional and emanate from natural classroom experiences. It should progress logically from earlier activities, not from contrived settings and artificial topics. "Teachers who are successful in promoting writing in their classes start with learning experiences or broad themes they believe contain valid and interesting content for children" (Barenbaum 1983, p. 17). In addition, teachers must help students recall relevant experiences and connect them with their understanding of the writing task, the purposes for writing, and the intended audiences. These activities may include leading discussions about the subject, participating in brainstorming sessions, and exchanging parallel experiences and role playing, all of which help students generate and shape substance, clarify rhetorical circumstances, and suggest structural possibilities (Daigon 1982). They are particularly important to mildly handicapped students who may require a great amount of structure and organization prior to writing.

Rjunyan (1981) has developed a model of the writing process, which provides a useful framework for teachers to use in organizing their strategies for written language instruction.

Prewriting Skills

   I. Determine purpose and audience.
  II. Choose appropriate form of writing to achieve purpose.
 III. Generate ideas and information from past experiences and knowledge.
      A. Brainstorming.
      B. Visualizing (forming sensory imagery).
 IV. Gather information using more than one source.
      A. Seeing:
          1. Reading-researching.
          2. Careful observation.
      B. Listening:
          1. Interviewing.
          2. Attentive listening to prepared material.
          3. Attentive listening to environmental sounds.
      C. Touching.
      D. Tasting.
      E. Smelling.
  V. Relate new information to present knowledge and past experiences.
 VI. Organize information.
      A. Taking notes from the sources used.
      B. Mapping and/or outlining schema information.

Students must understand the purposes for writing and the intended audience. Purpose helps students to organize their writing and creates an awareness of writing as a natural process of communication. When refining the purpose of writing, teachers help students to attend to the demand of the topic, to be more reflective regarding how to attain the writing goals, and to be actively involved in the writing stages.

There are two general purposes for writing—expressive or creative writing and functional or utilitarian writing (Polloway, Patton, and Cohen 1981). Expressive writing emphasizes personal communication of experiences and thoughts in an original way. Functional writing conveys information in a more structured way. Expressive writing affords flexibility in selecting and developing the content for a theme and capitalizes on students' abilities to use both divergent and convergent thinking. Divergent thinking encourages students to explore innumerable ideas and topics of interest within the boundaries of the writing assignment prior to narrowing the scope of the topic and selecting the relevant information (convergent thinking).

Functional writing requires that students understand the objective of the task, be aware of the target audience, analyze the task demands, and select an appropriate framework to enhance the purpose of communication. Handicapped students may need assistance in learning that writing is a means of communicating with a wide variety of audiences. The questions included in table 7-1 help students to focus on the purposes of expressive and functional writing. Prewriting activities help students to structure their thoughts prior to beginning a first draft. Daigon (1982) believes that "the cognitive foreplay of prewriting is essential to the writing act. Teachers need to provide time for it in their composition classes" (p. 244).

Teachers can use the questions in table 7-1 to generate and guide discussion during the prewriting phase. Extended discussion, with the teacher serving as a facilitator, is perhaps the best vehicle for the idea production and organization that are the essential products of the prewriting phase of the writing process.

Students can then be taught the strategy of producing "patterned" notes as a summary step or written product for the prewriting phase (Buzan 1976). Patterned notes consist of key words or phrases related to the writing topic. These are generated and written down during the discussion phase recommended above. Either during the discussion or immediately afterward, the key words can be organized into a pattern that can then be used as an outline for writing (see figure 7-1).

Buzan believes that these patterns have clear advantages over the linear form of notetaking or outlining. These advantages include:

TABLE 7-1   Determining Purpose for Expressive and Functional Writing

EXPRESSIVE	FUNCTIONAL
Why is this topic interesting?	What is the task objective?
What do I know about the topic?	What is the intended audience and how
Is additional information needed?	knowledgeable are they about the topic?
How can the old and new information be integrated?	What does the audience need to know?
How can this reconstructed information be organized?	How can I conduct additional research on the topic?
Do I have personal opinions about the topic?	How can the writing be arranged and organized to meet the objective?
How can I convey my personal feeling in writing?	

Adapted from E. A. Polloway, J. R. Patton, and S. B. Cohen. Written language for mildly handicapped students. *Focus on Exceptional Children* 14 (1981), no. 3, 1–16.

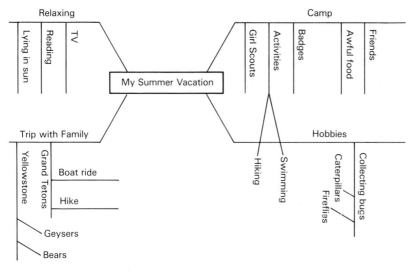

FIGURE 7-1 Keywords Organized into Patterns for a Writing Outline.

1. The center or main idea is more clearly defined.
2. The relative importance of each idea is clearly indicated, as more important ideas are nearer the center and less important ones nearer the edge.
3. The links between the key concepts will be immediately recognizable because of their proximity and connection.
4. The nature of the structure allows for the easy addition of new information without messy scratching out or squeezing in.
5. The open-ended nature of the pattern will enable the brain to make new connections far more readily. (Buzan 1976, p. 89)

We have found that even children in the early elementary grades quickly catch on to this approach and can then use it as a prewriting strategy for all types of writing assignments throughout their school years. Initially, the patterns can be produced in groups and with intensive modeling by the teacher who is guiding their creations; later, students can follow this procedure on their own.

In summary, we believe that prewriting activities are probably the most cognitively important component of the writing process. It is at this stage that writers get to know about their topics and their audiences and how they will communicate the one to the other. Clearly, communication is the main purpose of writing. The teacher who wants to develop strong written language competencies in students will make the prewriting exploration and discussion activities as extensive and thorough as possible. The brief pep talk and short review of some relevant content that often constitute the prewriting or motivational phase is simply not enough writing preparation for handicapped students. We urge you not to rush through this part of your writing program in order to "get to" the writing phase, which because of the resulting written product may be mistakenly over-emphasized as the most important element.

Writing Strategies

Mildly handicapped students may be overwhelmed by the notion that they must create an original piece of written expression. However, if teachers have provided for the elaborate prewriting exploration and discussion that we have just described, including the production of a patterned outline, the writing task itself should be a reasonable accomplishment for students. Assistance in the actual writing task will vary in quantity and content as students gradually grow in their understanding of the elements involved. As always, it is the teacher's role to understand and guide students' thinking, to serve as a model, to provide reassurance, and to engage in dialogue when students ask questions. Frequent referral to the content of the prewriting discussions should be made so that students gradually learn how important that element is and how to make optimal use of the resulting material.

Since the writing step is followed by a rewriting or revision step, emphasis in the writing portion of the process should continue to be on the expression and communication of the writers' ideas and not on the transcription skills of spelling and handwriting. (These skills will be dealt with separately later in this chapter.)

Rjunyan (1981) suggests that lessons and teacher strategies at this stage be directed to the following areas:

1. Using the organization generated through prewriting skills to develop main ideas
2. Expanding main ideas according to the chosen structure (paragraph, sentence, stanza, etc.)
3. Selecting and using language appropriate for the chosen audience (formal-informal, dialect, selection of adjectives, etc.)
4. Using the skills of handwriting, spelling, capitalization, and punctuation (at the students' present ability or knowledge level)

The product created during this step of the process is often referred to as a first draft or rough draft. One elementary-school teacher we know has her students call it "the sloppy copy," not because she encourages messy work, but in order to emphasize the difference between work in progress and the revised, completed copy produced in the final stage of rewriting. Students need to understand that *formal* writing (both narrative and expository) cannot be properly achieved without going through these three stages and that the rough draft is a required step that will always be part of the process in your classroom and probably in their other classrooms as well. Perhaps this is a procedure that could be agreed upon by all teachers in a school.

Production of rough drafts is a helpful procedure, but additional strategies are required for the production, organization, and expression of the initial written product in the writing phase. The remainder of this portion of the chapter describes some specific teacher and student strategies that we believe are helpful in this stage.

The patterned outline produced during the prewriting phase is a helpful tool in bridging the gap between just talking about a topic and writing about it. Copies can be made of the pattern if it was produced in a group setting. It is often a good idea to help the student express the first sentence or two and then discuss where the writing might go from there, referring to the patterned outline as one progresses. Again, lots of modeling and dialogue are useful here in helping the students get off to a running start. We often think of this starting-off part of the writing process as being analogous to a wind-up toy. Your goal is to wind up the spring, to help produce the potential and momentum that students need to get started. Don't think that you're doing the work for them and avoid this step. Get involved!

Dehouske (1982) suggests that teachers provide an organizing structure for students by dividing their papers into four blocks, which provide the basic format for a story: beginning, middle, elaboration of middle, and end. This format can be extended to six blocks or more as students develop in their writing ability. Of course, students can probably do the paper dividing themselves, too, and should discuss with the teacher *why* this type of step is helpful. Suggestions and discussion about the type of information to be placed in each block can be included (with examples) in a master chart posted in the classroom for student referral.

Another starting-up strategy is the use of a drawing to help the students think about what they are going to write (Grinnell and Burris 1983; Calkins 1979). These authors point out that younger writers move back and forth between drawing and print as they are learning to communicate in writing. Drawings can also be used with older students who are slow starters. Grinnell and Burris provide an extended discussion of the interaction and complementary nature of drawing and print in the early written expression efforts of children. Often, the print component is enhanced in its meaning by the drawing and vice versa. Neither element alone contains as much information for the reader as the two together. Students are frequently asked to illustrate their *completed* stories. We suggest that you might want to *start* with the illustration.

Strategies for Improving Organization: Sentences and Paragraphs

Teachers frequently turn to exercise books to have children "practice" writing sentences and completing paragraphs written by others. We believe *children need to write* in order to learn about writing. Their own writing should also be the focus of dialogue about specific sentence and paragraph elements. Of course, the occasional use of exercises designed to reinforce some particular element in a child's growing understanding of sentence and paragraph production might be of value.

Sentences

Rhodes and Shannon suggest helping students discover when their sentences are not informative or descriptive enough by asking the one who wrote the sentence questions about what is not clear. This may lead children to the idea that they must tell the reader more. Try involving all students in discussions about sentences written by various members of the class. Groups of from three to six children can look over dittoed copies of sentences selected from their writings and analyze them. We find that students soon become thoughtful discussants of syntax, vocabulary usage, and sentence clarity with this technique. Their writing often shows improvement that appears to result from the discussions.

Another helpful activity that can be used to assist students in developing sentence "sense" is to have a short period of time each day or so when all communication must be in writing. Students are given small sheets of paper, and they pass notes back and forth to each other, responding physically or in writing to whatever instructions or information is contained in the note. Students soon find out from the responses of their peers if their sentences are adequately explanatory and they can amend them accordingly. Students can ask each other specific questions: "Do you mean I should stand up and turn around counterclockwise or that I should just use my finger to make a counterclockwise circle on the desk?"

Sentence-combining activities can also be helpful in giving students practice in creating a single, more elaborate sentence from several short, choppy sentences. *Sentence Combining* by William Strong (1973) provides many and varied sentence-combining activities that are graduated in difficulty. A sample exercise (obviously suitable for older children) is given below. These sentences can be combined orally in small groups at first. Later, students can write them and share their written efforts with the group. This exercise also helps students see that there are many different ways of combining sentences that are all correct.

IN TOUCH

1. Children are remarkable for something.
2. The something is an ability.
3. The ability is to remain "in touch."
4. They know themselves well.
5. They acknowledge their feelings.
6. They show their joy.
7. They show their curiosity.
8. They show their excitement.
9. They do not repress feelings.
10. They are still in touch.
11. They respond with openness.
12. Their openness is to the world.
13. Their openness is to others.

(Adapted from *Sentence Combining*, p. 17)

154

Students can start with much simpler exercises that require them to combine only two sentences:

1. John is a fireman.
2. John lives near the firehouse.

1. Horses are fun to ride.
2. Horses can run fast.

1. I like french fries.
2. I like ice cream.
3. I like hamburgers.

Choppy sentences from children's own writing can be noted, presented, and combined during group time.

   Sentence-expansion activities are designed to help students add more information or detail to their sentences. The sentences used can also be drawn from student writing or suggested by the teacher. A kernel sentence such as "I like hamburgers" might become "My brother and I like big juicy hamburgers cooked medium-rare with pickles, onions, ketchup, and mustard." Take one part of the kernel sentence at a time and have students generate expanded sentences. After several have been done orally in groups, students can be given some to do by themselves in writing and then can present the resulting expanded sentences to each other. This is an excellent opportunity for teachers to start introducing such concepts as adjectives, adverbs, conjunctions, prepositional phrases, and clauses. At first, however, put the emphasis on *creating* sentences with such elements, not on what the elements are *called*.

Paragraph-Writing Strategies

   Since the paragraph is the primary vehicle for presenting and elaborating the main points the writer intends to make, it has received considerable attention in the literature related to teaching writing. Paragraph-writing strategies tend to focus on two main steps:

1. Identifying and stating the main idea one wants to discuss.
2. Elaborating upon the main idea by adding various kinds of information about it.

By emphasizing this two-step procedure, the teacher can gradually lead students to understand (and then to create) the interrelated nature of the sentences within a paragraph. Strategies should stress *organization* as the key to producing an orderly paragraph that clearly communicates one's idea and then supports it with corroborating details. By providing a pre-organizer, the patterned notes discussed earlier can be a helpful starting point for paragraph generation.

Statement-Pie Strategy

The purpose of statement-pie is to teach the reader (and hence the writer) to look for two different levels of concepts. The primary concept, or "statement," is the main idea, and the secondary level, or "pie," is the supporting *p*roofs, *i*nformation, and *e*xamples that are related to the statement (Hanau 1974).

A simple graphic representation of this strategy might be drawn on a classroom chart as shown below (Hanau 1974, p. 25).

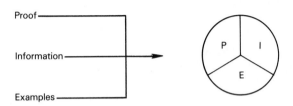

The statement-pie strategy has been adapted for use with mildly handicapped children by Englert and Lichter (1982). They suggest that teachers provide children with a preprinted model of the statement-pie structure (p. 165):

St _____

Pie _____

Pie _____

Pie _____

The basic structure, accompanied by the graphic PIE, gives students a simple framework for paragraph production. As always, start by giving many specific and concrete examples to students such as:

St—John is my best friend.
Pie—We play together after school almost every day.
Pie—We sit next to each other at lunch.
Pie—He helps me get my chores done at home so we can play.

Then have students work together to produce "pies" for statements you give them, and finally have students produce both statements and pies in a group setting. Once the basic two-part structure is clearly understood, students can start writing statement-pies of their own, perhaps initially from teacher- or group-prepared (and discussed) statements and later with both parts produced individually by students. Also, paragraphs from student writing and from their various reading and library books can be analyzed for statement-pies. If "pies" are a bit skimpy (unfilling—the reader is still "hungry" for more details), students can add more information to give the pie more filling. We believe that this strategy can be used effectively with both elementary and secondary students and that it is a good starting point for formal instruction in paragraph writing when this step becomes appropriate within the child's writing development.

Paragraph-Organization Strategy

The rationale for teaching the following paragraph strategy is, once again, that the organization of ideas is the central issue in writing. Moran, Schumaker, and Vetter (1981) were successful in teaching learning disabled adolescents to write three different types of paragraphs using their *Paragraph Organization Strategy* (Moran, Schumaker, and Vetter 1981). The three types of paragraph styles, listed in the order taught, were the enumerative, the sequential, and the compare-and-contrast paragraphs. The authors describe an enumerative paragraph as one in which the writer just wants to list a number of things (such as a paragraph about favorite record albums). A sequential paragraph describes a series of steps in a specific order (how to build something, a recipe procedure, and the like). A compare-and-contrast paragraph presents the similarities and differences between two or more items (such as individual versus group sports or classical versus rock music).

The same basic steps were used in teaching the students to write each of the three types of paragraphs:

1. Write a topic sentence.
2. Write at least three detail sentences.
3. Write a clincher sentence. (Moran, Schumaker, and Vetter 1981, p. 11)

The similarity between these steps and the statement-pie approach is helpful for students who have been taught statement-pie and who are ready to add a concluding or clincher sentence and to pay more attention to varying the types of paragraphs used in their writing.

As with any of these strategies, teachers may want to set up a simple scoring system to help in evaluating progress. Moran et al. assigned points for fulfilling requirements for a specific paragraph style: up to three points for a topic sentence (statement), up to one point for each detail sentence (pie), and up to three points for each clincher sentence. Partial points were given for approximations. Mastery of each paragraph type consisted of a score of 85 of the total points possible. We would recommend very direct and specific discussion with students about why a particular point score was given: "You earned two points for this topic sentence because _____. I didn't give you the full three points because _____. How could you change your topic sentence to make it into a three-pointer?"

It is of interest that Moran et al. successfully taught their paragraph-organization strategy to small groups of learning disabled adolescents rather than needing to use more expensive one-to-one instruction. The authors also found that the students seemed to generalize from the enumerative to the other two paragraph types. In other words, less instructional time was needed to achieve mastery on the sequential and compare-and-contrast paragraph types. Also, mastery on all three paragraph types was achieved by all students involved in the project after only fourteen to twenty-four hours of instruction. The paragraph-organization strategy illustrates the effectiveness of direct, specific instruction in a strategy once students are at a cognitive level where their basic understanding or knowledge needs to be codified or made more orderly.

Composition Strategies

Alley and Deshler (1979) suggest the use of a method developed by W. J. Kerrigan (1974) that has been used to teach students to write compositions.

The steps of the method as presented by Alley and Deshler are:

1. *Write a short, simple declarative sentence that makes one statement.* Work with students to help them produce sentences about which more can be written. Sentences about ideas are best, but almost any open-ended sentence is adequate. ("Cats are felines" would not be a particularly good sentence. "There are a large variety of felines in the world" or even "I love cats" would be much better.)

2. *Write three sentences about the sentence in step 1 that are clearly and directly about the whole of that sentence, not just about something in it.* Each of these sentences is going to become the topic sentence for a different paragraph. To help them write these sentences, students can be encouraged to think of the kinds of questions a reader might ask about the initial sentence.

3. *Write four or five sentences about each of the three sentences in step 2.* Again, each of these sentences is to be about the *whole* of its topic sentence and relate directly and clearly to it.
    For example:
    X I dislike winter.
    (a) I dislike the winter cold.
    (b) I dislike having to wear the heavy winter clothing that cold weather requires.
    (c) I dislike the colds that, despite heavy clothing, I always get in the winter.
    X I dislike winter.
    (a) I dislike the winter cold. It makes me shiver. It chaps my lips. It can even freeze my ears.
    (b) I dislike having to wear the heavy winter clothing that cold weather requires. I have to wear earmuffs. I have to wear galoshes. I have to wear a heavy coat. I have to wear long underwear.
    (c) I dislike the colds that, despite heavy clothing, I always get in the winter. They stop up my nose. They give me a cough. They give me a fever. They make me miss school. (Kerrigan 1974, p. 26)

4. *Review the sentences you've written in step 3 and make them as specific as you can. Give details. Give examples. Say more about what you have just said. Your goal is to say a lot about a little.* This step focuses on making the material more concrete. Use the sentence-expansion activity described above to enhance this step. Eliminate vague words and substitute specific ones. Add details and modifying words. Discuss synonyms that make the meaning more precise. This is a good place to bring in vocabulary discussions.

5. *In the first sentence of the second paragraph and every paragraph following, insert a clear reference to the idea in the preceding paragraph.* This step has to do with the

cohesiveness of the writing. We like to describe the purpose of this step to students as "verbal stapling." Transitions are often overlooked by inexperienced writers because the connection between one paragraph and another is already clear in their own minds. Ask students, "Why did you start this paragraph like this? What does this have to do with what you said in the preceding paragraph? Staple it on!"

6. *Make sure every sentence in your composition is connected with, and makes clear reference to, the preceding sentence.* This is the appropriate time to use word repetitions, synonyms, and pronouns to refer back to the previous sentence. Each sentence must contain an idea (that the student can state to you) *about* the idea contained in the previous sentence. (Adapted from Kerrigan 1974; Alley and Deshler 1979)

Steps 5 and 6, and to a lesser extent, step 4, are what might be called revision or rewriting steps. The revision conference described below is a good time to work on these steps.

Perhaps the greatest value of Kerrigan's model is that it provides a detailed procedure for producing unified, extended writing. Practice can be provided on each step as needed, and the steps are well suited to group discussions. Specific dialogue can be conducted about success on each step with each student. While the strategy may seem cumbersome if rushed through, it can provide the framework for a whole year's composition class for students ready to expand their writing skills at this level. Expect to spend a great deal of time on this strategy, with much effort directed toward helping the students translate the steps into a student strategy that guides their writing.

Rewriting

The revision process may be considered the real task of writing, as it affords writers the opportunity to respond to their first draft—that is, to reconcile their original intentions with what has materialized as a first draft. Revision allows the writer to modify both the draft and concept through a process of continual refinement in which words, sentences, and paragraphs are rehearsed and blended (Daigon 1982). The revision process allows student writers to clarify and to understand what they wish to express in writing.

Students will need assistance with the revision process of editing and refining the original draft. This will be particularly important for mildly handicapped students who have problems with semantics, syntax, and spelling. A revision conference may provide an opportunity to discuss the students' ideas, the strengths and weaknesses of their written work, and ways to improve their writing efforts. The revision conference should take place in a very supportive environment in which students view their teacher (as well as themselves) as an editorial colleague rather than as a discoverer and corrector of errors. The focus of the revision conference, then, is to identify those problems that require the most attention in an attempt to increase students' ability to communicate effectively in writing.

Rjunyan (1981) suggests the following as a guideline for the revision or rewriting phase.

Rewriting Skills

I. Examine the first draft to determine relative strengths and weaknesses of writing:
   A. Edit (whole class, teachers, peers, or self).
   B. Determine if it accomplishes the purposes.
   C. View the piece of writing first as a whole, then by sentences, and finally by words.
   D. Determine ways of improving and expanding on the writing.
II. Rewrite, making improvements in form, style, content, structure, and language.
III. Proofread for errors:
   A. Grammar and usage.
   B. Capitalization.
   C. Punctuation.
   D. Spelling.
IV. Recopy.

This framework can provide the agenda for the revision conference, whether it is used with small groups or individuals. Try reproducing the composition being reviewed on a transparency so the group can use an overhead projector to view the work under discussion. Dittoes are fine, too. Have the writer start out by telling you or the group orally what he or she was trying generally to do in this piece of writing. Then proceed with the revision, following Rjunyan's format. Since students have written the first draft on every other line, the suggested changes can easily be written in. Extra sentences or transition words can be added to clarify the writer's meaning.

This is an appropriate time to address vocabulary and word usage. Make specificity and descriptiveness the goal. Generate synonyms or more concrete words that will help make the meaning clearer. Redundancy can be discussed and eliminated at this step. Use of a thesaurus or topical-word lists can be introduced. Vocabulary discussions should be directly related to the piece of writing under discussion.

Syntactic considerations can be included at this phase, also, in terms of student's knowledge and use of specific grammatical skills. The most appropriate instructional approach for this area may be to discuss a small number of structural errors in a specific assignment. Errors should be selected for correction based on their value in clarifying students' communicative efforts. Students' written assignments should be considered in terms of consistency with their oral-language ability as a means of helping them to be aware of grammatical errors. Specific discussions about an individual error can be an effective way of helping students learn to correct their written work.

Another important consideration within the mechanics of written language is sentence structure. Well-developed sentences will help handicapped students to think more clearly and to express themselves in complete thoughts that enable them to communicate successfully. Quite often handicapped students rely on simple and repetitive sentence structures that result in less fluent writing. The instructional focus should be on teaching students to extend sentences into additional types of patterns. They can learn sentence extension by combining activities in which they modify an original simple sentence or sentences. Such activities have been discussed earlier in this chapter.

Organizational considerations include helping students to attain paragraph sense and organizational integrity. *Paragraph sense* refers to the transition from syntactically correct sentences to well-written extensions into paragraphs. Paragraph sense relies on students' abilities to organize their written composition coherently in an attempt to communicate effectively. Polloway et al. (1981) indicate that paragraph sense is a developmental function in which students learn the following sequential abilities:

1. Paragraphs must be related to a single concept or idea.
2. Topical sentences should provide a lead-in for the reader.
3. Subsequent sentences should support the concept developed.
4. Final sentences in a long, detailed paragraph should serve as a summary.

Instructional techniques for paragraph development should assist students in stating a basic premise, and then expanding their thoughts in an organized manner as in the paragraph-writing strategies discussed earlier in this chapter. Remember that it is the students' own work that is being considered and revised here and not responses to contrived activities in exercise books.

Proofreading

The primary goal of proofreading is to help students learn to monitor and recognize what is correct and what is incorrect about their writing. This is the step that has probably received most attention in classrooms, but most teachers would probably agree that mildly handicapped students are very poor proofreaders. Children are told to proofread their papers before they submit them (which they do not know how to do). Or they are commanded: "Check your work!" But what does that mean *exactly*? Most children seem to shrug off this admonition as being something that adults (especially teachers) always say to children but that cannot be translated into anything specific. A quick glance at the paper constitutes "checking" for most students. "Looks OK to me," they say, as they place it on the pile, knowing that it's bound to come back covered with red marks anyway.

The teacher's goal is to teach the children something definite and specific to do when they check or proofread their papers. Donald Deshler (1983) has suggested the use of the "COPS" procedure to help accomplish this goal. We have used this procedure effectively with children from second grade through college seniors. Basically, when told to check a paper, the student just goes through the COPS steps, one at a time. The steps should be printed on a poster and displayed in the classroom, although most students learn them very quickly:

COPS

Capitalization
Overall Appearance
Punctuation
Spelling

Capitalization

Students should be taught to check three things at this step:

1. The first letter of each sentence
2. Names (of people and places)
3. The letter *I*

Most other capitalization rules are infrequently used and really not very important from our point of view.

Overall Appearance

Deshler includes such items as margins and handwriting considerations at this step but also suggests that individual sentences be checked here for meaningfulness and clarity. Since we have already dealt with these issues in the revision conference, they need not be repeated here (unless the student has not participated in a conference).

Punctuation

Check all end punctuation (periods and question marks only) and commas (items in a series only). Again, we consider the other punctuation marks to be less important. Reserve hyphens and semicolons for your more advanced writers.

Spelling

Have students circle each word about which they are unsure or had doubts when they wrote it. Correct spellings can then be *given* to them so these correctly spelled words can be included in the final copy. Your goal here is merely to have students separate out those words that "look" correct or that they think are correct from those that they feel unsure about. We have found that this is a useful first step in teaching students to monitor their spelling errors. A more extensive discussion of spelling appears later in this chapter.

In order to encourage students to find as many errors as they can, you may want to set up a simple chart on which the students record the total number of errors they find on each piece of writing, using COPS, and the number of additional errors the teacher finds in a separate column. The student's goal is to find increasingly more errors than the teacher finds.

Most students seem to improve quickly in their proofreading when they use COPS, especially in the specific areas included. Other specific components can be added to the procedures as students mature (subject-verb agreement, paragraph development, and so on), but most teachers are pleased at how many of the commonly made writing errors in mechanics fall within the four basic COPS steps.

Spelling Development

While spelling is certainly not the most important element in writing, good spelling skills can be beneficial in helping the writer express ideas more freely because more of the writer's attention can be directed to the ideas and less to figuring out how to spell the words. Poor spelling distracts the reader or audience, makes the written product appear to be of poor quality, and is generally associated by society with lack of education. As Gerber (1984a) has pointed out, good spelling is accorded unusual value in our society (e.g., much-publicized spelling bees), and the difficulty of becoming an excellent speller is well recognized.

The learning disabled population has frequently been described as being especially poor in spelling (Poplin et al 1980; Boder 1971). Boder emphasized a relationship between poor spelling and subtle neurological damage or minimal brain dysfunction often cited at that time as being typical of learning disabled populations. More recently, however, research has supported the interpretation that poor spelling ability in LD youngsters is related to an immature cognitive developmental level in their knowledge about spelling (Graham and Miller 1979; Gerber 1984a). In other words, rather than being aberrant or idiosyncratic spellers, LD students perform similarly to younger normal children in spelling, and the types of errors LD children make in spelling are typical errors for their developmental stage.

There is a typical sequence of spelling development that Gerber (1984b) has organized into a classification system with five levels or categories:

Levels of Spelling Development

CLASSIFICATION	CRITERIA
1. Preliterate (p g r 2 L)	Unintelligible symbol strings mixing letters and nonletters.
2. Prephonetic (m n)	One or more, but not all, phonemes are plausibly represented.
3. Phonetic (m n s t r)	All phonemes are represented, but correspondence is based upon articulation of letter *names* (*eighty* might be spelled "*a t*").
4. Transitional (m o n s t o r)	All phonemes are represented legally; knowledge of orthographic marking system is demonstrated.
5. Correct (m o n s t e r)	Conventional spelling is produced.

Spelling produced by students can be codified according to these five levels, which helps the teacher to evaluate a given student's spelling ability on this cognitive developmental continuum. It is then possible to determine what type of spelling knowledge the child possesses and what types of spelling knowledge are still needed. Clearly, a child who spells the word *peeked* as *peecked* knows much more about English orthography than one who spells it *pte*. Both renderings are "wrong," but the latter is "wronger." The speller who produced *peecked* knows about *ck* spelling the *k* sound, about *ed* as the traditional way of writing the past tense ending, and also knows that *all* sounds in a work must be represented somehow. This spelling would be graded as being at the "transitional" level. The speller who produced *pte* would be at a "prephonetic" level: some, but not all, phonemes are represented. Clearly, he knows *something* about spelling but not nearly as much as the first speller (Gerber 1984a). From this perspective, it becomes the teacher's task to help students build from their present knowledge level vis-à-vis spelling to reach higher levels of spelling knowledge.

Present-day spelling instruction would appear to be inadequate to produce the spelling ability we would like to see in our students. Graham and Miller (1979) believe that unsatisfactory spelling progress can be attributed to several factors:

1. Inadequate contemporary classroom instruction.
2. Poorly designed commercial materials.
3. Failure to base spelling programs on research findings.

Furthermore, instruction is not being individualized but instead follows an almost universal pattern of daily exercises similar to this:

Monday: All students are introduced to the same list of words for the week (perhaps a shorter sublist is used for poorer spellers).
Tuesday: Write each word x number of times.
Wednesday: Use each word in a written sentence.
Thursday: Phonics activities, alphabetizing, or other fill-in-the-blank exercises from the spelling book.
Friday: Posttest.

Graham and Miller also indicate that commercial materials heavily influence spelling programs for which they often serve as the only component. While some of these programs might be described as "teacher-proof," that would be desirable, if at all, only if the content reflected worthwhile spelling-instruction technique. Unfortunately, this is not the case. In their review of the literature on spelling programs, Graham and Miller report findings that indicate some commercially prepared exercises actually had a negative effect on learning while others were only ineffectual. However, reassigning the responsibility for direct spelling instruction to the teacher will not automatically produce the desired results either. The review goes on to report that researchers have found that teachers rarely use research-supported practices in their classrooms. Graham and Miller conclude that spelling instruction should

1. be teacher directed (and individualized)
2. contain a variety of relevant instructional options
3. be based on a foundation of research evidence

Research evidence that should direct a teacher's selection of instructional options will be presented later in this section.

Spelling Strategies

Spellers spontaneously use the strategies relevant to their developmental level of spelling knowledge. A phonetic-level speller may sound out a word and represent each phoneme so that the word can be read by mature readers, especially if it is embedded in a context. However, little knowledge of orthographic conventions is shown at this level so that inflectional endings, double letters, silent letters, and other finer points of the system are not included in the speller's strategy. This results in the production of odd-looking words. The transitional speller's strategy will include the elements used by the phonetic speller but will incorporate more knowledge about conventions so that *-tion* is not spelled as *-shun* nor *schools* as *skoolz*. This process indicates to the teacher the type of knowledge needed by a student in order to improve his or her spelling. It would appear, therefore, that when one teaches spelling, one is really teaching about the structure of language.

Obviously, spelling requires a variety of knowledge and skills, such as sound-symbol relationships (including variant and invariant sounds and phonic rules), knowledge of word structure, the use of mnemonic devices and associations, as well as auditory discrimination and memory. Strategies should relate to enhancing students' knowledge and abilities related to these areas and should not be geared to rote-memory techniques that tend to be effective, if at all, only for the very short term and only for the specific word being studied.

Research-based general guidelines for teaching spelling and generating strategies include the following:

1. Use a test-study-test method rather than a study-test method because the former helps focus attention on studying the words the student does not already know.
2. Presenting words in a list or column is preferable to presenting them in sentences and paragraphs perhaps because it focuses student attention on each word to be learned.
3. The single most important factor leading to improved spelling ability is having the student correcting his or her own spelling test, as the teacher directs.
4. Games enhance student interest.
5. Spend at least sixty to seventy-five minutes a week on spelling instruction, that is, *actively* teaching spelling (Graham and Miller 1979, p. 10).

Interestingly, some frequently used spelling activities have been demonstrated as not being effective in teaching spelling. These include writing words in the air, writing words several times in a row, studying the "hard spots" in words, and allowing students to develop their own method for studying spelling words (Graham and Miller 1979).

While no single method of word study is clearly superior, word-study methods that are most effective emphasize the whole word and require the student to pronounce the word, visualize it (imagery) and provide for auditory and/or kinesthetic reinforcement and for systematic recall.

Since correcting one's own errors immediately after taking a spelling test has been demonstrated as being so effective, any of the following procedures might be employed:

1. Teacher spells the word orally while the student corrects it in writing by marking through the incorrect letters and writing the correct letters above them (omitted letters will also need to be added).
2. Teacher writes word correctly next to the misspelled word, and the student then rewrites the word correctly (Kauffman et al. 1978).
3. Teacher writes an exact imitation of student's error and then writes the word correctly. Student writes the word correctly (Kauffman et al. 1978).

In order to maintain correct spelling over time, words should be periodically reviewed and retested using the word-study procedures. It is probably best to teach only a few words a day to handicapped students and also to include review words daily rather than using the typical twenty-words-per-week approach (with final test on Friday).

We recommend selecting words for each day that illustrate a particular spelling pattern or rule. Gradually your students will acquire a knowledge of English spelling principles because of the systematic emphasis you have placed on them through your word selection. The LEAD Program (Grush and Fennel 1975) can be a useful guide in word and rule selection. The lessons in this program present words in an order that progresses from the most regular and frequently used spelling patterns to the more irregular and less frequently used patterns. Since learning disabled students often have difficulty in abstracting spelling patterns on their own, this type of program provides a well-sequenced structure to help in the construction of spelling knowledge.

Monitoring Spelling Errors

Many learning disabled and other mildly handicapped students have difficulty in monitoring their spelling errors. Students need to learn monitoring skills that, in time, will develop an awareness of when a word does not look right. This awareness leads the sophisticated writer to stop and check for correct spellings as needed. The typical classroom procedure is for the *teacher* to point out spelling errors. Obviously, this does not encourage self-monitoring. It would be better to list only the *number* of misspelled words in a piece of writing and have the students locate their own errors or to have students exchange papers and seek misspellings in each other's work. As in the COPS procedure discussed earlier in this chapter, students may start by circling those words about which they feel unsure in order to help them develop the sense of knowing what they know about spelling. The goal is to bring students to a stage where they can say, "This is right and I know it" or "I'm not sure of this one" (or "I know this one's wrong")—"I'd better check it" (look it up or ask someone).

Gerber (1984b) evaluated metacognitive awareness of spelling knowledge in learning disabled second-through-sixth graders. The children in his study were asked to predict how well they would do at spelling various words and then to report how sure they were that a word was correct once it was written down. He found that LD students were able to predict the few words they spelled correctly almost as well as normally achieving students but were very poor at predicting which words they would not be able to spell and in identifying errors once the words had been written. Hypothesizing that LD students had failed to use their knowledge about spelling in order to produce more accurate spellings, Gerber had LD students evaluate various misspellings of words that were presented to them in addition to the correct spellings. The LD students were consistently able to select either the correct or next-best spelling and usually dismissed poor-quality spellings (such as *pte* for *peeked*) as being impossible. Based on these findings, a strategy was developed and taught to students in two twenty-minute training sessions. Training included modeling by the teacher, imitation by the students of the teacher's procedures, and practice of self-questioning that led the speller to be more likely to apply his knowledge to the word at hand. Gerber suggests using questions such as:

1. Have I seen this word before?
2. Do I know any words that look/sound like this word?
3. What part(s) of the word am I uncertain about?
4. What are some different ways to write this word? (Gerber 1984b, p. 162)

This training procedure was especially effective for the older children in his group (eleven-to-twelve-year-olds), but, remember, there were only two twenty-minute training sessions used. We would encourage teachers to use the method with younger children, too, but would remind them to be sure to provide additional training using questions that are relevant to a child's developmental level in spelling.

Handwriting

Legible handwriting is another area that, like spelling, is not the main issue in written communication (indeed, typing is always an option) but that assists the reader in gaining access to the writer's message. We believe that poor handwriting has been overemphasized as a problem in writing, often at the expense of the primary purpose of writing—communication of thoughts. However, it is often necessary to provide direct remedial assistance in improving the handwriting of mildly handicapped students to a level where it is legible and automatic enough so that the student's greatest effort in writing can be directed toward communicating ideas and not to forming the individual letters correctly.

We do not believe that the manuscript- versus cursive-writing issue is highly significant but suggest that the teaching of whichever form is being used by the child can be enhanced through the use of a specific strategies approach. Perhaps poor handwriting skills are as much a result of inadequate teaching and practice as any skill dealt with in the schools. Therefore, we would recommend that handwriting instruction be scheduled regularly (daily when initial learning is occurring) and follow definite procedures. Remember, the goal is for handwriting to be legible, not necessarily pretty. Legibility is affected by various components of handwriting such as:

1. *Size* of letters (should be fairly uniform)
2. *Spacing* (between letters and words)
3. *Form* of letters (correct forms)
4. *Slant* of letters (should be fairly uniform)

The primary purpose of handwriting strategies is to bring the students' attention to these factors so that they can learn to monitor and modify the components as needed. Both initial instruction in handwriting and remedial instruction can follow the same basic teaching strategies, but remedial instruction will focus more directly on the specific problems being exhibited by each student.

Handwriting Strategies

The usual procedure for handwriting instruction is to start by over-learning letters in isolation through the use of intensive drill and practice. Gradually, the letters are used in a written context as writing instruction is introduced into the curriculum. Since we believe that writing should be a part of the curriculum from preschool onward, we believe that formal handwriting instruction should be concurrent with emphasis on writing for communication rather than preceding it. Why spend a great deal of time learning correct forms if all you are going to write is your name on your paper or single words in blanks on worksheets?

Procedures to use in teaching letter formation would include the following, in this general sequence:

1. *Modeling:* The teacher writes and names the letter. Attention is called to the number, order, and direction of the strokes.
2. *Noting critical attributes:* The letter is compared with other letters with similar formational characteristics.
3. *Physical prompts and cues:* Arrows or colored dots are used to outline letter shapes. When needed, the teacher physically guides the student's hand in forming the letter.
4. *Copying:* The student copies the letter on paper or in wet sand.
5. *Self-verbalization:* The student verbalizes the steps as the letter is written.
6. *Writing from memory:* The student writes the letter unassisted by cues.

7. *Repetition:* The student practices the letter.
8. *Self-correction and feedback:* The student corrects improperly formed letters using charts prepared by the teacher or with direct teacher supervision.
9. *Reinforcement:* The teacher provides reinforcement suitable to the age of the student. (Adapted from Graham and Miller 1980, pp. 9–10)

Self-instruction strategies have been shown to be effective in handwriting instruction (Kosiewicz et al. 1982). The typical sequence in self-instruction procedures as suggested by Meichenbaum and Goodman (1971) include:

1. Teacher modeling the task while the student watches.
2. Child performing the task while the adult verbalizes or describes the relevant features or procedures.
3. Child performing the task but this time verbalizing the instructions by himself or herself (teacher monitors and gives corrective feedback).
4. Child performing the task while whispering the self-instructions.
5. Child performing the task while self-instructing silently. Using this sequence, Kosiewicz et al. (1982) improved the handwriting of a ten-year-old boy whose handwriting was notoriously poor. The tasks involved in each day's handwriting lesson were the same (although specific words and paragraphs changed daily). The first task each day was to copy each of a list of twenty-eight single words handwritten by the teacher in column form next to the word, and the second task was to copy a paragraph, also handwritten by the teacher, below the paragraph on lined paper. The self-instructions were as follows:
   1. Student said aloud the word to be written.
   2. Student then said the first syllable.
   3. Student named each letter in that syllable three times.
   4. Student repeated each letter as it was written down.
   5. Steps 2–4 were repeated for each succeeding syllable. (Kosiewicz et al. 1982, p. 73)

Later, a self-correction or monitoring component was added in which the student circled errors he had made on the previous day's assignment before he copied the new assignment. It would appear that such a procedure helps to focus the student's conscious attention on handwriting, therefore providing more meaningful practice than rote copying. The monitoring step is recommended because it makes legible handwriting the student's responsibility rather than the teacher's. Whatever the strategies or teaching procedures used in handwriting instruction, one should emphasize the *active* involvement of students in observing, describing (orally), and producing (as one verbalizes either overtly or covertly) the various features of letters and letter connections (if cursive).

SUMMARY

We have indicated that written language ability emerges along a predictable developmental continuum. Formal instruction in written language should occur after the student has already become a writer—a communicator of thoughts in writing. Ways of enhancing this development were discussed, and emphasis was consistently placed on the meaningfulness of the written message. Instructional strategies to be used in teaching the mechanics of writing were presented, but we believe that such instruction should always be considered as secondary to the content of writing.

REFERENCES

ALLEY, G., AND D. DESHLER.   *Teaching the Learning Disabled Adolescent: Strategies and Methods.* Denver: Love Publishing Co., 1979.

ALVAREZ, M. C.   Sustained timed writing as an aid to fluency and creativity. *Teaching Exceptional Children* 15 (1983), 160–62.

BARENBAUM, E.   Writing in the special class. *Topics in Learning and Learning Disabilities* 3 (1983), 12–26.

BODER, E.   Developmental dyslexia: Prevailing diagnostic concepts and a new diagnostic approach. In H. Myklebust, ed., *Progress in Learning Disabilities,* vol. 2. New York: Grune & Stratton, 1971.

BUZAN, T.   *Use Both Sides of Your Brain.* New York: E. P. Dutton and Co., Inc., 1976.

CALKINS, L. M.   Andrea learns to make writing hard. *Language Arts* 56 (1979), 569–76.

CHOMSKY, C.   Write first, read later. *Childhood Education* 47 (1971), 296–99.

CLAY, M. M.   *What Did I Write?* Auckland, New Zealand: Heinemánn, 1975.

DAIGON, ARTHUR.   Toward righting writing. *Phi Delta Kappan* 64 (1982), no. 4, 242–46.

DEHOUSKE, E. J.   Story writing as a problem solving vehicle. *Teaching Exceptional Children* 14 (1982), 11–17.

DESHLER, D.   Intervening with learning disabled adolescents: A learning strategies perspective. Presentation at 7th Annual Kephart Memorial Symposium, Aspen, Colo., 1983.

ENGLERT, C. S., AND A. LICHTER.   Using statement-pie to teach reading and writing skills. *Teaching Exceptional Children* (March 1982), 164–70.

GERBER, M.   Solving spelling problems: Learning to appreciate competence in LD youngsters. Presentation at 8th Annual Kephart Memorial Symposium, Aspen, Colo., 1984a.

—————.   Orthographic problem-solving ability of learning disabled and normally achieving students. *Learning Disability Quarterly* 7 (1984b), 157–64.

GRAHAM, S., AND L. MILLER.   Handwriting research and practice: A unified approach. *Focus on Exceptional Children* 13 (1980), 1–17.

—————.   Spelling research and practice: A unified approach. *Focus on Exceptional Children* 12 (1979), 1–16.

GRINNELL, P. C., AND N. A. BURRIS.   Drawing and writing: The emerging graphic communication process. *Topics in Learning and Learning Disabilities* 3 (1983), 21–32.

GRUSH, H., AND P. FENNEL.   *LEAD Program.* Lexington, Mass.: Alpha Press, 1975.

HANAU, L.   *The Study Game: How to Play and Win with Statement-Pie.* New York: Barnes & Noble, 1974.

HOLT, J.   *The Underachieving School.* New York: Pitman, 1969.

HORN, E.   Phonics and spelling. *Journal of Education* 136 (1954), 233–35.

JOCHUM, J. M.   *The Teaching/Learning Cycle of the Language Disabled Adolescent: Studies of Reading and Writing Literacy.* Published Doctor of Education dissertation, University of Northern Colorado, 1982.

KAUFFMAN, J., U. HALLAHAN, K. HAAS, T. BRAME, AND R. BOREN.   Imitating children's errors to improve spelling performance. *Journal of Learning Disabilities* 11 (1978), 33–38.

KERRIGAN, W. J.   *Writing to the Point: Six Basic Steps.* New York: Harcourt Brace Jovanovich, 1974.

KOSIEWICZ, M., D. HALLAHAN, J. LLOYD, AND A. GRAVES.   Effects of self-instruction and self-correction procedures on handwriting performance. *Learning Disability Quarterly* 5 (1982), 71–78.

MARTIN, B., JR.   *Brown Bear, Brown Bear, What Do You See?* New York: Holt, Rinehart & Winston, 1970.

MEICHENBAUM, D., AND J. GOODMAN.   Training impulsive children to talk to themselves: A means of developing self-control. *Journal of Abnormal Psychology* 77 (1971), 115–26.

MORAN, M., J. B. SCHUMAKER, AND A. VETTER.   *Teaching a Paragraph Organization Strategy to Learning Disabled Adolescents* (research report no. 54). Lawrence: University of Kansas Institute for Research in Learning Disabilities, 1981.

POLLOWAY, E. A., J. R. PATTON, AND S. B. COHEN.   Written language for mildly handicapped students. *Focus on Exceptional Children* 14 (1981), no. 3, 1–16.

POPLIN, M.   Assessing developmental writing abilities. *Topics in Learning and Learning Disabilities* 3 (1983), 63–75.

————, R. GRAY, S. LARSEN, A. BANIKOWSKI, AND T. MEHRING.   A comparison of components of written expression abilities in learning disabled and nonlearning disabled children at three grade levels. *Learning Disability Quarterly* 3 (1980), 46–53.

RHODES, L. K.   I can read! Predictable books as resources for reading and writing instruction. *Reading Teacher* 34 (1981), 511–18.

————, AND J. L. SHANNON.   Psycholinguistic principles in operation in a primary learning disabilities classroom. *Topics in Learning and Learning Disabilities* 1 (1982), 1–10.

RJUNYAN, Y.   *A Model of the Writing Process*. Boulder, Colo.: Boulder Valley Public Schools Written Language Curriculum, 1981.

STRONG, W.   *Sentence Combining: A Composing Book*. New York: Random House, 1973.

CHAPTER EIGHT

Strategies in Mathematics and Arithmetic

- How is the clinical interview technique used in planning remediation of students' disabilities in mathematics?

- In what ways does learning at the enactive level support higher-level (iconic and symbolic) learning in mathematics?

- Why are norm-referenced tests so limited in value when planning remediation in mathematics? What alternatives should be considered?

- What is the Life Savers test?

- Why is an understanding of reversibility and conservation so important in mathematics?

- How may a teacher reduce the confusion that results when students do not fully understand the concepts of ordinality and cardinality?

- Why is it so important to learn to express numbers as entities rather than as a sequence of numbers?

This chapter was written with the assistance of Barbara Rhine.

INTRODUCTION

The primary focus of instructional intervention for students with mild-to-moderate learning difficulties traditionally has been in the area of language development. As a result, there is a limited research base for planned instructional intervention in mathematics. In commenting on this situation, Cawley (1981) noted that information related to the assessment and intervention of students' mathematical problems is so sparse that there is not a sufficient historical perspective to generate issues and controversies. However, students identified as mentally retarded, emotionally disturbed, and learning disabled do manifest unique needs in their understanding and application of mathematical concepts and skills (Capps and Hatfield 1977). Recent studies by various prestigious professional groups indicate the need to assist students who have learning problems in the area of mathematics (National Commission on Excellence in Education 1983; National Council for Teachers of Mathematics 1981).

It is important to distinguish between the terms *mathematics* and *arithmetic* prior to discussing major theoretical perspectives and concomitant instructional interventions and strategies for students who have mathematical difficulties. Mathematics is the systematic development of mental structures that deal with the magnitude of forms and quantities that may be expressed symbolically and the temporal and spatial relationships between them. Mathematical understanding is a prerequisite for arithmetic understanding and computation.

Arithmetic, on the other hand, is the most elementary branch of mathematics. It is a method or process of computation with figures that includes the basic operations (addition, subtraction, multiplication, and division); the commutative and associative properties of addition and multiplication; the distributive property for multiplication over addition; and the inverse operations of addition and multiplication. These properties are illustrated in figure 8.1.

FIGURE 8-1 Arithmetical Properties

Commutative property (ordering numerals does not affect the results)

Addition: $3 + 4 = 4 + 3$
                       $7 = 7$
Multiplication: $3 \times 4 = 4 \times 3$
                       $12 = 12$

Associative property (grouping numerals does not affect results)

Addition: $(3 + 4) + 5 = 3 + (4 + 5)$
                       $7 + 5 = 3 + 9$
                          $12 = 12$

Multiplication: $(3 \times 4) \times 5 = 3 \times (4 \times 5)$
$12 \times 5 = 3 \times 20$
$60 = 60$

Distributive property   (relates multiplication and addition)

$4(5 + 6) = (4 \times 5) + (4 \times 6)$
$4(11) = 20 + 24$
$44 = 44$

Inverse operations   (relate to opposite operations and aid students in monitoring their computation)

Addition and Subtraction: $1 + 2 = 3$; $3 - 2 = 1$

Multiplication and Division: $3 \times 4 = 12$; $12 \div 4 = 3$

THEORETICAL PERSPECTIVES: MATHEMATICS AND LEARNING DIFFICULTIES

There appear to be three major theoretical orientations that affect teachers' conceptualization of students' difficulties in the area of mathematics and concomitant intervention strategies—a neuropsychological/mental-abilities approach; an educational/task-deficits model; and a cognitive developmental perspective (McEntire 1981; Kosc 1981).

Neuropsychological Perspective

The neuropsychological/mental-abilities approach presumes a cause-effect relationship between the site of the cerebral insult and variance in a student's mathematical difficulties. Neurologists' attempts to differentiate specific areas of the brain as being responsible for mathematical behaviors were of great interest to educators who delineated various dyscalculias, or mathematical dysfunctions, that resulted from neurological impairment. For example, dyscalculias related to body orientation and position in space may be viewed as disturbed perceptions of spatial relations and directionality and, thus, the cause for a student's inability to recognize and understand place value.

The neuropsychological/mental-abilities model recognizes the existence of separate mental faculties and emphasizes training the component processes of mental ability, that is, sensory perception, sensorimotor integration, and memory (McEntire 1981). Kosc (1981) believes that this approach to remediating learning problems oversimplifies complicated brain-behavior relationships, especially when dealing with slight, neurologically unidentifiable symptoms in children. Neuropsychologists question the isolation of separate mental abilities, their sequential functioning in complex mathematical areas, and the training of discrete psychological-processing abilities as prerequisites for learning mathematics (Luria 1980). They also believe that we cannot measure and monitor cognitive processes accurately because they share a unique reciprocity in the performance of any intellectual activity (Flavell 1977; Neisser 1976). As a result, many educators question the efficacy of perceptual training as a means of increasing students' academic achievement (Ysseldyke 1978; Vellutino 1977; Myers and Hammill 1976).

Educational Perspective

The education/task-deficit model considers mathematics as a set of knowledge and skills acquired through learning and experience (Kosc 1981). This model is based on a psychological/learning-theory perspective that views learning as the formation and strengthening of associations or learning connections between environmental stimuli and individuals' responses. These associations are strengthened by similarity, contrast and contiguity, and pleasure (McEntire 1981; Garwood 1983). Learning theory fostered the belief that we could increase the amount and rate of students' learning in mathematics and measure students' learning change precisely through their responses on normative-referenced standardized tests. In addition, complex mathematical knowledge was viewed as being arranged hierarchically and dependent on mastery of subordinate skills and concepts (Gagne and Briggs 1974). Complex mathematical concepts theoretically could be task analyzed and sequenced into subskills.

Instructional strategies, from the educational/task-deficit viewpoint, should focus on a behavioral paradigm that (1) specifies final mathematics performance to be achieved, (2) assesses observable and measurable student behaviors in mathematics, (3) formulates and implements a contingency program (based on schedules of reinforcement) designed to attain the desired goal, and (4) evaluates the efficiency of the program in achieving that goal. Students' mathematical deficiencies are corrected by expanding instructional content to a total scope and sequence of mathematical skill performance; changing instructional strategies; and conditioning the learners' mathematical responses through manipulating environmental contingencies (McEntire 1981).

The educational-task-deficiency view of mathematics difficulties is based on an atomistic and additive view of learning in which complex mathematical behaviors are task analyzed into discrete and separate elements and sequenced for instruction in a "building-block" approach. It views students' learning as passive and based on manipulation of environmental variables. Such an approach fosters dependency, learned helplessness, and external locus of control (Grimes 1981; Moses 1981). It tends to ignore students' active internal processing and construction of knowledge based on their environmental interactions (Reid and Hresko 1981; Piaget 1973). Current research questions the acquisition of mathematical knowledge based on rote memory and the writing of correct responses to reflect or match a copy of reality. These approaches may inhibit students' mathematical-problem-solving abilities and may be detrimental to developing active, self-confident, autonomous learners who are able to generate and test alternative solutions to problems in mathematics and life in general (Kamii 1982, 1984; Luria 1980; Piaget, 1973).

Cognitive-Developmental Perspective

A cognitive-developmental perspective emphasizes the learner's interaction with, and adaption to, environmental expectations as the basis for intellectual growth. This constructivist view combined with information-processing theory stresses students' abilities to select, extract, maintain, and to use environmental information.

The organization of mathematical knowledge appears to be universal in nature and to consist of three hierarchical levels of conceptual complexity—enactive, iconic, and symbolic (Bruner 1966). These levels or kinds of knowing seem to correlate with Piaget's levels of cognitive development and may be applicable when working with mathematically handicapped students.

During the sensorimotor period of development, children's knowledge is primarily instinctive, and action based. They perform many coordinative motor movements through a stimulus response and trial-and-error procedure. Very young children have no language with which to describe their motor skills and knowledge; their knowing is primarily enactive, that is, based in their actions. Adults also know many things at the sensorimotor stage; and even though they have language, they may be unable to describe their motor knowledge—for example, how they walk.

During the preoperational and concrete-operational periods of development, children's knowledge is physical-sensory knowledge and based on their perceptual and visual spatial abilities. Children think with mental images of concrete objects. For example, they picture, mentally, the collection of two blocks and three blocks that make five blocks. Adults also rely on visual imagery and may visualize imaginary "maps" to help them get from one location to another. Visual-perceptual organization describes and dominates iconic knowing.

During the developmental stage of formal or logical mental operations, students can perform mental manipulations on abstract symbols, such as those that occur in highly organized and symbolized forms in mathematics. Concrete referents are not required for thinking and reasoning, which may originate with hypotheses. The level of formal operations is a never-ending stage, that is, an open system, in which new understandings lead to the reorganization and refinement of previous information. Logico-mathematical knowledge is based on relational-symbolic representations of information; that is, reflective abstraction in which we create relationships among objects by joining them together or placing them in ordinal succession either in the "real" world or in restructuring mental abstractions (Copeland 1979).

It is important for teachers to consider students' levels of cognitive development and their concomitant levels of mathematical-concept acquisition when working with mentally retarded, emotionally disturbed, and learning disabled students who have mathematics difficulties. Too often instruction in mathematics centers only on the iconic (visual-perception and imagery strategies) and symbolic (verbally oriented) response modes. The unique interaction of Piagetian and Brunerian perspectives will undoubtedly enhance students' learning of mathematical processes. Since new mathematical learnings appear to develop sequentially through the enactive, iconic, and symbolic levels, teachers may wish to consider introducing new concepts at the concrete level. Through motor impressions, students may acquire the concept at an intuitive or nonverbal level (which appears to result independently of the reasoning process) from a total perception of an experience. Children may not be able to explain the meaning of place value; they can, however, group twelve popsicles into a group of ten popsicles with two left over (enactive-concrete knowing). At the next level, children can work with pictures of objects, by encircling a group of ten (iconic-pictorial knowing); and finally, they can work with numerical symbols (symbolic-abstract knowing). In essence, students must be provided with opportunities to experience complex concepts on their own and to know them intuitively before they are formalized in terms of mathematical equations and elaborated verbal concepts.

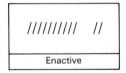

Enactive

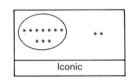

Iconic

	10
	2
	12

Symbolic

Piaget and Inhelder also believe that instructional methods and techniques should accommodate students' natural thought processes (Gallagher and Reid 1981). While they may question the concept of intuitive thought (because awareness or conscious realization is a process of reconstruction of knowledge rather than sudden insight), Piaget and Inhelder maintain that students should be confronted with concrete experiences that challenge their existing levels of thought. For example, we may even be able to teach the concepts of Euclidean geometry to students who are functioning at the concrete operational level, provided they are studied through materials that students can handle rather than through complex mathematical expressions. Concrete experiences that do not emphasize verbalization and abstract mathematical notation serve as the foundation for more sophisticated learnings.

In summary, it appears that students know mathematics at various levels. The most basic way of knowing is through motor activity (enactive), which provides intuitive investigations of sophisticated concepts prior to encountering them through perceptual (iconic) and abstract representational (symbolic) experiences. Capps and Hatfield (1977) believe that this "instructional triad of concrete-semiconcrete-abstract is critical to students with learning deficiencies in mathematical skills and/or concepts. Many learning deficiencies might not occur in the first place if this instructional triad were the universal basis for all instruction in mathematical concepts" (p. 2).

ASSESSMENT OF STUDENTS' NEEDS IN MATHEMATICS AND ARITHMETIC

Assessment of students' mathematics performance should provide a comprehensive picture of their understanding of our system of numbers and numeration, the strategies used in problem solving, and their actual achievement in arithmetical operations. Kosc (1981) suggests that assessment of students' mathematical abilities should be considered in light of their overall symbolic-communicative systems and include the following:

1. determining if students' mathematical deficiencies are isolated or whether they exist in concert with overall deficits in the students' symbolic-communicative functions;
2. determining the structure of students' mathematical abilities and the extent to which their verbal, memory, and reasoning abilities interrelate to indicate patterns of strengths and weaknesses, as a means of differentiating among the students' mathematics difficulties;
3. determining the developmental level of students' mathematical-abilities structure, that is, if they are functioning at the enactive, iconic, or symbolic levels;
4. specifying the neuropsychological correlates of the mathematical disability and how students "transcode" information across symbolic systems;
5. examining students' problem-solving strategies and the compensatory techniques (verbal or written) used to enhance their problem solving;
6. determining the efficacy of previous remedial attempts in mathematics and students' attitudes and orientation toward mathematical learning; and
7. establishing an educational hypothesis, based on students' neuropsychological (mental) structures and their thinking processes in mathematical problem solving, as a basis for instructional interaction.

Kosc's suggestions are based on contemporary theories of brain-behavior relationships and seem consistent with a constructivist perspective to education. They are integrated throughout our discussion of assessing students' mathematical abilities.

Formal Assessment

Formal assessment of students' mathematical abilities has traditionally focused on the administration of standardized normative-referenced and criterion-referenced tests, many of which survey students' overall mathematics achievement. Most such tests are global and provide limited insight into students' problem-solving abilities and limited help in our efforts to develop effective instructional strategies. They provide a means of determining a student's relative standing in comparison to the performance of other students but are not appropriate for determining the types of errors made by students and their problem-solving strategies, both of which are needed for instructional purposes.

Criterion-referenced tests have been used recently in education and behavioral psychology to determine students' mastery of particular mathematical skills and abilities. Test items on criterion-referenced tests are based on task analyses of mathematical skills. They sample sequential skill development and most often are linked to specific instructional objectives. Measurement from this perspective emphasizes individual program planning; it helps to delineate mathematical-skill-development strengths and weaknesses and to relate assessment to curricular content. Criterion-referenced tests (like norm-referenced instruments) may contain relatively limited samples of behavior.

Informal Assessment

Informal assessment of students' mathematics abilities most often relies on the observation of the students' everyday classroom activities and their performance on computational tasks. Assessment instruments may include informal teacher-made skill tests designed specifically to assess one or more particular mathematics skills, informal survey tests that sample a wider range of mathematics behaviors, and task analyses. Each of these informal assessment techniques is closely related to ongoing instructional programs. They approximate the skills and objectives of individualized instructional programs and provide data that are applicable directly to various educational procedures and strategies. The focus of these assessment techniques is similar to that of criterion-referenced assessment—that is, determining the level of attainment of particular skills as a means of planning instructional programs and techniques. Many teachers are already familiar with and use informal teacher-made tests and skill inventories to assess students' mathematical abilities. Therefore, our discussion will consider task analysis as an additional means of assessing students' learning needs.

Task analysis helps to delineate students' learning problems and may guide the development of an effective sequence of instructional planning. Task analysis is a procedure in which a complex skill is reduced to discrete units or steps as a means of identifying students' performance errors. Once the steps have been identified and arranged in a hierarchical sequence, students are presented with each sequential task as a means of determining their errors and the level at which they function successfully. Analysis of students' performance and errors made in the task-analysis hierarchy provides the successive teaching steps for attainment of a complex task. The task-analysis-assessment procedure facilitates the delineation of a target objective, the identification of discrete and sequential steps necessary for attaining an acceptable level of success, and a breakdown of the task into manageable learning units (Guerin and Maier 1983). The sequentiality and discreteness of the task analysis are the hallmarks of the "building-block" theory of skills learning and are consistent with the educational-task-deficit orientation to teaching mathematics. Each skill is a successive approxima- tion of the final task. In addition, each step is so discrete that it involves only one aspect of the task at a time (Myers and Hammill 1976). Informal assessment must progress beyond identifying whether students' problems are specific in nature and related only to their ability to perform arithmetic computation. It must also be determined whether there is a basic lack of understanding of mathematical concepts.

Error analysis is often used to identify systematic error patterns that underlie students' mathematics performances. It may be used with task analysis and usually consists of examining students' computational re- sponses and classifying their errors as a basis for making instructional decisions. Implicit in the use of error analysis is the expectation that learn- ers' mistakes are not random or the result of carelessness. Rather, errors are viewed as indicative of students' current mental structures. Analysis of students' error patterns may provide some insight into their current mental structures and how they think about the task.

An early study by Roberts (1968) identified four error categories in students' computational performances:

1. Wrong operations in which students may add instead of subtract, that is, $5 - 3 = 8$.
2. Computational errors in which students apply the correct operation but make an obvious error in recalling a basic number fact, that is, $8 + 4 = 13$.
3. Defective algorithms in which students apply the correct operation and recall basic facts, but employ the wrong problem solving patterns. For example, the child may add all digits with no regard to place value $48 + 75 (4 + 8 + 7 + 5) = 24$.
4. Random responses in which there appears to be no discernible relationship between the problem and the problem-solving process. These errors may result from distractibility, lack of completion time, or students' inability to understand the concept and to stabilize their cognitive structures.

Roberts's study indicated that careless errors and incorrect addition and multiplication computational errors were distributed across all ability levels; however, random responses and incorrect operations occurred more frequently in low-scoring and low-ability students. Analysis of stu- dents' errors ex post facto does not help us to identify procedural errors in attaining a particular answer (Goodstein 1981; Bachor 1979). Error analy- sis that examines students' thinking often yields information that is in sharp contrast to analysis based solely on answers to a specific task. For example, what may appear to be a complete lack of understanding of a mathematical concept may be an inappropriate application of a problem- solving pattern.

Procedural errors are the mistakes made by students in the step-by- step process of thinking through a task and arriving at a correct response. Understanding procedural errors is helpful in hypothesizing how students think and in developing intervention strategies to facilitate "how" students learn. Bachor (1979) suggests two forms of error analysis that allow us to analyze students' errors—interstudent error analysis and intrastudent error analysis. Interstudent error analysis focuses on the degree to which students in a group or class understand a particular mathematical concept or skill and helps to assess teacher effectiveness. Interstudent analysis, it would appear, provides little information that may be of value in remediation. Intrastudent error analysis, however, analyzes errors across task and content areas and provides insight into students' procedural errors. Intra-individual error analysis is concerned with the frequency, consistency, and type of errors made, that is, errors in input, elaboration, and output (Bachor 1979).

Input errors occur in conjunction with the cognitive process of paying attention—students scan the problem and do not focus on the salient features of the content. For example, a student may calculate an addition problem as one of multiplication. Therefore we may wish to teach students more effective attentional strategies for scanning and searching the environment.

Elaboration errors occur as students attempt to solve the mathematics problem; they include errors of simplification, omission, and inappropriate strategy use. Simplification errors may result when we treat each element of the problem as discrete. For example, in multiplying 598×3 a student may obtain the answer 152724 by multiplying each number separately. Omission errors occur when an essential task component is omitted and may result from confusion when processing extraneous information. Inappropriate strategy use may also result in an incorrect answer. For example, students may use an inappropriate rule of carrying in multiplication, which could result in any of a wide variety of errors.

Output errors occur in the process of communicating, or expressing, the response. Output errors may be corrected by helping students to estimate and to monitor the correctness of their responses. The inability to estimate hinders students from checking to determine the reasonableness of their answers. The ability to estimate is closely associated with understanding mathematical concepts. Students need to learn strategies to monitor each computational step in their problem solving, to help determine where an error occurs.

Error analysis helps us to determine how students think about and process mathematical information. It is a basis for generating educational hypotheses about students' strategies in computational problems and for designing appropriate educational interventions. Error analysis complements, and may be used in conjunction with, the clinical-interview format as a means of identifying students' mental structures in completing mathematics problems.

Clinical interview.   Piaget developed a clinical-interview technique as a means of assessing a student's level of conceptual development regarding a particular concept. In the procedure, students are presented with a concrete problem or a verbal question related to the concept, and they are asked relevant questions. Students' responses, whether accurate or inaccurate, are followed by additional questions and requests to determine the nature of their reasoning and their level of understanding of the concept. The clinical interview related to a particular concept is terminated only when the examiner has identified the students' level of understanding and is able to make inferences about students' understanding from their reasoning. From a Piagetian perspective, students' understanding and reasoning are as important as their answers. Students may often provide a correct response; yet their reasoning is incorrect. Correct responses and reasoning are both necessary in determining whether students have constructed a concept (Piaget 1963).

The clinical interview has been extended to a process of critical exploration, which is a method of questioning students that involves creating cognitive conflict, or disequilibrium. The purpose of critical exploration is to determine the stability of the students' cognitive constructions related to the concept under discussion and to pose additional questions that conflict with their reasoning. In mathematics, for example, students may be presented with problems similar to those they have solved previously, to determine the stability, accuracy, and completeness of their mental structures and their ability to generalize those structures to similar problem-solving situations. They are often presented with a second problem which, if solved by the same procedure, would result in an incorrect answer. The creation of cognitive dissonance helps the teacher to determine students' current mental structures as well as whether the dissonance that has been created causes a mismatch between *their thinking* and *how they must think* to accomplish the task successfully in the future (Gallagher and Reid 1981; DeRuiter and Wansart 1982). The creation of productive cognitive conflict seems necessary to facilitate students' learning. DeRuiter and Wansart refer to the procedure of generating disequilibrium as the "Columbo method." Additional discussion of the Columbo method may be found in chapter 3.

THE CLINICAL INTERVIEW TECHNIQUE

The clinical interview technique developed by Piaget and adapted by many teachers (as a way to determine students' cognitive structures) may be used to attempt to determine students' difficulties in mathematics. In the following illustration, we see an example of the difficulties students may have when they focus solely on mechanical procedures for the production of correct answers.

* * * * * * * * * *

Nancy is a fifth-grade student with above-average intelligence who has difficulty adding fractions. For example, when asked to add $\frac{3}{8} + \frac{1}{8}$, she proceeded as follows:

$$\frac{3}{8} + \frac{1}{8} = \frac{4}{16} \text{ or } \frac{1}{4}.$$

The following discussion illustrates the teacher's technique in determining her strategy for adding fractions.

TEACHER: Okay, Nancy, tell me how you got the answer ¼ in this addition sample.

NANCY: Well, when adding fractions we're supposed to reduce the answer to lowest terms and that's what I did.

TEACHER: Tell me what you did when you got the answer ⁴⁄₁₆?

NANCY: Well . . . I . . . uh added the top numbers and the bottom numbers in the fractions and got the answer. That's what we learned in addition of fractions.

TEACHER: Okay, so when adding fractions, we add both numbers—the top number called the *numerator* and the bottom number called the *denominator*, right?

NANCY: Yes, that's what we're supposed to do . . .

TEACHER: Suppose we had a whole pepperoni pizza. We can cut the pizza into eight slices. If you ate ⅜ of the pizza and decided to eat another slice (⅛) of pizza, how many pieces did you eat?

NANCY: Four pieces, or ⅛ of the pizza. Hey, that means that I ate ½ of the pizza.

TEACHER: Good, you *did* eat ½ of the pizza because we can rename the ⅛ to ½. Now is that the same as eating ⁴⁄₁₆ or ¼ of the pizza?

NANCY: No. ¼ of the pizza is less than ½. Now I know, you're only supposed to add the numerators when adding fractions.

TEACHER: Right. Now let's try another example. Suppose we . . .

* * * * * * * * * * *

It appears that Nancy relied solely on an incorrect procedure when attempting to add fractions. She had little confidence in her own mental structures or understanding of the processes needed to obtain the correct answer. The teacher's role is to discover how students are determining the incorrect answers, and then to help them understand both correct processes and meaningful concepts about the problem areas under consideration.

Critical exploration as an extension of Piaget's clinical interview process is a good illustration of a holistic approach to assessment in which informal assessment and individualized instruction may be combined into a single assessment-intervention process. This technique in the area of mathematics is illustrated in the box.

COLUMBO METHOD

The Columbo method is a general teaching strategy that is consistent with a constructivist approach to learning because it focuses on students' active involvement in their learning. The primary purpose of the Columbo method is to create disequilibrium in students' mental structures by asking probing questions about their approach to the attainment of a particular task. Disequilibrium is the motivation for the acquisition of new learning when students recognize that their strategies for accomplishing a goal are inefficient and that they must devise a new strategy. Once the strategies are developed and applied to learning new information, they are transferred to comparable situations.

Example: Clarification of student strategies used in regrouping in addition of whole numbers

1. Teacher presents an addition example and requests student to perform addition. Student adds 14

$$\begin{array}{r} 14 \\ +8 \\ \hline 112 \end{array}$$

2. Student reads one hundred twelve as the answer, and teacher probes to determine the process of student's answer as a basis for instruction; teacher sets paper aside.
3. Teacher presents student with twenty-two items (toothpicks) and groups them into two groups of fourteen and eight toothpicks.
4. Teacher asks student to count the toothpicks and writes the appropriate number by each group thereby symbolically representing the example: 14

$$\begin{array}{r} 14 \\ +8 \\ \hline \end{array}$$

5. Teacher asks student to add the toothpicks; student counts a total of 22 toothpicks, verbalizes the correct answer, and writes the total under the new example.
6. Teacher brings back the old example and asks student to compare answers.
7. Faced with the obvious contradiction, student is asked to explain the disparity between 112 and 22 and to make a judgment as to which is more correct.
8. This leads to teacher's explanation of the carrying process:
   (a) Using objects from above;
   (b) Grouping by tens;
   (c) Carrying in the ones column; and
   (d) Writing problems while manipulating real objects.
9. Application of procedure to new but similar problem to determine student's ability to transfer learning to a similar situation.

Cawley (1975) developed a clinical mathematics interview, which considers the content to be learned; the instructional mode; and the algorithm, or rule, for solving arithmetic problems. Cawley's process is threefold and includes:

1. Presenting students with a relevant test of arithmetic computation.
2. Eliciting students' explanations for their algorithmic solution for incorrect problems.
3. Presenting similar problems to students using alternative instructional modes, which may include enactive (manipulating objects), iconic (graphs and pic-

tures), and symbolic (oral presentations that include number sentences and abstract equations) experiences.

The process espoused by Cawley helps students generate alternative solutions to problem solving, to anticipate the results of their actions, and to evaluate and monitor the efficiency of their problem-solving strategies. In addition, the clinical mathematics interview enables teachers to determine more effective instructional interventions that are rich and varied and allows students to construct their own knowledge, based on numerous experiences with similar concepts. Finally, it facilitates the transition from assessment to intervention.

The interview techniques discussed in this chapter are harmonious with a cognitive viewpoint of mathematics learning, which is concerned with students' mental structures and the strategies they employ in solving problems. The techniques allow teachers to move beyond the assessment of skill deficiencies and to ascertain the students' levels of readiness for mathematics skills, their logico-mathematical development, and their cognitive style (reflective versus impulsive).

THE LIFE SAVERS TEST

The five-flavor package of Life Savers candies can be used in an informal assessment of many elementary readiness skills related to mathematics. The information derived from this informal assessment is not to be regarded as a formal assessment in itself. Rather, it is an excellent warm-up interaction between student and teacher, which by careful observation provides some good indicators of the student's skills in a number of areas. From this information, a more extensive assessment can be completed. The package of Life Savers contains eleven candies in the order of lemon, cherry, orange, lime, pineapple, cherry, lemon, lime, pineapple, cherry, and orange. It contains three red Life Savers and two each of the other colors.

Motor skills can be observed by asking the student to roll the package, toss it in the air, then open it. However, before opening the package, other skills can be assessed. An indication of the student's ability to identify letters and numbers can be obtained by using the letters and numbers on the package. For example, word-attack skills may be indicated by asking the student to read the words on the wrapping.

Language skills may be noted by asking the student to explain or tell all she knows about Life Savers. In this informal language sample, the use of vocabulary, the length of sentences, and the grammatical structure may be observed. The student may be asked why she thinks the candies are called Life Savers. The explanation should be followed with sufficient questioning to probe the child's reasoning and to determine where she thinks she obtained that information.

The child can now be asked to open the package. It is important to note if her actions are coordinated and whether she uses the pull string or mangles the package as it is opened. The teacher should remember this is an informal observation, and therefore one should avoid the temptation to form any assessment/conclusion about the child. Informal assessment with Life Savers is to create an awareness of possible areas that need a more intensive follow-up assessment.

The next step is to determine how the student follows directions. The child is asked to take the candies out of the package and to put them on a sheet of paper or on the table. It is important to observe her organization. Is there a pattern? Is there any classification into subgroups of colors and the flavors? The teacher should note what the child does with the pineapple and the lemon flavors. Are they both the same yellow, or does the child use a discriminating label to indicate the difference in shading? If she does not, the teacher may ask if the colors are the same or different. Both discrimination and language skills should be noted.

With some children, the teacher may wish to check simple spelling skills— *red, green, lime.* Next, the teacher may wish to ask the child to sort the candies by either color or flavor. If the child can do this, the teacher should move to the next classification step—inclusion—and ask, "Are there more red or more green Life Savers?" "Are there more red or more yellow candies?" The student may be asked to reclassify the candies. This is accomplished by mixing them up and asking the student to sort them into piles of red and not red. This allows us to check negation ability, that is, can the child sort "what is" and "what is not"?

One-to-one correspondence and conservation of numbers may be assessed next. In this task, the teacher should lay out a row of five candies and ask the child to put out another row with just as many candies in it. The teacher then observes the child's strategy—does she make a placement match, use a non-placement match, use counting, or fail to make a one-to-one correspondence? If the correspondence is made, the teacher may wish to spread one row and ask, "Are there as many in each row, or does one row have more?" Next, the teacher pushes the candies into a random grouping and asks the child to count the number of candies. Does the student arrange the candies in a pattern when counting? Does she use a system? Is the total correct, or have some been omitted or counted twice? Teachers should check for ordinal and cardinal understanding by putting the candies in a row and asking the child to "give me three candies; give me five more." The candies are then repositioned, and the child is requested to "give me ten candies." The candies may be repositioned and the child asked to "give me the third candy," and so on.

Simple number facts can be checked by saying: "There are three red Life Savers. If you had two more red Life Savers, how many red Life Savers would you have?" Subtraction can be checked with the "if you ate" approach. Multiplication can be checked by asking, "How many orange Life Savers would you have if you had three packages?"

Also, if one is inclined toward assessing information-processing abilities, visual memory can be checked by asking the child to reproduce a color sequence; auditory memory can be checked by asking the child to repeat a sequence of flavor names.

The Life Savers test is a good informal assessment of students' understanding of mathematics-readiness skills in addition to their cognitive, language, reading, and motor abilities. It helps to structure additional assessment activities and provides a base for instructional intervention.

We wish to thank Dr. Judy Gilbert, who created the Life Savers Test for her methods classes.

CHARACTERISTIC DIFFICULTIES IN MATHEMATICS

The assessment of students' mathematics deficiencies from a cognitive-developmental viewpoint recognizes the influence of diversity in students' cognitive functioning, in environmental differences, and in the dynamic and mutual interactive effects between students and the environment on students' mathematics functioning. Discussion of variance in students' mathematics abilities recognizes that students' errors are not capricious or random. Rather, students' errors reflect their mental structures, which are constructed as a result of continual interaction with the environment.

The following considerations have been hypothesized as affecting students' mathematics performance—cognitive-developmental readiness, cognitive-processing factors, affective factors, language and reading abilities, and inadequate instruction (Guerin and Maier 1983; Mercer 1983; McEntire 1981).

Cognitive Developmental Readiness

Understanding how students learn and their level of mathematical conceptual development are important prerequisites to instructional intervention. Piaget's developmental theory provides one approach to understanding students' mathematical performance. The notion of mathematical readiness is important to arithmetic instruction, since students' ability to understand higher-level mathematical concepts depends on their mastery of lower-level arithmetic skills. Mathematical readiness requires that students understand the basic concepts of spatial representation, one-to-one correspondence, classification, ordering and seriation, reversibility, and conservation; and they must have the language to describe the concepts of number, comparing, contrasting, and problem solving. We recognize, however, that from a Piagetian perspective, students may know more than they can verbalize, and conversely, they may verbalize the correct responses without true understanding of a concept.

Spatial relations includes the abilities to perceive and to compare spatial forms accurately and to visualize the separateness of an object's size, depth, and distance, all of which are related to object permanence. It is needed for visualizing geometric shapes and for understanding vertical and horizontal notation, measurement and estimation, and geometric concepts.

187

One-to-one correspondence is the basis for counting with comprehension and refers to the student's ability to understand that one object in one set is the same as one object in another set, regardless of their characteristics. It is a prerequisite to understanding the concept of zero and counting using cardinal and ordinal numeration. One-to-one correspondence may be fostered by giving young children a cookie for each hand or asking them to set the table with a place and utensils for each member of the family. In school, they may be requested to distribute a beanbag to each boy in the class.

Classification is the process of understanding relationships and grouping objects according to certain defined characteristics, that is, likenesses and differences. Classification is a prerequisite to understanding set notation and grouping. We must provide as many opportunities as possible for students to classify and sort concrete manipulative objects. Students should be permitted to sort blocks according to color and geometric shapes (circles, squares, and triangles) according to "what is" (affirmations) and "what is not" (negations), that is, "circles" and "noncircles." These activities should emphasize perceptual characteristics and include things that students know about to complement their egocentricity. As students progress to the iconic level of knowing, we may wish to use pictorial representations and ask students to indicate which does not belong and to explain their reasoning. For example, when presented with pictures of a shoe, pants, and a cat, students may be asked to explain "which does not belong" and to "tell why." The Sesame Street song, which refers to things which are not like others, or ones which do not belong, provides a good activity to foster the development of students' abilities to classify objects at a relatively simple level prior to progressing to multidimensional classification activities that may include size, shape, and color. For example, students may be asked to pick out large, yellow triangles from a group of geometric shapes.

Ordering and seriation relate to students' abilities to sequence objects without consideration to how they relate quantitatively (topological ordering) and on the basis of change in one or more characteristics such as length, weight, or color (seriation). Ordering and seriation are needed for counting in both cardinal and ordinal numeration, counting by twos, threes, and tens, and using a number line. We can help students to develop the concepts of ordering and seriation by allowing them to stack boxes of different sizes and asking them to line up by height (using mirrors), to facilitate the concepts of smaller and bigger.

Reversibility, or flexibility, of thought includes the ability to recognize that objects when changed and rearranged may return to their original condition. Reversibility is a prerequisite for understanding and using arithmetical operations, that is, the commutative and associative properties of addition and multiplication; the inverse functions of addition and subtraction, multiplication and division; and the distributive property for multiplication over addition. Reversibility of thought means, for instance, that one's father may be someone else's brother or uncle. We can help students to understand reversibility or flexibility of thought by providing concrete manipulative experiences in grouping objects for addition. For example, when illustrating the commutative property of addition, students may use buttons or M&Ms to determine that 4 + 6 is the same as 6 + 4 whether in horizontal or vertical notation (****) + (******) = (******) + (****). Students must be provided with a variety of experiences that relate to the same basic concept prior to true understanding.

Conservation is fundamental to more advanced mathematical reasoning and refers to students' ability to recognize that the quantity or number of objects in a set remains the same regardless of spatial arrangement or shape of the object(s). Conservation is a prerequisite to understanding place value and grouping, measurement, and problem solving.

Each of these cognitive concepts is essential to students' understanding and their ability to abstract complex mathematical operations. In most instances, they are developed by the time students have progressed from Piaget's stage of concrete operational thought to the stage of formal operations. Students' progress through the stages varies; therefore, teachers must determine the students' level of mathematical readiness and plan instructional interventions that harmonize with students' level of concept development. Teachers' knowledge of students' functional level with each of these mathematical concepts and their awareness of students' understanding at either the concrete (enactive), semiconcrete (iconic), or abstract (symbolic) level serve as a solid foundation upon which to construct mathematical intervention strategies. For example, students who function at the concrete (enactive) level may count on their fingers when asked to complete simple addition problems. Therefore, teachers may wish to provide concrete manipulative materials (cookies, blocks, straws) to facilitate arithmetical computation. If a student has difficulty with one-to-one correspondence and is functioning at the enactive level, he may be requested to distribute a pencil and a piece of paper to each child in a group.

The information included in table 8.1 illustrates the relationship of these cognitive concepts to students' readiness for mathematics at the sensorimotor, preoperational, and concrete operational stages of Piagetian thought. Understanding of Piagetian theory helps teachers to conceptualize an integrated mathematics program that relies on structural learning, has a solid theoretical foundation and is one in which they develop their own methods based on students' needs. This is in contrast to a cookbook approach that emphasizes procedural learning and is based on separate and unrelated units. Very often, this perspective emphasizes a "closet" approach to the selection of activities based on the mathematics "kits," or programs, that are available in the teacher's closet.

Cognitive-Processing Factors

Cognitive-processing difficulties have been hypothesized by a number of authorities (Bley and Thornton 1981; Kaliski 1967) as being related to students' arithmetic problems. These problems appear to be related to the processes of attention, perception, and memory. The information included in table 8.2 specifies the cognitive process and behavioral manifestations related to mathematics. We recognize that students' mathematical difficulties, attributed to cognitive-processing factors in attention, perception, and

TABLE 8-1 Mathematical Readiness from a Piagetian Perspective

COGNITIVE CONCEPT	MATHEMATICAL READINESS		
	SENSORIMOTOR: BIRTH–TWO YEARS	PREOPERATIONAL: TWO–SEVEN YRS.	CONCRETE OPERATIONAL: SEVEN–ELEVEN YRS.
Spatial relations	Visual differentiation among objects. Motor activity yields kinesthetic information.	Visual discrimination between similar objects first based on obvious distinctions and then on more subtle differences.	Identification and memory of visual patterns and symbols.
Object permanence	Visual perception and memory for objects when hidden partially from field of vision.		
Size	Differentiation based on gross distinction.	Distinguishes differences based on two characteristics and recalls differences from personal experiences.	Identifies results and associates similarities based on previous personal experiences. Orders based on one or more characteristics.
Distance	Develops concepts through motoric exploration.	Knows distance within personal experiences and begins to think about distances using concrete experiences.	Thinks about distances based on experiences; concrete referent is not always needed.
Time	Relates solely to basic physical needs.	Remembers first and can delay activities according to daily schedule. Understands temporal concepts of today, tomorrow. Anticipates and plans based on own experiences. Understands length of minute, hour, and day and tells time to the hour.	Sequences days, months, seasons. Estimates time lapses and length of time to complete an activity. Tells time to the minute.

TABLE 8-1 *(Continued)*

COGNITIVE CONCEPT	MATHEMATICAL READINESS		
	SENSORIMOTOR: BIRTH–TWO YEARS	PREOPERATIONAL: TWO–SEVEN YRS.	CONCRETE OPERATIONAL: SEVEN–ELEVEN YRS.
One-to-one correspondence		Recognizes that birthdays are repeated. Little understanding; at first counts and recites by rote memory; then performs with some assistance. Assumes that characteristics other than spatial concepts influence numerosity.	Understands and isolates characteristics under consideration from others; can place separate pair groups into pairs.
Classification		Classifies based on single characteristic/ attribute but cannot generalize to larger category owing to lack of understanding of class inclusion.	Classifies based on multiple characteristics and according to class inclusion. Understands subclasses.
Ordering and seriation		At first does not seriate; cannot consider all characteristics of object. Can seriate objects that are equally separate from each other; difficulty with random sizes and shapes.	Orders according to size, weight, and volume.
Reversibility		Performs conservation task of pouring water from beaker to beaker BUT does not understand concept.	Flexible/reversible thought establishes concepts of conservation.

(continued)

TABLE 8-1 *(Continued)*

COGNITIVE CONCEPT	MATHEMATICAL READINESS		
	SENSORIMOTOR: BIRTH–TWO YEARS	PREOPERATIONAL: TWO–SEVEN YRS.	CONCRETE OPERATIONAL: SEVEN–ELEVEN YRS.
Conservation		At first, concentrates only on static end characteristics, i.e., how object looks. Conserves number with assistance; remembers one-to-one correspondence with assistance when objects are separated and rearranged. Understands conservation of quantity.	Conserves weight (9–10 years) and volume (11–12 years).

Adapted from G. R. Guerin and A. S. Maier, *Informal Assessment in Education.* Palo Alto, Calif.: Mayfield Publishing Company, 1983.

memory are related and cannot be separated as discrete problems. For example, the inability to attend to a particular mathematics task may be related to memory and the inability to recall similar experiences and to motivational considerations related to a prior success-and-failure orientation. In addition, students' distractibility and inattention may be interpreted as an indication of poor initial understanding and construction of knowledge.

Affective Factors

Students may develop attitudes of learned helplessness when teachers correct their answers in arithmetic computation and problem solving, thereby reinforcing dependence in a controlling environment. Teachers' correction of students' responses does not ensure understanding and internal evaluation and construction of knowledge. If students are encouraged to anticipate the results of their actions, and to compare and evaluate their answers, they accept and recognize their errors more readily and try to resolve the error without external direction and coercion. In addition, students may continue to make the same errors, or they may not be able to generalize their responses to different situations (Kamii 1984, 1982; McEntire 1981).

TABLE 8-2 Cognitive-Processing Factors Related to Students' Mathematics Difficulties

COGNITIVE PROCESSES	BEHAVIORAL MANIFESTATION
Attention	
Impulsivity	Rapid guessing and incorrect and unstable responses.
	Careless computational errors.
	Attention to extraneous details in problem solving.
Distractibility	Off task and unable to complete assigned work within prescribed time.
	Inability to complete one problem or arithmetic example prior to proceeding to next problem.
	Difficulty sequencing and completing multistep computational tasks.
Perseveration	Overattention to task—works slowly and reviews work several times.
	Inability to switch from one operation to the next (addition to subtraction).
Perception	
Visual spatial	Inability spacing manipulatives into patterns and sets.
	Problems copying shapes and writing examples in straight columns on paper.
	Directional problems are noted in vertical computation (addition) and horizontal regrouping (subtraction), in aligning numbers in multiplication and division computation, in appropriate placement of decimal point, and in using number line.
Visual figureground	Loses place on worksheet and is unable to complete problems on page.
	Difficulty with place value and reading multidigit numbers.
Visual discrimination	Difficulty differentiating between numbers, coins, operational symbols $(+, -, \times, \div)$, and hour and minute hands on the clock.
Visual motor	Difficulty copying and writing numbers legibly with speed and accuracy.
Auditory temporal	Difficulty with before and after concepts and telling time.
	Inability to follow auditory number patterns and to count in a sequence.
	Difficulty sequencing and writing numbers from dictation.
Memory	
Sequential	Difficulty counting rationally.
	Inability to complete sequential steps in multistep computation examples and word problems.
	Inability to remember math facts on a short-term and long-term basis.
	Forgets meaning of operational symbols $(+, -, \times, \div)$ and other mathematical symbols $(=, >, <)$.
	Difficulty remembering steps and rules in an algorithm.

Adapted from N. S. Bley and C. A. Thornton, *Teaching Mathematics to the Learning Disabled.* Rockville, Md.: Aspen Systems Corp., 1981.

Language and Reading Abilities

Students who have difficulty with mathematics performance in school often exhibit delays in their developmental language abilities (McEntire 1981). Quite often, they are unable to derive meaning from mathematical information, to express mathematical concepts using appropriate vocabulary, or to verbalize the necessary steps in solving a word problem. The process for solving mathematical word problems depends on students' understanding and use of mathematical language in which students have to deal with vocabulary, syntactic complexity, and linguistic demands and be able to identify extraneous information (Goodstein 1981; Sharma 1981).

Students' language acquisition involves (in most cases) an orderly progression from using single words to noun and verb phrases and then simple, compound, and complex sentences. We cannot expect students who speak in short noun and verb phrases to understand and respond to mathematical tasks that require complex language structures. A study on the effects of syntactic complexity by Larsen, Parker, and Trenholme (1978) indicated that the complexity of sentence structure affected the accuracy of students' performance. Students were able to perform more accurately on word problems that contained simple sentence structures in contrast with sentences that contained combinations of simple and complex interrogative sentence or compound/complex sentences.

Successful mathematical problem solving is related to the linguistic demands of the problem and requires student recognition of nouns, adjectives, and verbs and the ability to use referential language clues (Sharma 1981). The presence of cue words such as *take away* may help students to determine the appropriate mathematical operation and influence the accuracy of their problem-solving abilities. However, cue words may not help students connect linguistic models (How much taller?) with the interpretation of the mathematical concept of ordinal numbers (Sharma 1981).

Finally, it appears that the presence of extraneous information in word problems affects students' problem-solving abilities (Goodstein 1981). This may result from their inability to organize the incoming information. Students need to identify, analyze, and organize the information provided in a word problem in a logical and coherent sequence prior to determining the appropriate computation skills for effective problem solving (Guerin and Maier 1983; Sharma 1981).

Inadequate Instruction

Instruction in mathematics has most often focused on teaching students isolated bits of information and training discrete computation skills, an approach that may be both arbitrary and deleterious to the development of mathematical concepts. It relies heavily on the attainment of correct responses and seems to ignore the importance of students' thinking processes and of their understanding of mathematical concepts. Quite often skills are introduced and learned by rote without sufficient time to practice and deal with the concepts in a variety of ways to ensure understanding. Students seemingly may understand a concept and be able to apply it.

However, they must be afforded additional opportunities to generalize the skill to a variety of experiences, to note similarities, and to establish associations and relations among their experiences. The assimilation of new information depends on students' abilities to form interrelationships between new environmental information and relative aspects of their existing cognitive structures. Students' experiences with mathematical concepts should be structured and based on a transition from concrete to semiconcrete and abstract involvement with the concept. A lack of understanding and practice at a lower level will hinder higher level performance. Kamii (1982) believes that arithmetic worksheets and story problems may not provide students with the needed physical and environmental experiences and social interaction necessary for developing mathematical understandings. She believes that children would develop much more rapidly in their abilities to think logically and in their arithmetic abilities if provided opportunities for social interaction, which encourages them to exchange ideas and to argue among themselves. Kamii states that we need a fundamental reconceptualization of objectives for mathematics instruction that encourages independent thought rather than correct responses. Logical mathematical knowledge is an internal process of constructing and reconstructing personal knowledge to higher abstracted levels based on individual experiences.

INSTRUCTIONAL STRATEGIES

Teachers' understanding of the characteristics of students' difficulties in mathematics and arithmetic computation complements the design of instructional-intervention strategies to facilitate their learning. Instructional strategies from a cognitive developmental perspective focus on either teacher-directed instruction or learner response to problem solving (McEntire 1981). Teacher-directed instruction emphasizes the role of the teacher in structuring students' learning and the attainment of mathematical concepts. This approach most often relies on the structured presentation of a concept using concrete-semiconcrete-abstract symbolic experiences. Students are guided in developing and testing a hypothesis about a particular mathematical concept and in generating strategies for developing conceptual relationships and problem solving.

The learner-response model of teaching follows a Piagetian perspective and views the teacher in a nondirective role as facilitator of students' learning. Programs are student centered and most often focus on students' learning "how to learn." The teacher's role as facilitator includes:

1. Presenting puzzling situations appropriate to students' conceptual developmental level in mathematics
2. Eliciting students' responses to, and justification of, the problematic situation and creating cognitive dissonance through countersuggestions and questions to determine the stability of their mental structures
3. Presenting related situations to determine the generalizability of students' mathematical knowledge to other situations

The discussion, related to instructional strategies, emphasizes a cognitive developmental perspective, which recognizes that the primary focus of teaching is the acquisition of mathematical concepts. Students' facility in arithmetic computation is secondary to their conceptual mathematical development. Students' understanding of the relationships of space and time, number, classification, seriation, and conservation is more essential to mathematical learning than is the memorization and manipulation of mathematical symbols. Students must have these basic cognitive prerequisites before they can develop the language and symbolic concepts needed for arithmetic operations. These prerequisites, as noted earlier, are developed through students' actual physical and subsequent mental manipulation of objects. As educators, we cannot impose the assimilation and accommodation of knowledge, but rather we must facilitate students' active and meaningful involvement as a foundation for their learning. Kamii (1981) states:

> It is often the clash among ideas about number that motivates the individual to make choices or to reconcile differences between competing ideas. These actions enable the individual to construct more adequate levels of conceptualization. . . . By focusing on areas of conflict, one may be able to expose the sources of difficulty that . . . learners encounter, in grappling with the numeration system. [p. 49]

Readiness Strategies

Basic readiness activities for developing mathematics concepts include counting, cardinal and ordinal numbers, and grouping and writing numerical symbols.

Counting.   When learning to count, children may be requested to count familiar objects within their immediate classroom environment such as the number of tables in the room or the number of books on a desk. Quite often children will touch or move each object as they are counting. If the naming and the touching sequence correspond, in all probability, the student has mastered the concept of one-to-one correspondence. However, students will need additional practice to develop mobility in their thinking (automaticity) to a level where counting is automatic and not related to touching each object. Once students are able to count concrete objects, they should progress to the next hierarchical level of complexity, at which they count pictures. Eventually, students counting should be at an abstract level, where they can represent numbers symbolically.

Cardinal and ordinal numbers.   Children's concept of cardinal versus ordinal numbers is often confused at early developmental stages. Cardinal numbers answer the question "How many?" whereas ordinal numbers position and locate and ask the question "Which one?" Many children may not understand that ordinal numbers have a cumulative designation of a collection of things and that they must perceive the collection as an entity. Therefore, when asked to pick up four blocks in a sequence or to get three paper clips, they will pick up the fourth block or retrieve the third paper clip. It seems that they view ordinal and cardinal numbers as being the same. There appears to be confusion in the students' minds between the idea that numbers can signify position in a series and a whole amount (Kamii 1981). The children do not seem to understand that an ordinal number represents all of the preceding numbers in a sequence. This confusion may result from having heard numbers out of sequence—as when used in telephone numbers.

Though some children appear to develop both ordinal and cardinal concepts up through four or five almost intuitively, children with learning difficulties may require specific training and experience to master these concepts. To determine whether a child understands ordinality, we may ask him to sit in the third chair, open the second drawer, or bring the fourth block. If it appears that he has not mastered and integrated the concepts of ordinal and cardinal numbers, we should provide varied experiences in counting familiar objects. In so doing, we should also include the concept of zero as a term that indicates no items.

As children are counting, they may be encouraged to group objects and to indicate the entity, that is, "one, two, three"—thereby illustrating the correspondence of the number name to each object. Then with a sweep of the hand, they should indicate the total group—that is, "We have three candies." Children may then be requested to count objects and to summarize the groups within a variety of contexts to ensure varied experiences with a concept as a basis for reconstructing their knowledge to higher levels of complexity. A plastic fly-fishing box is an excellent device to help students group and count various numbers of objects. The clear plastic provides separation of groups but allows students to view the whole. They should be encouraged to count using rows, circles, and various spatial arrangements and placements for the objects. These experiences facilitate the development of conservation of substance and allow the modeling of organizational strategies as the teacher counts and moves the objects into various symmetrical or asymmetrical patterns.

Children's counting should continue up through the number 9. When presenting counting concepts, we may wish to begin with a set of four objects and add the needed quantity for each new number. This activity is the beginning of developing an understanding of addition, which is the foundation for the three other arithmetic operations. Once students understand the numbers 0 through 9, they should be provided opportunities to learn the numbers 10 through 20. When students are counting concrete objects, the objects should be grouped by tens and the additional amounts. Students' understanding of cardinal numbers is then based on an understanding of place value—in contrast with teaching the concept of place value as a separate mathematical concept.

Learning disabled students very often have difficulty integrating and generalizing their learning; therefore, instruction should provide opportunities to integrate their knowledge and to transfer concepts to new settings. In addition, young children enjoy physical experiences that indicate differences in quantity. Clapping activities are not cumulative and will not impress children with the idea of increased quantity or quantity of differences. Jumping, on the other hand, helps children experience the difference between five (jumps) and nineteen (jumps). The increased fatigue of the nineteen jumps emphasizes the increased quantity.

Grouping and writing numerical symbols. Written numerical symbols should not be introduced until students understand the concepts of spoken symbols and cardinal numbers from one to twenty as being representative of specific quantities. The following sequence, as illustrated in Figure 8.2, may assist in developing students' concepts of *grouping* and written numerical symbols:

1. Children assemble groups of concrete objects (buttons, pennies) and match their object groups with pictorial representations of various quantities (dot cards). The teacher should model the verbal mediation of the associations for the students (three buttons match the three dots on the card).
2. Once students are successful in matching concrete objects with pictorial representations, the printed numerical symbol may be introduced for each group.
3. The students then match the groups of objects with the appropriate pictorial representations and the printed numerical symbol. Symbols should always be associated with the quantity of the group. Therefore, it is important for the teacher to discuss with the students the association between the quantity and the shape of the printed numerical symbol. For the numerals 0 through 5, the dot impressions of touch math may be an effective mnemonic of the quantity-symbol association.
4. The groups are then presented in random order, and the students are requested to represent the appropriate printed symbol card with the correct group of concrete objects, which are replaced gradually with the pictorial representation. Eventually, students will associate the concept of quantity with corresponding written symbols.

FIGURE 8-2 Grouping and Printed Numerical Symbols

Step 1   Group Objects

Step 2   Match Dot Cards

Step 3   Match Printed Numerical Symbol

Step 4   Random Presentation of Object Cards and Printed Symbols

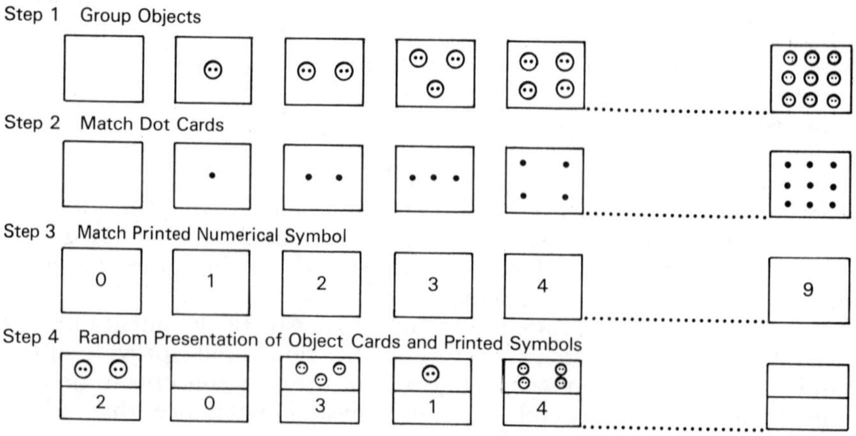

The techniques employed in any *symbol-writing* task may be used to teach students to write the numerical symbols: that is, tracing, copying, and reproducing from memory. The written symbol is always related to the quantity it represents (through concrete and semiconcrete (pictorial) experiences), to avoid rote learning. A pegboard with the correct number of holes for peg insertion and a rough-textured numerical symbol provide an excellent tracing device. Color cues can also be used to indicate the beginning point for writing the symbol. Young students and those who are learning disabled, emotionally disturbed, and mentally retarded may be perceptually bound. Therefore, it is important not to use cues that are too intensive and which may interfere with concept development.

Students' writing errors often include reversals of the numerals 2, 3, and 5 and confusion of the numerals 6 and 9. Cognitive behavior modification techniques may be used to direct students' attention to problem reversals and to guide their writing behavior. An awareness that the numerals 4 and 5 are the only "two-stroke" numbers often helps in symbol writing; or, these numbers may be taught as "one stroke" numbers. If 5 is taught as a one-stroke number, the child may be guided by the fact that all numbers are written with the initial movement to the right or down (with the exception of 5 and 9). The shape of each numeral should be discussed when the written symbol is introduced. When learning to write the numerals, first students should be presented (randomly) with groups of concrete objects, for which they write the numerical symbol. Next, the number should be presented orally, and the children should write it and group the objects. Finally, students should be able to write the number and to draw the objects to indicate the quantity. It is important to remember that as we teach students to write numerals and to associate them with groups of objects, we begin with a set and increase the set (as the basis for addition), in contrast with counting from zero to the appropriate number for each group.

When teaching the numerals above 10, students should be told that the "ty" ending on twenty, thirty, forty, and so on, equals 2 or 3 or 4 groups of 10s. This occurs at all levels except the "teens," which are written in reverse with respect to the verbal symbol. Learning disabled students often have difficulty with this type of pattern detection and will probably require some structured guidance to help them to discover the pattern. It is important that students be afforded learning activities to discover this knowledge for themselves. Therefore, they should be provided with opportunities for accommodation of their mental structures versus the assimilation of information. When presenting this concept, teachers should begin with concrete objects and proceed through the hierarchy to semiconcrete and abstract symbols. For example, when counting through the teens to nineteen, we may wish to start with a group of 3 or 4 blocks or beans, count to ten as a group and continue through nineteen. The student learns that ten and nine blocks = nineteen blocks. The activity may be changed to a stamp-pad picture activity in which students count groups of pictures to match a given number and then write the numerical symbol in extended notation.

Problem-Solving Strategies

This separate section on problem-solving strategies is included for discussion purposes only. We believe that verbal *problem solving should be an integrated component of a total mathematics program* for all students but it is specific for students identified as mildly mentally retarded, emotionally disturbed, and learning disabled. Teachers should not foster the idea that problem solving is a separate function, especially for students who may be unable to organize and to integrate incoming environmental information meaningfully and to perceive relationships among information. It appears that these students lack the integrative processes needed to adapt their knowledge systems to problem situations. They seem unable to link mathematical concepts and language with general problem solving (Sharma 1981). Some students may have problem-solving strategies available to them; however, they may not recognize when to use them. Since it appears that they are unable to generalize problem-solving strategies, it is important to teach strategies and to help students transfer their knowledge to other situations. This approach may help them to avoid adopting the only strategies they can comprehend easily—rote learning.

Mathematical word problems have the potential of helping students to develop their reasoning and evaluative skills and language- and reading-comprehension abilities in addition to mathematical conceptualization. Word problems will help students to focus on essentials, to analyze and organize information, and to determine language patterns that relate to mathematical operations.

Verbal problem solving is a multifaceted process, which involves *situational* variables that are related to the environment; *individual variables* that concern students' prior knowledge, interests, attitudes and motivational needs, and abilities; and *instructional* variables that include methods and strategies and materials (Cawley et al. 1979). Each of these variables is critical if we wish to facilitate students' problem-solving abilities and to bridge school and real-life experiences. "Problem-solving processes cannot be learned without content, and similarly content learned without actual applications to real-world problems may not be of any significant or lasting value" (Sharma 1981, p. 65). Burns and Richardson (1980) indicate that students' inability to connect arithmetical processes to real-life situations is the foundation for their difficulties in problem solving. In most situations, we teach abstract computational skills prior to, and independently of, problem solving. Too much emphasis on computational drill and rote memorization can be counterproductive in developing the cognitive flexibility needed for problem solving. It would be much more relevant for students to acquire problem-solving skills through word problems that relate to real-life contexts. Students need to see the acquisition of computational skills as an integral and useful component to solving problems, in contrast to viewing them as abstract recipes for attaining answers—as arithmetic worksheets.

The acquisition of a mathematics-symbol system solely may lead to a loss of students' intuitive problem-solving abilities (Carlson, Gruenwald, and Nyberg 1982). We should capitalize on students' daily natural language and environmental experiences as catalysts to developing and understanding the importance of computational skills and the ability to recognize, describe, and solve complex mathematical concepts.

Word problems seem to be an appropriate vehicle for introducing arithmetic concepts because they afford a multitude of rich and varied experiences upon which students can construct their mathematical knowledge. Initially, word problems should appeal to students' egocentricity and be presented as real-life situations to help them to understand and to generalize the language of mathematical operations (as it appears in real situations) to an abstract symbol system. Students' success with word problems depends on their ability to analyze problem components and to determine appropriate processes needed for a correct solution.

It would seem that word problems should appeal to students' intuitive senses. They should offer opportunities to manipulate physical objects and materials as students progress from a level of concrete operational thought to formal-operational thought, in which they consider verbal statements and propositions. In addition, the ability of children to categorize the environment into what is critical and what is not critical—that is, to observe the environment selectively and to analyze information—occurs at approximately the same time. We must remember that students are in a continual stage of transition from one stage to the next. The environment therefore must provide sufficient experiences at a concrete level and with manipulations to help students transfer mathematical-language concepts and mental operations to the more abstract level needed for problem solving.

The discussion on problem-solving strategies that follows is considered as both a prerequisite to, and an integral component of, the other instructional strategies presented in this chapter (computation, money and time, fractions and decimals, and higher mathematical concepts). Problem-solving strategies should be infused into the total mathematics program; word problems appeal to students' intuitive sense and are the foundation for developing complex mathematical abilities.

Developing problem-solving experiences. Word problems should enable students to improve their problem-solving abilities and to develop an understanding of arithmetic processes. According to Goodstein (1981), verbal problems should:

1. Rely on a natural language format in contrast to mathematical symbols to communicate quantitative information
2. Provide the data as a means to acquiring the information needed for correct solution to the problem
3. Direct students' cognitive processes obtaining an answer to a specific question
4. Require students to process the information actively, that is, to understand the meaning of the problems prior to generating the correct response
5. Afford students opportunities to evaluate their performance based on appropriate use of strategies and decision making in contrast to attainment of the correct response

Word problems should reflect the real world and be meaningful and interesting to students. They should be consistent with students' cognitive capabilities and interests and help them to organize and integrate mathematical ideas and processes as an impetus for developing their mental structures. The activities that follow are helpful in developing students' problem-solving abilities.

Word problems should incorporate anything that relates to students' environmental experiences and use props, students' names, and *action*. Students should be provided opportunities to act out the verbal directions in a problem to aid their understanding and interpretation. This approach focuses on students' experiencing real-life situations; the action appeals to their intuitive sense and helps them to verify and monitor their predictions. Word problems should complement students' cognitive functioning. At first they may be relatively simple, and they should increase in complexity as students mature and develop a knowledge base upon which to relate new information.

Once students have acted out the word problems, the teacher may introduce the mathematical symbols and record the appropriate equation for each problem. This approach helps students to connect the symbols with their actual experiences, and it focuses on the importance of translating action into a numerical sentence or equation (Burns and Richardson 1981). Eventually, students themselves record the mathematical equations. Students should also have the opportunity to generate their own word problems, for which the teacher serves as recorder. This variation on a language-experience approach allows teachers to incorporate numerical equations as a "shortened" version of the story.

Problem-solving activities at first should rely heavily on the use of concrete manipulatives (cars, dolls, balloons, cookies) and then progress to the use of "token" manipulatives (blocks, buttons) to represent the information presented in the word problems. Students need opportunities to build physical models of mathematical symbols to demonstrate their understanding prior to writing equations.

An extension of this approach to verbal problem solving relies on using pictures in conjunction with manipulatives to facilitate students' active processing of information in their solution of verbal problems. Story problems can be generated around a specific theme (a grocery store) or student interest (jogging). Visual aids also help teachers to analyze students' problem-solving strategies as they arrange and rearrange the manipulatives to construct their responses. The reader is referred to Cawley et al. (1979) for a more extensive description of the use of visual aids for verbal problem solving.

Additional activities that facilitate students' problem-solving abilities include drawing pictures to illustrate equations, writing individual word problems for other students to act out and to solve, and completing unfinished word problems. This activity focuses students' attention on the questions in word problems because they must write the math question based on the situation described in the unfinished story and must also solve the problem (Burns and Richardson 1981). A variation on this theme is providing students with problems that cannot be solved because information is missing. In this case, students must determine the missing information, supply the information, and solve the problem.

The cloze procedure is also an activity that requires students to determine missing information before they can solve the problem. A cloze procedure requires that students insert words or mathematical terms that have been deleted. It helps to direct students' attention to the relevant information contained in a problem (Cawley et al. 1979), and to organize and structure the data needed to solve the problem.

In summary, problem solving focuses students' attention on the questions asked and helps students to recognize relevant data needed to solve a problem. Once they have isolated this information, it must be processed by encoding it into a mathematical sentence or equation. In addition, students must remember the actions associated with the operation needed to solve the equation. This requirement includes remembering details and proper sequence. As a result of the requirements for successful problem solving, we may attain a concomitant benefit of increasing students' reading comprehension skills. Word problems help students to understand complex mathematical processes in a way that makes sense and can be transferred to their daily experiences. Problem solving is an inquiry process in which students make observations, organize information, and express mathematical ideas as a basis for understanding their environments.

Computational Strategies

All arithmetical operations should be introduced through the use of study problems. Research by Carlson, Gruenwald, and Nyberg (1982) indicates that many children use intuitive reasoning to solve addition problems in the context of everyday situations. Intuitive reasoning may be considered as the base for developing students' conceptual understanding of the arithmetic operations. *Addition* is combining groups into larger groups. If students understand this concept and have an understanding of number symbols as indicators of a given quantity of actual objects, common errors such as $23 + 6 = 89$ will occur less often. Also, if students understand the concepts of quantity, conservation, and place value, errors such as $16 + 9 = 115$ will not occur.

The use of familiar situations and objects in word problems will help to develop a concept before the symbols of the plus (+) sign or the equal (=) sign are introduced. Children can be presented with questions such as: "If we have 4 oranges *and* 2 bananas, how much fruit do we have?" The problems should incorporate familiar objects—students at the concrete-operational level are often egocentric and unable to operate with unfamiliar objects.

This is also an appropriate time to introduce the commutative property of addition, in which word problems are introduced in two ways—that is, "If we have 2 green balls *and* 4 red balls, how many balls do we have?" and, "If we have 4 red balls *and* 2 green balls, how many balls do we have?" Discussion should concern whether the manner in which we group or talk about objects makes any difference in "how many" objects we have altogether. Groupings of token objects may be used to represent real objects, such as, 3 girls (one pile) and 4 boys (a second pile) are 7 children when the piles are pushed together.

The abacus is also an excellent tool to use in moving the child from the manipulation of the actual concrete objects to a symbolic level. The abacus is a manipulative device. The abacus designed for the blind is constructed with only one five counter. It has a firm backing to prevent accidental movement of the counters, thereby making it an excellent device for learning disabled students. Since all the counters on the abacus for the blind are white, the confusion of perceptual interference is eliminated for the learning disabled student. Students should be allowed to explore their strategies as they intuitively find the answer, either through the actual physical manipulation or through the mental manipulation of the objects. Teachers should model the language of the operation without the specific vocabulary, that is, "4 oranges and 2 bananas are 6 fruits" when summarizing the child's activity. The next step involves allowing students to summarize their own activities prior to introducing the symbol.

When introducing the plus sign, the teacher may wish to make a three-by-three-inch card with the + symbol and one with the = symbol. The plus sign is then inserted between the two groups and read as *and*. The mnemonic strategy of the sign can be explained as two parts being joined together, that is, "This part is put with this part." When students understand this concept, they can be introduced to the word *plus* as another word meaning *and*. It is often helpful to generate other words that can be used, such as *with*. A second pile may be constructed to match the total quantity of the two piles rather than pushing the piles together. Students continue to talk their way through the operation. The equals sign can then be introduced as the symbol for the word *are*, or *makes*, which has been used in the verbal operation.

Piaget points out that addition (the union of groups into a larger group) is the basic operation upon which all other computational operations are constructed. It is important therefore that the concept is well understood because it is a basic mathematical structure upon which other mental structures are reconstructed to higher levels of complexity.

Teachers should avoid the temptation of substituting procedural learning for the sake of moving on to the next objective. By using the concrete groupings and the symbol cards as guides, students begin to write the equation for the operation, first in the horizontal array and then in the vertical array. The concrete manipulatives and iconic representations are then phased out of the activity, and the children work only with symbols. However, additional activities should continue to tie the symbol to a real quantity—such as 2 *Mars* bars and 3 *Hershey* bars. Students should be encouraged to make up story problems for written equations and, conversely, to write equations for story problems. We should be very careful to avoid teaching students to look for key words or cues in word problems. Key words may cause students to rely on procedural computation without understanding. Also, key words may occur in misleading usage.

Once students understand the basic concepts, the basic facts may be learned by rote for efficiency. The facts of $+ 0$, $+ 1$, and $+ 2$ seldom are a problem to learn at an automatic or rapid response level. Most children also find the doubles easy to learn. If the combining of groups has emphasized the commutative property, students should not have a large number of facts to commit to memory. Flash cards and various reinforcement activities may be used. Five to ten minutes of practice each day will usually result in mastery of the basic facts if the concepts are well understood. Rather than learning all the $+ 3$ facts and all the $+ 4$ facts, it is often better for students to subdivide a given number into all the possible subgroups that may be combined to that total and to learn that set of facts. Grouping to 10 or using a known fact and "one more" can often help with learning the facts. Often finger counting is used efficiently by children in the early stages of computation, but it may become an inefficient and limiting crutch in later computation. The internalization of the dot on the symbol or of a number line is more efficient if the child seems to need a reminder.

When teaching two-digit addition, teachers should avoid referring to the digit in the "tens" position as a single-digit number. Rather, it should be named as twenty or thirty during the regrouping process. In addition, teachers may wish to use regrouping blocks with "fair trade" during the concrete-grouping activity. When moving to the symbol use it should be rewritten with expansion.

$$23 = 20 + 3$$
$$12 = 10 + 2$$
$$\overline{35 = 30 + 5}$$

The process should be rewritten with expanded notation first in computations that do not require regrouping. When regrouping is necessary, the children can see the integration of all operations and not as separate or extra operations. All computations should be tied to word problems to avoid procedural learning. When students are regrouping, the term *carrying* should be avoided because it often encourages a procedural computation. Also, teachers should model and encourage the use of an adequate amount of paper and organization in the spacing of problems.

Students should be required to estimate the answer before the actual computation and to monitor their work. "Does this answer make sense?" or "Does this answer seem like it is right?" If the student has developed a structural understanding of the computation, many common errors will not occur, and the student can often catch the errors that do occur. It is important to emphasize the process by which students attain the answer rather than the "right" or "wrong" of the final product. When children have a sound understanding of the mathematical and computational concepts, they often enjoy checking their own work using a calculator. When an error is made, students should be encouraged to check that problem for an error. If a student does not recognize the error, the problem should be reworked while thinking aloud to help determine the student's mathematical reasoning and the basis for his or her understandings or misunderstandings. We should then remediate misunderstandings before attempting any further instruction. One strategy to remediate students' difficulties in arithmetic computation is the Columbo method as illustrated on pages 183–184.

Subtraction should be taught as an extension of addition by beginning with word problems. For example, "Sue brought 3 dolls and Mary brought 2 dolls. How many dolls are there altogether?" After the child answers, "There are 5 dolls," we may continue by saying, "Mary took her 2 dolls home. How many were left?"

A HELPFUL HINT

The ultimate goal is to facilitate the students' regular classroom activities. For this reason, students must learn to copy and work problems from a text. The simple strategy of circling the number of the problem will avoid the common error of adding it as part of the problem. If a child has difficulty writing the numbers in proper alignment, the use of grid paper will often help. Using spirit duplication on low pressure, run off grid paper of an appropriate size so that the guide lines serve to place the work without causing visual interference for the child. If the child has difficulty isolating the problem to be copied during the copying process, a file card with an appropriate-size window cut will help to isolate the problem from the others on the page. If the child tends to mix the lines of the problem, an acetate covering over the window with a narrow black line can help direct the copying process. Students should be taught to express a number as an entity rather than as a sequence of numbers to help avoid the problem of mixing the numbers. That is, students should think of and read the number 242 as two hundred forty-two rather than two-four-two.

Students then should move to the following type of problem: "There are 7 cookies. Bob ate 3 cookies. How many cookies are left?" Again, concrete aids may be used to help students to develop the understanding that just as addition puts subgroups together into a larger group, the larger group can be then divided into the subgroups. It is important to follow the same format used in developing the concepts of addition. First, we should work with concrete manipulatives and then integrate the use of token concrete or semiconcrete representations, add the symbols, and move to the written equation. The minus sign can be designated mnemonically as the finger that pushes objects out of a group.

The learning of the basic facts must be tied to the basic addition facts. For some children the use of "8 and what make up 12?" is more integrative and easier to learn than the "12 minus, or take away, 4" approach. Many mnemonics and strategies, such as signing the facts or using rhymes, exist. However, it is best to avoid those that do not aid in conceptual understanding and are only imposed gimmicks because they encourage relying on crutches and superficial learning and may interfere with students' conceptual understanding.

Regrouping often causes difficulty for learning disabled children. If the child has a firm grasp on place value, many errors do not occur. The common error is to subtract the smaller number from the larger number: $43 - 16 = 33$. When teachers introduce subtraction as a "taking some out of a group" it is best to work with word problems and concrete manipulatives that involve regrouping. "There are 21 children in the classroom; 16 of them are eating hot lunch. How many children are eating cold lunch?" Students should work the problem intuitively if possible. They can then represent the problem with the place-value blocks. Students will have to "trade" or regroup. If the concepts are developed as an integrated whole, they are less likely to use a procedural approach on computation and will monitor both process and product. Again, it is important for students to estimate the answer and to write the estimate to the right of the place for the answer. They can then place a box around it as a way to monitor their work at the end of the computation, that is, "Does it make sense?" Students may use cognitive behavioral strategies to guide their work as in the box below. This strategy is taught using the classical five-step procedure as outlined by Meichenbaum and Goodman (1971) and illustrated in chapter 10.

When giving the child problems to work, it is important to keep the major focus on the use of the operation in life situations. In other words, word problems should be relevant to a student's life experiences. (If the problems are written, the reading level should be at such a level that the child can read the problem with ease. It may be necessary to present the problems orally.) Whether giving the problems as word problems or written equations, the operations of addition and subtraction may be mixed to avoid the use of rote computations.

Multiplication should be introduced as repeated addition. For example, "Joe bought 3 cookies and Bob bought 3 cookies. How many cookies do they have?" The students display the tokens for the two groups of cookies. (The students are probably beyond the need for the actual object itself by this time. The token can be used as a counter for the real thing. Again, the objects in the problems should be related to the students' environment.) After the students have answered for the two groups, the complexity of the problem may be increased to "Joe bought 3 cookies, Bob bought 3 cookies, and Harry bought 3 cookies. How many cookies do they have?" The activity should continue, increasing the number of classmates who are bringing the cookies.

COGNITIVE BEHAVIORAL STRATEGY

"What am I going to do? The sign is subtraction." *or* "The problem asks how many are left" *or* "The problem asks how much of the ———— is ————, so I will subtract.

I start with 26 so my answer will be less than that. I'm going to take away 8. 8 is close to 10 so my answer will be close to 16.

Will I need to trade? I have 6 ones and I want to take away 8 ones.

Yes, I will need to trade one of the tens for 10 ones. That will leave 1 ten and make 16 ones. 16 ones take away 8 ones leaves 8 ones (or 8 and what number makes a group of 16. 8 and 8 are 16. So I'll have 8 left).

Now I'll do the tens column. I have 1 left there and I'm not going to take away any tens so I'll have 1 ten in my answer, ok, I have 1 ten and 8 ones. My answer is 18. I figured it would be close to 16. Is it close to 16? Yes, I must be right."

Multiplication should be introduced as a shortcut for adding the same number over and over. If the child has a structured concept of addition, the concept of multiplication is a simple extension of a quicker way to add. Students should be provided repeated addition experiences to illustrate the benefit of a shortcut. Again, the problems should be in the context of real-life situations.

When moving to the written equation, the multiplication symbol can be presented as the addition symbol twisted ($\times$) to a faster speed. The teacher should present the idea of the problem as being written in all arrays. The basic facts can be presented and then memorized for efficiency. Often students will benefit from constructing their own multiplication tables by grouping and adding. For the higher values, this may be a task that consumes time beyond the return. Most children have little difficulty with the twos and the doubles. These basic facts can often be used with addition to facilitate the learning of the other facts. Again, as with the basic facts of addition and subtraction, it is best to provide short repeated practice of small parts until the facts are known at the automatic level. Many mnemonics are available, but these may increase the memory load or complicate the computational process.

When working with multiple-digit numbers, the students' common errors include adding rather than multiplying; splitting the process and combining addition and multiplication; not adding in the regrouped values, or adding them before multiplying. Another source of error is the incorrect placement of numbers and consequently an incorrect addition sequence. Teachers should emphasize that the number in the tens position is a tens value and should not refer to it as a ones number. In the problem 23×12, teachers should *not* refer to the 20 in 23, as a 2 or to the 10 in 12 as a 1. In writing the problem, the process is to work from right to left, rather than left to right. If the child is trying to use only a procedural method, confusion often results. If students are operating from the conceptual cardinal-number orientation, they will realize that the ones are completed prior to multiplying the tens and so on. This also will help in spacing, because students realize that they are multiplying by 10, not 1, and they can monitor the process. Cognitive behavior modification strategies can be used to help students to generate their own monitoring strategies.

Division should be presented as the breaking up of a large group into a number of smaller but equal groups. "Fair sharing" is a concept that children can understand. For example, "We have 12 flowers, and there are 6 children. How many flowers can each child have?" "If we have 4 children, how many flowers can each child have? If we have 3 children, how many flowers can each child have?" Students may work with manipulatives or token counters until the idea of equal groups is firmly established. Then the number of groups may be increased until the child realizes the efficiency of short-cut methods. Once students understand the concept of division, facts may be presented. Students should be led to see the relationship between the multiplication and division facts. If students can generate the nature of the relationship on their own, understanding will be more complete. As with the use of the addition facts to facilitate the learning of the subtraction facts, the multiplication facts may be used to facilitate the learning of division facts, that is, "3 times *what* equals 24."

Working with multiple-digit numbers can be very difficult for some students. We can help them to realize that errors have been made if they monitor the idea that the answer must be smaller than the large group that they are breaking into smaller groups.

Common division errors include: repeatedly dividing rather than increasing the divisor and using only part of the divisor. Problems with zero in the answer cause difficulties. Students should be taught to round out and estimate for division. The multiplication for this estimate should be completed at the side of the paper and the number monitored to determine if it is too large. Next, one additional divisor should be added to check, "Will one more sharing make it too much?" The number is adjusted or entered into the division problem. This work should be written at the side of the paper until the students are fairly proficient at estimating to avoid having the problem obscured by the regrouping notations. It may be necessary to use a tachistiscopic card to block off the portion of the problem with which the child is working, since the numbers can become bewildering. It is important to emphasize the placement of numbers in the quotient in relationship to the place value of the dividend. Again, care should be taken in using mnemonics to avoid the use of procedures in lieu of conceptual understanding.

Division by zero is sometimes taught in an abstract method that is too difficult for learning disabled children to understand. An effective way to teach division by zero is to use a bag of marbles or M&Ms. For example, the teacher may say, "I'm going to divide this bag into groups of zero for you." and then reach into the bag and take out a group of zero. This activity may be repeated over and over until the students realize that we can put our hands in the bag and bring out zero for many, many times. *Infinity* is a term already in the vocabulary of many and can be introduced and explained to the others in conjunction with this activity.

Strategies to Learn About Money and Time

Money. Instruction about money should follow a sequence through-out students' education. Money is an area that should be taught with small, frequent, and interspersed lessons. Real money should be used if possible when dealing with coins. Children will usually accept the trust that is given them and not take real coins. However, often they may regard play money as not having any real value and walk off with it. For many children the manipulation of the real coins, with their weight and texture, aids the learning process. Replicas of coins are needed to help students progress from actual coins to the abstract symbol system. The sequence for teaching money is as follows:

1. Discuss the use of money to develop the concept of value and the understand-ing that it is used in exchange for goods and services. We must be careful to use terms within the child's vocabulary to avoid imposed verbal learning.
2. Children learn the names of the coins and to recognize them on sight.
3. Develop an understanding of the values of the coins and introduce the cent sign (¢). It is often confusing to learning disabled students that the smaller dime is worth more than the larger penny and nickel. Therefore, teachers should be very careful in their use of *larger* and *smaller*.
4. Learning the equivalent value of coins is the next step. For most children, it seems easier to learn first that 5 pennies equal a nickel and, second, that 10 pennies or 2 nickels equal a dime, rather than that 5 pennies equal a nickel, 10 pennies equal a dime, and 25 pennies equal a quarter.
5. Counting groups of mixed coins totaling less than $1.00 is next. It is impor-tant to include odd amounts such as 62¢ or 78¢. Students should be taught to start with the larger coins and to use counting by 5s or 10s, counting the pennies last. If they have a large number of pennies they should be taught to group them by 10s.
6. Students should next be given amounts less than $1.00 that they can match with coins. They should use several different groupings to reach each amount.
7. Making change for amounts up to $1.00 is next. Students should learn to count change and check their work with a calculator. A menu from a popular restaurant is useful for this activity.
8. Bills larger than $1.00 may be discussed now. Many children are intrigued by large-denomination bills, and a field trip to the bank may be an interesting learning experience.
9. Students should next learn to write amounts larger than $1.00 and to count those amounts.
10. The next step is to add amounts of money. This is also a foundation for decimals. Newspaper ads and catalogs are useful.
11. Making change for amounts over $1.00 is learned next.
12. Older children should learn to write checks. They are often surprised that the cursive signature is required. Bank accounts (both checking and savings) should be introduced to junior high school students. The topic should be an important unit for high school students.

Time. The first instruction in time should be to develop an understanding of the concept of time as a unit and as a sequence of events. Then students are ready to learn to tell time using a clock and to understand the standard designations of time. The sequence for developing this understanding is as follows:

1. Students must understand the ordering and the sequencing of the day. Discussion of what they do from the time they get out of bed in the morning until the time they go to bed at night will help them develop this concept. Pictures to represent these activities can be drawn and sequenced.

2. Discussion of time can be extended to longer periods such as the week, month, and year, or other combinations of time periods, using the activities with which the child is familiar. Holidays can often be used to help the students develop this sequence.

3. Children also need to develop an understanding of the passage of time. The concept of "How long?" can be developed on familiar activities such as the length of TV shows and classroom activities. Short intervals of time can be understood by such activities as tapping a foot for one minute and then two minutes or standing on one foot.

4. Children should then estimate the duration of one minute in a variety of activities, such as closing their eyes and listening to music. They often suppose that the speed of the activity determines the speed of the passage of time. For example, learning disabled students may feel that time goes faster when they run rather than when they walk. A wide variety of activities are needed to help students develop the concept of time duration.

5. Once students understand the concept of time and the vocabulary of time (minute, hour, day, week, month, and year), they are ready to learn to tell time and to use a calendar.

The first step in teaching how to tell time is to have the child count from 1 to 60 on a number line. The child then superimposes a 1-to-12 number line on the 1-to-60 number line (the 1-to-12 number line should be the same *actual length* as the 1 to 60), counts off every five units, and marks them in different colors. This number line is then placed on a large clock with the hands removed or on a teacher-made clock face of the appropriate size without hands.

The 1-to-60 number line will correspond with the minute markings on a clock, and the 1-to-12 number line will correspond to the hour markings on a clock. This will help the child understand the function of the clock face. The minute hand is then attached and used to indicate the passage of time in minutes. This hand can be used to mark off the passage of activities in the classroom. When this concept is well understood, the hour hand may be attached and used to indicate how many times the minute hand has gone around.

Piaget points out that confusion occurs when the language "before the hour" is used in learning to tell time because of the negative aspect it imposes about the passage of time. For this reason and because digital clocks are so common, it is important to use the form related to "so many minutes" after each hour. This form will also help to preserve the continuum of the time line; and it matches digital time. It must be pointed out to students that the hour hand does not remain on the one-hour designation and then jump to the next hour after sixty minutes have gone by, but rather it creeps along between the designations as the minute hand is marking off the full turn. This can be illustrated by using a clock with an easily movable hour hand and making the abrupt move. Children will observe and note that such an abrupt movement does not really happen. For some children, looking at the gears inside the clock helps to explain the slow movement of the hour hand during the hour.

Strategies to Learn about Fractions and Decimals

Fractions.   Fraction concepts should be developed slowly by using familiar situations. In addition, work with fractions should be practical and simple. For example, 23/56 is not a fraction that occurs commonly in real life; its use is only a computational procedure for most children. A variety of concrete materials are necessary at all levels of fraction learning. Much of the difficulty children have with fractions is due to the fact that fractions can represent part of a single unit (one-half of a cookie) or part of a group of units (one-half of ten cookies). Therefore, materials should be of different shapes, dimensions, and groupings.

Children often understand that fractions are parts, but they do not understand that the parts must be equal parts—"You took the big half" indicates this misunderstanding. If children do not have operational conservation structures, they will be bound by the perception and believe that cutting the object into parts has increased the quantity "because it looks like more." Children at this level are only able to understand that fractions are parts. Once they do have operational conservation, they are ready to learn the meaning of fractions and how to use them. The sequence for learning fractions that seems to work best includes: separating the fraction into equal parts and the naming of those parts; reading and writing fraction symbols; comparing and ordering fractions; finding equivalent parts; and relating mixed fractions and improper fractions.

Students may begin by cutting a variety of objects into equal parts; graph paper can guide their divisions. Halves, thirds, and fourths should be presented first. Students' understanding of fractions is indicated when they know that fractions are divided into equal parts, and the naming of the parts indicates the number of parts taken (the first number) and how many equal parts comprised the whole of these fractions (the second number). In other words, they know that one-fourth means one part out of four equal parts. Once students have mastered this concept they are ready to learn about fifths, sixths, sevenths, and eighths. After working with concrete objects and cutting fractional pies, students should move to coloring parts of pictured objects and graph-paper shapes.

As students learn the vocabulary that designates parts, they can be introduced to the written symbol. The bar in the fraction can be described as meaning "out of." In the verbalizations during the previous activities, students usually learn this step with little difficulty. Practice should be provided for a wide variety of fractions and with a wide variety of materials. Students should cut objects and designate each fractional part. They should display the groupings for written fractions and then write the fraction for these groupings.

The concept of the fraction as division of a group of units may be presented when students understand the fraction as a division of a single unit. A variety of groups should be used. Large circles divided into fractional units may serve as a guide for the fractional groups and can be a valuable aid.

For learning equivalent fractions, students should make their own fraction kit. All sheets of paper used to make the kit should be the same color. Learning disabled children are often perceptually bound and will learn color equivalency rather than fractional equivalency. Squares are easier to cut into equal parts than are circles; therefore, the child should use square shapes. (The teacher should make a classroom kit using circles that the child can use later to help generalize the concept of equivalency.) The child should have an uncut sheet for the unit of one and equal-size sheets that are divided into halves, fourths, eighths, sixteenths; and thirds, ninths, and twelfths. Students should write the symbol for each fractional part on the parts as they make them. This kit is useful to compare fractions. The child should write the equivalency during the comparisons—$\frac{1}{2} = \frac{2}{4}$. In addition, students should predict what an equivalency will be and check the prediction with the kit.

Before actual formal computation of fractions is introduced, the use of story problems will help students to develop the concept. Teachers may use problems such as, "If you have one-half of a pie and I have one-half of a pie, how much do we have altogether?" and "If you have one-half of a pie and I have one-fourth of a pie, how much do we have altogether?" Students should be provided the time to understand that the pieces must be of equivalent size to be added. The most common mistake children make in adding fractions is this kind: $\frac{1}{2} + \frac{1}{4} = \frac{2}{6}$. If students have handled concrete fractional parts and added the concrete parts, they will not accept an answer of $\frac{2}{6}$ to the above problem.

Teachers may introduce the written equation once the students have had many experiences with addition using their own fractional kits and the classroom circles kit. First experiences with the written equation should rely on using the fraction kit to guide the addition and then to check the addition. Students should be permitted to express fractions using written equations only when they have internalized concepts of fraction equivalencies and can use them as a guide and check. Fractional problems should be expressed in both horizontal and vertical arrays.

Students should also use the organizational format of rewriting with equivalent fractions. Simple- and mixed-fraction problems may be included throughout the discussion. Some children will handle easily the mixed fractions and regrouping while other children will need repeated experiences. The materials and problems can be varied to provide interest.

Subtraction of fractions should follow the same pattern as addition of fractions. For example, patterns such as the following, "If you had a pie and you ate one-fourth of that pie, how much pie would you have left?" "If you had three-fourths of a candy bar and I had one-half of a candy bar, how much more do you have?" should be used until students (working first with the concrete kit) have internalized the concepts and can answer with ease. Then the written equation may be introduced. It is important to include mixed-fraction problems and problems with regrouping. We should avoid destroying a conceptual whole by breaking it into many different lessons. Learning disabled students often tend to approach each task as a new and different concept rather than to generalize to an entire concept. Therefore, it is important to keep all computations and all concepts unified.

In working with multiplication of fractions, it is difficult to use manipulatives. The conceptual understanding is easier for students if the multiplication term *of* is used interchangeably with *times*. An intuitive approach with word problems should be used to introduce multiplication of fractions. For example, "The recipe for cookies calls for one cup of chocolate chips, and you want to make only half a recipe. What is one-half of one cup?" After the child responds the teacher continues: "The recipe also calls for one-half cup of butter. What is one-half of one-half?"

A number of story problems of this type, which rely on familiar situations, may be used to develop the concept that in multiplication of fractions, the answer will be a smaller quantity rather than a larger quantity, as in multiplication of whole numbers. The algorithm is easier to use than the algorithm of addition or of subtraction since the fractions do not need to be equivalent. However, teachers should avoid the temptation to teach only the procedural computation. We may use a number of familiar situations of taking a part of a part to develop the understanding prior to using written equations. After the child can multiply simple fractions, satisfactorily, we can advance to the multiplication of mixed fractions.

Division of fractions can be developed from the multiplication concepts by comparing the relationship between multiplication and division of fractions with the relationship between multiplication and division of whole numbers. The first step in teaching division of fractions is to divide whole numbers by fractions and to count the number of units. For example, "If you had two pies and divided the two pies into fourths, how many pieces would you have?" Concrete manipulatives should be used. Students should then be introduced to dividing fractions by fractions. "If you have three-fourths of a pizza, how many pieces that are three-eighths of the pizza could you cut from this?" Again, manipulatives can be used to help the child find that the answer is two. This type of activity helps students determine the method of solving the problem and to write the algorithm. An explanation that division is the opposite of multiplication helps students to determine the procedural method of turning the fraction upside down prior to multiplying. With conceptual understanding, students are able to monitor their answers: "Does that make sense?"

Decimals.   Decimals follow fractions and may be introduced as another way to write a fraction that has a denominator of 10 or 100 or 1000.

The decimal point and the *th* ending are developed as the indicators of decimals. The relationship between decimal and whole-number place values may be developed by using number lines in which the 1 is used as the pivot point, in contrast to the decimal. Often children are confused about the absence of "oneths" if they think of the decimal as being the pivot point. Meter-long lengths of adding-machine tape cut into ten strips and marked for comparison, used with blocks of 100 graph-paper squares, will help students to develop the idea that as the pieces get smaller, it takes more pieces to be an equivalent amount.

Money can be used also to reinforce the decimal concepts, with pennies, dimes, and dollars. It is important that students think of the penny and dime as subunits of the dollar rather than as unique units. Students should be provided with a multitude of varied, hands-on activities to develop the concept of equivalency especially since many children may regard .23 as being larger than .5 based on their experiences with whole numbers in which 23 is larger than 5.

Addition and subtraction of decimals are usually easy for students to conceptualize from their experiences with money. The computations of multiplication and division of decimals are best taught by using the decimal in the fraction form of $\frac{3}{10}$, $\frac{6}{10}$, or $\frac{5}{100}$. The solution can then be computed again by using the decimal form, based on the understanding of the fractional computation.

Strategies to Learn About Higher Mathematical Concepts

Ratio.   Ratios are a particular type of fraction that may be introduced with informal activities in familiar situations. Students may be requested first to write ratios in the form of "8 chairs and 2 tables." When students write a number of these expressions to show relationships, they should be requested also to count the objects for the relationships as a prerequisite to the idea of comparisons. Once students have an understanding of these relations, the ratios should be reworded to the form of "8 chairs to 2 tables." Discussion should follow that indicates that in arithmetic we use special symbols instead of words to show how numbers fit together and that elicits from the student any ideas for showing this kind of relationship without using the word *to*. It is important to consider any systems that the students suggest. If students do not generate the proper notations, then we may wish to remind them of the meaning of the fraction designation and, after discussion, to have them rewrite the relationships in ratio form. At first, they should use labels when writing the ratios: 8 chairs/2 tables. If the students do not suggest renaming the ratio in its simplest form, they should be led with questions such as, "Is there a simpler way to show how many chairs there are to tables?" By using a number of relationships, students can write the ratios, gradually phasing out the labels. Students should then be presented with ratios of familiar things and asked to label the objects that are representations of those ratios. For example, there are (usually) four legs to each chair, two wheels to a bicycle, four wheels to a car, etc. A similar approach may be used in making a scale drawing of the classroom in which one inch equals five feet, or whatever scale (ratio) is appropriate for the area being drawn and the size of paper used.

Percent.   Percent may be seen as a group "out of" 100 and/or related to the decimal statement of a relationship. This is a common usage in everyday life and should be given enough time to develop a solid under-standing and computation ease. Sales tax may be used to facilitate students' understanding. Again, we should rely on many real-life situations to devel-op students' understanding. The most common error that students make in determining percentages is to use the quantities of the subgroups rather than the one subgroup and the total group. It is important that the term *out of* is used to reinforce the understanding of the relationship to the entire group.

Integers.   The concept of integers is often very difficult. Piaget points out that until students can visualize the position changes and trajectories of rotations, they cannot understand the concepts of integers. Often the anal-ogy of having money or borrowing money is used to develop the concept of integers. However, this may result in confusion because of language dis-abilities. A better approach may be to use a number line with both negative and positive numbers. The student should be able to move forward and backward on the number line with ease, on both sides of the zero, and to cross the zero during moves. This concept can be developed by using tokens. Then we can remove the actual number line and ask the student to move forward and back using the internalized line. For example, "You are on the positive (or plus) 6, and you move a negative (or minus) 3. Where are you?" Another example may be, "You are on the positive 5, and you move a negative 7. Where are you?" or "You are on the negative 7, and you move a negative 2. Where are you?" This activity should be repeated until the student can perform it with ease. Students should not be rushed as they develop this skill. Once the skill is mastered, we can introduce the written equation. If the student needs the structure of the concrete number line, it can be used in the introduction of the written equation, but it should be removed as soon as possible.

Exponents.   Exponents may be introduced by requesting the students to write the doubles of the multiplication table, and then asking if they would like to know a shorter and more efficient way to write doubles. Students may then be shown the "square sign" and requested to rewrite the doubles using the square. The concept may be developed further by asking students to complete such problems as 16 squared (16^2) or 126 squared. Since students must concentrate on the concept of the exponential designa-tion, they should be permitted to use the calculator for the calculations. They should write out the equations using the following form: $16^2 = 16 \times 16 = 256$.

When the students can compute squares with ease, the concept of cubes should be introduced by writing 2 cubed (2^3) and asking students what they think it means. If students have been writing the squares in extended form, most will realize that it means $2 \times 2 \times 2$. Again, using the calculator and writing the equation in expanded form, students should practice working a number of cubes. Next they should be exposed to higher exponents.

The next concept involves scientific notation in which 10 squared (10^2) and 10 cubed (10^3) are used to help students see the pattern. They may need some structured questioning to guide them in perceiving the pattern. Then they should move to larger numbers such as 10 to the 18th power (10^{18}) and 10 to the 23rd power (10^{23}). *To the* should be added to their vocabulary as students progress in the activity. Students should then be asked to estimate and write a number for the blades of grass on the football field and then attempt to write the number in the expanded form. Finally, the concept of 8×10 to the 16th power should be introduced and related to students' science courses and its application in that setting.

SUMMARY

The primary focus of instructional intervention for mildly and moderately handicapped students has been on facilitating overall language development in the areas of listening, speaking, reading, and writing. However, there has been growing interest and research emphasis within recent years concerning students' learning difficulties in mathematics and arithmetic. Characteristic difficulties relate to cognitive and affective factors, language and reading ability, and inadequate instruction. There are various theoretical perspectives around for which educators design instructional approaches that can be used to develop mathematics and arithmetic competencies. These approaches include neuropsychological, educational, and cognitive developmental perspectives, each of which has implications for the assessment of students' learning needs. Traditionally, assessment included both normative-referenced testing and informal assessment based on skills inventories in arithmetic. Both of these approaches were related to an empiricist view of learning. Little consideration was given to how students learned arithmetic skills and solved word problems. One new approach includes a clinical interview in which teachers question and probe students' thinking to determine their mathematical problem-solving strategies. These strategies then become the basis for designing instructional interventions that harmonize with students' thinking and their cognitive structures in mathematics.

Instructional strategies include using readiness activities as prerequisites for learning basic computational processes, and for understanding money and time, fractions and decimals, and higher mathematical concepts. It is important to stress problem-solving strategies in all instruction in mathematics. This approach helps to facilitate students' understanding that problem solving is an integral component of mathematics learning and not a separate unit. It is also important for teachers to help students organize their mathematics learning as a gestalt. Teachers often assume (perhaps inaccurately) that if students understand the mathematical operations involved in a given problem, they will be able to solve that problem. However, this may not be true, since problem solving appears to pose particular difficulties for mildly and moderately handicapped students. It may be necessary to develop students' mathematical language and vocabulary as a prerequisite to organizing and sequencing information needed for decision making and problem solving.

REFERENCES

BACHOR, D. G.   Using word samples as diagnostic information, *Learning Disability Quarterly* 2 (1979), 45–52.

BATTISTA, M.   Interrelationships between problem solving ability, right-left hemisphere processing facility and mathematics learning. *Focus on Learning Problems in Mathematics* 2 (1980), 53–60.

BLEY, N. S., AND C. A. THORNTON.   *Teaching Mathematics to the Learning Disabled.* Rockville, Md.: Aspen Systems Corp., 1981.

BRUNER, J. S.   On cognitive growth. In *Studies in Cognitive Growth.* New York: John Wiley and Sons, 1966.

BURNS, M., AND K. RICHARDSON.   Making sense out of word problems. *Learning* (1981), 27–30.

CAPPS, L. R., AND M. M. HATFIELD.   Mathematical concepts and skills. *Focus on Exceptional Children* 8 (1977).

CARLSON, J., L. J. GRUENWALD, AND B. NYBERG.   Everyday math as a story problem: The language of the curriculum. *Language Disorders and Learning Disabilities* (1982), 59–69.

CAWLEY, J.   Commentary. *Topics in Learning and Learning Disabilities* 1 (October 1981), 89–94.

————.   Math curricula for the secondary learning disabled student. Paper presented at a Symposium in Learning Disabilities in the Secondary Schools, Norristown, Pa., March 1975.

————, A. M. FITZMAURICE, R. A. SHAW, H. KAHN, AND H. BATES.   Math word problems: Suggestions for LD students. *Learning Disability Quarterly* 2 (1979), 25–41.

COHN, R.   Developmental dyscalculation. *Pediatric Clinic of North America* 15 (1968), 651–59.

COPELAND, R. W.   *How Children Learn Mathematics: Teaching Implications of Piaget's Research.* New York: Macmillan Co., 1979.

DeRUITER, J. A., AND W. L. WANSART.   *Psychology of Learning Disabilities.* Rockville, Md.: Aspen Systems Corp., 1982.

FLAVELL, J. H.   *Cognitive Development.* Englewood Cliffs, N.J.: Prentice-Hall, 1977.

GAGNE, R. M., AND L. J. BRIGGS.   *Principles of Instructional Design.* New York: Holt, Rinehart & Winston, 1974.

GALLAGHER, J., AND D. K. REID.   *The Learning Theory of Piaget and Inhelder.* Monterey, Calif.: Brooks-Cole, 1981.

GARWOOD, S. G.   *Educating Young Handicapped Children.* Rockville, Md.: Aspen Systems Corp., 1983.

GOODSTEIN, H. A.   Are the errors we see the true errors? Error analysis in verbal problem solving. *Topics on Learning and Learning Disabilities* 1 (October 1981), 31–46.

GRIMES, L.   Learned helplessness and attribution theory: Redefining children's learning problems. *Learning Disability Quarterly* 4 (1981), 91–100.

GUERIN, G. R., AND A. S. MAIER.   *Informal Assessment in Education.* Palo Alto, Calif.: Mayfield Publishing Co., 1983.

HRESKO, W., AND D. K. REID.   Five faces of cognition: Theoretical influences on approaches to learning disabilities. *Learning Disability Quarterly* 4 (summer 1981), 238–43.

KALISKI, L.   Arithmetic and the brain injured child. In E. Frierson and W. Barbie, eds., *Educating Children with Learning Disabilities: Selected Readings.* New York: Appleton-Century-Crofts, 1967.

KAMII, C.   Autonomy: The arm of education envisioned by Piaget. *Phi Delta Kappan* 65 (February 1984), 410–15.

——.   Encouraging thinking in mathematics. *Phi Delta Kappan* 64 (December 1982), 247–51.

KAMII, M.   Children's ideas about written numbers. *Topics in Learning and Learning Disabilities* 1 (1981), 47–59.

KOSC, L.   Neuropsychological implications of diagnosis and treatment of mathematical learning disabilities. *Topics in Learning and Learning Disabilities* 1 (October 1981), 19–30.

LARSEN, S. C., R. PORTER, AND B. TRENHOLME.   The effects of syntactic complexity upon arithmetic performance. *Learning Disability Quarterly* 1 (1978), 80–85.

LEZAK, M. D.   *Neuropsychological Assessment*. New York: Oxford University Press, 1976.

LURIA, A. R.   *The Higher Cortical Functions in Man*. New York: Baser Books, 1980.

——.   *The Working Brain: An Introduction to Neuropsychology*. New York: Penguin Books, 1973.

MCENTIRE, E.   Learning disabilities and mathematics. *Topics in Learning and Learning Disabilities* 1 (October 1981), 1–18.

MEICHENBAUM, D., AND J. GOODMAN.   Training impulsive children to talk to themselves: A means of developing self-control. *Journal of Abnormal Psychology* 77 (1971), 115–26.

MERCER, C. D.   *Students with Learning Disabilities*. 2d ed. Columbus, Ohio: Charles E. Merrill Publishing Co., 1983.

MOSES, N.   Using Piagetian principles to guide instruction of the learning disabled. *Topics in Learning and Learning Disabilities* 1 (1981), 11–19.

MYERS, P. I., AND D. D. HAMMILL.   *Methods for Learning Disorders*. New York: John Wiley and Sons, 1976.

NATIONAL COMMISSION ON EXCELLENCE IN EDUCATION.   *A Nation at Risk: The Imperative for Educational Reform*. Washington, D.C.: U.S. Department of Education, 1983.

NATIONAL COUNCIL FOR TEACHERS OF MATHEMATICS.   *An Agenda for Action: Recommendations for School Mathematics of the 1980's*. Reston, Va.: National Council for Teachers of Mathematics, 1981.

NEISSER, U.   *Cognition and Reality: Principles and Implications of Cognitive Psychology*. San Francisco: W. H. Freeman and Co., 1976.

PIAGET, J.   *The Child's Conception of the World*. Paterson, N.J.: Littlefield, Adams, 1963.

——.   *To Understand Is To Invent: The Future of Education*. New York: Viking Press, 1973.

REID, D. K., AND W. P. HRESKO.   *A Cognitive Approach to Learning Disabilities*. New York: McGraw-Hill Book Co., 1981.

ROBERTS, G. H.   The failure strategies of third grade arithmetic pupils. *Arithmetic Teacher* 15 (1968), 442–46.

SALVIA, J., AND J. E. YSSELDYKE.   *Assessment in Special and Remedial Education*. 2d ed. Boston: Houghton Mifflin Co., 1981.

SHARMA, M. C.   Using word problems to aid language and reading comprehension. *Topics in Learning and Learning Disabilities* 1 (October 1981), 61–72.

SHAW, R.   Designing and using non-word problems as aids to thinking and comprehension. *Topics in Learning and Learning Disabilities* 1 (1981), 73–80.

VELLUTINO, F. R.   Alternative conceptualizations of dyslexia: Evidence in support of a verbal deficit hypothesis. *Harvard Educational Review* 47 (1977), 334–54.

WHEATLEY, G., R. FRANKLAND, R. MITCHELL, AND R. KRAFT.   Hemispheric specialization and cognitive development: Implications for mathematics education. *Journal of Research in Mathematics Education* 9 (1978), 20–32.

YSSELDYKE, J. E.   Remediation of ability deficits in adolescents: Some major questions. In L. Mann, L. Goodman, and J. L. Weiderholt, eds., *Teaching the LD Adolescent*. Boston: Houghton Mifflin Co., 1978.

CHAPTER NINE

Social Development: Theory and Strategies

- What major factors influence social development? How do they interrelate?

- What are the observational learning components that appear to have the greatest influence on social development?

- How does the "successful resolution of conflict" concept affect social development, and what is the teacher's role in assisting students with such resolution?

- How similar, and how different, are the social-development age trends described by Freud, Erikson, Piaget, and Kohlberg?

- How may the life-space interview technique be used to build understanding of a given student's needs with respect to a crisis situation?

- How do the differing theories of empathy influence the manner in which a teacher may approach the question: How do I assist the student to develop acceptable, prosocial behavior?

INTRODUCTION

Social development is a multifaceted process in which children acquire competencies and behaviors that allow them to function, within a social environment, in a manner that is mutually beneficial to their well-being and that of others. Through social development, children and youths establish interpersonal relationships, acquire a sense of sex-role identity, and develop social standards and a sense of conscience.

Social development is influenced by many different socialization forces. These affect children's acquisition of the habits, values, and knowledge that facilitate their attainment of goals and enable them to function satisfactorily as members of society. In other words, children learn a complex network of clues that indicate the appropriateness of their actions for specific situations. For example, students' behavior in one teacher's classroom may be very different from their behavior in another classroom or on the playground.

A variety of social agents, or determinants, influence the socialization process needed for effective social interaction. These social determinants may include biological factors, social structure and cultural-group membership, the unique social interactions that children and adolescents have with parents and other caretakers, cognitive development, and situational determinants.

Children are not just passive recipients in their acquisition of social behaviors; rather they are active participants in their environments (Garwood 1983). Through their social interactions, students actively incorporate the standards of external social agents, and they process those mental structures that enable them to construct schemes or programs that facilitate appropriate behavior in other social situations.

Social development varies with children's social and cultural systems. Children are enculturated differently based on their cultural backgrounds and on parental beliefs related to the nature of children and how they should behave as adults. For example, American Indian, Oriental, and Anglo-American children are enculturated to have different values and behaviors. However, it appears that children's acquisition of social traits and skills is independent of culture and that the process of social development is similar across cultures and social systems (Garwood 1983).

The focus of the socialization process is on the acquisition of prosocial behaviors, which tend to draw people together and to diminish social distance. Prosocial behaviors enable us to deal with other people individually and in groups; to respond appropriately to expectations and standards; and to handle positive and negative emotions toward others in socially acceptable ways, each of which requires a delicate balance between dependency and autonomy. Prosocial behaviors are actions that aid or benefit another person or group of persons without the anticipation of external reward (Mussen and Eisenberg-Berg 1977). They include altruism, nurturance, cooperation, and participation in activities designed to reduce social injustices, inequities, and brutality. These behaviors seem to rely on early experiences in which children associate reward, satisfaction, and pleasure with the presence of other people. As children get older, their motives for assisting others are less dependent on external rewards and punishment and approval of authority. It appears that they have acquired internal motives and rewards as the basis for their prosocial behavior. This internalization may be due to their ability to decenter and to see others' perspectives and viewpoints.

Antisocial behaviors, on the other hand, tend to disrupt interpersonal behaviors and therefore increase social distance. These behaviors include aggression, anger and hostility, and acting out behaviors, all of which result from frustration of individual desires. Those who must cope with frustration may learn that aggression is rewarding and that they can attract attention from others. The consequent growth of antisocial behavior may be thus reinforced.

Our purpose in this chapter is to consider factors that influence the acquisition of prosocial behaviors, various theoretical approaches related to social development, and strategies to facilitate the development of prosocial behaviors among students. There is a relatively heavy emphasis on the various theoretical perspectives to social and emotional development. Theory can provide a solid foundation for understanding students' current school behaviors by providing insight into the influence of parents, peers, and other social agents on students' development. In addition, theory is the basis for conceptualizing methods to facilitate students' prosocial behaviors.

DETERMINANTS OF SOCIAL DEVELOPMENT

It is difficult to pinpoint one specific overriding factor that determines how an individual will react in social situations; however, a number of factors seem to influence social behavior.

Biological factors have been hypothesized as playing a critical role in social development. Fadely and Hosler (1980), Thomas and Chess (1977), and Thomas, Chess, and Birch (1968) suggest that inborn temperamental differences, which may be sex linked and/or have a genetic component, influence children's response to their caretakers. Temperament implies a general behavioral set that may be identified soon after birth and is somewhat distinctive to each child. Children's initial birth temperament and interaction with the environment influence the development of a child's unique personality. This dynamic interaction of nature and nurture shapes all aspects of social and emotional development (Fadely and Hosler 1980). For example, it is generally recognized that certain methods of child rearing work better with some children and have different outcomes, based on children's temperament.

Thomas and Chess (1977) have identified three temperament types to help predict children's behaviors in various situations. The "easy" child is fairly adaptable, has a high tolerance for frustration, shows positive response to new situations, and is able to transfer solutions from one situation to the next. The "difficult" child, on the other hand, shows poor adaptability, withdraws from new stimuli, is frequently negative and irregular in biological functions, and may react to frustration with explosive and tantruming behavior. The "slow to warm up" child is a combination of the easy child and difficult child, whose uncertainties in new or frustrating situations may cause clinging behaviors but who eventually adapts satisfactorily.

Temperament then appears to be an important consideration to help explain a child's total personality and the concept of socialization. Some children seem more irritable than others; some are more easily soothed. Some are more interested in their environments than others. It is difficult to apply universal themes to children's social development because of these differences.

Social structure and cultural-group membership influence children's behavior, their psychological functioning, and their proclivity toward prosocial behaviors. Parents raise their children within specific cultural and social systems. Therefore, it is important to consider those social variables (parental role and home ecology) that affect the family today as a basis for understanding children's behaviors within the context of society as a whole.

Social structure and cultural-group membership are powerful forces in shaping children's personality characteristics, social values, and sense of social responsibility. It is difficult, however, to determine the impact of cultural influences on prosocial behaviors. Therefore, we must look at socialization practices within cultures and at the influence of *socialization agents*, such as parents and other caretakers, peers, and teachers, to determine the development of prosocial behaviors.

Parents are the earliest and perhaps most significant socialization agents. This is evidenced by the fact that children's personal characteristics and behavioral dispositions acquired in a family setting seem to endure and resist change (Mussen and Eisenberg-Berg 1977). The following variables appear to affect children's overall social development and their acquisition of prosocial behaviors: modeling and identification, nurturance, disciplinary techniques, and maturity demands.

Children's observation of, and exposure to, powerful and nurturant models who perform prosocial acts is likely to increase their level of generosity, helping, and sharing. Parental modeling, generosity, and commitment to justice and equality are powerful antecedents of children's sharing and prosocial behaviors. These variables seem to produce a strong parent-child identification. This identification in turn increases children's tendencies toward imitating their parents' patterns of generosity and altruism. The old adage that actions speak louder than words appears to hold true. Prosocial behaviors seem to result from observing strong and consistent models who are nurturant and loving and who exhibit prosocial attitudes and behaviors, all of which strengthen children's tendency to identify with and to imitate parental models.

Parental nurturance, when accompanied by a consistent pattern of child rearing that features prosocial modeling, is effective in strengthening children's predisposition toward prosocial behaviors. Nurturance itself, through the demonstration of consideration, kindness, and sympathy, is a type of modeling of prosocial behavior. However, nurturance alone does not ensure that the child will exemplify altruistic behaviors.

Disciplinary techniques also affect children's attitudes toward themselves and others and help to mold their prosocial inclinations and behaviors. Parental control by physical force and aggressive behavior and the withdrawal of love and material resources teaches children that aggression can achieve desirable goals (Mussen and Eisenberg-Berg 1977). These power assertions are not very effective in stimulating children's interest in others because parents communicate external power and authority rather than praise for altruistic actions toward others. In addition, power is not conducive to internalizing control because it elicits hostility in children and provides a model for expressing outward hostility. Power assertions also make children's need for love less salient and interfere with arousing empathy. Finally, power assertions sensitize children to the punitive responses of adult authority and contribute to an externally focused moral orientation.

If parents reason with their children and stress the social implications of behavior, they model consideration for others and thereby strengthen children's moral autonomy and empathic tendencies toward others. Discipline through reasoning with children about the painful consequences of their actions is more conducive to developing prosocial attitudes and behavior. Through reasoning, parents demonstrate respect for their children and, at the same time, demonstrate that they maintain high standards for them (Kamii 1984; Thibault and McKee 1982).

Maturity demands and pressures for children to behave in mature ways, to achieve according to their abilities, and to assume affective maturity consistent with their chronological age are significant forces in students' manifestation of social responsibility toward others. Children gain in prosocial behaviors if they are encouraged to assume responsibility for others.

These factors—modeling and identification, nurturance, power assertiveness or reasoning, and maturity demands—are interdependent influences on children's prosocial behaviors. Other socialization agents, including peers and teachers, also influence students' behavior, motivation, and attitudes. Peer actions, whether they are aggressive or prosocial behaviors, are powerful models in the acquisition or modification of prosocial responses. We can assume, therefore, that repeated exposure to prosocial peer models might promote the development of strong, generalized, and enduring prosocial dispositions, as does exposure to parental and teacher prosocial models. Teacher rewards, punishment, and modeling also influence children's behavior. Unfortunately, there is little systematic research related to the influence of peer and teacher modeling of prosocial conduct in naturalistic or classroom settings. Strategies for facilitating the development of moral autonomy and prosocial behaviors may be found on pages 232–233.

All behavior is influenced by our interactions with environmental situations, and those interactions are regulated by personal characteristics, motives, needs, and cognitive abilities, as well as by the specific and immediate circumstances or social contacts. We have a tendency to behave consistently in social situations and over a period of time owing to internalized qualities, predispositions, and orientations. These factors seem to be shaped by socialization experiences, our capacity for empathy, role-taking ability, and the stage of moral reasoning we have attained. Individual differences in personal characteristics account for differentiated reactions in similar stimulus situations. However, the immediate situational context also helps to determine our reactions.

Situational determinants include unique events that alter an individual's personality and life patterns and propensity toward social behavior. Temporary external conditions, singular experiences, and transient feelings and moods are situational determinants that have short-term effects on our prosocial behaviors. Therefore, we must examine the immediate situational context to understand variable personal reactions to situations.

In summary, there appear to be numerous factors that influence the development of prosocial behaviors. Altruistic children appear to be self-confident and active; they are advanced in their moral reasoning, role taking, and empathy. They come from nurturant parents who are good models of prosocial behavior, use reasoning as the primary disciplinary technique, maintain high standards, and encourage early acceptance of responsibility for others.

At present, there is no comprehensive widely accepted theory of prosocial development. Construction of a comprehensive and meaningful theory of prosocial development should reflect the complexity of prosocial development and account for the interaction of cultural, familial, cognitive, and situational determinants.

SOCIAL DEVELOPMENT: AN EXPLANATORY STATEMENT

Theoretical perspectives to explain social development evolve from two divergent viewpoints—learning theory and developmental theory. Learning theorists view children's social behaviors as products of their environmental experiences; that is, children's behaviors are shaped by environmental consequences. As noted in chapter 1, learning theorists espouse a mechanistic view of a world that is composed of discrete elements that function in time and space. This mechanistic approach is related to an empiricist philosophy that views human beings as passive learners who are motivated, and acted upon, by external forces. Learning theorists emphasize quantitative changes in children's development. These changes in amount, frequency, and degree are gradual and occur in small increments as children develop (Miller 1983).

Developmental theorists view social development as a continuous and active process of change and refinement in which children's behavior becomes increasingly more complex, mature, and refined. Developmentalists maintain that the world is composed of individuals who are active and organized wholes that evolve continuously from one state to another. Developmental changes, from an organismic perspective, are qualitative changes that cannot be reduced to discrete elements; rather, they are characteristic changes that emerge at particular developmental stages. Most developmentalists, however, agree that changes are both quantitative and qualitative (Miller 1983). For example, as children become older, they are able to retain more items that are memorized in a rote manner (a quantitative change). At the same time, however, they may have developed a strategy for retaining information (a qualitative change), such as checking items on a grocery shopping list according to particular categories.

SOCIAL DEVELOPMENT: A LEARNING-THEORY PERSPECTIVE

The learning-theory approach to social development is derived from a viewpoint that reflects the influence of external factors (positive and negative reinforcement) on social behaviors. According to this perspective, children's social behaviors are shaped by parents and teachers.

The traditional learning-theory approach to social development relies on external environmental factors; that is, stimulation and reinforcement are the determinants of behavior. The student is a passive recipient of these external factors. Social development depends on antecedent (stimulus variables) and consequent (reinforcement/punishment variables) events as they relate to a particular response. Traditional learning theorists conceptualize social development as a learning process in which new social skills and abilities are acquired primarily because performance of these behaviors is rewarded by significant persons in the child's environment. Those behaviors that are not valued by a particular social system may be punished or at least go unrewarded—consequently, nonvalued behaviors slowly drop out of a child's behavioral repertoire.

Social Learning Theory

Social learning theory is a relatively new theoretical framework that is an outgrowth of the learning-theory perspective (Garwood 1983). It focuses on observational learning in social situations as the basis for acquiring new behaviors, and therefore considers modeling and imitation important to social development. Accordingly, learning is a combination of psychological principles and social conditions; learning that occurs through observation results from manipulation of internal cognitive variables (Miller 1983).

Social learning theory views learning as an unobservable process. It recognizes the importance of cognition to learning and focuses on an individual's active cognitive processing to select, extract, and maintain environmental information and to generate meaning from that information. This is in contrast to traditional learning theory, which distinguishes between learning and performance. Social learning theorists believe that we can observe someone's behavior and acquire new knowledge without actual performance. Performance is merely an overt manifestation of a learned behavior and an index of learning. For example, a child's performance on a test may indicate how much a child has learned in a particular subject area.

According to social learning theorists, reinforcement is not needed for learning, but rather, observation teaches the possible consequences of behavior. We learn through vicarious reinforcement in which we formulate expectations concerning behavioral outcomes without direct action or overt performance of a behavior. Learning is a cognitive process that is influenced by observation and modeling. Children learn from both live models and symbolic models (television or books) in which they acquire information in the form of symbolic representation of modeled activities. Another form of symbolic modeling is verbal mediation or instruction, which is translated into overt behaviors. An example of verbal mediation may be a driver-education teacher's instruction and demonstration to a student on how to drive a car.

Social learning theorists believe that students acquire social skills from their observation and imitation of others' social behaviors. Imitation is critical to the socialization process and is increased if children's models are powerful. In addition, social learning theory recognizes the importance of cognitive processes in mediating children's behavior as the children interact with the environment. Changes in behavior result from the reciprocal interaction of children with the environment. Social learning theory integrates operant conditioning and reinforcement with socialization and information processing. The accuracy of students' learning is influenced by cognitive capacities (attention and retention) and reinforcement (direct and vicarious), both of which serve as the basis for abstracting behavioral norms. Performance of social skills is determined by the accuracy of students' learning (attending to behavioral events and encoding and retaining those events), by motor reproductions that are based on physical integrities, and by motivation. Cognitive factors influence what is observed, how a person or event is perceived, how new information is organized for the future, whether observational learning has a lasting effect, and the effect of that learning on students' behavior (Miller 1983).

The quality of social development, it seems, results from the appropriate social behavior emitted by significant others in a child's environment. Children act like their parents, who play a crucial role in the early socialization process. Parents are the most consistent and salient models of behavior and dispensers of reinforcement. It would appear that if children are exposed to undesirable modes of behavior and excessive forms of punishment, they will have difficulty adapting to societal norms. Therefore, socialization during early childhood is critically important to children's overall development.

Children's early prosocial responses may be viewed as the consequence of reinforcement. If children are rewarded by praise, attention, or gifts for sharing or helping others in distress, these early responses will be strengthened and the likelihood of their subsequent repetition is increased.

As children become older, most prosocial urges, such as helping and generosity, appear to be controlled internally without any apparent external rewards. It may be assumed that the original controls were extrinsic; however, behavior soon becomes independent of external sanctions, and children administer their own rewards and punishment. Consequently, children learn which responses bring external praise, and they begin to praise themselves for these reinforced actions. They gradually acquire an internal cognitive representation of external rewards and are able to exercise control over their own behaviors; that is, they construct values and guidelines needed for self-regulation.

Social learning theory, however, appears incomplete since it does not consider the cognitive developmental forces that determine children's reactions to their socialization experiences. Does a child's level of cognitive development determine which adult behaviors will be observed and imitated and incorporated into previously acquired repertoires? It would seem that developmental changes are not just an outgrowth of socialization experiences. Rather, development intersects dynamically with environmental input to determine students' responses. We believe that social development results from students' critical interaction with their environment.

SOCIAL DEVELOPMENT: A DEVELOPMENTAL PERSPECTIVE

Discussion of social development from the developmental viewpoint will include the psychodynamic theories of Freud and Erikson and the social-cognitive theories of Piaget and Kohlberg. Developmental theory attempts to explain the course of development through a set of general principles or rules that specify the antecedents for change and identify those variables that modify the rate or nature of change (Miller 1983).

Psychodynamic Theory: Sigmund Freud

The psychodynamic theory of Sigmund Freud conceptualized human development in terms of unconscious motivation, which provides the impetus for behavior. From this perspective, social development is the acquisition of skills and abilities to control these unconscious motivational forces in a socially acceptable manner. Freud believed that children's early lives had great influence on their subsequent development. He was especially concerned with parents' reactions to children's emotions of fear, anger, love, and sexuality. In addition, he believed that there was a natural sequence of events that governed the expression of emotions and the acquisition of controls over these emotions. The primary task of early childhood, according to Freud, was the resolution of conflicts between an individual's inner needs and external pressures and demands, conflicts that often resulted in the erection of defenses against the individual's emotions. Freud believed that the first few years of life are critical in forming children's personalities. The early interactions between children's internal drives and their social environments set the pattern for later learning, social adjustment, and the ability to cope with anxiety. He believed that children could not be educated in the intellectual sphere until these emotional defense barriers were established.

Freud stressed the idea of a maturational timetable that controlled children's development. Progression from one psychosexual stage to the next occurs in an invariant manner and is determined by biological maturation. Movement occurs whether or not children are ready to progress to the next developmental stage. Each Freudian stage is characterized by a dominant trait that is integrated loosely into the next stage. The psychosexual stages do not evolve into succeeding stages, but rather each stage builds upon and dominates the previous stage. Freud's stages do not replace previous stages; therefore, regression to earlier behaviors or experiences may cause unbearable tension (Miller 1983).

Freud's theoretical perspective was rich with ideas concerning children's social development. He focused on children's internalization of parental or adult standards of behavior through identification—a defense mechanism in which children resolve conflicts by inculcating the adult standards of those they emulate—and on the superego, or conscience, which enables children, by themselves, to perform some of their parental- or adult-controlled functions. Altruistic predispositions and humanistic values are explained in terms of defense mechanisms and reaction formations. The concept of identification with parents helps to explain the acquisition of prosocial behaviors, that is, moral conduct and values. Identification influences the internalization and incorporation of humanistic values and patterns of prosocial behaviors as do parental and societal prohibitions (Mussen and Eisenberg-Berg 1977). Children often adopt their parents' nurturant, generous, and altruistic characteristics.

Psychosocial Theory: Erik Erikson

Ego psychologists are disciples of Freud who stress the dominant role of ego processes rather than instinctual self-gratification. These more recent psychoanalytic theorists reject the belief that the internalization of parental values and standards is the sole determinant of moral behavior. Rather, they emphasize both the influence of identification with significant others and the role of moral principles. Erik Erikson is an ego psychologist, who deemphasized Freud's biological approach and focused on the impact of societal influences on social development (Miller 1983). Erikson's theory presents a comprehensive social matrix that consists of the child, mother and father, other primary caretakers, the extended family, and the child's historical and cultural heritage.

Erikson accepts the basic tenets of Freudian theory, but he is more interested in the relationship between psychoanalysis and education. Erikson rejects the sexual nature of human motivation; he views ego development as more than the mere expression of sexual desires and aggressive urges. Ego development occurs as children synthesize the developmental and social tasks with which they are confronted during different stages of their lives and is responsible for an individual's overall social competency. It is a function of children's experience with reality and develops and matures as they decenter and no longer view the world as an extension of themselves.

Erikson's major contribution—the psychosocial stages of ego development—is the view of development as a continuous process that extends from birth to old age. According to Erikson, physical maturation and the social environment determine and exert societal demands on individuals, which help to shape their development. The successful resolution of these demands leads to the acquisition of social competencies, or ego capabilities, which enable individuals to resolve future conflicts.

Inherent in Erikson's theory is a maturational notion, or epigenetic principle, which states that anything that grows has a ground plan out of which the parts arise to form a functioning whole (Erikson 1968). Not all ego capabilities are present at birth, but rather each part has a time or a stage in which to emerge. During a particular stage, the focus of development is on a certain ability. The focus changes with each succeeding stage in the life cycle. Erikson stresses the successful resolution of conflicts or crises at various ages as opportunities for developmental progression. His theory is optimistic and focuses on children's affective development as an affirmation of their unique individuality within their social worlds.

Erikson's theory, like those of other developmental theorists, meets the requirements of stage theory. He has conceptualized eight stages of psychosocial development, each with varying environmental demands or crises, that are critical to the acquisition of particular ego capacities. The crises are described in terms of both positive and negative outcomes and change as children progress from one stage to the next. Ideally, children develop a favorable ratio in which the positive aspects dominate the negative outcomes. In table 9-1 is a brief description of Erikson's eight stages of psychosocial development. Further discussion can be found in Erikson (1968), Crain (1980), Biehler (1981), and Miller (1983).

Since physical maturation and societal expectations create the emotional crises or issues that must be resolved, children are often propelled into the next developmental stage even though a particular ego capability may not be developed fully at the preceding stage. For example, the physical changes of adolescence and the ensuing environmental demands may force a young adolescent into Erikson's stage of identity versus role confusion even though the youth has not resolved successfully the demands of the preceding stage of industry versus inferiority. Erikson believes that to become a fully functioning social individual, it is important to develop the ego capabilities inherent in a particular stage during that developmental stage. If childhood crises are not handled satisfactorily, the person continues to struggle in later life. Erikson is optimistic, however, that it is never too late to resolve any of the crises. Each stage is based on previous stages and influences future stages. Most people progress through the eight developmental stages; however, individual progress is unique owing to differ-

TABLE 9-1   Erikson's Stages of Psychosocial Development

Trust vs. mistrust (birth to 1 year)	Consistency, continuity, and sameness of environmental experience lead to trust; inadequate, inconsistent, and negative care may assure mistrust.
Autonomy vs. doubt (2–3 years)	Opportunities to explore world and develop skills lead to autonomy; overprotection and lack of support lead to doubt about self-control or environment.
Initiative vs. guilt (4–5 years)	Freedom to engage in activities and use language to express understanding leads to initiative; restrictions and parental failure to respond lead to guilt.
Industry vs. inferiority (6–11 years)	Freedom to be industrious and to create leads to industry; limitations in activities and criticism lead to inferiority.
Identity vs. role confusion (12–18 years)	Recognition of continuity and sameness in personality lead to established sex roles and occupational choice; inability to resolve identity crisis leads to role confusion.
Intimacy vs. isolation (young adulthood)	Fusing identity with another leads to intimacy; competition and combative interrelationships lead to isolation.
Generativity vs. stagnation (middle age)	Establishing and guiding next generation lead to generativity; concern with self leads to stagnation.
Integrity vs. despair (old age)	Acceptance of one's life leads to integrity; feeling that it is too late to compensate for missed opportunities leads to despair.

ent growth patterns. Social development, according to Erikson, is the acquisition of a multitude of ego capabilities that leads to identity and allows the individual to cope effectively with society. An individual is always a personality in the making; that is, an evolving system that develops and changes qualitatively as we progress from one stage to the next. The solution of the dilemmas of each phase generates the struggles for the next developmental conquest. The progression from a central problem or dilemma of one stage to the next is universal. Each person deals with the dominant theses of individual psychosocial phases. These theses are a series of critical steps, or turning points, that provide the possibilities for new solutions of previous struggles. The growth of human strength occurs in a sequence of stages that represent the development of the various parts of a whole psychosocial personality.

Social development is the successful resolution of conflict from opposing forces as we progress from one stage to the next. Erikson has an optimistic view of human nature in which children and adults seek to develop a positive sense of identity that gives coherence to their individual personalities. Development is a lifelong process in which some childhood conflicts may not be resolved satisfactorily until childhood is passed.

Erikson's theory helps us to place the current social status of mildly and moderately handicapped students in perspective. Did they have opportunities to develop a basic sense of trust during infancy, which resulted in a sense of autonomy and initiative? Or were their environments so meager in meeting their basic needs that they developed a sense of mistrust and concomitant feelings of shame, doubt, and guilt? As students entered school, were their feelings of industriousness thwarted by repeated failures and a sense of threat, which lead to inferiority? Students who experience failure, even though they are working harder, need to experience success to develop positive self-esteem and a sense of control over their lives that they *can* perform school tasks. Perhaps educators should help students to "work smarter" as opposed to working "harder," by teaching them strategies for learning "how" to learn. Finally, if students have not resolved the social crises and acquired the necessary ego capabilities at each of the previous stages, what is the impact on their sense of role identity during adolescence?

Erikson's theory highlights the effects of social influences and environmental forces that interface as children evolve into totally functioning and unique personalities. His observations help to clarify the qualitative differences among students' behaviors and serve as a guide to foster appropriate growth at each developmental stage. Erikson provides a framework for helping students to negotiate the social crises that occur in school. The information in table 9-2 outlines some inappropriate behavioral manifestations of students who have not acquired the necessary ego capabilities at Erikson's first five stages of psychosocial development and suggestions for teachers when working with these students.

TABLE 9-2   Characteristic Behaviors and Suggested Environmental Adaptations

ERIKSON'S STAGE	INTERVENTION STRATEGIES
TRUST VS. MISTRUST	
Unable to discriminate appropriate behaviors in a social setting.	Teach appropriate social strategies and help students "walk through" behavior.
Gullible and unsure of self.	Develop a sense of self-trust by providing successful experiences.
Continually "testing" others' responsiveness.	Set limits within safe boundaries and allow choices for decision making.
Fear of rejection and loss.	Provide an atmosphere of stability and acceptance.
AUTONOMY VS. SHAME AND DOUBT	
Inability to complete tasks and destruction of products.	Structured environment of natural consequences with clear behavioral expectations; required finished products.
Defies authority and disruptive outbursts.	Define boundaries and means of expressing self within boundaries.
Intolerance of frustration.	Design work within students' capabilities; provide success, which leads to self-esteem and pride.
Inability to control self or to tolerate control of others.	Establish one-to-one working relationship and simple peer activities and role playing to allow for expression of opinions.

TABLE 9-2 (*Continued*)

ERIKSON'S STAGE	INTERVENTION STRATEGIES
INITIATIVE VS. GUILT	
Energy is stifled; guilt over goals leads to lack of zest and disinterest in exploration activities	Reinforce exploration; develop realistic goals that lead to success and provide opportunities for practice in an enriched and varied environment.
Dependent and unable to assume responsibility for behavior	Decision-making activities within a structured environment.
INDUSTRY VS. INFERIORITY	
Low esteem and apathetic—sense of worthlessness and isolation.	Create successful climate in which industry is an acceptable goal.
Rebellious and aggressive attempts to create self-worth	Avoid comparative grading; positive feedback for initiative and cooperation.
Overdependence on others and need for approval.	Avoid reinforcing rebellious behaviors; teach strategies for self-control and self-worth.
	Accept efforts within judgment; teach strategies to attain learning goals independently.
IDENTITY VS. ROLE CONFUSION	
Peer group dominates; tendency to overidentify; little sense of self; total conformity.	Develop positive peer culture and awareness and understanding of behaviors; appropriate sexual identity.
Delinquent behavior and switching group allegiance.	Discussions about various role models; present positive and negative alternatives.
Erratic mood swings and feelings of aggression or depression.	Supportive and knowledgeable teacher, who is human and trustworthy and supports emotional changes.
People viewed as "good" or "bad"—no grey areas.	Discussions about moral issues and dilemmas to increase awareness of different perspectives.
	Student-initiated/centered activities that foster personal exploration and evaluation.

Moral Development: Jean Piaget

Piaget's interests in children's cognitive development were the foundation for his research into children's concepts of justice and morality. His research, therefore, attempted to trace the transformation in children's moral reasoning from a level of objective responsibility to that of true moral understanding. Piaget relied on the critical interview technique to ascertain the reasoning and motivation behind children's behaviors. He determined that all normal children progress through a hierarchical sequence of moral development, even though there are differences in nationality, race, socioeconomic level, and intelligence. Differences in rate of progress seem due to variations in cognitive maturity, opportunities for reciprocal role taking, moral education, home life, and other environmental factors.

Piaget determined that there were two stages in moral development—moral heteronomy and moral autonomy—which are linked by a transition period. Moral heteronomy is sometimes referred to as moral realism or morality of constraint. Moral heteronomy characterizes children whose thinking is below the level of concrete operations. Younger children maintain that rules are fixed and absolute and expect them to be handed down by some prestigious authority. Rules, therefore, are external to the child's mind and must be followed unconditionally. Children base their moral judgments on whatever the adult authority or the law commands and on the consequences (rewards and punishments) of behaviors rather than on intentions or motivations for behavior. Their moral reasoning is characterized by the absoluteness of their values and their belief that everything is either totally right or wrong and that punishment for behavioral transgressions will be severe.

The moral reasoning of younger children can be understood if we consider their cognitive structures. Young children are very egocentric and unable to recognize others' viewpoints. They believe that everyone shares their own perspective. In addition, their thoughts are realistic; they have a tendency to conceive of psychological phenomena such as thoughts, dreams, and rules as physical entities. Moral realism is fostered by their belief in adult constraints and by the unequal relationship that exists between children and parents.

A transition occurs when children interact more extensively and on an equal basis with peers and thereby free themselves from adult authority. They begin to realize that rules are not fixed and absolute, but rather rules are social agreements accepted by all on the basis of cooperative actions. Children change drastically in their orientation toward rules. They become realistic and recognize that rules exist among equals, as products of social interaction, and can be changed by concerned parties. Their sense of autonomy or egalitarianism emerges and begins to take priority over authority. Their beliefs in imminent justice and severe punishment are superceded by ideas of reciprocal punishment consistent with the severity of the behavioral transgressions.

Moral autonomy occurs during the preadolescent years as students enter the formal operational stage of cognitive development. This stage is characterized by moral relativism or morality of cooperation in which equity dominates students' thinking about justice. Moral judgments are now influenced by extenuating circumstances, motivations, and intentions. Adolescents reject arbitrary punishments, moral absolutism, and blind obedience to authority. Their attainment of mature and autonomous concepts of justice results from decentration, which permits recognition of another's perspective, and results in cooperation and reciprocity among peers. Ego-centrism is diminished as our concern for others' welfare and rights increases. Absolute authority figures do not exist among peers; therefore, adolescents develop ideas of equality, cooperation, and solidarity. Differences in Piaget's stages of morality are illustrated in table 9-3.

Piaget believed that moral thinking changes as children mature. *However, children do not seem to progress through orderly sequences of moral development as they do with cognitive development.* Piaget believed that the different types of moral thinking overlap. Children are moral realists or moral decision makers, depending on the situation. A more detailed discussion may be found in Piaget's text *The Moral Judgment of the Child* (1932, 1965).

Moral Judgment: Lawrence Kohlberg

Kohlberg's theory of moral development amplifies Piaget's initial formulations. Kohlberg's stages of moral development are more complex and extensive. They reflect the different social orientations that occur as individuals progress through middle childhood, adolescence, and adulthood. He conceptualized six stages of development that are universal across cultures and represent increasingly differentiated and abstract ways of judging moral matters (Kohlberg 1969, 1981). The successive stages are arranged in an invariant and hierarchical sequence, which Kohlberg believes is universal and intrinsic to all human beings. Kohlberg's theory is consistent with a constructivist approach. The six stages of development differ qualitatively; each represents a structured whole that embraces a

TABLE 9-3 Differences Between Piaget's Moral Heteronomy and Moral Autonomy

MORAL HETERONOMY	MORAL AUTONOMY
Single, absolute moral perspective (behavior is either right or wrong).	Awareness of different viewpoints regarding rules.
Rules are unchangeable.	Rules are flexible.
Extent of guilt is determined by amount of damage.	Consideration of a wrongdoer's intention when evaluating guilt.
Definition of moral wrongness is based on what is forbidden or punished.	Definition of moral wrongness is based on violation of spirit of cooperation.
Punishment should stress atonement; and does not need to "fit the crime."	Punishment should involve restitution or suffering a fate similar to that of the victim of wrongdoing.
Peer aggression should be punished by an external authority.	Peer aggression should be punished by retaliatory behavior on the part of the victim.
Children should obey rules because they are sacred pronouncements by an external authority.	Children should obey rules because they are mutual agreements based on concern for the rights of others.

Adapted from Robert F. Biehler, *Child Development: An Introduction.* Boston: Houghton Mifflin Co., 1981, p. 466.

new, more comprehensive and coherent cognitive organization of moral thinking. Each stage, then, represents cognitive advances over the previous stages. Progression from one stage to the next results from the interaction of environmental experiences, with cognition as the basis for judging right and wrong.

According to Kohlberg, moral maturity depends on a person's level of cognitive development. The attainment of a particular stage of thinking and reasoning is a necessary precondition for achieving a parallel stage of moral development. Mature moral reasoning relies on the cognitive judgmental processes of classification, grouping, and conservation, each of which contributes to children's ability to balance claims of justice and to understand the concept of reciprocity. In other words, children must understand that change in one dimension compensates for change in a second dimension.

Morally advanced individuals, unlike those who are egocentric in their reasoning, can look at a situation objectively and understand others' perspectives, that is, their wants and needs, in making moral judgments. Further discussion of role taking and empathy is found later in this chapter. This difference is accounted for by the cognitive processes of empathy and role taking.

Empathy is the sharing of another's emotional responses. It is a motivational process that mediates the perception of others' needs and prosocial acts. Empathy includes both cognitive and affective components, each of which is a necessary prerequisite to the execution of prosocial behaviors. The cognitive component of empathy includes the comprehension of a social situation. Individuals must be able to discriminate others' affective states and to assume another's perspective and role. The affective component includes an emotional responsiveness that matches an individual's personal feelings and emotions with another's positive or negative emotion.

Social role taking, or *perspective taking,* is a very influential experiential factor in moral development because it enhances our ability to perceive others' perspectives and to empathize with them. Perspective taking facilitates our ability to communicate effectively and to cooperate with others. It affords us an awareness of discrepancies between our own judgments and actions and those of others. The resolution of conflicts between differing viewpoints brings the individual to higher, more mature and stable stages of moral development. Perspective taking is the assessment of other people's knowledge and their needs to deal with the situation that confronts them.

Educational implications from Piagetian and Kohlbergian viewpoints emphasize increasing students' moral reasoning abilities to a level of moral autonomy. This may be accomplished by encouraging students to exchange alternative points of view and to consider others' perspectives as prerequisites for constructing moral values needed for decision making and prosocial behavior. Accordingly, if students are to develop moral autonomy, they must acquire mutual affection and respect for one another and the significant adults in their environments. This may be facilitated by creating a climate of positive social interaction in which students exchange viewpoints, interpret and evaluate others' ideas, and develop relationships among their own thoughts and values. Students must be allowed to construct their own thoughts and value ideals. They respect the rules and goals they make for themselves, and they work hard to attain those goals (Kamii 1984). If students are respected for the way they think and feel, they are more likely to respect the thoughts and feelings of others.

Students must be involved actively in the reorganization of their thinking in order to progress to a higher level of moral thought. Their reasoning should be probed and challenged as a means of getting them to look at their ideas more carefully and to formulate a better position.

Theories of Empathy

The traditional theories of empathy follow one of two perspectives— a learning theory or a psychoanalytic viewpoint. The learning theory explanation is based on the belief that empathy is acquired early in life by conditioning or association. Accordingly, empathy develops through a repeated pairing of pleasurable feelings with another's expression of corresponding feelings (Aronfreed 1968). A psychoanalytic perspective, on the other hand, emphasizes that empathy develops from infant-caretaker interactions in which the caretaker's moods are communicated to the infant through touch, voice tone, and facial expression (Ekstein 1971).

A third perspective, that of altruistic motivation, emphasizes the cognitive and affective aspects of empathy (Hoffman 1975). Hoffman believes that empathic reaction depends on an individual's cognitive sense of another person as a distinct and separate individual. This development of a sense of other interfaces with an individual's early empathic responses and becomes the basis for altruistic motivation. Empathic affective reaction develops during early infancy and is explained by "built-in" human tendencies or by conditioning theory. Hoffman believes that children experience empathic distress before they can differentiate themselves from others. Therefore, they sometimes behave as though distress in others is happening to them. As children acquire a cognitive sense of others as distinct from themselves, at approximately one year, empathic distress is transformed into reciprocal sympathetic concern. Children, however, are still egocentric and cannot see others' perspectives. They do not realize that others have their own feelings and traits.

At two years of age, children have developed a social comprehension and are able to distinguish emotions such as happy and sad. In addition, they begin to see other individuals as distinct human beings with their own feelings, thoughts, and emotions. They have acquired rudimentary cognitive aspects of empathy and evaluating others' distress. From approximately six to nine years of age, children's empathic responses are limited to another individual's immediate, transitory, and situation-specific distress. Further cognitive development allows children to comprehend the plight not only of individuals but also of an entire group of people, such as the mentally retarded, social outcasts, or victims of war or an impoverished economy.

Hoffman views empathy from a broad developmental perspective that changes with increasing age, cognitive development, and maturity of affective processes. Cognitive role taking, then, is a complex facet of empathy and a forceful antecedent of prosocial behavior.

From an affective aspect, empathy is the chief mediator of altruistic behavior. There is a direct link between empathy and prosocial behaviors. A person's predisposition to empathic responses is an acquired capacity. Therefore, as educators, we must attempt to raise children's levels of empathy through special training in perspective taking. Consequently, if empathy is a powerful determinant of prosocial behavior, an increase in empathic ability should be reflected in increments of prosocial behavior. It would appear that an individual's level of empathy is a potent factor that governs tendencies to behave prosocially and that the capacity for empathy, therefore, can be strengthened through training and experience (Mussen and Eisenberg-Berg 1977).

COMPARATIVE SYNTHESIS OF
DEVELOPMENTAL THEORIES

The developmental theories of Freud and Erikson when compared with those of Piaget and Kohlberg appear to focus on different areas of experience. Freud and Erikson concentrate on children's emotional development and their social interactions. Piagetian theory addresses more areas of behavior than any other developmental theory. Although he had very little interest in delineating the implications of his theory for social and emotional development, Piaget's contributions to social development included work in moral judgment, egocentrism, and communication. Piaget considered cognitive and affective development as sharing a unique complementary and reciprocal relationship. He believed that intelligence provides the structure for learning and that affectivity or emotions are the energetic and motivational forces that influence cognitive development.

Kohlberg is primarily a Piagetian who concentrates on children's moral reasoning, that is, children's active formulation of moral standards based on social interchanges.

One common thread that unites the theorists is the concept of *invariant stages*. Each theorist proposes that children of all cultures proceed through a series of universal stages in an invariant manner. Freud and Erikson propose that children proceed through stages in which they cope with specific crises that are stimulated biologically. Invariant order for Freud evolves almost entirely from physical maturation. Freudian theory falls within an organismic perspective in which the individual is a loosely organized, active, and self-regulating whole. This holistic approach is based on the idea that behavior is influenced by the id, ego, and superego, each of which is a component of a structured whole.

In addition, Freudian theory focuses on a dominant trait at each developmental stage. His stages form layers, which are integrated loosely into the next stage with each stage building on, and dominant over, the previous stages. The previous stages however are not assimilated entirely into the following stages, thereby permitting children to regress to former levels. According to a Freudian viewpoint, children are passive but are forced into action by instinctual drives. However, children also may be considered active in their attempts to cope with these instinctual drives and external forces and to maintain a state of balance. The ego, as the executive function, is the most active agent of the personality. It organizes incoming internal and external environmental and social information and directs the behavior that is chosen. Freud's organismic theory focuses on the whole as being more than the sum of its parts.

Erikson believes that individuals normally progress through all eight stages of psychosocial development. Biological maturation and social expectations propel us through the stages, whether or not the conflicts of the previous stages were negotiated successfully. In other words, we are forced to face the crises of each succeeding stage. Erikson conceptualizes each stage as building upon previous stages and influencing the development of later stages. His theory of integration lies somewhere between Freud's loosely knit whole and Piaget's tightly knit equilibrated whole.

Erikson accepts the basic notions of Freud's theory in which nature determines the sequence of stages and sets the limits within which nurture operates. However, he emphasizes the role of personal and sociocultural influences in nurturing the child. He also disputes Freud's claim that development is completed within childhood. Erikson believes that development is a lifelong process in which identity gives coherence to personality. For Erikson, the development of identity is a positive affirmation of self that evolves from infancy to old age.

Freud's and Erikson's notions of stage development are different from Piaget's theory, which emphasizes that one stage must be completed prior to progressing to the next stage. For Piaget, invariant order results from physical maturation, physical and social experiences with the environment, and the equilibration process. Piaget's stages each form a tightly knit structured whole that is transformed into the succeeding stage as children reorganize and reconstruct their knowledge to higher and more complex levels. His organismic theory views an integrated and equilibrated tightly knit whole in which individuals are inherently active and self-regulated.

Kohlberg expanded and modified Piaget's stage approach to moral reasoning. He believes that individuals progress through six stages of moral development in an invariant manner. Each succeeding stage represents cognitive advances over the previous stage. The stage sequence is universal to all cultures; however, cultural experiences can alter the rate and extent of moral development. Kohlberg also disagrees with the socialization argument that an individual's moral reasoning and attitudes result from cultural transmission. Rather, he focuses on students' active formulation of moral standards based on social interchanges.

A second commonality that is woven throughout each of the theories is the notion of *equilibration*. Freud, Erikson, and Piaget each present a "trouble" theory in which development proceeds because of disturbances in the child's system. When these disturbances occur, children strive to establish a relative state of calm, or equilibrium. Freud's sources of conflict include physical maturation, both external and internal frustration, personal inadequacies, and anxiety, all of which cause an unpleasant state of tension that must be rectified. Erikson's epigenetic principle describes the forces that underlie movement through the psychosocial stages. These forces include physical maturation, societal and cultural expectations, instinctual drives, and frustrations that arise from external and internal forces, creating crises or issues that must be resolved. Piaget presents a dynamic equilibration system that harmonizes physical maturation and physical and social environmental experiences with our current knowledge to attain a state of balance.

Freud views equilibration as a process of reducing or eliminating disturbing elements, or tensions, that is, emotionally laden thoughts and psychological pain. He is concerned with the role of emotions in forcing the development of personality and thought as the child strives to cope with emotions. Qualitative changes in psychological organization depend on the superego and acquisition of defense mechanisms needed to assuage dominant sexual drives. His system of equilibration is closed and more resistant to change owing to a limited amount of energy that can be changed.

Erikson views development in the resolution of conflict from opposing forces as opposed to Freud's internal focus on sexual drives. Like Piaget, he espouses a positive or optimistic view of human nature in the quest for identity as opposed to Freud's negative or pessimistic approach to defense against unpleasant tensions. Erikson believes that we are in a continual process of "becoming" throughout our lives and that identity is reaffirmed at each successive stage of development.

Piaget views equilibration as a process of attaining balance and logical consistency regarding objective and physical environmental information. Piaget speaks of continual assimilation and accommodation of new experiences, that is, the rational individual searching for epistemological truth.

In summary, social development, from a developmental point of view, regards children as active participants in their environments. Developmentalists focus on children's thoughts, feelings, and actions as emanating spontaneously from within. In essence, children structure their own behavior as a result of their developing interests.

Each of the developmental theorists focuses on environmental and cultural influences as playing a significant role in human development; they emphasize individual autonomy as the central agent in determining personal development. In addition, they believe that educational environments can be designed to foster rather than retard human development. *It is critical, therefore, for teachers to be sensitive to students' developmental differences and to their active involvement in conflict resolution as a basis for learning and the attainment of optimal levels of cognitive and social development.*

SOCIAL COMPETENCE

Students' academic performance is influenced by their learning problems, feelings of competence, and perceptions of others' expectations for their behavior. These feelings and perceptions are reflected by students' social interactions and peer relationships. Very often mentally retarded, emotionally disturbed, and learning disabled students behave inappropriately in social situations and are rejected and isolated by their peers. They may also be viewed negatively by significant adults in their lives. They appear to be socially incompetent and unable to deal with life's challenges and respond effectively to them.

The concept of competence implies that socially skilled persons can recognize that social situations require the differential use of social patterns and sequences, determine the appropriateness of specific social skills, and perform in a socially acceptable manner that increases the likelihood that the behavior will result in positive consequences (Deshler and Schumaker 1983). Appropriate social behavior is a composite array of complex and varied skills that must be performed in an appropriate sequence to facilitate interpersonal functioning. The socially competent are those who are motivated to have social goals, can perceive social situations by attending to social cues and stimuli, can interpret and assign meaning to social patterns and sequences, and can perform the appropriate behaviors within the specific social context. In addition, they are sensitive to social feedback and can integrate that feedback to enhance further, acceptable social interaction (Kronick 1983; Deshler and Schumaker, 1983).

An emphasis on the improvement of students' social skills and competencies should assist them to profit from their educational experiences, to function more efficiently in mainstreamed settings, and to increase their employability (Deshler and Schumaker 1983). The following discussion is concerned primarily with the social competence of learning disabled students; however, it is applicable to many students identified as mildly mentally retarded or emotionally disturbed.

Handicapped students' inappropriate social behavior may result from incorrect perceptions of social situations. Such perceptions reflect the difficulties they have in selective attention and inhibition. Quite often it seems that they have problems detecting and understanding contextual clues, that is, reading body language, facial and clothing cues, or environmental situations. It appears that they are unable to identify emotional and social relationships and to understand others' thoughts, feelings, and perceptions. They are either too impulsive or too reflective with regard to their responses and therefore may not notice critical stimuli assign appropriate meaning to these stimuli. In addition, they may lack imagery of sequence and an understanding of cause-effect relationships in social situations. They seem unable to take another's perspective (that is, "walking in another's pair of shoes"), which may explain why their communications appear unfriendly and socially inappropriate. Quite often, such students have not learned the appropriate behavior for specific situations and the need for differential conversation with adults and peers. They may not notice how people respond to their behavior and may misconstrue social detail and inflection (Kronick 1983; Pearl, Bryan, and Donahue 1983).

In other situations, students do perceive social cues and recognize that present social experiences are similar to previous experiences. However, they do not seem to have the appropriate social responses available in their behavioral repertoire to perform in a socially acceptable manner. Deficits in syntactic structures and in generating and retrieving vocabulary to express themselves may interfere with their ability to communicate effectively. These language deficits may cause awkward social interactions and thus make the individuals less skillful in maintaining conversations. Atypical conversation practices are often responsible for students' lack of popularity and rejection by their peers (Pearl, Bryan, and Donahue 1983).

Students may not realize their responsibility for the outcome of a social situation or are unable to generalize the availability of strategies to specific situations. In this instance, they may possess the appropriate skills and strategies, but they do not know which behavior is appropriate for the situation at hand. They can verbalize attitudes concerning prosocial behaviors, but they do not know when to use them. Students seem unable to initiate desirable behaviors and instead fall back on inappropriate strategies. It would appear that they need a structured learning situation and direct instruction concerning behaviors relevant to specific settings.

Students' atypical behavior may not result from a lack of interest and caring about social acceptance, as educators often assume. Rather, their behavior may reflect a poor self-concept and an attitude of being less competent socially than their peers, both of which are a result of rejection and isolation.

These explanations have a variety of implications for initiating intervention strategies in the area of social competence. For example, teaching particular social behaviors may not be appropriate or effective for students who lack the social perceptions to know when to apply them or for students who have mastered appropriate behaviors but who lack the motivation to use them. We do know, however, that social-skill intervention can be successful and that students can be taught social competence.

INTERVENTION STRATEGIES: GENERAL CONSIDERATIONS

In general, intervention strategies are mediation processes between students and their environments that attempt to reduce disturbances and to increase appropriate behavior and positive mental health. They include instructional methodologies and management techniques designed for students who have secondary social and emotional difficulties that may result from learning disabilities and mental retardation as well as for students who have primary emotional behavioral disorders that cause their learning difficulties.

Sanders (1983) indicates that there are roughly three groups of students with whom we must be concerned in planning educational and psychotherapeutic interventions—students who are healthy, those who have learning problems that are organically based, and those who are emotionally disturbed. The "healthy" students are those who are intact neurologically and whose learning problems do not emerge until they enter school and must interact with an academic and social environment. Their learning difficulties do not affect personality development during the early formative years. Therefore, psychological development appears to be age appropriate and to afford pleasure and an appropriate level of self-esteem. These students are generally open and straightforward about their learning problems and maintain friendships with peers and stable and respected positions within their families. Their learning and behavioral difficulties appear to be transient and related situationally to personal idiosyncracies, and they do not interfere with productive relationships.

Students whose learning and behavior difficulties are organically based are characterized by the presence of diffuse neurologically based problems that exist concurrently with academic failure. These students often have difficulty with selective attention and may be unable to filter out extraneous stimuli. In addition, they may be unable to inhibit cognitively or socially unacceptable responses. Sanders (1983) believes that these students do not have *major* social and emotional problems; however, they often experience frustration and unhappiness, a result of the incompetency and isolation that are concomitant with inadequate selective attention and inhibition. Such learning difficulties are pervasive and interfere not only with students' academic functioning but also with all aspects of their lives at home, in school, and within the community. Learning disabilities that result from uneven cognitive functioning and interfere with the normal learning processes may cause feelings of frustration and anxiety, and impinge on students' self-concept, peer and family relationships, and social interactions (Sanders 1983; Silver 1983). These students may have difficulty maintaining close friendships with their peers, and they are often vulnerable to prolonged dependence on their parents. Therefore, we must be cognizant of the potential emergence of secondary social and emotional overlays that result from various types of learning difficulties.

Students may require specific instruction in social situations to facilitate the organization of incoming stimuli and outgoing responses. Interventions must be planned based on full knowledge of students' total environment. In essence, our goal is to provide students with positive opportunities to construct automatic and integrated successful response patterns.

It is important to differentiate among social and emotional difficulties that reflect stress *caused by* learning disabilities and those that are the *cause of* students' academic problems. Students who may be considered emotionally disturbed have emotional conflicts that interfere with the remediation of learning difficulties. Their social-emotional conflicts appear to be unrelated to their learning difficulties and began to emerge prior to their enrolling in school. Some students with emotional problems seem unable to focus their attention on school work because all of their energies are absorbed with the emotional problems that preoccupy their thoughts. Other students tend to exploit their learning problems as a means of maintaining their distorted perceptions of the world. Very often students seem unable to cooperate or to direct their personal efforts toward overcoming their learning failures. This in turn creates additional inner conflicts that impede future attempts at remediation. Intervention therefore must consider students' conflicting feelings and thoughts of inadequacy (Sanders 1983).

We recognize that no one theory or intervention strategy is unanimously accepted and applicable to all students. The strategies included in this chapter are those specialized approaches that are referenced most frequently in the education of students whose social and emotional difficulties interfere with their learning.

Emotional problems most often manifest themselves through acting-out and withdrawal behaviors, social isolation, anxiety, lying, and defensiveness and immaturity, all of which threaten students' self-esteem and motivation to achieve academically. Threats to self-esteem and motivation may result in additional maladaptive behaviors and further withdrawal from academic tasks, and consequently students become emotionally distant from remedial intervention. The situation appears to be cyclical; therefore, we must be supportive and caring of students' self-esteem and motivation to achieve by providing learning activities and strategies that help them to experience their environment in a positive way. It appears that self-esteem results from both internal feelings of competence and external acceptance by others. It is a critical variable in students' positive cognitive development and social acceptance.

Failure in school threatens students' internal feelings of competence as well as their acceptance by parents, peers, and teachers. In addition, failure to negotiate the societal challenges presented at the different developmental stages may cause regression to the emotional positions of earlier stages, as well as stagnation and failure to progress emotionally through the crises. Students' positive feelings about themselves as valued and worthy individuals with good qualities lend to positive attitudes toward school, which in turn foster appropriate verbal expression and participation in classroom activities. Intervention strategies therefore must attend to students' self-concept and sense of adequacy in an attempt to effect cognitive changes (Rich 1982; Meyer 1983). Failure in both academic and social experiences may result in pervasive feelings of inferiority and helplessness that inhibit students' coping mechanisms, and it may also foster prolonged dependence on others and an inability to make independent judgments and decisions (Meyer 1983; Kamii 1984).

A positive teaching environment contributes to students' motivation to achieve and to their perceived control over achievement outcomes and task persistence. This environment may be enhanced by allowing students to make conscious choices and by increasing an awareness of their own control over behaviors and social interactions. In essence, we must help students to analyze academic and social situations, to consider alternatives, and to evaluate the outcome or consequences of their behaviors (Meyer 1983). In addition, a supportive teaching environment helps students to set realistic goals and expectations for success based on an understanding of their capabilities and disabilities. Positive expectations influence students' perceived control over the situation and task persistence and help to avert an attitude of helplessness. Finally, we must provide students with strategies for coping with failure and frustration. Students must learn to monitor their own reactions, recognize feelings of frustration, and make use of conscious strategies that enable them to cope constructively with these feelings (Meyer 1983). Discussion of metacognitive strategies and cognitive behavioral training may be found later in this chapter.

Quite often mentally retarded, emotionally disturbed, and learning-disabled students' inappropriate behavior in social situations elicits negative responses and attention from their peers. They seem to be lacking in self-control, ego strength, and social personal adjustment, all of which are necessary for establishing positive interpersonal relationships. There is a need therefore to design educational interventions that emphasize social and interpersonal skill development to help students acquire prosocial behaviors.

Psychoeducational Intervention

Feelings influence students' academic performance in the classroom; therefore, we cannot separate cognitive and affective states that interact throughout students' daily lives. Students' cognitive performance is enhanced by mastery of affective experiences, which in turn are influenced by intellectual mastery (Fagen and Long 1979; Fagen, Long, and Stevens 1975). For example, our memory process (cognitive abilities) may be disrupted by anxiety and emotional stress (affective experiences). Conversely, the identification and expression of feelings necessitate the retention and use of verbal concepts (anger and joy). Quite often, students identified as mentally retarded, learning disabled, and emotionally disturbed are unable to identify their affective states or feelings because they are unable to generate and to retrieve appropriate labels (words) to express those feelings. Psychoeducational intervention is holistic and relies on students' attitudes, interests and skills, and their active involvement in learning. The major purpose of psychoeducational intervention is to provide students with planned learning situations that integrate thoughts and feelings and stimulate the constructive expression of affective experiences needed for appropriate social interaction and academic achievement.

Our intellectual abilities enable us to expand the world of cognition and to use our emotions in an enriched manner (Fagen, Long, and Stevens 1975). The basic assumptions upon which psychoeducational approaches are founded indicate that civilized behavior emerges from the appropriate use of our emotions in negotiating life's experiences. Frustrations are often a natural consequence of our dealings with reality. Therefore, we must teach students how to manage frustrations so they can deal appropriately with unpleasant feelings. In essence, frustration is necessary for personal growth and enriched human relations, both of which depend on our willingness to accept, share, and appreciate personal emotional states and those of others. We must blend affective education (teaching and learning about feelings and emotions) with cognitive skills and processes needed to cope with external environmental stimuli. The psychoeducational perspective is the foundation for crisis intervention and life-space interview techniques (Morse 1971; Redl 1959), reality therapy (Glasser 1975), the self-control curriculum (Fagen, Long, and Stevens 1975) and social-learning therapy (Goldstein 1981; Goldstein et al. 1980, 1979), each of which helps students to develop positive feelings and internal control over their behavior.

Crisis Intervention

The notion of crisis intervention was developed to meet the needs of public-school teachers who worked with students in least restrictive environments. Crisis intervention focuses on managing students' surface behaviors while simultaneously dealing with the deeper meaning of the incident. Students need to know how to cope with stressful situations if they are to grow and change. This may be accomplished by verbal intervention and environmental manipulation, both of which facilitate students' ability to cope with academic and social pressures. Intervention may take the form of life-space interviewing or remedial instruction. Morse (1971) believes that the person who conducts the life-space interview must be well versed in interviewing techniques and the skills necessary to effect behavioral change.

Life-Space Interview

Life-space interview, developed by Fritz Redl (1959) and William Morse (1976), is a technique through which adults can help students to understand the effects of their unconscious thoughts and feelings and the actions of others. Life-space interviewing centers on a crisis when and where it occurs and is intended to help students gain insight into a problem and develop positive alternatives for dealing with situations that culminate in conflict and crisis. It is a form of perspective taking in which teachers help students to understand and deal appropriately with stress. The goals of the life-space interview are to foster deeper insight and understanding of a situation through critical exploration and to reach resolution, or to offer emotional first aid in which teachers support students in a calming manner to help dissipate the excess emotion.

Life-space interview consists of as many as seven steps (Morse 1976) that may be used to facilitate students' understanding of the conflict:

Step 1. *Investigating conditions:* Investigate the child's perception of the problem situation, that is, the actual location and conditions of the incident.

Step 2. *Testing depth and spread:* Determine the child's level of involvement, degree of internalized concern, and the generality of behavior. Is the current incident part of the child's lifestyle, or is it an isolated occurrence?

Step 3. *Content clarification:* Clarify the issue or the theme of the incident and highlight for students how their behavior affects others. This must be done nonjudgmentally.

Step 4. *Acceptance of feelings:* Enhance the students' acceptance by recognizing their feelings without necessarily condoning the behavior.

Step 5. *Avoiding value judgments:* Explore with students the feelings they are experiencing and how those feelings may be controlled. Strategies for self-control and other coping skills are taught at this time, as the student is helped to see the consequences and implications of the nonadaptive behaviors.

Step 6. *Exploration of internal mechanisms:* Explore internal mechanisms for change based on students' feelings of anxiety, guilt, or remorse. Students' feelings and values may be the means of deriving mutually agreed-upon and realistic solutions.

Step 7. *Two resolution phases:* Attempts at resolution include presenting the adults' views of the situation (description of consequences, behavior standards, expectations); and looking for a solution that may prevent future disruptions (specific plans for change that might involve others in the students' environment).

The life-space interview helps students cope with and resolve conflict situations. The foregoing steps may be modified to match students' needs. A related technique includes reality therapy as a means of managing disruptive classroom behavior.

Reality Therapy

Reality therapy is a specialized learning process that helps students to face reality and fulfill responsibility for meeting their two basic needs: love and self-esteem. Reality therapy has a distinctively psychodynamic orientation; yet it focuses on changing students' overt behavior in a manner that is realistic, responsible, and right.

Realistic behavior involves recognizing the long-term impact and consequences of personal actions rather than ignoring reality and projecting problems on external sources. Responsibility refers to the ability to fulfill one's needs in a manner that does not interfere with another's ability to meet his or her basic needs. The acquisition of responsibility is a complicated lifelong process in which we learn to behave according to acceptable societal standards. The right-wrong aspects of reality therapy refer to people's inappropriate rationalizations, justifications, and other exploitative activities that nurture their inappropriate behavior. The principles for efficient implementation of reality therapy are presented in the box on page 248.

Glasser (1969) offers a plan for redirecting the focus of modern education that involves three types of classroom meetings. Social-problem-solving meetings are concerned with the individual's social behavior and group problems. The meetings are designed to teach students responsible behavior and control over their own destiny. Open-ended meetings center on discussing intellectual/thought-provoking subjects, and educational diagnostic meetings are related directly to academic content and student's understanding of the curriculum. Glasser's techniques are designed for educational applications. They attend to the natural consequences of behavior and insist on individual responsibility for behavior.

Self-Control Curriculum

The self-control curriculum is a process-oriented approach to affective-skill development that provides students with the skills to cope flexibly and realistically with life's situations, and teaches them to have better feelings about themselves and to appreciate other's feelings. Fagen, Long, and Stevens (1975) believe that students' capacity for self-control depends on cognitive- and affective-skill clusters that enable them to direct and regulate personal actions in a flexible and realistic manner.

Fagen, Long, and Stevens (1975) cite eleven conceptual attributes that identify psychoeducational approaches to working with students.

1. Cognitive and affective processes are in continuous interaction.
2. Behavior comprises verbal and nonverbal expressions of a totally functioning person, and it is that person, not the expression, that is most important.
3. Behavior is a source of concern when it promotes or perpetuates personal unhappiness, conflict, and self-deprecation; or when it creates serious disturbance with existing social norms, thereby resulting in feelings of rejection and alienation.
4. Understanding behavior means understanding phenomenally relevant aspects of a child's life space. For the teacher, this means appreciating transactions between the child and the teacher, the curriculum, the peer group, and the educational system.
5. Understanding behavior requires an awareness of cognitive, affective, and motivational processes in self and others.
6. Understanding behavior is achieved through assessment of, and communication with and about, learners and significant others in their space.
7. Changing or modifying self-defeating behavior involves a process of establishing identifiable objectives that are set in relation to total personal functioning.

8. Understanding behavior facilitates the ability to create conditions for optimal behavior change.
9. The ultimate criterion for personal growth is the extent to which positive behavior derives from self-control rather than external control.
10. Emotions are critical personal events that must become understood, accepted, and valued.
11. The scope of learning involves increasing understanding and satisfaction in relationship to things, symbols, the self, and others.

This humanistic orientation to education recognizes that we must facilitate the acceptance and expression of feelings as alternatives to destructive behavior, promote new positive learning, allow for awareness and increase of more constructive and satisfying feelings in contrast with negative and unproductive ones, and facilitate mutual understanding and problem solving.

The acquisition and application of cognitive information must have personal relevance and interest. Teaching strategies are designed to enable students to direct and regulate their behavior flexibly and realistically. Recommended strategies include games, role playing, and discussion.

Games have great learning potential, create lasting impressions, and can be changed to suit the group's wishes. They are the basis for imaginative and exciting learning activities; the skills acquired are applicable to the life cycle and are the basis for moral autonomy and reciprocal justice.

Role playing is useful in helping students to manage and appreciate personal frustration and feelings, to anticipate consequences, and to recognize others' viewpoints. Role playing allows students flexibility and imagination in role identification, which makes it a realistic and effective learning experience. In addition, it helps students to focus on decision-making alternatives and to ascertain the consequences, each of which is related to self-esteem and perceived control over situations. *Discussion* involves the presentation of academic content and other information in small groups or on an individual basis.

Fagen, Long, and Stevens (1975) offer detailed suggestions for implementing a psychoeducational approach to instruction that allows the parallel development of students' cognitive and affective needs. They provide specific goals, objectives, and learning activities to facilitate cognitive processes (attention, perception, memory, cognition, and expression) and affective experiences (appreciating feelings, managing frustrations and inhibitions, and learning to relax). Table 9.4 provides an overview of the self-control curriculum and instructional units.

Social Learning Therapy

Goldstein (1981), Goldstein, Sprafkin, Gershaw, and Klein (1980) and Goldstein, Sprafkin, and Gershaw (1979) believe that students need help dealing with feelings of stress and aggression and in developing social-planning skills to facilitate their interaction with peers, parents, and teachers. They have designed a psychoeducational intervention called struc-

TABLE 9-4   The Self-Control Curriculum: Overview of Curriculum Areas and Units

CURRICULUM AREA/DEFINED	INSTRUCTIONAL UNITS
Selection: accurate perception	1. Focusing and concentration 2. Mastering figureground discrimination 3. Mastering distractions and interference 4. Processing complex patterns
Storage: retention of information	1. Developing visual memory 2. Developing auditory memory
Sequencing and ordering: organizing and planning actions	1. Developing time orientation 2. Developing auditory-visual sequencing 3. Developing sequential planning
Anticipating consequences: relating actions to outcomes	1. Developing alternatives 2. Evaluating consequences
Appreciating feelings: identification and constructive use of affective experiences	1. Identifying feelings 2. Developing positive feelings 3. Managing feelings 4. Reinterpreting feeling events
Managing frustration: coping with negative feelings	1. Accepting feelings of frustration 2. Building coping resources 3. Tolerating frustration
Inhibition and delay: postponing actions	1. Controlling action 2. Developing partial goals
Relaxation: reducing internal tensions	1. Developing body relaxation 2. Developing thought relaxation 3. Developing movement relaxation

Adapted from S. A. Fagen, N. J. Long, and D. J. Stevens, *Teaching Children Self-Control.* Columbus, Ohio: Charles E. Merrill Publishing Co., 1975.

tured learning therapy, which focuses on developing students' prosocial, interpersonal, and stress-management/coping skills and also confidence in their abilities to resolve conflict. The social-skill training components include modeling, role playing, performance feedback, and transfer of training. *Modeling* emphasizes learning by imitation as an effective and reliable technique for learning and strengthening behaviors. Modeling teaches students what to do; however, students need practice in, and sufficient reward for, behaving in a certain manner. *Role playing* provides students with the opportunity to practice and learn how to behave in a certain way, to focus on others' perspectives, and to develop empathy. Role playing must be accompanied by a motivational, or incentive, component to ensure lasting change. *Performance feedback* affords constructive criticism, social reinforcement, and rewards following role playing. Praise and encouragement, however, must be paired with the transfer of training components in which students apply their newly acquired behaviors in natural, real-life situations at home, in school, and in the community. *Transfer of training* provides students with organizational concepts and principles that explain successful skill selection and implementation. Real-life reinforcement helps students to maximize the transfer to natural settings and to ensure endurance—it helps students learn why they should behave in appropriate ways.

VIGNETTE: INTEGRATION OF SELF-CONTROL SKILL CLUSTERS

1. Jane receives appropriate materials needed for a class assignment and begins working despite extraneous talking and noise in the classroom (selection).
2. Jane's progress in the class assignment is hampered by difficult vocabulary, so she raises her hand to solicit the teacher's assistance (managing frustration). However, the teacher is helping another student.
3. Jane would like to ask another student for help; however, she wants to follow class rules and not discuss the assignment during the work period (managing frustrations and anticipating consequences).
4. Jane raises her hand again (managing frustrations, inhibitions, and delay).
5. The work period is almost over. If the assignments are not completed in class she must finish it as a homework assignment (anticipating consequences).
6. Tonight Jane's best friend is having a surprise party (sequencing and ordering, storage) and she won't be able to attend unless her assignment is complete (anticipating consequences, appreciating feelings, and managing frustrations).
7. Jane raises her hand again (managing frustrations) but her teacher is still with another student. So, Jane asks her friend Nancy for assistance with the assignment (managing frustration and inhibition).
8. The teacher gives Jane and Nancy a disapproving look (appreciating feelings).
9. Jane tries to figure out the word, but she still has difficulty.
10. She raises her hand (managing frustration, inhibition, and delay) and finally . . .
11. The teacher calls on Jane (relaxation) who explains her problem with the vocabulary (managing frustrations and being able to relax).
12. The teacher asks other students if they are having similar difficulties, and basing her decision on the number of positive responses (appreciating feelings), the teacher decides to review the lesson the next day and to allow completion of the assignment in class.

Social learning therapy includes fifty skills designed to facilitate successful social interaction. Each of the skills is accompanied by training activities and suggestions for implementation. The program begins with basic social skills, such as listening and starting a conversation, and proceeds to highly sophisticated skills, such as dealing with contradictory messages and making a decision. The information in table 9-5 is representative of the skills included in social learning therapy.

In conclusion, the interventions just discussed are based on the assumption that students' affective states precipitate disruptive behaviors. Therefore, we must create an appropriate and supportive educational environment that complements students' cognitive and affective needs and facilitates interpersonal management and positive mental growth. Interpersonal techniques include listening to and interpreting students' feelings, maintaining open lines of communication as a means of identifying problems and alternative solutions, emphasizing natural consequences as a result of negative experiences and behaviors, and providing opportunities to communicate and to explore feelings and appropriate ways of fulfilling basic needs. The interpersonal-management process is a personal learning experience for students that emphasizes understanding of feelings and emotions and how to translate them into appropriate and acceptable behaviors (Rich 1982).

Conflict Resolution: A Constructive Approach

Conflict resolution in the classroom should be based on an exemplar, or model, that represents appropriate prosocial behaviors and a problem-solving orientation that deals with conflict in a nonjudgmental manner. The focus should be on communication and respect for students in order to develop appropriate values that encourage their intellectual and moral autonomy. Communication is the basis for discussing students' academic and social concerns, their feelings, and sensitive moral issues, and as such depends on interpersonal relationships between teachers and students that are based on mutual respect. Effective communication is based on ground rules that include: (1) active listening and looking at the person who is speaking, (2) using descriptive instead of judgmental language, (3) dealing with specific issues and concerns that can be changed, and (4) providing appropriate feedback. Just "plain talking" with students, in which teachers ask questions ("go fishing" to determine issues and problem situations) and respond to students' comments, conveys mutual respect and has a powerful effect on developing self-control and self-esteem. Therefore, we must attempt to create a diverse communication environment within the educational setting that makes social interaction between students and teachers and among peers the basis for discussing personal problems and brainstorming alternative solutions to problems. Social interaction leads to decentration, perspective taking, and the development of empathy, all of which are prerequisites for becoming an autonomous decision maker.

Communication helps students progress through the stages of moral reasoning. Whatever their age, we can capitalize on their desire to be treated fairly. Therefore, when solving problems we should focus on a construc-

TABLE 9-5   Social-Skills Curriculum

GROUP I. BEGINNING SOCIAL SKILLS

1. Listening
2. Starting a Conversation
3. Having a Conversation
4. Asking a Question
5. Saying Thank You
6. Introducing Yourself
7. Introducing Other People
8. Giving a Compliment

GROUP II. ADVANCED SOCIAL SKILLS

9. Asking for Help
10. Joining in
11. Giving Instructions
12. Following Instructions
13. Apologizing
14. Convincing Others

GROUP III. SKILLS FOR DEALING WITH FEELINGS

15. Knowing your Feelings
16. Expressing Your Feelings
17. Understanding the Feelings of Others
18. Dealing with Someone Else's Anger
19. Expressing Affection
20. Dealing with Fear
21. Rewarding Yourself

GROUP IV. SKILL ALTERNATIVES TO AGGRESSION

22. Asking Permission
23. Sharing Something
24. Helping Others
25. Negotiation
26. Using Self-Control
27. Standing Up for Your Rights
28. Responding to Teasing
29. Avoiding Trouble with Others
30. Keeping Out of Fights

GROUP V. SKILLS FOR DEALING WITH STRESS

31. Making a Complaint
32. Answering a Complaint
33. Sportsmanship after the Game
34. Dealing with Embarrassment
35. Dealing with Being Left Out
36. Standing Up for a Friend
37. Responding to Persuasion
38. Responding to Failure
39. Dealing with Contradictory Messages
40. Dealing with an Accusation
41. Getting Ready for a Difficult Conversation
42. Dealing with Group Pressure

GROUP VI. PLANNING SKILLS

43. Deciding on Something to Do
44. Deciding What Caused a Problem
45. Setting a Goal
46. Deciding on Your Abilities
47. Gathering Information
48. Arranging Problems by Importance
50. Concentrating on a Task

From A. P. Goldstein, R. P. Sprafkin, N. J. Gershaw, and P. Klein, *Skillstreaming the Adolescent: A Structured Learning Approach to Teaching Prosocial Skills*. Champaign, Ill.: Research Press Co., 1980. Reprinted by permission.

tive and fair approach based on mutual respect and equality between students and parents and teachers. Such an approach to conflict resolution involves expressing viewpoints and listening, to find a common ground for resolution. We must help students to translate their moral reasoning to prosocial behaviors and fair and appropriate interpersonal relationships.

Lickona (1983) indicates that components of a constructive-fairness approach to conflict resolution includes mutual understanding, solving the problem, and follow-through. Mutual understanding of others' feelings involves the following: (1) stating the purpose of the discussion and the intent to listen to all perspectives, (2) describing the problem from a personal perspective and eliciting others' feelings, and (3) paraphrasing others' viewpoints to ensure understanding. Problem solving includes: (1) listing possible solutions, (2) developing a written agreement that describes solutions that are fair, and (3) a follow-up discussion to determine if the agreement is working. This phase of the fairness approach involves compromise and empathic listening to others' perspectives. Follow-through is a follow-up discussion at a later time to determine the effectiveness of the plan.

The constructive-fairness approach helps to lessen students' dependence or heteronomy and to foster autonomy. It requires a certain degree of "structured flexibility" in adults' relationships with children and adolescents in which they set limits and standards for appropriate behavior. Parents and teachers must have confidence in their basic moral authority and in setting expectations and maturity demands for students in an attempt to foster their prosocial development. Authority should be fair, and not arbitrary and dictatorial. Fairness lends to a balance between control (heteronomy) and independence; it is the basis for moral autonomy. Parents and teachers must be models of prosocial behaviors for students.

Strategies to Develop Prosocial Behavior

Intervention strategies that facilitate students' acquisition of a caring and altruistic orientation and encourage concomitant prosocial behaviors should be an integral component of educational programs for all students. This is especially true for students identified as mentally retarded, emotionally disturbed, and learning disabled whose cognitive, affective, and social development may differ from their peers and affect their interpersonal relationships. Therefore, educators must make a conscious effort to provide appropriate role models to encourage prosocial peer interactions and to use prosocial media as vehicles for developing students' prosocial behaviors. Newspapers, television, and radio, for example, provide a wealth of information about local, national, and worldwide problems that have a negative impact on people. Discussions about these issues should relate specifically to students' lives, whenever possible, and encourage empathy and perspective taking, both of which facilitate affective decentration and lead to moral and intellectual autonomy.

Kobak (1979, 1981) and Self (1981) state that "caring" and the development of prosocial behaviors of cooperation, commitment, and concern can be infused into students' educational programs on an ongoing and consistent basis. Kobak believes that students should be afforded opportunities for involvement in varied and enriched caring experiences to help strengthen their internal comfort level—that is, their feelings and attitudes—as a basis for expressing prosocial actions. Second, she states that caring activities help to reduce the psychological threat and the concomitant "risk" involved in expressing caring qualities. The notion of caring may stimulate unresolved and unconscious feelings in some students that can touch off fears of identification with, or contamination by, those who are different. Quite often these fears produce guilt feelings, which in turn cause pain and stress. Unfortunately, the way in which people survive these anxieties, especially if they are not understood, is through the defense mechanisms of rejection and withdrawal, both of which are pervasive and insidious behaviors that perpetuate the cycle of self-centeredness and a sense of alienation. We need to help students to recognize the plight of others and to regenerate ethical and altruistic attitudes and behaviors. Kobak and Self indicate that caring can be the vehicle for the solution of global problems related to hunger, poverty, racial inequities, war, and terrorism.

Intervention strategies therefore should encourage responsible behavior and promote ethical and altruistic behaviors among students. These activities may include dialogue, creative or action projects, and role playing.

Class dialogues may be planned as spontaneous discussions that focus on developing a caring orientation among students. Discussions are designed to create disequilibrium and to cause students to consider and empathize with others' perspectives. There are three types of class dialogues: (1) mutual-help dialogues, which aid students with personal problems or dilemmas; (2) anger and justice dialogues, which question the effectiveness of students' behaviors as a means of understanding and changing the actions of others; and (3) resistance dialogues, which center around ethical values based on personal experiences or societal norms.

Discussions may begin with an opening question designed to promote self-assessment and behavioral change. Examples of opening questions include:

—*Empathy questions:* "What are some of the problems that confront your parents?"
—*Philosophical questions:* "Why would anyone ever consider warfare?"
—*Identification questions:* "Who is the saddest person you know?"
—*Alternative questions:* "How can you settle a disagreement with a friend?"
—*Problem questions:* "While visiting your house, a friend borrowed a cassette tape that belongs to your older brother and did not return it. How can you retrieve the tape?"

Discussions of moral dilemmas and issues will help students to reorganize their thinking and adopt universal ethical principles. To attain this goal, we may wish to induce cognitive conflict and create disequilibrium and imbalance in students' mental structures. Eventually, the resolution of the conflict will lead to reorganization or reconstruction of moral thought and more advanced and comprehensive understanding. Cognitive and moral development occur not only through external reinforcement or imitation but through active problem solving and reconstruction of existing information, based on internal motivation and the need to seek a state of equilibrium.

Creative projects that revolve around art, music, and literature are excellent ways to help students express their emotions. They are also catalysts for discussion about caring and working cooperatively toward the attainment of particular goals. Group and team learning is a good means of problem solving and encourages cooperation, listening to others' thoughts and feelings and taking their perspective, expressing thoughts and feelings, and deriving satisfactory solutions.

Action-oriented projects foster students' active participation in altruistic behaviors and are designed to help others. For example, students may be encouraged to "adopt a family" and to donate food and clothing to them during the Thanksgiving season. The key to the success of such an endeavor, however, revolves around the complementary discussions about sharing, caring, and responsibility.

Another action-oriented project includes active exploration of caring among students, in which they share acts of kindness and study each other's similarities and differences. These activities help students to discover personal values, strengths, and abilities and eventually lead to an atmosphere that recognizes diversity and encourages toleration and understanding of differences (Self 1981).

Role playing and sociodrama that focus on issues and dilemmas will help students to understand others' feelings, to recognize issues, and to become more tolerant of others. Role playing also helps students to be more responsible for their own actions and to appreciate the reciprocal effects and consequences of their behaviors on others and themselves. Students should be provided with opportunities for making choices and decisions about their actions, both of which will enhance their self-concept. Responsible behavior elicits positive, responsible behaviors from others and helps students to work cooperatively in their problem-solving endeavors.

An integral component of each of these activities is positive feedback for students' efforts. Positive feedback helps students to overcome feelings of shyness and shame or anxiety in demonstrating caring behaviors. Feedback strengthens students' comfort levels and encourages their continued involvement in caring activities (Kobak 1981).

Metacognition

Kronick (1983) suggests a metacognitive approach to the development of social competence. Some learning disabled students need assistance in generalizing social skills across social areas; therefore, we must assist them to view social situations objectively and to determine alternative approaches to problem solving. Students need to stand back from difficult social situations and ask, "What shall I do?" Even if students may be aware of information-processing difficulties, they may lack strategies for initiating appropriate social behaviors. Once students possess the necessary strategies, they must become active in remediation efforts and monitor their own behaviors. Metacognitive approaches include:

1. Self-monitoring of selective attention processes to ensure attention to the social situation—asking the following questions: "Am I paying attention?" or "What did I miss?"
2. Strategies to facilitate memory—rehearsal and chunking.
3. Awareness of task difficulty, based on previous situations and the appropriateness of the strategy to the outcome and established goals—prediction.
4. Learning the strategy through practice and generalization to real-life situations—implementation.
5. Assessment of one's own actions as being correct or incorrect. If incorrect, did the problem result from lack of strategy awareness or inappropriate use of the strategy?

Cognitive Behavior Modification (CBM)

Cognitive behavior modification is an executive control strategy that is allied closely to metacognition. It can be used to help students organize their thought patterns and social learning behaviors. Cognitive behavior modification parallels research into behavioral self-control, social problem solving, and self-instructional training. It evolved as a result of the difficulties incurred by children in maintaining and generalizing socially appropriate behaviors and learning strategies. As an intervention strategy, CBM helps children to control their own social and learning behaviors through self-treatment techniques (self-assessment, self-verbalization, self-instruction, self-guidance, self-monitoring, self-recording, and self-reinforcement) that provide a structure for organizing incoming environmental information. Cognitive behavior modification is based on how language affects cognition. Students who have language deficiencies may not understand the nature of social requests or directions, and as a result they may guess impulsively and have problems associating ideas and concepts and in forming new concepts. Quite often, students have production deficiencies in their spontaneous problem-solving abilities. In these situations, they may lack ready access to information-processing strategies and fail to produce socially relevant verbalizations and strategies. Once the access is acquired and they process appropriate language mediators and strategies, some students may persist in the inability to produce strategies or to generalize them to similar social situations. As educators, we must move beyond these production deficiencies and investigate students' executive-functioning abilities, which include assessing, monitoring, and sequencing information needed for social-problem-solving activities. If students are unable to review information and make organizational and executive decisions, their social performance can be affected. Finally, some students who have language-mediation abilities may not be able to use those abilities to guide or regulate their behaviors. These mediation deficiencies may be evidenced in students' inability to express themselves efficiently in social situations.

We must assist students in making executive decisions and in improving their social performance. Cognitive behavior modification strategies help students to organize incoming information and to monitor their responses. The key component of cognitive behavior modification is self-instructional internal dialogue in which students ask questions about organizing information and making decisions. CBM is applicable to social situations and involves verbalizations and modeling that follow a defined sequence (Meichenbaum and J. Goodman 1971). *Verbalizations* are overt at first and are used to guide students through a series of steps that produce effective cognitive, affective, and social behaviors. *Modeling* is the primary means of instruction that enables students to verbalize their progress steps. In addition, many cognitive procedures may teach students to deal with their social responses so they can evaluate different alternatives. CBM regimens cited most frequently include training in problem solving and self-instruction.

Training in problem solving has been effective in reducing behavior problems and aggression, controlling impulsivity, and increasing social interactions (Craighead et al. 1978; Spivack and Shure 1974). Mastery of problem-solving strategies requires students to become aware of their cognitive processes and abilities. Once that is accomplished, they can learn when and how to employ social-problem-solving strategies.

There are several factors involved in developing social-problem-solving strategies with children (D'Zurilla and Goldfried 1971; Spivack, Platt, and Shure 1976). These include:

1. Acknowledging the fact that environmental events may control or be related to the problem
2. Defining the problem and generating alternative solutions
3. Examining alternatives in light of their acceptability and their short- and long-term effectiveness
4. Devising a plan for implementing selected alternatives; that is, specifying the steps necessary for social-problem solving
5. Recognizing and understanding the natural consequences of behavior and the fact that social interaction is a reciprocal and interactive process
6. Implementing and evaluating the plan

Problem-solving training has helped students with behavior problems to identify emotions, consider others' feelings, generate solutions to social problems, and evaluate the results of their activities in social situations with peers (Spivack and Shure 1974).

Self-instructional training has promising implications for efforts with students who have attentional problems, difficulty with academic tasks, and impulsive behaviors when responding to social situations. Since these students have not learned to use their cognitive processes and affective experiences effectively, it seems logical to provide assistance through direct cognitive training. Self-instructional training helps to alleviate learned helplessness and to improve students' self-esteem by providing a mechanism to interpret the social sequences in which they must engage, to organize their thought processes, and to understand expectations for their social behavior.

Training in cognitive behavior modification is built around four major steps in which specific verbalizations are taught in the following modeling and rehearsal sequence (Meichenbaum and S. Goodman 1979):

1. Cognitive modeling: the teacher performs the task to be learned, talking aloud while the student watches and listens.
2. Overt guidance: the student performs the task using the same verbalizations demonstrated by the teacher; the teacher assists as needed.
3. Faded self-guidance: the student performs the task, self-instructing in a whisper with no assistance from the teacher.
4. Covert self-instruction: the student performs the task guided by covert speech (thinking the self-instruction that was verbalized previously).

In addition to these four steps, there are six kinds of self-statements that are modeled by the teacher and rehearsed by the students (Meichenbaum and J. Goodman 1971; Meichenbaum and S. Goodman 1979):

1. Problem definition: "What do I have to do in this social setting?"
2. Focusing attention: "I have to think about what is happening."
3. Planning and guiding responses: "Be careful; look at only one aspect of the situation at a time."
4. Self-reinforcement: "That's good—I'm doing fine" or "So far . . . so good."
5. Self-evaluation: "Did I follow my plan and look at each component of the situation?"
6. Coping and error correction: "That's OK—if I make a mistake, I can backtrack and go a bit more slowly."

These statements enable students to understand the nature of the social situation confronting them, to produce appropriate strategies and verbalizations, and to direct and mediate their social behavior. Self-instructional statements can be used across a variety of situations and may reflect either social components or learner characteristics that might interfere with performance (impulsivity, learned helplessness, or external locus of control).

Self-instructional training emphasizes the students' active and collaborative role in designing, implementing, and evaluating their training regimens. It encourages students to "talk to themselves" before, during, and after a social behavior. Self-instructional training is flexible and responsive to individual students' unique needs. Students act as their own trainers as they analyze their cognitive and affective processes and identify the steps through which they must proceed in attaining a social goal.

The intervention strategies included in this chapter complement the theoretical perspectives espoused by psychodynamic and cognitive developmental theorists. Most of the interventions are teacher strategies and focus on the role of the teacher in facilitating the development of prosocial behaviors. The metacognitive and cognitive behavior modification approaches are student strategies that emphasize students' active involvement in their own learning. Other student strategies that foster appropriate prosocial behavior may be developed by teachers, following the guidelines presented in chapter 3.

SUMMARY

The development of social skills and competence is influenced by a number of variables that are highly interrelated. These variables may include biological and ecological factors, individual socialization agents, and situational determinants, all of which contribute to the uniqueness of students' personalities and their social behavior.

Social development begins with good social contact and relationships with adults, usually parents, and proceeds to a variety of social contacts with other children and individuals. This overall process of socialization has been conceptualized according to a number of theoretical orientations.

Traditional learning theory focuses heavily on environmental factors as determinants of social behavior. Reinforcement of the desired social behavior by significant adults in the child's environment is considered a powerful influence of social development at the early ages. A more recent conceptualization—social learning theory—recognizes the interaction of students' information-processing abilities and reinforcement in mediating their social behavior. Social learning theory considers the importance of learning through imitation and observation.

From a developmental viewpoint, social development results from the dynamic interaction of students and their environments, as they progress through various stages or levels of socialization. The developmental theories considered in this chapter include the psychodynamic theory of Sigmund Freud, which focuses on unconscious and instinctual self-gratification in personality formation and the development of morality. Erikson's theory of psychosocial development is an extension of Freud's conceptualization of human development. He believes that children's psychosocial development is influenced by historical and cultural values and attitudes in addition to internal factors.

Discussion of cognitive developmental theory centered in the works of Piaget, and Kohlberg is a framework for understanding morality and the acquisition of prosocial behavior. Piaget believed that social interaction is important to cognitive development and that children's liberation from egocentrism is an important consideration in their social interactions. Piaget's conceptualization of the development of moral judgment is aligned closely to his theory of cognitive development.

Kohlberg's stages of moral reasoning are an extension of Piaget's work. He believes that an individual's conceptualization of moral issues and of the motives that underlie these issues seems to change with age and cognitive maturity. Closely related to the development of moral reasoning is the concept of prosocial behavior, which involves acting in a caring and altruistic manner toward others. Caring and altruism are both related to empathy and perspective taking.

Students identified as mildly and moderately mentally retarded, emotionally disturbed, and learning disabled often have difficulties acting in a socially acceptable manner. Their inappropriate behavior may be influenced by atypical social experiences that are related to their learning handicaps. It is critical, therefore, that teachers have a solid theoretical understanding of social development as a means of initiating intervention strategies to facilitate students' moral-reasoning abilities and prosocial behaviors.

We have related intervention strategies to specific theoretical perspectives, where possible. The majority of them are general teacher strategies and techniques that are applicable to students identified as mildly mentally retarded, emotionally disturbed, and learning disabled. Specific student strategies to facilitate appropriate social behavior included a discussion of cognitive behavioral training and metacognition. These approaches help students to develop an awareness of, and to monitor, their social interactions with peers and significant adults—parents and teachers—in their daily environments.

Social competence must be learned through social interaction rather than through formal teaching. If we accept this idea, then parents and teachers must structure and organize students' environments so there is maximum opportunity for students to develop into socially competent individuals who function at a high level of moral reasoning and act prosocially toward others.

Concomitantly, we must remember that it is difficult to "teach" special educators how to deal with all of the social and emotional problems encountered in their interactions with students. Each situation will differ; therefore, we can only provide a general theoretical framework from which to understand students and to develop intervention strategies that will foster their acquisition of appropriate social behaviors.

REFERENCES

ARONFREED, J. *Conduct and Conscience: The Socialization of Internalized Control over Behavior.* New York: Academic Press, 1968.

BANDURA, A. *Social Learning Theory.* Englewood Cliffs, N.J.: Prentice-Hall, 1977.

BIDDELL, T. Piaget's theory of affectivity. Unpublished paper, 1980.

BIEHLER, R. *Child Development: An Introduction.* Boston: Houghton Mifflin Co., 1981.

CHENEY, C., AND W. C. MORSE. Psychodynamic interventions in emotional disturbance. In W. C. Rhodes and M. L. Tracy, eds., *A Study of Child Variance,* vol. 2, *Interventions.* Ann Arbor: University of Michigan Press, 1972.

CRAIGHEAD, W. E., B. WILCOXON, L. CRAIGHEAD, AND A. W. MEYERS. New directions in behavior modification with children. In M. Hershen, R. M. Eisler, and P. M. Miller, eds., *Progress in Behavior Modification,* vol. 6. New York: Academic Press, 1978.

CRAIN, WILLIAM C. *Theories of Development.* Englewood Cliffs, N. J.: Prentice-Hall, 1980.

DAMON, W.   *Early Conception of Justice as Related to the Development of Operational Reasoning.* Published Ph.D. dissertation, University of California, Berkeley, 1974.

DESHLER, D. D., AND J. B. SCHUMAKER.   Social skills of learning disabled adolescents: Characteristics and intervention. *Topics in Learning and Learning Disabilities* 3 (1983), 15–23.

D'ZURILLA, D. J., AND M. R. GOLDFRIED.   Problem solving and behavior modification. *Journal of Abnormal Psychology* 78 (1971), 107–26.

EKSTEIN, R.   Psychoanalysis and education for the facilitation of positive human qualities. *Journal of Social Issues* 28 (1971), 71–86.

ERIKSON, E.   *Childhood and Society.* 2d ed. New York: W. W. Norton, 1968.

FADELY. J. L., AND V. N. HOSLER.   *Development Psychometrics.* Springfield, Ill.: Charles C. Thomas, 1980.

FAGEN, S., AND N. J. LONG.   A psychoeducational curriculum approach to teaching self-control. *Behavior Disorders* 4 (1979), 68–82.

————, AND D. J. STEVENS.   *Teaching Children Self-Control.* Columbus, Ohio: Charles E. Merrill Publishing Co., 1975.

FLAVELL, J. H., AND L. ROSS, EDS.   *Social Cognitive Development.* Cambridge: Cambridge University Press, 1981.

FREUD, S.   *A General Introduction to Psychoanalysis.* Translated by J. Riviere. New York: Washington Square Press, 1965.

GALLAGHER, J. M., AND D. K. REID.   *The Learning Theory of Piaget and Inhelder.* Monterey, Calif.: Brooks/Cole, 1981.

GARWOOD, S. G.   *Educating Young Handicapped Children.* 2d ed. Rockville, Md.: Aspen Systems Corp., 1983.

GLASSER, W.   *Reality Therapy: A New Approach to Psychiatry.* New York: Harper & Row Publishers, 1975.

————.   *Schools without Failure.* New York: Harper & Row Publishers, 1969.

GOLDSTEIN, A. P.   *Psychological Skill Training.* Elmsford, N.Y.: Pergamon Press, 1981.

————, R. P. SPRAFKIN, AND N. J. GERSHAW.   *I Know What's Wrong But Don't Know What to Do About It.* Englewood Cliffs, N.J.: Prentice-Hall, 1979.

————, AND P. KLEIN.   *Skillstreaming the Adolescent: A Structured Learning Approach to Teaching Prosocial Skills.* Champaign, Ill.: Research Press Co., 1980.

HOFFMAN, M.   Developmental synthesis of affect and cognition and its implications for altruistic motivation. *Developmental Psychology* 11 (1975), 607–22.

————.   Empathy, role taking, guilt and development of altruistic motives. In T. Lickona, ed., *Moral Development and Behavior.* New York: Holt, Rinehart & Winston, 1976.

KAMII, C.   Autonomy: The aim of education envisioned by Piaget. *Phi Delta Kappan* 65 (1984), 410–15.

KOBAK D.   A philosophical rationale and practical guide to raising the CQ—caring quality— A moral imperative in global education. *Journal of Children and Youth* (fall 1981), 11–15.

————.   Teaching children to care. *Children Today* 8 (1979), 6–7. Department of Health, Education and Welfare.

KOHLBERG, L.   *The Philosophy of Moral Development.* San Francisco: Harper & Row Publishers, 1981.

————.   Stage and sequence: A cognitive developmental approach to socialization. In D. A. Goslin, ed., *Handbook of Socialization Theory.* Chicago: Rand McNally, 1969.

KRONICK, D.   *Social Development of Learning Disabled Persons: Examining the Effects and Treatments of Inadequate Interpersonal Skills.* San Francisco: Jossey Bass Publishers, 1983.

LICKONA, T., ED.   *Moral Development and Behavior.* New York: Holt, Rinehart & Winston, 1976.

————.   *Raising Good Children.* New York: Bantam Books, 1983.

MEICHENBAUM, D., AND J. GOODMAN.   Training impulsive children to talk to themselves: A means of developing self-control. *Journal of Abnormal Psychology* 77 (1971), 115–26.

MEICHENBAUM, D., AND S. GOODMAN.   Clinical use of private speech and clinical questions about its study in natural settings. In G. Zivin, ed., *The Development of Self-Regulation Through Private Speech.* New York: John Wiley and Sons, 1979.

MEYER, A.   Origins and prevention of emotional disturbances among learning disabled children. *Topics in Learning and Learning Disabilities* 3 (1983), 59–70.

MILLER, PATRICIA H.   *Theories of Developmental Psychology.* San Francisco: W. H. Freeman and Co., 1983.

MORSE, W. C.   Crises interventions in school mental health and special classes for the disabled. In N. J. Long, W. C. Morse, and R. G. Newman, Eds., *Conflict in the Classroom: The Education of Children with Problems.* Belmont, Calif.: Wadsworth, 1971.

————.   Worksheet on life space interviewing for teachers. In *Conflict in the Classroom.* 3d ed. Belmont, Calif.: Wadsworth, 1976.

MUSSEN, P. H., AND N. EISENBERG-BERG.   *Roots of Caring, Sharing and Helping.* San Francisco: W. H. Freeman and Co., 1977.

PEARL, R., T. BRYAN, AND M. DONAHUE.   Social behaviors of learning disabled: A review. *Topics in Learning and Learning Disabilities* 3 (1983), 1–14.

PIAGET, J.   *The Moral Judgment of the Child.* Translated by M. Gahain. New York: Free Press, 1932/1965.

REDL, F.   The concept of life space interview. *American Journal of Orthopsychiatry* 29 (1959), 1–18.

RICH, H. LYNDALL.   *Disturbed Children.* Baltimore: University Park Press, 1982.

ROUSSEAU, J. J.   *Emile, or Education.* Translated by B. Foxley. London: J. M. Dent and Sans, 1948.

SANDERS, M.   Assessing the interaction of learning disabilities and social emotional development. *Topics in Learning and Learning Disabilities* 3 (1983), 37–47.

SCHUMAKER, J. B., C. S. PEDERSON, J. S. HAZEL, AND E. L. MEYER.   Social skills curricula for mildly handicapped adolescents: A review. *Focus on Exceptional Children* 16 (December 1983), 1–16.

SELF, E.   Education for caring. *Journal of Children and Youth* (Fall 1981), 16–23.

SILVER, L. B.   Therapeutic intervention with learning disabled students and their families. *Topics in Learning and Learning Disabilities* 3 (1983), 48–58.

SPIVACK, G., J. J. PLATT, AND M. B. SHURE.   *The Problem Solving Approach to Adjustment.* San Francisco: Jossey Bass Publishers, 1976.

SPIVACK, G., AND M. B. SHURE.   *Social Adjustment in Young Children: A Cognitive Approach to Solving Real Life Problems.* San Francisco: Jossey Bass Publishers, 1974.

THIBAULT, J. P., AND J. D. MCKEE.   Practical parenting with Piaget. *Young Children* 38 (1982), 18–27.

THOMAS, A., AND S. CHESS.   *Temperament and Development.* New York: Brunner/Mazel, 1977.

————, AND H. BIRCH.   *Temperament and Behavioral Disorders in Children.* New York: New York University Press, 1968.

A SPECIAL PREFACE TO
CHAPTER TEN

The emphasis in this text might be described as developmental, as constructivist, or as emphasizing cognitive strategies. We believe that as children develop cognitively, they are creating valuable new learning strategies, based primarily on their previous experiences. We are convinced that such concepts as metacognition and executive control are practical and useful tools in assisting students to improve basic cognitive and social skills and to thus maximize their school achievement and later to adapt to adult society.

But we (the authors) are also pragmatists. We believe that there are some situations in which the behavioral point of view may be of value and that when it is, it should be utilized. Therefore, we have included chapter 10, relating to behavior management techniques and strategies. Not to include it would mean ignoring instructional ideas that are effective in certain situations and with specific students. Chapter 10 is philosophically out of step with much of the rest of the text, but because we are most concerned with helping teachers to more effectively teach mildly and moderately handicapped students, we felt compelled to include it.

CHAPTER TEN

Behavior Management Techniques and Strategies

- What are the limitations of behavioral theory and applied behavior management?
- How may behavior modification techniques be considered "good"; how may they be considered "bad"? (What is the *real* "truth"?)
- What is the difference between negative reinforcement and punishment?
- Can teachers become overdependent on behavior management techniques?
- How do primary reinforcers, conditioned reinforcers, and token reinforcers differ?
- What guidelines exist for establishment of effective contracting systems?
- What factors limit the effectiveness of behavioral approaches in actual classroom implementation?

INTRODUCTION

In this chapter we will consider a number of specific techniques and strategies that have been found to be useful in modifying unacceptable classroom behavior and in promoting the learning of skills, content, and concepts that are part of the overall educational program. These techniques and strategies are known as behavior modification, operant conditioning, and applied behavior analysis, and have been given many other, similar terms, labels, and titles. All have their roots in behaviorism, as originated by J. B. Watson (1913) and other psychologists and brought to the field of education by B. F. Skinner (1953, 1968). In the remainder of this chapter, we will consider: (1) the theoretical/historical origin of behavior management strategies, (2) basic behavior modification terminology, (3) using behavior modification techniques to increase desirable behaviors, (4) using behavior modification to reduce or eliminate undesirable behaviors, and (5) variations of behavior modification approaches. Certain specific approaches, such as contingency contracting, will receive more attention than others. In addition, we will review a number of case studies in applied behavior management and consider the basic limitations to behavioral approaches. However, before considering these major topics, we want to share some thoughts on the use of behavior management techniques and their relationship to the rights of the student to "personal freedom." We share these thoughts because there appear to exist at least some vestiges of concern about "behavior-changing" procedures and their acceptability in a free society. The essence of our thoughts include the following:

1. There is a body of information that may be called behavioral science, which indicates that behavior falls into certain regular patterns, in turn permitting the development of a number of behavioral laws and principles.
2. Behavioral science is incomplete (not fully developed) and has the potential for being used for both "good" and "bad" purposes. (One example of "bad" use—for those who object to the methods of certain religious cults—is the use of behavioral principles to encourage young people to totally reject society, family, and so on, and believe only the teachings of the leader of the cult.)
3. As with the other sciences, we must not reject this science and its valuable applications simply because of its potential to produce effects or results that may be negative to society.
4. Children's behavior *is* being managed, by a variety of forces; that is, it is *caused by some thing,* and to the extent that such behavior is unacceptable, educators should attempt to modify it.

We believe that students in our schools deserve the opportunity to develop adequate academic, social, and decision-making skills, and have the right to develop a full repertoire of those abilities that will permit them the broadest possible range of future life choices. We further believe that analysis of student behavior and the use of behavioral approaches are often of value in assisting students to develop these abilities. Our discussion of behavior management techniques and strategies is intended to help the teacher to assist more effectively in the development of academic skills and socially acceptable behavior. We believe that individuals with a broad range of skills and abilities are more "free" of the possibility of improper behavioral controls; thus behavior modification, when used to develop a broad range of skills, may actually reduce the possibility/effectiveness of future behavior modification. With these thoughts in mind, we will proceed with a consideration of the theoretical/historical origin of behavior management strategies.

THE THEORETICAL/HISTORICAL ORIGIN OF BEHAVIOR MANAGEMENT STRATEGIES

The psychologist John B. Watson provided part of the original impetus for behavior modification as presently applied in our schools when he contended that "certain stimuli lead the organisms to make the responses . . . [and] given the response the stimuli can be predicted, given the stimuli, the response can be predicted" (1913, p. 167). His statement was near heresy in the field of psychology, which had been dominated by psychoanalytic theory and concern with the elements of the mind, consciousness, mental states, and the like. He proposed that psychology be considered an objective, experimental branch of the natural sciences and believed that its major goal was the study, prediction, and control of behavior.

Between 1913 and the midtwentieth century, a number of studies were reported in which behavioral principles were used to change behavior, but it was not until the publication of a book by B. F. Skinner in 1953 that more serious consideration was given to changing from the psychoanalytic model to the behavioral model. In his book *Science and Human Behavior* Skinner noted that behavior had not been accepted as an entity "in its own right" but "only as an indication of something wrong somewhere else" (1953, p. 373). Between 1953 and the publication of *The Technology of Teaching* (Skinner 1968), many important contributions were made by a variety of behavioral researchers and practitioners, and the decade of the 1970s saw the publication of dozens of texts and thousands of journal articles relating to behavior modification. Behavior modification had arrived as an important tool for use in the classroom.

The theoretical origin of behavior modification may be considered either simple or complex. It may be considered simple in that it is based on the simple idea that observable behavior can be changed if we arrange or alter significant environmental events. Also, stated simply, there is no concern for "inner causes"; it is, in effect, a rejection of the medical model, "causal" theory.

If in considering theoretical origin, we include the research that attempts to support and expand these simple ideas, then behavior modification can be considered complex. Procedures used in behavior modification are based on experimental results, but as noted by Sulzer and Mayer (1972), although "in many cases there are adequate data on humans to back up an assertion or suggestion, . . . in others, only data from the animal laboratory are available" (p. 2). This is the case because it would be unacceptable to conduct the required carefully controlled research on humans just for the sake of obtaining the needed research results. Therefore, actual application of certain types of behavioral intervention with humans must be based on research with animals, which leads to considerable complexity in some instances. The situation, however, is not too different from what happens in medical research, where a considerable amount of testing on animals must precede the use of new surgical procedures or application of new types of medication with humans.

Establishing a solid theoretical base for applied behavioral intervention is further complicated by the wide variety of outside factors that have an effect on individual humans and that cannot be controlled (in most cases) when dealing with children in school settings. As a result, carefully controlled research is extremely difficult to plan and implement. Despite these difficulties, through a wide variety of experimental studies with school-age boys and girls, the efficacy of behavior modification has been established. It is a recognized vehicle for change, and behavioral change is the major purpose of the schools.* Some might protest that "learning" or "personal development," or some other term(s) might better define the major purpose of schools, but all such terms include the need to change. Parents expect their children to learn to read and write (or to read and write more effectively), and that is certainly change. They expect social and emotional growth, and that is change. In fact, change is the purpose of education, and the behaviorist is a scientist who specializes in change. Behavioral changes that have relevance to the classroom are the focus of the remainder of this chapter.

BEHAVIOR MODIFICATION TERMINOLOGY

There is some possibility of confusion in relation to the specific terminology of behavior modification; therefore, several terms will be briefly defined in this section. This will permit the discussion of application of behavior modification methods without the interruption of thought that would be necessary if such definitions were to be a part of each such discussion.

Behavior modification is a technique wherein environmental events are arranged so as to produce a specific change in observable behavior (Ullmann and Krasner 1965; O'Leary and O'Leary 1977; and others). An

---

*Many authors in the field of child development, learning theory, and related disciplines have noted that change (development) is inevitable, and that the purpose of education is to guide that change in those directions that are consistent with the goals of society. (Those goals, of course, vary in various geographical areas of the world.) Many quotations might be used to illustrate this point, but perhaps few are more effective and more simply stated than those of Bloom, Hastings, and Madaus, as found in their monumental *Handbook on Formative and Summative Evaluation of Student Learning* (1971). They note that "education . . . is a process which changes learners. Given this view we expect each program, course, and unit of education to bring about some significant change or changes in the students. Students should be different at the end of a unit than they were before it" (p. 8).

alternate definition by Sulzer and Mayer (1972, p. 2) is that "when the methods of behavioral science and its experimental findings are systematically applied with the intent of altering behavior, the technique is called behavior modification." The general term *behavior modification* is often used to include more specific terms, such as operant conditioning, contingency management, contingency contracting, and behavioral modeling. However, in each case it will be noted that the individual utilizing behavior modification (in whatever form or forms) is applying the methods of behavioral science in the attempt to alter behavior. A third, and very effective, description of the basis for behavior modification is provided by Alberto and Troutman (1982). They describe a hypothetical "Professor Grundy," who eventually, through trial and error, gets his professorial world under control and evolves some simple principles. These include: (1) learning occurs as a result of the consequences of behavior; (2) behavior followed by pleasant consequences tends to be repeated and thus learned, and (3) behavior that is followed by unpleasant consequences tends not to be repeated and thus not to be learned. Behaviorists, through behavior modification, attempt to apply these three principles to reinforce behavior they wish to be repeated and to change behavior they feel to be unacceptable.

Operant conditioning, a term made popular by B. F. Skinner (1968), can best be described by contrasting it with *respondent conditioning.* Skinner noted that there are just these two types of observable human behaviors— *respondent* and *operant.* Respondent behavior would include such reactions as children clapping their hands in joy (in response to some happy event), or shrinking back in fear (in response to a much larger child raising his fist). In contrast, operant behavior may be viewed as "voluntary" in nature. With operant (voluntary) behavior, the likelihood or frequency of repetition of such behavior is influenced by the events that follow (the consequences) of that behavior. Operant conditioning is one major type of behavior modification and, according to Swanson and Reinert (1979), is "the most thoroughly investigated approach for the classroom teacher" (p. 51). In very simple terms, in operant conditioning, the teacher determines which behavior should be changed, selects procedures that will likely modify that behavior (either positive consequences or aversive consequences), and applies a systematic program to attempt to bring about the desired change. If an *increase* in behavior is desired (for example, an increase in attendance to a reading assignment at the student's desk), it should be accomplished through *pairing positive consequences,* or a *reduction in aversive consequences,* or through the *use of aversive stimuli.* This procedure is commonly called punishment, and of course has been used for decades, perhaps centuries. This pairing of certain planned consequences with the behavior under consideration is called operant conditioning. Though often used as synonymous with behavior modification, it is actually a more specific term.

Target behavior is the behavior we wish to modify, and it is important that we define behavior quite specifically (for example, at what point does "pushing" or otherwise touching another student become "hitting"?).

Contingencies are relationships between behaviors and whatever events follow the behavior. Some contingencies may occur "naturally"; for example, if a student steps in front of a batter while she is swinging the bat, he gets hit. That is a natural contingency. However, teachers will ordinarily be most concerned with planned contingencies, which may be used to maintain, strengthen, weaken, or eliminate behavior. To properly apply behavioral approaches, it is important to plan and specify contingencies in advance. (*Contingency contracting* is a process whereby such contingencies are part of a written contract. It has value at all age levels, but has been particularly useful at the upper-elementary and the secondary levels.)

Extinction is the process of removing reinforcement for a behavior (which the teacher wants to be reduced) until it is significantly reduced or is no longer exhibited. This procedure may permit us to avoid the use of punishment.

Shaping involves the reinforcement of behaviors that approximate some desired terminal behavior. It requires systematic reinforcement of successive approximations, which are, in effect, moving the student closer to the desired behavioral goal. Shaping is essential when the desired behavior is quite complex, or when the desired response (behavior) is never exhibited by the child.

Modeling relates to the tendency of individuals to model or imitate the behavior of others. Modeling is ordinarily encouraged by reinforcement and may make use of a shaping procedure.

Reinforcement is any factor or event that results in the maintenance or increase of behavior. It should be noted that teachers must think not only of reinforcement for *desired* behavior but also of those procedures or events that are reinforcing *undesirable* behavior. Behaviorists often speak of types or schedules of reinforcement. The two major types of reinforcement schedules are continuous reinforcement (reinforcement after each desired response) or intermittent reinforcement. The four generally recognized types of intermittent reinforcement schedules are indicated in table 10-1.

In addition to the information on application contained in Table 10-1, Craighead, Kazdin, and Mahoney (1981) indicate the following generalizations with respect to the various schedules: (1) fixed-interval schedules may lead to considerable pauses after the reinforcer is delivered (the subject apparently learns to wait until near the end of the interval to provide the target response); (2) higher rates of response are usually obtained through ratio, as compared to interval, schedules; (3) variable schedules tend to produce more consistent patterns of response; (4) variable schedules are important to develop resistance to extinction; and (5) as performance is attained under a given schedule, the schedule may be made "leaner" (longer time interval or requiring more responses between reinforcement in ratio schedules), moving toward high performance with minimum reinforcement.

Negative reinforcement involves the removal of an aversive stimulus. Therefore, to be able to use negative reinforcement, an aversive stimulus must be present or at least viewed by the child as "possible." (That is, it could happen or take place.) In negative reinforcement, the child's behavior is reinforced by the removal of an aversive (undesirable, unwanted) stimulus. In contrast, *punishment* means the presentation of (providing) an aversive stimulus. In negative reinforcement, the child's behavior is what

TABLE 10-1   Types (Schedules) of Reinforcement

TYPE	DESCRIPTION	APPLICATION*
Continuous	Reinforce after each desired response.	Best for initial effort in establishing or shaping new behavior.
Fixed-interval schedule	Reinforce every *n* minutes (fixed *time* interval).	For infrequent behaviors.
Variable-interval schedule	Reinforce at *variable* time intervals.	When fixed-interval is not too effective, this may provide higher probability of response and maintain behaviors at a higher rate. Also used after fixed interval to maintain behavior.
Fixed-ratio schedule	Reinforce after every *n* number of responses.	May be used to maintain new behaviors but may be less effective than variable schedules.
Variable-ratio schedule	Reinforce after a variable number of responses (i.e., after 4, then 11, then 7, etc.).	Valuable for maintaining desired behaviors.

*Reinforcement schedules can be named and described with some assurance, but application is not so clearcut.

stops the aversive aspect of the experience; in punishment, the teacher decides when to stop. (The use of the term *reinforcement* alone usually means "*positive* reinforcement"; however, technically the definition of *reinforcement* could also include "negative" reinforcement. Therefore, most authors qualify the type of reinforcement by indicating positive or negative.)

Generalization refers to the "spread" or application of a behavior learned in one stimulus situation to other situations. This is the process most parents and teachers hope for with respect to study habits, good social manners, and a host of other areas of performance. It must be noted that students may generalize both "good" and "bad" behaviors.

There are additional terms that might be defined in this section, but these few might be called key terms, and others (if the meaning is not fairly obvious through context clues) will be defined as their use is required in the following discussions.

INCREASING THE EXISTENCE
OF EXISTING DESIRABLE
BEHAVIORS

Though some teachers' referral forms might lead one to believe that the child (who is the subject of the referral) has *no* good behavior, in fact, even the most disruptive student has a moment or two each day in which his behavior approaches acceptability. It is, of course, the other 95 percent of the day that contributes to teacher "burnout." One major application of behavior modification is to find ways to increase that 5 percent of the day in which the student exhibits acceptable behavior, thus automatically decreasing the percentage of the time in which the student is exhibiting unacceptable behavior. For years, perhaps centuries, we (parents and teachers) have tended to think in terms of "punishment" that may decrease the unacceptable behavior. Obviously, our real goal is to *increase acceptable behavior.* One of the most effective ways to achieve these dual goals (decrease of unacceptable behavior, increase of acceptable behavior) is through positive reinforcement of those behaviors we want to see increased.

Positive Reinforcement

Positive reinforcement requires a contingent stimulus that will maintain or increase the targeted response. In the case of the teacher who wants to modify a given child's behavior, this means carefully determining the target behavior to be increased, and *selecting a reinforcer that is truly a reinforcer for that student.* We emphasize the matter of selection of the reinforcer since, in our experience, this is where many attempts at behavior management break down. Let us consider, for example, the behavior we like to see in young children that involves raising the hand to ask to speak. Then after the child is recognized, we like the child to say (for example), "May I go to the restroom?" We have often heard teachers say, "I don't see why John can't raise his hand before he speaks. I know he understands what I want him to do."

In fact, it is not a simple procedure, especially for some students. For most students it means changing from a "home procedure" that may include any of the following: (1) simply going to the bathroom area of the home; (2) (if, after going to the bathroom area at home, John finds it occupied by his brother Sam) banging on the bathroom door and yelling, "Sam, get out of there, I've gotta go"; or (3) (if Sam is in the bathroom) going to his mother (without raising his hand or being recognized in any way) and saying, "Get Sam out of the bathroom or I'll go on the floor!" Most readers will recognize some similarities to events that have taken place in their own homes. Earlier experience does not necessarily prepare a child to exhibit all of the various types of behavior we require in school, and for some students it is difficult to learn to follow the new rules and requirements.

But, we may ask, why do most of the students learn to follow the many requirements of the schools, while those few "troublesome" ones do not? The behaviorist will probably answer "because there was insufficient positive reinforcement for those who did not learn to conform." When it comes to social/behavioral habits and rules, most children learn to conform because they want parent and teacher approval. In this case, the reinforcement is a smile, words of approval, and the like. For some children, that is not enough. When it is not, the behavioral point of view is that we must find another reinforcer. When we find the right reinforcer, we should be able to increase the behavior in question.

In the case of the child who has not learned to follow the rules and social patterns expected in the school, it should be apparent that the normal positive reinforcers have not been sufficient. In some cases (it is very difficult to predict a percentage of cases, without specific information about the behavior in question), more of the same type of reinforcement used with other children may work. But in many instances, "more of the same" is not the answer. Then the question is just what reinforcer(s) should be used.

There is no answer that will fit all situations. An obvious truism is that it must be a reinforcer *for the child in question.* For example, we have known situations in which extra time working with computers may prove to be strong reinforcement. But if the child has his or her own computer at home or knows so little about computers that additional computer time is meaningless, then computer time may not be effective as a reinforcer.

Primary reinforcers by definition include food, water, sex, warmth, and similar life-maintaining or perpetuating stimuli. Of this group, food is most often used in the school setting. But what about the ethics of using food as a reinforcer? Our answer is that used with judgment, it can be both acceptable and effective. Sulzer and Mayer (1972) point out that when a teacher waits for her class to line up quietly before they may go to the lunchroom, she is using food as a primary reinforcer for orderly behavior. In a similar manner, class parties featuring food may be contingent on behavior, and the list could be lengthened considerably.

Conditioned reinforcers are also effective in many cases. According to Sulzer and Mayer, "A conditioned reinforcer is a stimulus, an object, or an event that initially was neutral but, through frequent pairings with primary or strong conditioned reinforcers, has assumed reinforcing properties" (1972, p. 26). Axelrod (1977) notes that although there is a tendency to view conditioned reinforcers as something less than "real" reinforcers, they are quite potent and are an important source of reinforcement in the school. Most children are subject to strong reinforcement from a number of conditioned reinforcers long before they enter school; however, the strength of these reinforcers varies in relation to their early experience and perhaps in relation to other factors that are not fully understood. The early pairing of smiles, pats, and comments such as "You're a good girl," with food, has led most children to respond favorably to attention, praise, and smiles. The attention, praise, and smiles have become essentially just as strong as food, the primary reinforcer. But when a student will not respond to the usual teacher repertoire of conditioned reinforcers, primary or, at the very least, unusual or particularly strong conditioned reinforcers must be used.

It is quite possible that more teachers have heard of *token reinforcers* than of conditioned reinforcers. Token reinforcers are simply a special kind of conditioned reinforcer, one that is particularly applicable in the classroom. Tokens might include stars, check marks, poker chips, trading stamps, or anything that the student recognizes as representing real value (exchangeable for any of a variety of other items, activities, or privileges). In the terminology of the behaviorist, a token may be anything that can acquire conditioned reinforcing properties. The token, given after the child exhibits the required behavior, then may be accumulated along with other tokens, to exchange for a *back-up reinforcer*. The back-up reinforcer is then the real "power" behind the token and may include any of a long list of activities, privileges, responsibilities, or real items. O'Leary and Drabman (1971) indicate that tokens should have certain properties. They should (1) be easy to dispense, (2) be readily portable, (3) have a value easy to understand, (4) not require extensive out-of-class teacher effort, and (5) be easily identifiable as belonging to the recipient.

Whatever the token, the back-up reinforcer is highly important. According to Lahey and Drabman (1981), certain reinforcers are of more value at specific ages (their comments are based on the results of a number of studies). For example, young or retarded children respond well to activities such as running errands, cleaning the room, or serving as a teaching assistant. Candy, small toys, or trinkets are also valuable. Older students relate more positively to playing records, dancing, and playing games such as checkers, pool, or Ping-Pong. These "sound like" age-appropriate back-up reinforcers, but it is reassuring to read Lahey and Drabman's summary of research that supports this "logical" thinking.

The following list of possible reinforcers (these might be used as back-up reinforcers for a token system or used immediately following the desired behavior) are more directly applicable to young children or to older retarded children. This list is adapted from lists provided by Sulzer and Mayer (pp. 33–35).

model with clay	push someone around in swivel chair
cut out choice of pictures	write on blackboard
throw or roll ball	pour water through funnel
climb ladder or steps	into container
look at slides	look in mirror
listen to short recording	color pictures
watch short film or filmstrip	have extra time on playground
pop balloon, paper bag, etc.	equipment
string beads	play short game
play with magnet	turn off (or on) lights
play with flashlight	put blinds up or down
play with water gun	be leader in line
blow bubbles	pass out milk
record and listen to voice	run errand for teacher
on tape recorder	erase blackboard
play with typewriter	

It is admittedly more difficult to compile a long list of possible reinforcers for use with secondary-age students, but those already mentioned (dancing, listening to records, just talking, playing pool or Ping-Pong) are among the more popular, along with free time; that is, time in which the student is free to select from among a number of alternatives including just doing nothing of an academic nature. *Finally, we should not forget to try just asking students what they would like as a reward or reinforcer.*

Token reinforcement systems, implemented when social praise and approval are not sufficient, must be explained carefully to the class if they are to be successful. Such programs are at times initiated with just one or two students and at other times with the entire class. In either case, the entire class should have some understanding of the system. Swanson and Reinert (1979) suggest that at least three components are absolutely essential for a successful program. These components are (1) explaining how the target behaviors will be reinforced, (2) explaining how the token(s) will be contingent on behavior, and (3) clarifying the rules whereby tokens may be exchanged for the back-up reinforcers. Clarity and repetition are emphasized by all advocates of token systems. Daily review of the rules, clearly recorded results of each student's behavior, and (if there are a variety of possible back-up reinforcers) a readily available list of potential "rewards" are essential if token systems are to work effectively.

Token reinforcement systems were first used to improve social behavior and have been found to be of considerable value in such areas as reducing hitting/kicking behavior, reducing excessive swearing or other particularly objectional language, and ameliorating other socially unacceptable behavior. In most cases, the procedure was that of reinforcing more acceptable behavior. Token reinforcement systems have been used more recently to bring about academic improvement through such efforts as improving in-seat behavior or attending behavior. In such cases, if the student has the prerequisite learning skills, and if the educational material is appropriate and well organized, the result of more attention and less time moving around the classroom is usually improved academic performance. Used in these ways, token reinforcement systems (positive reinforcement through conditioned reinforcers with appropriate back-up reinforcement) can be highly effective in the education of many handicapped or disabled students.

Modeling and positive reinforcement go hand in hand. Modeling, or learning through the observation of others, is something that happens, whether teachers like it (or plan it) or not. It is likely that we all learn to a considerable extent through modeling. Modeling is of value in modifying the frequency of previously learned responses or in the development of new responses (Rosenthal and Bandura, 1978). However, Craighead, Kazdin, and Mahoney (1981) caution that we must be careful to distinguish between *learning* and *performance* when we consider the effects of modeling. For example, in a study by Bandura (1965) in which three groups of children observed aggressive responses in a film, there were differing performances by these groups in relation to additional films that they viewed. The subgroup who saw the aggressive behavior punished did not tend to model it when given an opportunity to perform similar aggressive responses. But the other two subgroups who saw the behavior being ignored or rewarded tended to model the behavior. Later, strong incentives were given to children in all three groups to perform aggressive responses. At that time, there were no differences in the responses of the three groups. Apparently all three groups had *learned* the aggressive responses, but until given strong incentives to exhibit such aggression, the group who had observed the film model being punished for aggression did not model such aggression. We might therefore conclude that children tend to *learn* through observation but *perform* because of observed consequences of the observed action or direct personal reinforcement to respond as the model responded.

In addition, it appears that a number of other variables help determine whether a given individual will actually model any given behavior. According to Craighead, Kazdin, and Mahoney, a variety of research indicates that observers are more likely to imitate (1) models who are similar to themselves, (2) models who are relatively high in prestige, status, or expertise, or (3) a group of models exhibiting the same, or similar, behavior.

Modeling has obvious implications in changing a student's social behavior and, as indicated in the beginning of this section, will more likely be successful if used in conjunction with positive reinforcement. Modeling may also be of value in academic situations in the area of study skills and attending behavior or in areas such as writing, in which specific motor acts are involved.

Shaping, like modeling, is more often used in conjunction with other types of behavior modification. It is of particular value in assisting the student to develop a response that is not in his or her repertoire of responses. This is usually some relatively complex response, but it may be relatively simple, yet very foreign to the experience of the student.

Modeling may be used in conjunction with shaping as, for example, in teaching handwriting. In most handwriting workbooks, the young child learns to go through various steps (lines of various shapes) in which more and more complex lines are formed, requiring increasing degrees of precision. When such efforts are observed by the teacher, reinforcement is supplied as the teacher says, "That's fine" or "You are doing very well, Sally." Another type of shaping is involved with very young children as they learn to articulate new words, or at school age, when they need to learn to correct speech patterns.

Another example of shaping in the social-behavior arena is the manner in which we teach children not to run in the hall or not to speak too loudly. Usually we reward them when they slow down to some degree, even if they have not really slowed to the speed we would desire. Similarly, if we can encourage a child to reduce a loud shout to a "soft" shout, it may be the first step toward that child's learning to speak at a normal speaking level, as required in a large classroom.

In shaping, we must carefully define the terminal behavior we want, and then plan the small steps which will likely lead to that behavior. We must also select reinforcing contingencies which are likely to actually be reinforcing to the child under consideration and which we can actually provide. As with all behavioral efforts, good record keeping is essential. In shaping, it is altogether possible that the teacher will have to reduce the amount of change (movement toward the desired goal) expected in each step of the procedure or, in some cases, the student may be able to move more rapidly than planned initially. The plan, along with careful recording of results, will provide the basis for such modifications, if such are desirable.

Contracts

A contract is just what the term indicates. It is a written agreement between the student and the teacher (sometimes also countersigned by the parent) regarding accomplishment or performance in given behavioral (including academic behavior) areas. It usually indicates that the student will _____ and the teacher will _____. Figure 10-1 provides

Figure 10-1

CONTRACT

This contract is hereby established between _____ and

(student)

_____. The conditions of this contract become

(teacher)

effective on _____ and remain in effect through _____.

Contract conditions will be reviewed on _____ and may be

renegotiated if both parties agree to the new conditions.

The terms of this contract are:

_____ agrees to _____

(the student)

_____

_____

_____

_____

_____ will then _____

(the teacher)

_____

_____

_____

Special conditions and provisions of this contract include:

1. _____

2. _____

_____ _____ _____

(signature)   (signature)   (date) an example of a contract that might be used at the secondary level or upper-elementary level. In general, contracts used in secondary schools tend to be "plainer" and also slightly more "legal" in appearance and construction. Contracts used with younger students may be embellished with pictures (for example, cartoonlike pictures) and in general are less formal and "legal" in their wording. In both cases, however, there are certain general rules that should be followed. Figure 10-2 provides an outline of the major rules for contracting, adapted from recommendations made by Homme. Figure 10-3 summarizes the major steps that should be taken in establishing the conditions of the contract.

In most cases, teachers who have not used contracting in their classes should attempt to find someone who has used it or should look for more detailed explanations of contracting in Homme's text, which is totally devoted to contracting, or in a behavior modification text that has a chapter on contracting. The information in this chapter, however, should provide fundamentals necessary for successful use of contracting. In concluding this section, we might note some cautions provided by Marsh, Price, and Smith (1983): (1) Tangible or primary rewards should be accompanied by social rewards for maximum effectiveness; (2) there may be difficulties because the required task is too easy or too difficult; (3) rewards may lose their effectiveness; and (4) some teachers do not evaluate the system with regularity and thus do not realize when things are going wrong. Finally, all authors note that, although the idea of a contract is to provide an established set of goals (something concrete), it is essential to be flexible as the contract is being implemented.

Figure 10-2   CONTRACTING GUIDELINES

1. Contract "payoff" (the reward promised the student if contract conditions are met) should be immediate.
2. *Initial* contracts should be consistent with the principles of shaping; that is, they should require, and reward, small approximations.
3. Contracts should be designed so as to reward frequently, with small amounts.
4. Contract conditions should be established so that *accomplishment, not obedience,* is called for.
5. Performance must be rewarded *after* it occurs.
6. Contracts must be fair and honest.
7. Contracts must be positive.
8. The terms and conditions of the contract *must be clear.*
9. To be most effective, contracting must be used systematically.

*Adapted from L. Homme, *How to Use Contingency Contracting in the Classroom.* Champaign, Ill.: Research Press, 1971.

Figure 10-3 SEQUENTIAL STEPS IN ESTABLISHING A CONTRACT

1. After assuring that rapport has been established, the purpose of the "contract meeting" should be carefully reviewed with the student.
2. The teacher should explain the process of contracting, give examples of contracts used in other arenas (i.e., a contract between a builder and a homeowner to pour a concrete driveway or between a farmer and a grocer for a given quantity of vegetables) and then tell the student that they are going to consider a contract.*
3. The teacher should explain that the contract is an advantage to most students, is a source of help, and assures, in writing, specific rewards if contract conditions are met. The purpose of this discussion is to convince the student that this process is favorable to the *student.*
4. Both the student and the teacher should suggest tasks that might become part of the project. Actual written lists are usually the best procedure.
5. The student and the teacher should then agree on a task for the initial contract.
6. The teacher should ask the student what activities he or she likes (what would be good for a reward). The teacher should already have a number of ideas but must remain open to new ideas.
7. The teacher and student should negotiate: (1) time frame, (2) reinforcers, (3) criteria for achievement (x problems in y minutes with z percent accuracy, etc.), (4) evaluation procedures, (5) how reward/reinforcer is to be delivered and other details essential to complete the contract.
8. The teacher and student should actually complete the project together, with the student playing as major a role as possible.
9. The teacher and student should review the contract together, making certain all is understood.
10. Two copies of the contract should be made and both signed by both parties. One is retained by the teacher; the other goes to the student.
11. In concluding the initial establishment of a contract, the teacher should assure the student that he or she views the contract as a positive step and should emphasize that any questions that arise should be made known immediately.

*The level of examples used and the amount of time taken in this step depend on the age of the student and his or her level of understanding of the concepts of "contract." With younger students, it may be a good idea to encourage *them* to think of other examples of contracts, to be certain that the concept is clear.

NEGATIVE REINFORCEMENT

Negative reinforcement is one possible way to increase the frequency of whatever behavior is the target of the behavioral procedure. Negative reinforcement is effective because the student performs the desired (target) behavior to avoid or escape the negative (aversive) consequences. There are times when use of negative reinforcement may be the best (most effective) system, but in general most authorities would advise that we try to use positive reinforcement whenever possible. One common use of negative reinforcement is the teacher's use of facial expressions that say, "Stop what you are doing, or you will be in trouble." This process, sometimes called use of a "teacher face," is effective with many, but not all, children. Another common example of negative reinforcement is for a teacher to motivate students to work by promising that she will not require homework for that day "if you all finish your worksheets by 3 P.M."

The problem with negative reinforcement is that it is quite easy for the teacher to get into a difficult situation through its use. (Axelrod [1977, p. 8] notes that "teachers sometimes unknowingly become trapped by negative-reinforcement arrangements.") For example, if the frown, or "teacher face," does not work, the teacher may eventually be shouting at students to achieve "order," and the result will be disastrous. And as pointed out by Alberto and Troutman (1982), the student, in attempting to avoid some particular aversive stimulus, may escape from the whole school setting (be truant), or in reaction to what he or she believes to be unfair treatment, may become aggressive and become involved in more detrimental behavior than that we are attempting to modify. Alberto and Troutman summarize the situation (regarding value of negative reinforcement) succinctly and effectively when they say that "mild aversive stimuli may sometimes be justified, but positive reinforcement is the procedure of choice for increasing or maintaining behavior" (p. 202).

REDUCING OR ELIMINATING UNDESIRABLE BEHAVIORS

For the most part, undesirable behavior should be reduced or eliminated by positive reinforcement of desirable behavior. All of the methods we have discussed are obviously applicable. Shaping, the use of contracts, token-reinforcement systems, modeling—all may be effective, depending on the situation. However, there are four approaches to the reduction or elimination of undesirable behavior that deserve particular mention here: the use of extinction, time out, response cost, and punishment.

Extinction

Extinction "is a procedure for reducing behavior which involves abruptly terminating the positive reinforcer [that is] maintaining an inappropriate target behavior" (Alberto and Troutman 1982, p. 212). Further, we may generalize that: (1) extinction is more often used by teachers to decrease behaviors that have been maintained by teacher attention; (2) teacher attention may be positively reinforcing, even if it includes criticism, correction, and threats; and (3) teachers are often unable to recognize that their actions are reinforcing inappropriate behavior. Alberto and Troutman suggest that it may be helpful to have another person observe teacher-pupil interaction to arrive at a more accurate determination as to whether the teacher is actually reinforcing the behavior he or she would like to extinguish.

Extinction can be very effective for reducing school-related behaviors that are unacceptable. One of its greatest strengths is that it is more long lasting than many other approaches. Another is that it is very effective when used in combination with other procedures (positive reinforcement of desired behavior, modeling). In a summary of procedures for reducing behavior, Sulzer and Mayer (1972) note that to maximize the effectiveness of extinction we must (1) identify all reinforcers for the response and withhold completely, (2) maintain the procedure long enough to show effect, and (3) provide reinforcement for other behaviors (p. 234). Alberto and Troutman (p. 216) suggest the following three important questions to be asked before implementing an extinction procedure:

1. Can the behavior be tolerated temporarily, based on its topography and on its current rate of occurrence?
2. Can an increase in the behavior be tolerated?
3. Is the behavior likely to be limited?

One additional question of great practical importance is whether alternative behaviors have been identified for reinforcement.

Sulzer and Mayer point out that although preferable to punishment, extinction has several potential disadvantages. These include the following:

1. Elimination of undesirable behavior through extinction takes time; in some cases (for example, situations that are dangerous to the student or others around him), we may not have the luxury of taking any time.
2. When first starting a program of extinction, there may be increases in rate and intensity of the undesirable behavior, and general aggression may increase.
3. It may be difficult to identify the reinforcer (which must be terminated), and thus we may originate our procedure with inaccurate information. Consequently, it will not be successful, and valuable time will have been lost.
4. It may be difficult to control the reinforcing consequences, for example, if reinforcement is provided by classmates, often without the knowledge of the teacher.

Time out is a procedure used to reduce inappropriate behavior, in which access to reinforcement (to the opportunity to be reinforced) is removed for some specified period of time. Time out is usually considered as a separate procedure for reducing inappropriate behavior but may also be considered by some as a type of punishment (Alberto and Troutman 1982).

Time out might include placement outside of the room in the hall (in a chair or on the floor), or in an established "time-out room." It is generally agreed that time-out in the hallway may be counterproductive because of various reinforcements that may be received there. A separate space in the classroom (e.g., an area enclosed by bookshelves), or placement in a time-out room is preferable and may have fewer potential legal ramifications. Another version might be, in a setting where all students are accumulating points through some token reinforcement system, "time out" from involvement in that system.

Various factors, such as the problem of legal responsibility for a student while in a time-out setting, must be carefully checked, and we must remain aware that what is an effective time-out procedure for one student may be totally ineffective for another (see legal guidelines for time-out room which follow). It is a negative procedure and has many of the same disadvantages of extinction and punishment, but it does have applicability in some cases. To maximize its effectiveness, Sulzer and Mayer recommend the following: (1) remember to remove *all* reinforcers for *all* responses, (2) apply consistently, (3) avoid time out from situations that are aversive, (4) use short time-out periods whenever possible, and (5) provide reinforcement for any of several alternative behaviors.

RECOMMENDATIONS FOR USE OF TIME-OUT PROCEDURES*

1. The teacher should have identified the reinforcers that are maintaining the inappropriate behavior.
2. Behaviors that will lead to time out should be explicitly stated in advance and clearly understood by the student.
3. All other forms of behavior management should be exhausted before resorting to seclusion time out.
4. The teacher should develop a concise, written statement of procedures for use in placing a student in time out. This statement might include (but not be limited to) the following:
   (a) Explain behaviors that will result in time out in advance. Then when implementing, just say "Mike, because you _____, you are going to time out for _____ minutes."
   (b) To assist students to assume responsibility for their actions, they should be given an opportunity to take their own time out.
   (c) Time-out periods should be brief (i.e., one to five minutes) in nearly all cases.
   (d) When a seclusion time-out space is used, it should be
      1. at *least* six feet × six feet
      2. properly lighted and ventilated
      3. free of fixtures, objects, etc., with which the student might possibly harm himself or herself
      4. continuously monitorable
      5. unlocked

---

*Adapted from D. Gast and M. Nelson, "Time Out in the Classroom: Implications for Special Education." *Exceptional Children* 3 (1977), 461–64.

5. Complete records of time-out utilization should be maintained, including such data as time, date, length of time in time out, cause of time out, other procedures used.
6. A school advisory committee should be used to evaluate the use and effectiveness of time-out procedures and make recommendations as appropriate.

Response-cost procedures are those in which reinforcers are removed as a consequence of inappropriate behaviors. If they are used properly, specific amounts of reward must be removed for specified behavior. Alberto and Troutman liken it to the system used to enforce motor-vehicle laws, in which citizens must pay fines for overtime parking, speeding, and the like. The reinforcers, in this case, are the dollars citizens already have in their possession. In applying response cost in the classroom, we must be certain that there are reinforcers to remove. This has been accomplished in some classrooms by "giving" all students *x* points or tokens at the start of each day, which may be exchanged for a variety of privileges or rewards (use of just one privilege would not necessarily be a reward for all students). Then, if certain behaviors are exhibited, students lose points. This system has proved effective in various research studies (Iawata and Bailey 1974; Kazdin and Bootzin 1972). In such systems it is important that students understand the rules, and it is usually best to penalize sparingly. A reserve of reinforcement from which to extract the "cost" is essential. If students have been "fined" for all they have by 10 A.M., it may indeed be a long day. That is especially true if the teacher has no other modification procedures planned.

Punishment is definitely less well accepted by behaviorists as a solution to undesirable behaviors but may be required in some instances. Punishment has different meanings to different individuals. For example, some parents may mean slapping a child's hands or spanking him. This type of punishment is meant to reduce the likelihood that the undesirable behavior will be repeated. Then there is psychological punishment, for instance, ridiculing a student in front of the class so as to shame or embarrass her, with the same intent as slapping the hands or spanking. Punishment involves presenting a stimulus (in this case slapping, spanking, or ridicule) contingent on the unacceptable behavior (whatever that may be). The stimulus is designed to reduce the rate at which that behavior is emitted.

Punishment is different from time-out or response-cost procedures in that the stimulus is *presented,* as opposed to something being *withdrawn.* For example, let us assume that a student is continually leaving his seat, and interfering with the work of others. In the time-out procedure, he may be required to leave the room for ten minutes. In this case, it is assumed that the room is a reinforcing environment, and it is *withdrawn* (he is removed from it). Or if a point system is used, which relates to the opportunity to do something of interest, he may lose ten points. Thus ten points that lead to reinforcers are *withdrawn.* If the conditioned aversive stimulus of a sharp "no" plus a strong grip on the shoulder is used, it is a matter of *presenting* the aversive stimulus (the punishment).

The major advantage to punishment is that it is more likely, in many settings, to immediately stop whatever target behavior is the concern of the teacher. In some situations, that is essential; in others it is not. A second advantage is that it may reduce the likelihood that classmates will do the same thing. (Sulzer and Mayer say that punishment can be "instructive" to class peers.)

Although it undoubtedly should be avoided if possible, when used, punishment should be used effectively, not just to ease the tensions of the teacher. To be most effective, Sulzer and Mayer suggest that the following be observed: (1) prevent the student from escaping the situation; (2) apply punishment consistently; (3) maximize the intensity of the aversive stimulus; (4) combine with extinction; (5) combine with positive reinforcement of alternative behaviors; and (6) be certain the student understands the rules applied (p. 235). Punishment may radically decrease behavior or stop it immediately, but there is no assurance that the behavior will not be repeated at some later time. And punishment can lead to a situation in which the child thinks primarily in terms of teacher versus child, with the child viewing the teacher as "the one who hurts." However, despite many disadvantages, punishment continues in common use by both parents and teachers. Our recommendation is that, if it is used, teachers should pay particular attention to suggestions 5 and 6, as outlined above.

Case Studies in Applied Behavior Management

The case studies that follow illustrate various ways in which behavior management has been used to effect changes in students in the schools. They are relatively simple, requiring a minimum of additional teacher time and funds, but they do require understanding of applied behavior management for successful implementation.

Case Study 1: Frank: A Distractible, Unmotivated Child

Frank was a source of concern to his teacher, Ms. Brown. Although he was not a sufficient problem to fit the typical "disruptive child" pattern, he was frequently off task, did not listen to instructions, and was very easily distracted. He regularly interrupted Ms. Brown when she was helping other students and asked questions that indicated he had not attended to her last attempts to help him. He was at least one year behind in all academic areas, although measures of ability indicated that he should be doing much better. In some ways, his troublesome behavior was little different from that of other students, but others did not cause the consistent and wide variety of problems that he did. It appeared that other students were imitating Frank, either consciously or unconsciously, the factor that led Ms. Brown to decide to contact the parents and ask them to come in for a conference.

Adapted from Hill Walker, *The Acting-Out Child: Coping with Classroom Disruption.* Boston: Allyn & Bacon, 1979, 234–40.

Frank's parents did not view him as a problem at home, and were not overly concerned with his school difficulties but wanted to cooperate. They agreed to work with Ms. Brown on a program designed to motivate Frank in the school setting. Their support seemed genuine, and performance-contract planning was initiated.

Step 1 was the establishment of *home-reward activities*, which would be made available to Frank *only* as he earned them through his school performance. The three top activities (ranked according to the parents' perception of Frank's preferences) were (1) going to a matinee movie, (2) having a friend stay overnight, and (3) going on a family picnic. A number of others were also listed, including extra TV time and not having to carry out the garbage at night. The plan was to develop a contract (between Frank and Ms. Brown) that would specify school tasks that would lead to these various home rewards.

Step 2 was development of the contract. The contract, developed by Ms. Brown, was a three-way document requiring three signatures, Frank's, Ms. Brown's, and Frank's parents'. The contract listed various things under the heading *Frank agrees* including items such as "to listen carefully to teacher instructions" and "to not interrupt the teacher when she is busy talking to someone else." Under the heading *Ms. Brown agrees* were listed statements such as "to check Frank's behavior and school performance regularly throughout the day," and "to review Frank's performance at the close of the day and award tickets based on how well he has done on each of the listed tasks." Under the heading *Frank's parents agree* was the pledge that his parents would make special privileges available that Frank could have in exchange for tickets earned in school.

Step 3 was a conference between Frank and Ms. Brown, in which the contract was reviewed. This was, in part, a pep talk, with Ms. Brown assuring Frank that he *could* accomplish the various tasks as outlined. Frank seemed to have some positive reactions but indicated that part of it was not fair. He noted that the rewards (home privileges) were things already available to him at home. Ms. Brown agreed but pointed out that his school behavior had become quite a problem and that she and his parents had agreed to this program to try to encourage him to do better at school. She reiterated her feeling that he could do what the contract called for and thus could have the home benefits. Frank was not really happy about the situation and said so but agreed to give it a try. He signed, Ms. Brown signed, and the parents' signatures were also obtained. The program, as established, was a private matter, known only to Frank, Ms. Brown, and Frank's parents.

The program was implemented (*step 4*), and tickets were made available on a basis that would make it possible for Frank to earn eighteen tickets if he had a "nearly perfect" day. Rewards were established so that the least preferred privilege required fifteen tickets and the most preferred (a trip to the movies) cost eighty tickets.

Program results for the first day were most encouraging. Frank earned fifteen of the possible eighteen tickets. There was no question but that he could behave acceptably when he tried. During the next five days, his daily totals ranged from eighteen down to a low of ten tickets. Frank's academic work improved more slowly than other areas, but it did improve. Then Ms. Brown decided to ask Frank's other teachers about his behavior during the past week. She discovered that there was no improvement; in fact, if anything his behavior had gone downhill. Ms. Brown explained the program to his other teachers, each of whom seemed interested in participating. A method was worked out whereby each of Frank's teachers was to rate him daily, which rating could be converted to tickets by Ms. Brown at the end of the day. The program change was explained to Frank and was implemented. There were immediate changes in all of Frank's other classes. Ms. Brown managed the program, which required minimum effort on the part of the other teachers. The program ran effectively for four weeks, and a major change was observed in Frank's academic-work output. The quantity of work nearly doubled, and the quality improved also. All concerned were very happy with the overall results. But Ms. Brown knew that eventually a means must be found whereby the good results might be maintained without the involved ticket system. A parent-teacher conference was called to discuss various possibilities.

In the parent-teacher conference (*step* 5) it was agreed that before long, the program should be modified, but both Frank's parents and his teachers were concerned that the excellent improvement should not be lost. Abrupt termination of the program was rejected, and after considerable discussion, it was decided that major components should be eliminated one step at a time. The first step involved elimination of the ticket system, and substitution of "plus" and "minus" ratings approximately once each hour of the day. (The new program was fully explained to Frank, and he agreed to the change.) Frank now earned home privileges with pluses and minuses. He earned about the same number, since the exchange ratio had been adjusted downward to reflect the fact that he had less opportunity to earn pluses than he previously had to earn tickets. There was little change in Frank's behavior, and all concerned were satisfied with the program. In a further change (agreed to by parents, teachers, and Frank) it was decided that there would be one high-magnitude reward available just once a week. There were thirty pluses possible during a week, and the high-magnitude reward required twenty-five. This change seemed to work just as well as had the previous one. Then, after several more weeks, Frank's program was modified to just one overall rating, on a daily basis. Ms. Brown checked with his other teachers, and if all said his behavior was satisfactory, he got a satisfactory for the day. In order to earn the home reward, Frank had to be rated satisfactory on four of the five days of the week.

As a final step, it was decided that the program should shift to an occasional home reward for good performance. Frank was told that when his performance warranted it, he would get a special note to take home, which would lead to the "occasional" reward. Under this system, considerable variability in Frank's behavior developed, but after a few weeks, his behavior began to approximate that which had occurred with the much more frequent rewards. This was the program that was maintained through the remainder of the year, and it led to notable improvement in both social and academic performance.

Case Study 2: Three Hyperactive Boys

Three hyperactive boys had considerable difficulty in managing their own behavior, could not stay in their seats, and tended to disturb others. At times they seemed to be "in another world," and unable (or unwilling) to follow class practice, which was that students must raise their hands if they wanted teacher help. These concerns were made the focus of their behavior management program, and several rules were posted on the wall, facing the boys: (1) stay in your seat; (2) work quietly; (3) don't bug others; (4) don't space out; and (5) raise your hand if you need help. A tape was made in which a bell rang at random intervals. The boys were given cards for the purpose of self-recording and were instructed how and where to make a mark on the card if they were following the rules when the bell rang.

For the first week, the taped bell rang at random intervals during each class work period. The schedule was changed for the second week, but the procedure remained the same. In this experimental setting, an observer was employed to record the same data, and bonus points were assigned each time the two records (the boy's tally and the observers' tally) agreed. The students had explicit instructions as to what each of the rules meant, and it was a matter of increasing awareness through this self-recording procedure. The result in this small-group experiment was that study behavior was improved significantly.

From a study by R. Barkley, A. Copeland, and C. Sivage, "A Self-Control Classroom for Hyperactive Children," *Journal of Autism and Developmental Disorders* 10 (1980), 75–89.

Case Study 3: Sue: Improvement, with a Little Help from Her Friends

In a timer-game study somewhat similar to case study 2 (a token-reward system, with tokens given for in-seat behavior) with sixteen subjects in a remedial classroom, nearly all subjects demonstrated improved in-seat behavior when tokens were redeemed for such primary reinforcers as clothing and candy. However, one student, Sue, showed little improvement. It was assumed that the group-reinforcement system was not sufficiently rewarding to Sue, so an individual version was established. A piece of construction paper with the numbers 50, 40, 30, 20, and 10 drawn on it was posted where Sue could clearly see it. Sue was told that she would start with fifty points but would lose ten points each time she was out of her seat when the bell rang. Then in another version of this procedure, the rules were changed so that the four students nearest to Sue were also part of the game. The new rules were that Sue would lose ten points each time she was out of her seat when the bell rang, but whatever points remained at the close of the session were divided equally between Sue and her four other students. Points lost depended entirely on Sue's behavior, but remaining points were divided five ways.

M. Wolf and others, "The Timer Game: A Variable Interval Contingency for the Management of Out-of-Seat Behavior," *Exceptional Children* 37 (1970), 113–18.

In the first of the new versions (fifty points for Sue alone), Sue's out-of-seat behavior reduced significantly. But in the second version (where Sue had to share the points) it was reduced even more. Peer encouragement (and pressure?) appeared to be even more powerful than the points.

Factors that Limit the Effectiveness of Behavioral Approaches

Many limitations of behavioral approaches are those that are specific to some particular approach (for example, the response-cost procedure will not work unless there are meaningful reinforcers to withdraw, it is difficult to arrange such reinforcers in every case, and certain approaches may lead to aggression and/or escape). Other limitations relate to the inability of the teacher to control the environment to a sufficient extent to make the procedure work. However, in many cases in which we have talked with teachers about ineffective behavioral approaches, it was the teacher's misunderstanding of which approach to use or how to use it that was the major difficulty. But beyond these limitations/shortcomings, there is one other factor deserving of special attention. That is the matter of establishment of appropriate goals.

Alberto and Troutman note that "ethical use of behavioral procedures starts with selection of appropriate goals" (p. 41). We would add that the effectiveness of behavioral procedures also depends upon the selection of appropriate goals. Martin (1975) noted a number of factors that should be considered by those (often a team of individuals in the IEP conference) establishing goals. These factors include (1) stating goals in understandable, objective, measurable terms; (2) making certain that the goal is established primarily for the benefit of the student, not for the convenience or comfort of the school; (3) establishing reasonable goals; (4) assuring that the purpose is positively oriented, that is, directed toward the development of appropriate behaviors, not just toward suppression of objectionable behaviors; and (5) establishing that the behavior to be changed is not protected by the student's constitutional rights. Martin's concern related more to legal questions than effectiveness of the program, but several of his points of concern also relate to program effectiveness. If we interpret his third factor as establishing *achievable goals*, it is of course highly relevant, and this question then relates to the point that will follow. *Behavior modification cannot "help" a student do something that is beyond his or her realm of abilities.* For most new tasks, particularly academic skills, there is available information as to required prerequisite skills. We *must* obtain this information and consider it as we establish academic goals. We must not expect too much of behavior modification. It is a technique, a means to an end.

SUMMARY

Behaviorists view all behavior as "learned" and believe that it is learned primarily as a result of its consequences. They believe that some consequences strengthen or increase the frequency of the behavior they follow, some weaken or decrease the behavior they follow, and others simply maintain the behavior they follow. When consequences increase the behavior they follow, the relationship is called positive reinforcement. The consequence, or stimulus, is called a positive reinforcer. If behavior is strengthened through an interaction that involves the avoidance of some aversive (undesirable) consequence, this is called negative reinforcement. When the event that follows a behavior has the effect of decreasing the behavior, it is called a punisher. Consequences that have no effect on the behavior they follow are called neutral consequences.

The major thrust of the efforts of the behaviorist is to arrange the environment so that consequences follow behavior in such a manner as to reinforce behavior they wish to have repeated and to decrease or eliminate behavior they feel is unacceptable. This approach is particularly valuable in efforts with students with learning difficulties (either learning disabilities, behavioral disorders, or mental retardation) and may be applied both to changing unacceptable social behavior and to promoting the learning of academic tasks. It is not necessarily applicable and/or practical in all instances and has its critics, but its frequency of use with students with special needs, and outstanding success in some instances, makes it an essential tool for the special education teacher.

In this chapter, we have reviewed the major behavior modification approaches and the terminology related to these approaches. This review of approaches included a consideration of the considerable strength of positive reinforcers of all types, the specific use of token systems and modeling, shaping, contracting, extinction, time out, response-cost, and punishment approaches.

In addition, a number of case studies were outlined to illustrate behavior modification. A final section on the limitations of behavioral approaches was included to provide what we feel to be a fair, objective perspective with respect to this question.

REFERENCES

ALBERTO, P., AND A. TROUTMAN. *Applied Behavior Analysis for Teachers.* Columbus, Ohio: Charles E. Merrill Publishing Co., 1982.

AXELROD, S. *Behavior Modification for the Classroom Teacher.* New York: McGraw-Hill Book Co., 1977.

BANDURA, A. Influence of model's reinforcement contingencies on the acquisition of imitative responses. *Journal of Personality and Social Psychology* 1 (1965), 589–95.

BARKLEY, R., A. COPELAND, AND C. SIVAGE. A self-control classroom for hyperactive children. *Journal of Autism and Developmental Disorders* 10 (1980), 75–79.

BLOOM, B., J. HASTINGS, AND G. MADAUS. *Handbook on Formative and Summative Evaluation of Student Learning.* New York: McGraw-Hill Book Co., 1971.

CRAIGHEAD, W. E., A. KAZDIN, AND M. MAHONEY, EDS. *Behavior Modification: Principles, Issues, and Applications.* 2d ed. Boston: Houghton Mifflin Co., 1981.

GAST, D., AND M. NELSON. Time out in the classroom: Implications for special education. *Exceptional Children* 3 (1977), 461–64.

HOMME, L. *How to Use Contingency Contracting in the Classroom.* Champaign, Ill.: Research Press Co., 1971.

IWATA, B., AND J. BAILEY. Reward versus cost token systems: An analysis of the effects on students and teacher. *Journal of Applied Behavior Analysis* 7 (1974), 567–76. ·

KAZDIN, A., AND R. BOOTZIN.   The token economy: An evaluative review. *Journal of Applied Behavior Analysis* 5 (1972), 343–72.

LAHEY, B., AND R. DRABMAN.   Behavior modification in the classroom. In W. E. Craighead, A. Kazdin, and M. Mahoney, eds., *Behavior Modification: Principles, Issues, and Applications.* 2d ed. Boston: Houghton Mifflin Co., 1981.

MARSH, G., B. PRICE, AND T. SMITH.   *Teaching Mildly Handicapped Children: Methods and Materials.* St. Louis: C. V. Mosby, 1983.

MARTIN, R.   *Legal Challenges to Behavior Modification: Trends in Schools, Corrections, and Mental Health.* Champaign, Ill.: Research Press Co., 1975.

O'LEARY, D., AND S. O'LEARY, EDS.   *Classroom Management: The Successful Use of Behavior Modification.* New York: Pergamon Press, 1977.

O'LEARY, K., AND R. DRABMAN.   Token reinforcement programs in the classroom: A review. *Psychological Bulletin* 75 (1971), 379–98.

ROSENTHAL, T., AND A. BANDURA.   Psychological modeling: Theory and practice. In S. Garfield and A. Bergin, eds., *Handbook of Psychotherapy and Behavior Change.* New York: John Wiley and Sons, 1978.

SKINNER, B.   *Science and Human Behavior.* New York: Macmillan Co., 1953.

———.   *The Technology of Teaching.* New York: Appleton-Century-Crofts, 1968.

SULZER, B., AND R. MAYER.   *Behavior Modification Procedures for School Personnel.* New York: Holt, Rinehart & Winston, 1972.

SWANSON, H. L., AND H. REINERT.   *Teaching Strategies for Children in Conflict.* St. Louis: C. V. Mosby, 1979.

ULLMAN, L., AND L. KRASNER.   *Case Studies in Behavior Modification.* New York: Holt, Rinehart & Winston, 1965.

WALKER, H.   *The Acting-Out Child: Coping with Classroom Disruption.* Boston: Allyn & Bacon, 1979.

WATSON, J. B.   Psychology as a behaviorist views it. *Psychological Review* 20 (1913), 158–77.

WOLF, M., AND OTHERS.   The timer game: A variable interval contingency for the management of out-of-seat behavior. *Exceptional Children* 37 (1970), 113–18.

CHAPTER ELEVEN

Organizing for Effective Instruction

- What physical aspects of the learning environment can be managed or organized to facilitate instruction?

- What factors may lead to the need for modified seating arrangements in the classroom, and what purposes can such modified seating satisfy?

- Why may there be greater need for organization of teacher and student materials when teaching handicapped students?

- How may symbols (other than alphabetic symbols) be used to communicate instructions? Why might such a substitute symbol system be needed?

- How do the teaching styles identified by Spaulding (1980) as "the director," "the entertainer," "the counselor," and "the story teller" differ?

- What is meant by planning for change? Why is it particularly necessary in the resource room for handicapped students?

- What modifications in evaluation procedures may be considered? Why are such modifications so difficult for educators to accept?

In the preceding ten chapters, we have considered a wide variety of instructional techniques and ideas. The possibilities available for various combinations of alternative methods and techniques are almost endless, limited primarily by the energy and ingenuity of the teacher and the flexibility of the school system in question. Yet too many teachers seem to prefer and use the same instructional methods year after year, with all students. The tendency to cling to the "tried and true" is understandable, and to some degree traditional methods are effective with the 80 to 90 percent of the student population who learn despite the limitations of teachers and/or methods, but they are unacceptable when we consider students with learning difficulties and the unique needs generated by these difficulties. For such students, a variety of program modifications must be considered, which will, in composite, lead to greater learning. It is not a matter of two or three different basic types of instruction, or two or three ways of organizing the physical surroundings in the classroom, or the learning materials with which students interact. Rather, it is a matter of understanding the potential value of many variables in several dimensions, realms, or domains. It is a matter of careful planning for the individual educational needs of students who cannot learn effectively in the "normal" setting, using the "standard" curriculum. We have chosen to call this process of combining and manipulating these variables *organizing for effective instruction.* In many respects, the IEP, required by federal and state regulations for handicapped students who are receiving special education services (see pages 41–42) is a statement of how we plan to organize for instruction, but we believe that it is important to further emphasize those variables that can and should be considered in the all-important teaching/learning process.

Teachers cannot develop a valuable educational program until they are fully aware of the variables over which they can exercise control and that can contribute to the final goal of more effective instruction. Throughout this text we have considered these variables, but for the most part we have been concerned with some particular subarea, such as reading strategies, written language strategies, or strategies that will encourage social development. Therefore, we want to integrate the ideas provided throughout the text as they relate to (1) the manner in which teachers can control the physical aspects of the learning environment and (2) literally "how the teacher teaches." Certain illustrations will be provided to attempt to clarify the concept of organizing for effective instruction. We do not intend them as an additional comprehensive listing of teaching suggestions. We suspect that many teachers do not fully appreciate the potential arsenal of teaching weapons they possess and thus never reach their full effectiveness as teachers. We would like to assist teachers to more fully understand the strengths of these teaching weapons and will start with a discussion of the physical aspects of the learning environment.

PHYSICAL ASPECTS OF THE LEARNING ENVIRONMENT

The physical aspects of the learning environment are among the easiest for the teacher to manage and organize for more effective instruction. Except where limited by unreasonable administrative rules or requirements or by rigidly restrictive financial considerations, they are within the control of the teacher. For purposes of this discussion we will consider as "physical aspects" those aspects that involve primarily solid objects as they interrelate with the students in the classroom. In most cases, physical aspects and how the teacher teaches, the second major topic of this chapter, are very closely related, in some instances, almost impossible to separate. We will, however, attempt to separate them for purposes of emphasis and clarification of our basic concern—how teachers organize for instruction.

One way to illustrate how the management of physical aspects of the classroom has changed is to point out how one aspect—seating—has changed over the years. At the time that we (or at least the senior author) started elementary school, all seating in most school districts was fastened to the floor, and desks were in long rows with aisles of a standard size between each row. In science labs in the secondary schools the furniture was not fastened down, but it was in the lecture sections of the science classrooms. Lower-elementary-level classrooms had low tables and small chairs for reading circles, but seating in the classroom proper was carefully aligned in rows parallel to the walls. This arrangement was viewed as essential to effective, orderly teaching.

Certainly, all readers are aware that this is not the rule today, nor has it been for many years. A wide variety of seating arrangements are utilized to good instructional advantage, an excellent example of organizing the physical aspects of the classroom. Another example is the development of open-space buildings with no walls between classrooms. In this case, many of us have open-space schools in which the teachers have "built" walls with bookcases, bulletin boards, etc. In a few cases, school boards have decided to add permanent walls to such buildings, thus reducing noise levels in the various classrooms. One final example is the use of carpeting in many classrooms, a practice that would have been unacceptable in most of the nation fifty years ago. In the discussion of managing/organizing the physical aspects of the classroom that follows, we will indicate *what* can be organized, *how* it might be changed, and *why* such organization might be worthwhile. In each instance of planning for a particular student, you will see that a variety of factors determine what should be done for that student. *Please note that the organizational ideas and concepts we discuss may be applied somewhat differently in the regular classroom than in a resource-room setting. The underlying principles are the same, but application may differ. However, it is the responsibility of the special education teacher to be able to advise the regular class teacher regarding these procedures as well as to implement the procedures in the resource room or other special setting.**

*Seating arrangements for a distractible student who has serious difficulty attending to instructional tasks provide one example of this difference. In a resource room, with perhaps only two or three

293

Seating and Grouping

Seating and grouping are perhaps the most obvious of the physical aspects of the learning environment that are subject to considerable control. For the resource-room teacher, it may be relatively easy to arrange seating so that the two, three, or four students in the room have minimum auditory or visual contact with others at those times when they are working independently, or when the teacher is working with one student while others are working independently. The use of study carrels, or room dividers, seating away from windows, use of headsets to muffle noise, and related modifications are standard practice in many rooms. In the regular classroom, where the student must learn along with thirty other students, it is a different and more difficult matter. Various seating and grouping possibilities are outlined in table 11-1.

For the most part, the alternatives suggested in table 11-1 should be self-explanatory; they might be called common-sense ideas. However, we might note that any one seating alternative may have a variety of effects on a student. For example, seating close to the teacher's desk may mean a bit more distraction if many students come to the teacher's desk for assistance or to ask permission to change activities or leave the room. But if the teacher's desk is in the front of the room, it may also mean that the student is not as often visually distracted by movement that he or she may see through peripheral vision. It also means that the student's activities are much more easily monitored. The decision on seating must be made on an individual basis; but it is essential for the teacher to remain fully aware of the possibility of different results for various seating arrangements.

As for assignment to groups for reading (for example), it is important to consider carefully the major result(s) expected from such grouping. Traditionally, students have been grouped according to reading ability in an attempt to develop homogeneous groups. For the students with learning difficulties, factors other than reading level may be more important. Also, it may be that any given student should be working with two groups, or with one group full time and with another group part time. Sometimes teachers forget that it is their prerogative to assign students to groups and that there are a variety of reasons for group placement.

A Student-Centered Environment

Although some teachers may have difficulty in organizing their room as a student-centered environment, it is the best arrangement. (We are here contrasting the concept of a student-centered classroom with a more traditional teacher-centered classroom, organized to facilitate lectures and authoritative control and making relatively passive use of space.) The stu-

---

other students in the room at the same time, it will be much easier to arrange to minimize the student's problems that result from distractibility. But it is essential, if we are to see maximum educational progress, that problems resulting from distractibility also be reduced in the regular class setting where the student spends a majority of his time.

TABLE 11-1   Seating Alternatives

SEATING ALTERNATIVE	PURPOSE/RATIONALE
A. Isolate: (1) to one side of room (2) study carrel (3) in time-out room (out of class) (4) behind temporary screen (for example, a bookcase)	To get away from: (1) distraction due to noise (2) distraction due to visual stimulation (3) certain other students (This means that the pencil sharpener, the wastebasket, windows, major aisles, the teacher's desk, disruptive students, etc., must be considered.)
B. Selected group clusters for purposes of group study: (1) groups whose members are not likely to trigger aggressive or inattentive behavior (2) groups that include students who will contribute academically and who accept the student (3) groups whose knowledge level and manner of participation will not threaten the student or lead him to be a nonparticipant	In various types of group work, the type of participation by other group members can influence social behavior, the degree to which the student participates, and the amount of learning by other group members. Teachers should develop original hypotheses about the likely influence of other students, but actual tryout of various arrangements is the only final way to be certain about effects.
C. Special placement owing to specific sensory-acuity disabilities	Students with hearing impairments may need preferential seating for purposes of speech reading. This may relate to distance from the teacher's desk, lighting needs, etc. Visually impaired students may also have special needs.
D. Special placement to keep special-needs student from negatively affecting others	Some nonhandicapped students are much more able to successfully complete their academic tasks, even though students next to them are at times disruptive.
E. Special placement to encourage withdrawn student to participate	Some withdrawn students begin to interact with specific other students in hallways, playground, and nonacademic areas before they begin to interact in the classroom. Sensitivity to various clues as to which students might motivate class interaction on the part of withdrawn students will permit the teacher to use seating assignments to facilitate interaction.

dent-centered, or informal, classroom organization provides a variety of individual learning areas, learning centers, interest centers, quiet areas, and study carrels but still provides for some small-group (traditional) instruction. When properly managed, such classroom organization is more effective for most disabled/handicapped students. It permits movement from space to space—some freedom but also some structure. It is also more effective for *all* students.

In such a classroom, there must be rules and a code of conduct. There should be certain general, overall rules, but there must also be specific rules for each of the areas in the room (see figure 11-1). For areas such as the computer center or listening center, the rules might relate to scheduling in advance and observing time limitations. In addition, there must be rules about care of equipment and consequences if an individual continually refuses to observe such rules. In the quiet area there would be rather specific rules about noise and physical interruptions. In all cases such rules must be carefully thought out and explained to students in advance. In addition, copies of the rules should be posted in affected areas.

Some students with learning problems may have difficulty with the more unstructured areas of a student-centered classroom, but if they can slowly learn to function in these areas, it is excellent preparation for moving out of special educational programming, a goal we should keep in mind

FIGURE 11-1   The Flexible Student-Centered Environment

This room is organized to accommodate up to four or five students at one time with only one teacher in the room, or seven or eight with two teachers or a teacher and a teacher aide. In the latter situation, another teacher's desk must be provided.

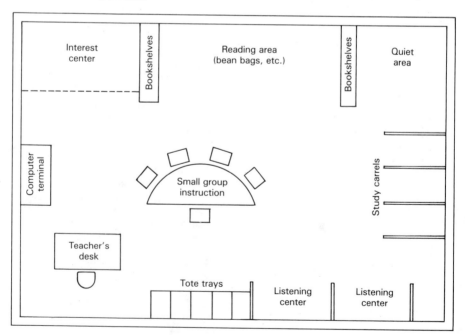

for all students. The student-centered classroom will *not* work unless it is carefully planned, has appropriate rules and guidelines, and is managed by an effective, organized teacher. With such planning and management, it can be an excellent setting for student learning.

Organizing Student and Teacher Materials

The matter of organization of both student and teacher materials is important with all students, not just the handicapped or disabled. But because there is greater likelihood that handicapped/disabled students may need materials that are different from those required by most of the class, it becomes even more important as applied to them. Most resource-room teachers we have observed have worked out systems whereby time may be saved and confusion reduced as students come into or leave the resource room throughout the day. It is particularly important to have such organization if overlapping time schedules lead to one student's coming into the room while the teacher is working with another student. Resource-room teachers are given smaller student loads with students who have unique educational needs so that maximum educational benefit can be derived. This situation dictates that the teacher use every possible minute of instructional time efficiently. In the case of overlapping schedules (a common occurrence), the teacher should not be obligated to immediately leave the student with whom she or he is doing individual work, but the student who just arrived in the room should not have to lose valuable time while waiting for the teacher. Though there may be a few students who absolutely require immediate teacher attention when they enter the room, most will respond favorably to organizational techniques that make it clear to them just what they are to do until the teacher comes over to monitor their work, talk to them, outline additional assignments, provide assistance, and so forth. A number of organizational ideas that may facilitate this goal are described in the following paragraphs.

The use of "tote trays" is one of the more common organizational practices in use in resource rooms. The tote tray (clearly marked with the student's name) should be in the same place each day so that there is a minimum of confusion. Students should be taught to immediately take the trays to their desks or work tables and check inside for further instructions. Depending on the situation (age of student, type of academic work required, ability to read, ability to handle distraction), any of the following ideas might be used to communicate with the student until the teacher comes to her table or desk with further instructions.

1. Standard cards might be used (as appropriate each day) that say, "DO THIS FIRST, DO THIS SECOND," and so on. They can be paper-clipped to the appropriate folders.
2. Cards with numbers (1, 2, 3, and so on) may be used.
3. Picture cards (chosen by the student) may be used to indicate to do one assignment first, and then second, and so forth.

Because some students may have difficulty with instructions as to how to proceed, innovative teachers have developed unique symbols that indicate what to do. After the student learns to associate the symbol with a particular concept, this system can prove to be very effective. Figure 11-2 provides samples of such symbols; teachers may work out their own, consistent with their unique needs.

The preceding ideas assume that the student can find his/her tote tray and has enough self-discipline to take it to a table or desk. With names on the trays, the trays placed in the same place each day, and signs or symbols to indicate where to start, it might seem that organization is complete. Not so, in our experience.

Some young students have so few directional and/or orientation skills that they must be taught to go to the right place on the shelves to find their tray. Otherwise they will regularly search through all the trays, often overlooking their name. For these students, it will be a valuable time-saver (and a type of good organization) for the teacher to specifically teach the student how to find the tray. For such students (usually younger students) it may be wise to place the trays at one end of the storage area and perhaps at the

Figure 11-2 Samples of Symbols That May Be Used to Communicate Instructions.
The symbols, and others as appropriate, may be on duplicated sheets, with space for additional instructions. It is important that the *concept* involved (for example, "match") be taught to the student, and that the student understands it. Then the symbol represents not only a word but also a concept.

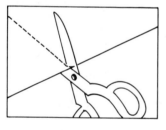

Indicates that the student is to get scissors and **cut** (according to whatever additional instructions are included).

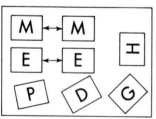

Indicates that the student is to **match** (according to additional instructions).

Indicates that the student is to **read** (whatever pages are indicated, or if one or two pages are attached, it means to read these).

bottom or top. Then they can learn to find it more quickly. In a somewhat similar manner, it may be wise to have them always use the same desk or table. When this is done, each desk or table may have a name card indicating the names of the three or four students who use that area. Care must be taken, however, that students are not scheduled in such a manner that two whose names are on the same desk are in the room at the same time.

Just as the resource-room teacher must develop organizational patterns and procedures that will maximize effective instructional time and facilitate instructional goals, so must that teacher assist the regular classroom teacher with respect to the special-needs student for whom they share joint responsibility. In most instances, idea-sharing conversations are effective; authoritative instructions (given the regular classroom teacher by the specialist) are more often counterproductive. Sharing of materials, filing, and storage ideas may be of great help; the special teacher will also get useful new ideas from the regular classroom teacher.

A variety of other practices that seem to fall under the general-organizational rubric include: (1) establishing a procedure for turning in completed work—for example, a completed work box; (2) establishing a method for students to ask for help without interrupting the teacher—for example, a "help" sign, which the student places vertically in a small wooden base when he or she wants help; or (3) other signs to be used with the wooden base depending on need (for example, a "finished" sign, indicating readiness for another assignment, or other signs indicating common student requests). There are many such techniques or practices that are of concrete value in accomplishing our goal of more effective use of instructional time and effort. In addition, and perhaps of equal importance, many of these practices are of value in assisting students to develop better organizational patterns and habits. It is quite likely that such external organizational assistance will lead to the development of better internal organization and structure. In the long run, this can be more important than the time efficiency that is the immediate gain.

Additional suggestions relating to organization of physical aspects of the learning environment have been interspersed throughout this text. Our primary purpose in this chapter, however, is to encourage teachers to think about how they may use better organization to improve instructional effectiveness. There is adequate evidence (and wide, general acceptance) in the areas of business and industry that better organization can greatly facilitate production and profit. We believe that this same principle applies in education. The educational payoff is more and better-quality academic work and more profitable utilization of instructional time.

HOW THE TEACHER TEACHES (ORGANIZATION AND THE INSTRUCTIONAL PROCESS)

The matter of organizing for success in the instructional process has a number of aspects, but the two that we consider basic are how the special teacher organizes for her or his work with students with special needs in the resource room and how the regular classroom teacher organizes to better meet the special instructional needs of the disabled or handicapped student in the mainstream. As noted with respect to organizing physical aspects of the instructional program, the special-program teacher has a definite responsibility to assist the regular classroom teacher; that assistance must be related to the teaching style of the regular classroom teacher, to be maximally effective.

The question, What is "teaching style"? can be answered in many ways, but one that seems to apply to both the regular classroom teacher and the specialist and that utilizes some interesting adjectives in labeling styles, was suggested by Spaulding in a presentation to the American Educational Research Association (1980). For illustrative purposes we will consider seven of his characterizations.

1. The director—one who establishes limits and gives directions and has clear rules, procedures, and standards. The director systematically redirects students who go astray, and in general, students comply.

2. The discovery teacher—one who attempts to elicit sorting, grouping, categorizing, and inductive thinking, and promotes attention to goals, objectives, and logical, sequential thinking.

3. The lecturer—one who describes, explains, illustrates, and asks students to recall or apply what was presented.

4. The entertainer—one who regularly digresses from subject matter—is open to student opinions and their self-expression and is not particularly goal oriented.

5. The rote-learning teacher—one who provides information, repeats for emphasis, and expects students to attend, practice, and regurgitate.

6. The counselor—one who listens, redirects behavior, and elicits student feelings, attitudes, and values.

7. The story teller—one who narrates, reads, tells that which is to be learned, and encourages sharing and participation in this process.*

Most teachers reflect some combination of styles, and the special education specialist must recognize these differences and provide assistance that complements existing styles. It is altogether possible that the organization for teaching that is useful for the specialist will not be useful for the regular classroom teacher. Sensitivity to this fact and willingness to develop ideas that will work with the teacher in question (this is individualization and is just as important as individualization with students) are absolutely essential to success with students. In addition, the specialist must make every effort "to avoid, in appearance or reality, intensification of daily teaching and clerical burdens for mainstream teachers" (Marsh, Price, and Smith 1983, p. 359).

---

*Adapted from R. Spaulding, "Relationships of Inservice Training to Classroom Teaching Models, Management Styles, and Student Achievement." (Paper presented at the American Educational Research Association Annual Meeting, Boston, 1980.)

Preacademic-Year Planning

In her text on teaching students with behavior disorders, Gallagher (1979) devotes an entire chapter to preacademic year planning. She notes that planning is a prerequisite to effective teaching and that good planning can "extend the teacher's tolerance for stress, heighten sensitivity to student behaviors, and enhance openness to new techniques" (p. 19). Advance planning takes many shapes and forms, including ordering of new materials and equipment, checking out old materials and equipment, and other "standard" practices known to all organized, experienced teachers. For the special educator, this means that whenever possible (and this will vary from setting to setting), all available information on the students who will be part of the program should be assembled and organized to provide a basis for determining what materials will be needed. Unlike a third grade, or a high school biology class, where the curriculum is established, the special education program can be established only after the individual students have been assigned to the program. When a teacher faces a new program with no students assigned or even tentatively assigned in advance, all that can be done is to attempt to make good "guesstimates" about the nature and needs of the students who are likely to become part of the program and to proceed from there. For most programs, it is likely that the names of many of the students to be served will be known. But names alone are of little value—what is needed is information about academic needs (including both strengths and weaknesses), social/emotional needs, ability to work in a small group, personal interests, procedures that have worked most effectively in the past, and other related information. This information is in addition to information about age, physical characteristics, home/family status, homeroom assignment (which then establishes which teacher will become the other team member), previous standardized test data, and the like.

In our experience, the best teachers with whom we have worked have developed their own list of data, which becomes the basis for preacademic-year planning. Some use loose-leaf notebooks, others use five-by-eight-inch file cards, but *all have a system*. In addition, although some have many years of experience, most use a system that includes a form with headings, which will direct their data collecting. The form is used because it is easy to forget to check some particular point, and that point may be the key to understanding the student's needs.

Planning for Change

In addition to gathering and recording the data that can help to provide better understanding and thus permit more effective planning for the student, it is important to maintain information about the student's daily schedule when he is not in the special program. This may be difficult to do with complete accuracy, owing to the manner in which students' schedules (in various programs such as music and physical education) may change periodically, but it must be attempted. Program changes may mean that the student comes to the special education program at different times than expected, which may mean reorganization (for that day) of what the teacher has planned for both the student in question and for others whose scheduled programs may be upset by the changes. Ordinarily, in the regular classroom, if a student has been out of the classroom and returns, the teacher attempts to assist him or her to reenter one of the group activities (or the total class activity) in progress. This may pose some difficulties, but it *is* the accepted thing to do. When a student comes to the resource room at a different time than previously scheduled it is highly unlikely that he or she can simply enter an ongoing activity. If the resource-room program is doing what it should be doing, the learning activity will be an individual, personalized activity for that one student. Therefore, daily schedule information can be of great importance. One practice we have seen used by teachers who have students in their program for one-half or more of each day is that of maintaining a small chart that outlines each student's daily schedule, posted on the bulletin board. Then when there are changes, they are temporarily tacked onto the schedule. This presumes that teachers are communicating with one another, often no small accomplishment in and of itself; but if there is no system to record and make such information readily available, even communication is relatively useless.

The possibility that a student might appear unannounced or at a time other than planned leads to a related need that must be anticipated, even if all students arrive and leave the resource room on schedule. Just as *all* teachers must plan for those days when a lesson goes faster than scheduled and there is a fifteen- or twenty-minute time period (or even a five-minute period) with nothing planned for the class, so must the resource-room teacher plan for each student served in the resource room. *Alternative assignments must be planned in advance.* They cannot (or should not) be "busy work"; the needs of students assigned to special education programs are too great to waste time on busy work. In addition to meaningful extra assignments that are similar to, and parallel with, regular assignments, there is need for planned work at both "higher" and "lower" levels than those presumed to be appropriate, based on information available on the student and on stated objectives in the IEP. In other words, especially at the initial stages of working with any given student (start of school year or just after a student is placed in the program during the school year), it is important that there be a standby plan with some alternative work conceptualized in case the initial work planned for the student is too simple or too complex. That does not mean detailed plans, work sheets, and materials for several days. It does mean that various possibilities have been considered and that there are notes and guidelines suggesting what might be tried next. This work is much easier to do in the quiet of a planning session, with no student across the table, than it is when the student is bored and/or frustrated and has just precipitated a minor emergency. What we have described is the essence of planning and organization for change.

Continuing Record Keeping for Instructional Guidance

It was earlier suggested that effective preacademic planning includes gathering all available pertinent information on each student in the program so as to be able to plan more useful, productive programs. In addition to this pre-implementation planning, it is essential to maintain continuing records that will indicate (in very brief form) the focus of daily lessons and the extent to which goals were or were not accomplished. In addition, such records should indicate which approaches or ways of presenting information or teaching new skills worked, and which did not.

Information of this type does not have to be recorded in some formal manner, utilizing complete sentences and precise punctuation. It is for the "teacher's eyes" only—a reminder that certain procedures or ideas were of value and that others were of less value or perhaps valueless. Over a period of many weeks, such information establishes a pattern that can guide the teacher for the remainder of the year and can be recorded (this time in more formal form) in the student's permanent records.

In commenting on the frequent complaint of teachers that record keeping requires too much time, Lund, Schnaps, and Bijou (1983) indicate that "teachers need neither fancy charts nor complicated coding systems. They need only to collect information that will answer two basic questions: (1) How are my children doing? and (2) Are the instructional programs working for each child?" (p. 155). They note that record keeping allows the teacher to monitor both the child's performance and their own management skills, and that "an analysis of the records enables the teacher to make necessary midcourse program corrections and to be responsive to each individual's unique needs" (p. 155).

Without some form of systematic record keeping, it is very difficult to remember, for example, just how well a given student was doing with specific arithmetic tasks three weeks ago, or which methods, approaches, or rewards seem to be related to improvement. Without a usable basic data system, it is most difficult to determine when program changes should be made and the nature of any change. At times, certain data that may have seemed to be totally unrelated suddenly provide definite guidelines for change when they can all be considered at one time.

Though there are no universally recognized guidelines for displaying data (once the data are recorded), simple charts or graphs may provide a very useful display mode. At times such visual displays make it quite obvious that (for example) when teaching-method C was used, improvement was accelerated, whereas when method A was used, improvement was negligible or nonexistent. The best advice is to use the most simple display possible to illustrate degree of change and to provide for analysis of relationships between pertinent variables. Brainstorming with other teachers may be the best approach in developing simple, effective graphical displays.

In addition to guiding the special education teacher, insights gained through evaluation of such records should be shared with the regular classroom teacher. In most instances, similar ideas can be tried in the regular classroom, and the results can be valuable information for the student's permanent record. At the risk of possible overemphasis, we would again point out that these procedures are a matter of planning and organization. To be successful, plans of this type must be carried out systematically with a considerable degree of consistency. Good planning and organization cannot take the place of good overall teaching skills, but they can increase the benefits of such skills in application in the classroom.

MODIFICATIONS IN PRESENTATION, RESPONSE, AND EVALUATION

Three important areas of consideration when dealing with disabled/handicapped students are (1) how the curriculum is presented, (2) how students are required (or permitted) to respond, and (3) how their efforts are evaluated. Modifications in these three areas require advanced planning to be successful, and some require a degree of organization not possessed by all teachers. We will outline a few such modifications to illustrate the degree of planning and organization involved and to suggest the type of modifications that may be effective. All of these suggested modifications will permit wider application, and our experience indicates that *all* curricular areas and *all* grade levels are subject to some useful modification. The two major factors are the teacher's knowledge of such practices and willingness to try something new and different—in other words, willingness to "think" in terms of modifications and adaptations of standard practices and procedures.

Modifications in Curriculum Presentation

Curriculum presentation tends to be "standardized" by subject or skill area and by grade level, but teachers develop their own style of presentation, which may be related to how they were taught or the instructional materials available in their school district or building. In addition, they are influenced by their own unique abilities or specialized training, how they plan to later evaluate student progress, how they think *they* will be evaluated by their principals or other administrators, and a host of other variables. Presentations may include various combinations of lectures (particularly at the secondary level), group projects, use of films or videotape, individual reports (either oral or written), library assignments, or a host of other teaching/learning approaches. Teachers do change their methods through the years, and some teachers may be so open to trying new approaches that they do not give the "old" approach a proper tryout. But it appears that many, perhaps most, teachers tend to have established ways to teach the various subjects or skills they are assigned to teach and tend to follow these ways rather consistently. That is certainly logical if these methods have proved to be effective for them.

But what of the student who does not learn efficiently, using the "standard" methods of curriculum presentation? Certainly, in some cases, other methods or modes of presentation may be no more effective. But to know whether they may be, they must be tried. Modifications of curricular presentation are particularly likely to be of value with some disabled/handicapped students and may include the ones in the following list or many others.

1. The full content of reading assignments may be presented on tape.
2. The content of reading assignments may be condensed and presented on tape.
3. Selected parts of the curriculum may be provided through the efforts of peer tutors.
4. Reading materials may be modified through color coding, underlining, or other methods of emphasizing certain essential parts of a lesson. Often one goal of such procedures is to teach the student how to do them for himself in the future.
5. An *outline* of material to be presented in class (through lecture or demonstration, for example) may be prepared and given to the student in advance. It might be provided on tape, in simplified written form, by peer tutor, and so on.
6. Technical vocabulary or other unusual words derived from lessons to be given in the near future may be explained in advance of the student's actually reading or otherwise taking part in such lessons. They may be provided in a variety of modes and might involve emphasis on understanding meaning of words, how to recognize (read) them, or whatever is appropriate to a given student's individual needs.
7. For classes in which a good deal of lecture or extended demonstration-and-lecture is used, the student may be provided with lecture summaries, either in advance or through use of a "buddy" or "partner."

In presenting the curriculum in a modified manner, the goal in all cases is *to provide instruction in a manner that increases the likelihood that the student will learn more efficiently*. This goal should be the intent of all teaching, but teaching to *groups* of students has led to the development of effective *group* methods that are not always effective with individuals. Disabled/handicapped students do not require modified curriculum presentation at all times for all skills and subjects, but when modification is required, it is highly important. Most teachers would not attempt to teach deaf students through purely auditory methods or blind students with printed materials, but they do not always see that there are comparable situations with respect to learning disabled, mentally handicapped, or behaviorally disordered students. Given this understanding and ideas as to how curriculum presentation can be modified, many teachers can and do provide instruction in a manner that enhances the learning of handicapped students.

Modifications in Accepted Modes of
Response to Class Assignments

Preparation of class assignments may often be a problem for disabled/handicapped students. The teacher may have multiple objectives with respect to required assignments; for example, in a social studies class a written assignment related to the process of electing public officials might have the following goals: (1) to develop skills in reading a variety of materials and understanding the major, critical issues; (2) to develop library research skills; (3) to develop the ability to summarize information; (4) to develop the ability to organize information in a logical sequence; (5) to develop/demonstrate grammatic, spelling, or other similar skills; and (6) to expand reading vocabulary. With disabled/handicapped students, some of these goals may be very difficult owing to the nature of the handicapping condition. At the very least, some may be so difficult that, if they remain a critical goal, others may not be attainable. Therefore, certain modifications in the permitted response mode may be necessary. The following modifications might be appropriate in certain circumstances:

1. The student may be permitted to complete certain assignments by developing his or her thoughts on tape.
2. The student may be permitted to respond to the assignment orally, to peers.
3. The student may be provided a simplified outline to guide written responses, and responses may be made in single words or short phrases.

In these or other mode-of-response modifications, certain instructional goals are by-passed, or given much less priority, so as to make it possible for the student to achieve goals that are determined by the instructor to be more important. It is a matter of making acknowledged "trade-offs," and without such trade-offs some disabled or handicapped students will not reach any of the desired goals. As with all other modifications, it is essential to plan ahead so that special equipment that may be required is available. Teachers must think ahead on a daily basis—what is needed for all special-needs students today (projector, tape recorder)—and on a weekly, monthly, or unit basis—what additional materials, alternate books, and so on, are needed. Specialists must help regular classroom teachers to be organized and must assist them in planning for special needs far enough in advance that regular class teachers are not unduly rushed or burdened.

Modifications in Evaluation
Procedures

Although the two types of modification we have mentioned so far require a great deal more time and effort on the part of the teacher, the question of modifications in evaluation may be the most difficult in the mind of the teacher. For some teachers it is a matter of professional ethics, and modifications in evaluation procedures may be viewed as a "lowering of academic standards." In thinking through the ethics of the matter, it may be of value to consider the situation of the blind student who is not asked to complete all work in handwriting and is, for example, often permitted to respond on tape, without penalty in evaluation. *If* we accept the disability or handicap of the student who is learning disabled, behavior disordered, or mentally handicapped as real, then the same philosophy could apply. The major question often relates to assignment of grades, and we know of no single, well-accepted practice in this regard. Various modifications of grading systems have been used, including the use of "credit" or "n.c." (no credit), or subscripts or superscripts added to letter grades. There may be nearly endless variations, and the best one to use is the one that is best accepted in a given school system. But in addition to this question, there is the matter of how to give tests or use other evaluative instruments. Certain modifications have been used with some success, including the following:

1. Tests may be modified as to the number of questions asked.
2. Tests may be modified through simplification of the wording of questions.
3. Tests may be given on tape, and/or students may be permitted to answer on tape.
4. Test questions may be presented orally (peer tutor or other), and oral responses may be permitted. (These may be taped for later evaluation.)
5. Combinations of 1, 2, 3, and 4 above, or other similar ideas.

The question of how to test is interrelated with the problem of how to assign grades, and the entire matter will likely continue as a source of difficulty for years to come. However, there are certain ideas that have been useful in various settings, including the following*:

1. When scoring a student paper, emphasize the positive aspects. Attempt to point out something the student did well.
2. Consider providing "prompts" or "cues" to students who have predictable difficulties. By providing cues, the teacher is rephrasing the question in such a way that students may understand. This is *not* "giving the students the answer."
3. Accept student errors. Provide feedback as to what they did incorrectly, but use the test as a teaching tool, not as punishment.
4. At the beginning of each term, give a "free grade." Record an A in every student's folder or in your grade booklet. (This applies to *all* students, not just those with disabilities.) This procedure may have very positive effects for a student who has never received an A. It serves as a strong motivational tool, and students may work diligently to maintain high grades.
5. Consider giving a test more than once. If we really want to know more about students' basic skills, or how much they have learned, we must often test more than once.
6. Utilize an advanced-warning system. Four or five weeks before the end of the term, meet with the student and tell her what her final grade will be. If it is low, give her several alternatives through which she may be able to earn a higher grade.

*Adapted from Gearheart and Weishahn, *The Exceptional Student in the Regular Classroom* (St. Louis: C. V. Mosby, 1984), p. 334–35.

7. Initiate joint planning with the student regarding the relative value of course assignments. The student may want to place greater emphasis on some special project (for example, for one-half of her grade), with lesser emphasis on examinations and class participation.

8. Allow time for teacher-student discussion concerning evaluation alternatives and student self-evaluation.

9. Establish evaluation/grading guidelines and/or agreements *in writing.*

It is important to note that although some of the preceding modifications can be provided in haste (with little specific planning), to be effective, planning and preparation are essential. For example, giving a student a different time frame for completing a lesson or assigning fewer problems require careful consideration. If not, program adaptations and modifications may be effective only in that they teach the student that he can get by with less effort than other students, or the selection of questions may by-pass some of the most critical skills. Willingness to modify is important, but willingness to take time to plan carefully and prepare modifications is much more important.

COMMUNICATION

We will consider one final area in which planning and organization play a major role. That is the area of communication. This includes, but is not necessarily limited to, communication with parents, communication with other teachers who work with handicapped/disabled students, and communication with the students themselves. Organization for better communication requires many of those aspects we already considered in this chapter, such as keeping adequate records, but our specific concern in this discussion is that teachers should *schedule and carefully plan* meetings with parents, with other teachers, and with students. The meetings with parents and other teachers can involve many topics but certainly would involve reporting on student successes or areas where there has been little success and on areas where joint efforts may pay bigger dividends. Such meetings should also include a variety of opportunities for parents or other teachers to provide information and make suggestions. If a number of such meetings are scheduled in advance and follow a structured format, parents and other teachers will more likely believe that they are important. In addition, it should be made clear to these important other adults in the student's life that any time they feel the need to talk about student progress, problems, or whatever, you (the teacher) are ready to arrange a conference.

As for the students, even though the teacher may work with them daily, there should be regularly scheduled "conferences" in which the teacher shares oral evaluations. These should relate to the goals the student knows have been established and should be as positive as possible. (For example, it is more positive to say, "You got fifty-six arithmetic problems right this week," than to say, "You missed twenty-four arithmetic problems this week.") So much has been said and generally accepted about the importance of communication that we may become insensitive to its real significance. But even given sensitivity to its importance, some teachers appear to communicate primarily as it is convenient or as the situation makes it essential to communicate. Of course, all communication is important, but our emphasis here is on *planning and organizing* for communication. This means planning regular times (time of day, days of the week, or intervals within the quarter or semester), what will be discussed, and how the topic will be approached and presented. Various systems have been used to ensure regular communication, such as one meeting (with other teachers) per day at an established time, with an outline of major topics to be covered. The use of an outline (as a general guide) helps make certain that important points are covered and that conferences do not turn into social visits. It increases the ability of the specialist to apply self-monitoring, to be certain that established conference goals are met. Teachers from whose classes the special-needs students were assigned may be scheduled on a revolving basis, with schedules established for several weeks in advance.

The proper conduct of parent conferences has been a topic of concern since such conferences became popular (some thirty to forty years ago, depending on geographics), and many larger school districts have comprehensive guidelines for parent-teacher conferences. However, some do not make specific provision for cases in which the student has both a regular class assignment and a special education, resource-room assignment. The one rule that should be applied in nearly all cases is that if the specialist schedules a conference with the parents, the regular classroom teacher should be invited to participate and should be made to feel really wanted. (There are "invitations" that are merely a polite formality and real invitations; this invitation should be the latter type.) In some cases the regular classroom teacher really doesn't want to participate, and in such cases they should at least be asked for input, via records or materials to be reviewed or comments that should be made. A joint conference is usually best, since the topics of concern—the student's academic and social performance, what can be done to more effectively accomplish educational goals, how to work jointly in the student's behalf—relate to *one* student, not to a student in the regular classroom and to another in the special education resource room. Established school-district policies must be followed, but if there are no special policies on joint conferences, there should at least be some written agreement as to how to proceed at each local school.

Regardless of written local policy for conferences, certain commonsense suggestions apply to this highly important communicative process. The following are among the more important:

1. *Prepare for the conference.* Have pertinent records, student papers, test results, and so on, in the order in which you intend to present them and in a separate folder.
2. *Make certain that what you say and the data you present are consistent with what will appear on the written report card.* Parents have a legitimate gripe when they hear one thing in the face-to-face report and read an altogether different thing in the written report.

3. *Arrange a private setting for the conference.* Other teachers walking in and out of the area can have a disastrous effect on an otherwise fruitful meeting.

4. *Start the conference on a positive note.* Don't "hit" the parent with a lot of negative information. Surely there is something positive that can be said.

5. *Plan in advance a number of verbal cues that will encourage the parents to make contributions.* Elicit suggestions from the parent whenever possible and delay most of your suggestions until at least midconference, unless they are required by direct questions from the parents.

6. *Plan together for the next cooperative steps on behalf of the student.* Experienced teachers learn a number of ways in which they may ask for and receive parent cooperation. Even though the same things may be suggested in 90 percent of the conferences, they are old only to the teacher. Parents do not often contact all other parents to see what the teacher has suggested to them.

7. *Establish a time limit at the start of the conference and stick with it.* If several conferences are scheduled on the same day, allow at least fifteen minutes between conferences to (a) briefly summarize what was discussed and what was decided in the conference, and (b) get out the materials and be ready for the next conference.

In conducting the conference, be aware of your language and its affective impact. There are many ways to convey your thinking, and the more positive expressions are usually better. A few examples of such alternative expressions are given in table 11-2.

It would be difficult to overemphasize the importance of communication and planning to make it more effective. It is at the very core of successful integration of the educational program as implemented by the regular classroom teacher and special instruction as provided by the specialist. Without such communication, teachers, parents, and students are losers.

TABLE 11-2   Watch Your Language—Suggestions for More Positive Expressions

WHAT YOU MAY BE THINKING	A MORE POSITIVE EXPRESSION*
Uncooperative	Should learn to work with others
Lazy	Should learn to try harder
Selfish	Has difficulty sharing with others
Stubborn	Always wants to have his own way
Cheater	Too often depends on the work of others
Wastes time	Should learn to make better use of time
Show off	Needs the attention of other students
Trouble maker	Often disturbs others in class
Steals	Takes things that belong to others
Sloppy	Should learn to do neater work
Rude	Should learn to respect the feelings of others

*When the teacher uses the more positive expression, parents at times may suggest the more negative label. However, it is then they who are "labeling" the student. In most cases, the same point can be made with the more positive expression, with less risk of causing direct offense, or anger, on the part of the parent. It is much better to describe the behavior or make suggestions for positive change than to apply labels.

With such communication, small problems can be solved before they are out of control, misunderstandings can be more easily resolved, and everyone benefits.

SUMMARY

Specialists who teach handicapped/disabled students and assist the regular classroom teachers to more effectively teach these students must be aware of a wide variety of instructional methods and techniques. They must be fully aware of the variation in needs of individual handicapped/disabled students and must be able to assess students, develop hypotheses, try out alternative approaches, and evaluate the effectiveness of such approaches. To accomplish these goals, teachers must learn to *organize* for instruction so as to make more efficient use of both student and teacher time.

In this chapter we have reviewed various physical aspects of the learning environment that are under the control of the teacher. These are among the easiest aspects of instruction for the teacher to organize and manage, but too often teachers do not utilize them to their fullest. For example, seating and grouping of students can be modified to meet a variety of goals, but many teachers seem to be unaware of the possibilities. In a similar manner, student and teacher materials may be organized so as to facilitate instruction by maximizing the time available for active learning, or as in some classrooms, students may spend 15 to 20 percent of their school day waiting to get a new assignment, waiting to talk to the teacher, waiting to have their work graded, and so on.

In addition to these physical aspects of the learning environment, there is the matter of how teachers organize their actual teaching tasks. A number of areas in which better organization can facilitate the teaching/learning process were outlined in this chapter. These included ideas relating to preacademic-year planning, deliberate planning for change, and maintaining records that permit evaluation of instructional goals. Modifications in presentation and the mode of response permitted from students and to means and methods of evaluation were also covered.

Finally, it was noted that effective communication is the element that permits optimum use of all other elements of the instructional program. For effective communication, it is essential that regular conferences or meetings be scheduled in advance and that guidelines for the agenda of such meetings be established. They may be made to appear or "feel" informal, but without planning and organization, they will be less than optimally effective.

REFERENCES

GALLAGHER, P.   *Teaching Students with Behavior Disorders: Techniques for Classroom Instruction.* Denver: Love Publishing Co., 1979.

GEARHEART, B., AND M. WEISHAHN.   *The Exceptional Student in the Regular Classroom.* St. Louis: C. V. Mosby, 1984.

LUND, K., L. SCHNAPS, AND S. BIJOU.　Let's take another look at record keeping. *Teaching Exceptional Children* 15 (spring 1983), 155–59.

MARSH, G., B. PRICE, AND T. SMITH.　*Teaching Mildly Handicapped Children: Methods and Materials*. St. Louis: C. V. Mosby, 1983.

SPAULDING, R.　Relationships of inservice training to classroom teaching models, management styles, and student achievement. Paper presented at the American Educational Research Association Annual Meeting, Boston, 1980.

CHAPTER TWELVE

Trends and Issues

- Which issues in special education are primarily political and philosophical, as opposed to "researchable"?

- How are technological change and the approaches and techniques spawned by such change affecting education of the handicapped?

- How may the accountability movement affect education of the handicapped?

- What modifications should be made in minimum-competency requirements (at the state level) as they relate to handicapped students?

- How are remedial and special education alike? How are they different? What one factor may tend to keep them separate?

- To what extent are the major issues in education of the handicapped interrelated? What influence does any such interrelatedness have on the search for adequate resolution of these issues?

Many trends and issues have been discussed throughout this text; some will be highlighted in this closing chapter. Trends and issues are closely related, with attempts to resolve issues often leading to new trends. One major example of this principle has been concern with reading approaches over the past seventy-five years. The issue—how to improve reading; the trend—some new (for that time) approach. Educators have vacillated between phonics-oriented approaches and whole-word approaches, or some combination of these approaches, for decades. Each time a new trend develops, it evolves into an issue, and another new trend eventually takes its place. This is noted not as a criticism of the process but rather as a statement of fact. In this chapter we will focus primarily on issues, but in so doing we will also consider trends for the reasons just outlined.

According to Ysseldyke and Algozzine, in the concluding chapter of their text *Critical Issues in Special and Remedial Education* (1982), "The critical issue in special and remedial education seems to be the demand for instant, simple solutions to incredibly complex problems" (p. 256). We agree with this basic idea and further agree that "we have not only demanded *the* programs (that will solve all our problems), but we have given them widespread use without examining our assumptions and/or requiring evidence of the safety or efficacy of the interventions" (p. 257). Given this belief, we will attempt to state issues clearly so as to provide a point of focus for further consideration, hypothesis, and investigation. In some instances, we will also make suggestions as to cautions and guidelines that should be considered in approaching these issues.

THE NATURE OF SPECIFIC
CATEGORIES OF HANDICAPS
AND DISABILITIES

This text is in part based on the assumption that there are categories of handicaps or disabilities that may be appropriately called mental retardation, learning disability, or behavioral disorders. Given the special education regulations relating to Public Law 94-142 and the regulations of the majority of the states, these categories exist, even though they may be expressed in slightly different language in different parts of the nation. The issue in the minds of some is, "Are they real, specific, and individually discrete?" This question is particularly important when we consider mild or moderate levels of mental retardation, learning disability, or behavior disorder.

Part of the difficulty and the resultant debate relate to the manner in which we have attempted to define each condition so that it can be identified as separate or different from other conditions. This need has not been viewed as so significant with respect to, for example, blindness and deafness. We have readily recognized that an individual can be visually impaired and hearing impaired, for these two conditions involve two sensory systems that are undeniably separate. But with mental retardation, learning disabilities, and behavior disorders, we are dealing with how a student behaves (social behavior, academic behavior), how the central nervous system and what we have called the mind processes and relates to information, and the resultant actions (behavior) of the human organism. Our interpretation of this behavior is based on incomplete, primarily unverified hypotheses about learning, and thus conclusions must be tentative. However, for legal purposes of "identifying" students for special educational services, we must make decisions that are often given the aura of absoluteness. At present, in most states we must decide that John Jones or Mary Smith *is* mentally retarded, learning disabled, or behavior disordered. Most of the pertinent regulations indicate that we must decide on the "primary" disability, that is, which disability is the major contributor to the student's need for special educational services. This, in and of itself, indicates the belief that these are conditions that are separately verifiable.

As implied in earlier discussion, the question may not be so difficult when we are dealing with *severe* levels of these three conditions. However, the great majority of the students who are presently receiving special education services in the public schools are those with mild-to-moderate levels of disability—the levels that lead to confusion with respect to correct identification. This issue of the existence of specific categories is a major one, with ramifications for assessment, educational programming, funding, and in fact, almost all aspects of what we provide in the way of educational programming and how we provide it. We have not attempted to make specific recommendations regarding a solution to this problem but would recommend that in looking for solutions, teachers attempt to remain highly flexible, including the consideration of some entirely new way(s) of analyzing the issue. In the meantime, given the lack of consensus, we recommend continuing special educational programming for students with apparent special needs, with minimum emphasis on categorical labeling, and with maximum emphasis on efforts to provide individually planned and tailored programs.

ASSESSMENT TOOLS AND TECHNIQUES

This issue is obviously highly interrelated with the question of the existence of specific categories of disabilities and handicaps. It is also related to other issues, such as how learning takes place and the value of various approaches. The validity and reliability of various assessment tools have been of concern to psychologists and assessment specialists since the beginning of the efforts to measure various psychological, sociological, and educational characteristics of students in our schools. This issue has been discussed in some depth in chapter 2, and suggestions of more promising and acceptable procedures were outlined there. Broadly speaking, the issue may be subdivided into two major areas: (1) assessment to determine type or category of disability and (2) assessment to provide guidance for intervention. Some tests may be used for both purposes, but others are primarily for either identification or program (intervention) planning.

Tests and other assessment techniques (such as, for example, systematic observation of student performance in a controlled-learning setting) have been shown to be subject to various degrees of bias, based on factors such as racial or ethnic background, a student's previous experience, personal motivation, language differences, and sex expectation of assessment personnel. Various court cases have led to decisions that many tests used in special education are unacceptable, yet we must assemble data on which to base decisions about how to most effectively assist students. Until the issue of categories is solved so that identification by category is no longer required, we must gather data that will permit a decision as to whether any given student "fits" one of the special education categories. Otherwise we cannot receive essential special education reimbursement from state and federal governmental sources. The issue is a major one, multifaceted, and despite the expenditure of a great deal of effort and millions of dollars, it remains critical and unsolved. We can explain the difficulty by noting that we are attempting to measure quantities and qualities that are nebulous and ill defined in subjects (human children) who are unbelievably complex. But the issue remains and likely will remain for some time.

The question of appropriate assessment to provide guidance for intervention strategies is a separate issue from that of assessment to determine eligibility for such services. Even if the tests in use were valid and reliable, even if we were certain we could avoid bias related to those completing the assessment, and even if there were *no* special education "categories," there would remain the question of which tests measure those characteristics, processes, or abilities that are most important to effective intervention. The questions in this issue relate to the nature of the learning process and those factors or influences that inhibit this process.

Commencing at an extremely simplistic level we might say: "So we can determine a student's height and weight with a fair degree of certainty; so what?" "So we can determine whether he can spell as well as, better than, or less well than other third-grade students; so what?" "So we can convert this spelling ability/skill/knowledge (or whatever) to grade equivalents, to percentile scores, or other objective representations; so what?" "So we can determine his visual discrimination ability; so what?" In actuality, all of these measures and many more are a part of the assessment we undertake with many students. But even if they can be measured through the use of valid, reliable instruments, there is the question of whether the quantity and quality they measure is important. The various issues surrounding assessment tools and techniques are indeed troublesome, and their resolution depends upon a variety of variables such as the one that is the topic of discussion in the following section.

HOW DO CHILDREN LEARN?/WHAT FACTORS INHIBIT LEARNING?

The question of how "normal" learning takes place, which is important to special educators primarily because they need to determine what factors may be inhibiting learning, may be partly resolved, but for the most part it is still a major issue. We might say partly resolved (though some would disagree) in that, for example, we know that most children need to experience a broad range of spoken language to be able to learn and develop adequate spoken language. This seems to be relatively well established through observation of deaf children who do not experience a broad range of spoken language and thus have considerable difficulty in developing adequate language. Similarly, in those very few cases where some child is *severely* deprived environmentally with respect to language experience, there is an effect on learning. Further, we know that children who score very low on individual tests of intelligence do not develop language as effectively as most of those who score average or above on the same tests of intelligence. Therefore, we conclude that experience with a broad range of language and normal or above intellectual ability (as we now measure intellectual ability) are important factors in learning language.

But what about children with normal hearing, normal mental ability, and normal "exposure" to language who do not learn normally? How and why is their language learning inhibited? What are the factors that lead to their learning difficulties? What types of assessment will provide information as to what to do to remediate such difficulties? The bottom line is, *How do children learn?* Though we know some of the factors that are essential to normal learning, there are some we simply do not understand. Thus, we must conclude that we may not know enough about learning to effectively intervene in some cases. Hypotheses abound, but established fact remains elusive. This certainly is a major issue that continues to confound special educators.

POLITICAL AND PHILOSOPHICAL ISSUES

Most issues have political and philosophical aspects, but some have more than others. For example, one of the most critical issues is that of the appropriate source of financial support of education. Another is the question of who is responsible to determine the proper scope of public education. These issues apply to all of education, not just special education, but there is much more immediate debate with respect to special education. Education of nonhandicapped students is generally accepted by all fifty states as a state responsibility that is properly theirs and that they *will* meet. However, litigation continues questioning whether local school districts are providing appropriate education for handicapped students. Most of this litigation relates, in the final analysis, to the cost of education and the existence of the Education for All Handicapped Children Act (PL 94-142). The various states certainly would continue many educational programs for handicapped students whether or not Public Law 94-142 was in effect and whether or not there was federal financial support for such programs. However, our experience convinces us that, if the federal law was repealed and all federal support withdrawn, some states would severely curtail such programs. Therefore, the twin issues of who should dictate the scope of education and who should pay for educational programs, especially the higher-cost programs for handicapped students, are highly important to the future of special education.

Another issue that has both political/philosophical aspects and aspects that may be scientifically researched is wrapped up in the very hazy concept of mainstreaming. The idea that all students should remain in the "mainstream" of the school (the regular class) whenever appropriate is one with which most would likely agree. The controversy comes with respect to determining the "whenever appropriate" part of the equation. For some, the concept of mainstreaming is an emotional one—"You *must* leave handicapped students in the regular class *whenever possible*," they might say. For many mildly-to-moderately handicapped students, it might be "possible" to leave them in the regular class at *all* times. But would they be receiving the special help they need? This obviously must be determined on an individual basis, but in the face of highly emotional appeals to "mainstream" students, decisions may be influenced in the direction which will reduce the likelihood of later complaints about too much separate programming. The situation in the mid-1980s is probably more objective than it was at the beginning of the decade, but some misunderstanding may still exist. This is an important issue, and compared to most other issues discussed in this chapter, it is more likely to be satisfactorily resolved in the near future.

The question of accountability in education is an issue that takes very different forms in different states. In some, the move to a required examination before awarding the high school diploma has led to problems for handicapped students. Their modified educational program does not always properly prepare them for such examinations, and even if they could answer the questions at a sufficient level to permit them to pass the exam, the required mode and time limits for taking the exam may lead to failure. If the state does not make special provisions for students enrolled in adapted or modified programs, serious problems may arise.

Some states have made such special provisions; an example is the state of Louisiana. According to Gillespie, an evaluation specialist for the state of Louisiana, the following individualization takes place (Gillespie and Lieberman, 1983):

1. The IEP committee decides whether a given special education student will be required to take the basic skills test. (Such testing starts in grade 2 in Louisiana.)
2. Students not addressing the Louisiana minimum-skills tests in their educational programs are considered to be in an "alternative to regular placement" program. They take separate minimum-standards tests developed by special educators and work toward a certificate of achievement rather than the standard high school diploma. Parents must agree in writing to this alternative plan. This alternative-placement decision is reaffirmed at least annually, and when appropriate, a change back to the regular high school diploma program may be made.
3. For students who may likely be successful in the standard basic skills test but require format or procedural modifications on the test, nine modifications are possible: (a) the test is available in Braille; (b) the test is available in large

print; (c) answers may be recorded by the test administrator (when student is unable to mark his or her own answers); (d) extended time may be permitted; (e) sign language may be used; (f) the student may mark in the test booklet and a test administrator will transfer the answers to an answer sheet; (g) individual administration may be provided; and (h) the math section of the test (but not the language-arts section) may be read aloud to the student.

The most important thing about the Louisiana program is that it specifically recognizes the special needs of disabled and handicapped students and makes a variety of provisions for those needs. Another alternative that might be considered when special provisions are not made is to deliberately "prep" students for the examination. But if the prescribed special education program, which has been established specifically for the needs of a given student, is aborted in favor of an examination-preparatory program, there are a number of predictable effects. First of all, this switch can mean deliberate subversion of the Individualized Educational Program established for that particular student. In such an instance, the "pledge" of the local district and state officials, via local guidelines and a state plan (signed by state officials and accepted and filed in Washington, D.C.) is being ignored. In the case of federal monitoring, or state monitoring of the local district, this could lead to charges of noncompliance. To avoid such charges, we might originally write the IEP so that one major goal is to pass the competency examination, but this would seem to be in contradiction to the spirit, if not the letter, of Public Law 94-142. Most important, if we emphasize practice to pass an exam, as opposed to efforts to assist the student to develop those skills and competencies that comprehensive assessment and lengthy consideration determined to be his or her particular special needs, we are undermining the basic purpose of special educational services.

Though not a major national issue as yet, this has been a legal issue in a few states and could become one in others. Chandler (1984) notes that courts have ruled that "handicapped students can be held accountable for at least modified competency requirements and that they also can be denied a diploma if they cannot pass the same senior year graduation exam which all other students in a state must pass" (p. 61). Special educators in states that have minimum-competency tests must make every effort to establish acceptable alternative provisions for students with specific handicapping or disabling conditions. Otherwise we may be faced with the problem of deciding whether to accept the situation where the special educational program remains meaningful, but the student cannot graduate from high school, or subvert the purposes of special education in favor of a curriculum designed almost exclusively to "pass the exam."

In a separate but related problem, legislators in some states have taken steps to attempt to penalize those school districts that admit to having students at the secondary level who are reading or otherwise achieving significantly below grade level. This is done in the name of "upholding academic standards" and thus increasing the accountability of school officials. Often the idea is that the high school should not be giving high school credit to students doing work that is not of "high school caliber." Penalties may include verbal harassment or in some cases financial retaliation. School officials become understandably paranoid about state-level reprisals against their school districts and as a result do not want to admit that they have special-needs students with such low-skill levels. This dilemma has an obvious negative effect on special programs.

Perhaps the most serious threat to badly needed special programs comes at the classroom level. When schools evaluate teachers on the basis of their students' achievement, with inadequate provisions to recognize the predictably low achievement of handicapped students, teachers may not want to accept low-achieving students in their classrooms. When it comes to possible reprisals that would reduce their pay, teachers are understandably concerned. Accountability in these cases leads to lack of acceptance of low-achieving students, "game playing" to avoid having their scores considered as part of a given class or school, and negative effects on the students concerned. Accountability, in principle, is a good idea. Accountability, in parctice, may be another matter.

LEARNING-STRATEGY INSTRUCTION

One major new instructional trend in teaching learning disabled students and, to a somewhat lesser degree, students with behavior disorders and the mentally retarded is that of learning-strategy instruction. This approach, often called a metacognitive approach, involves deliberate teaching of the skills required to acquire knowledge or information. Learning-strategy instruction involves assisting students to learn how they learn, and in most cases it includes the teaching of specific study strategies. (For example, Sheinker and Sheinker (1983) emphasize the teaching of four specific study strategies: skimming, summarizing, note taking, and outlining.)

A number of researchers, including Flavell (1979), Meichenbaum (1980), and Archer (1979), have established a theoretical base for learning strategy instruction and have provided some practical recommendations for implementation. But this approach remains to be fully verified in practice. Its frequency of mention in professional journals qualifies it as a major trend; it appears to be highly promising, but only time and additional use in a variety of settings will establish its eventual value.

The metacognitive approach, including cognitive behavior modification and various applications of learning-strategy instruction, was highlighted in chapters 3, 4, and 5 and will not be detailed here, but this concept is of sufficient potential value that it deserves special mention in this summary of trends and issues. If it proves to be as valuable as some believe it may be, and if teachers can learn to use this strategy effectively, it may eventually be recognized as having been a major breakthrough in our search for effective instructional methods.

INCREASED USE OF TECHNOLOGY IN SPECIAL EDUCATION

It seems certain that there will be a continuation of the present trend of increased use of technology in education, including applications in special education. In the past, "teaching machines" were utilized with various degrees of success in classes for handicapped students. Technological advances have had their greatest impact on education of the visually impaired and the hearing handicapped and will likely continue to play a major role in these two areas in the future. Technology, particularly in the form of various computer applications, now plays an important role in education of the learning disabled, mentally retarded, and behaviorally disordered—for instance, in the administration of special programs (reports to state officials and miscellaneous record keeping), in teacher training, both preservice and in-service, and in the instructional process. However, all plans that seem to hold great promise do not necessarily receive the needed support to succeed. For example, Gearheart (1973) wrote a short chapter entitled "Just Ask the Computer—a Coming Trend?" This chapter outlined an apparently successful system called Computer Based Resource Units (CBRU) based on the idea that "many more ideas, materials, instructional activities, and procedures are actually available somewhere in the nation than most classroom teachers are able to tap" (p. 138). In this system, effective teaching units, unique activities, and the like, were made available for teachers to "tap" through a statewide system. This system was in place in a number of eastern states, and the idea looked like one that could not fail. But it did not spread to the rest of the nation or even continue to be available in the states in which it originally developed, primarily because of fiscal problems. This was a federally funded project (part of the Special Education Instructional Materials Centers, a national network supported by the Bureau of Education for the Handicapped, U.S. Office of Education), and when the funds were not available, the project did not continue for long. This does *not* mean that all such projects will fail or that federally funded projects are never continued by local or state authorities once the federal funding ceases. It does indicate, however, that such failure or discontinuance is highly possible. It also illustrates another facet of the question of funding outlined on page 317–318 of this chapter.

However, aside from such lessons from the past, the rush of school districts throughout the nation to utilize microcomputers in the classroom in the 1980–85 time period seems to assure that this is a movement that will persist. The major questions seem to be those related to the role and function of microcomputers, questions that will be answered over time. Anderson believes that the microcomputer may be viewed from two angles—as a medium or as a tool. As a medium (their typical application) they "present material, either through tutorials, drill-and-practice lessons, games, or simulations" (Anderson 1982, p. 369). As tools, they are more flexible. Students may be given a freer rein to use computers to solve problems. These might be problems assigned by the teacher or constructed by the student. Anderson believes that students enjoy using computers for a variety of reasons and highlights two that have important educational implications. First, the computer is willing to wait for answers—students have control over the pace of instruction. Second, the computer provides immediate feedback to either their answers (they know if they were right or wrong) or their instructions. And "the computer is not dismayed by their frequent mistakes" (Anderson 1982, p. 369).

In addition to the more ordinarily recognized uses of computer technology, there are a number of less widely recognized uses such as use of the computer and the speech synthesizer in teaching spelling. According to Fisher (1983), in actual use with adults with learning disabilities, certain variations of this approach have been quite effective. As computer technology improves and particularly as additional software is available, there is considerable likelihood that techniques and strategies as yet unconceptualized may prove to be of great benefit to handicapped students.

One aspect of the new technologies available to education is of particular interest to special educators in rural areas. It relates to a greatly increased ability to communicate with other special educators and to gain information from a wide variety of sources that were previously unavailable because of distances. However, in discussing the potential strengths of such technological tools, Hofmeister notes a number of problems and issues, including the following:

1. The fact that we have a considerable potential in the area of technology does not necessarily mean that teachers and administrators will utilize it. Hofmeister (1984) notes that "while our children appear to be adapting quite readily to the hardware of the information age, many administrators, teachers, and teacher trainers do not share their enthusiasm" (p. 347).

2. We must learn the proper balance between electronic and personal contact, which is at present unknown.

3. Financing various technologically advanced programs may be a serious problem; the price of some equipment may be more than the schools are willing to pay.

4. The fact that certain equipment and/or programs are available does not ensure their use.

Although Hofmeister was referring primarily to technological tools, which relate more to communication than to direct instruction, his concerns would seem to be broadly applicable to the question of the use of advanced technology in special education.

The increased use of microcomputers and various other technology in instruction is an established fact in education in the 1980s; special education is no exception. How such technology will eventually be used, what new technology will appear tomorrow, next month, or next year is difficult to predict, and how effective it will be is equally uncertain. There is a possibility that certain technology will be much more effective at one age or academic level than at others. There is a possibility that certain equipment or techniques will be of value (for example) with the learning disabled and not the mentally retarded, or with the mentally retarded and not with students with behavior disorders, and so on. These questions may be answered by 1990 or not till the year 2000, but whatever the answers, the trend is toward much wider use of technology in special education.

"REMEDIAL" EDUCATION VERSUS "SPECIAL" EDUCATION

The issue of whether the special educator's work with many students is "remedial" or "special" education has been debated over the years. The special education category that has been the major subject of this debate has been learning disabilities; however, it might also apply to the mildly mentally retarded and perhaps to students with mild to moderate behavior disorders. This issue was a fairly controversial topic in the early 1970s (about the time that special education for the learning disabled was becoming a very strong national movement) and has been an "on-and-off" topic ever since. One of the earlier references to this concern, which received national consideration, was in an article by Hartman and Hartman (1973) in which it was maintained that there was little, if any, difference between students served by the remedial-reading specialist and those served by the learning disabilities specialist. Part of their reasoning was based on an assumption that the learning disabilities specialist was most concerned with "what's wrong with the child" and did not investigate the child's reading problems.

It is certainly true that prior to 1970 there was much dependence on perceptual training and the remediation of faulty processes, but this emphasis has changed radically, as witnessed by the focus of this text and many others. We might conclude that their concern (lack of attention to reading problems) in the early 1970s cannot be supported today, but the issue remains.

Actually, the issue today is in many ways similar to the issue in 1973. In some schools, the learning disabilities specialist may work with students with the same type and degree of difficulty as those whom the remedial-reading specialist serves in another school. However, in any given school, the learning disabilities specialist may work with students with more severe difficulties than those seen by the remedial-reading specialist. In addition, the learning disabilities specialist is trained to work with disabilities in arithmetic/mathematics, with social disabilities, and others. And the learning disabilities specialist *cannot* serve students unless they have been assessed (following parent approval) and staffed, had an IEP developed for them, and received parental permission for their modified program. There are no similar legal requirements with respect to remedial-reading services in most states. But probably the most significant difference relates to funding. In most states, the local educational agency will receive substantial special state reimbursement, which will pay a significant part of the salary of the learning disabilities specialist. Very few, if any, states provide such support for remedial-reading services. This funding may be the one most important reason why we have "special educators" rather than "remedial educators" in many of the nation's schools.

THE INTERRELATED NATURE
OF VARIOUS ISSUES IN
SPECIAL EDUCATION

It has been noted throughout most of the previous sections of this chapter that the issues that confuse and confound us most are not, in fact, clear-cut, separate issues. We have considered a number of such issues, but in no single discussion were all specifically interrelated. To permit consideration of thirteen such issues in one visualization, they have been summarized in figure 12-1. These are not all of the issues of concern, but careful consideration of these thirteen issues and how they interrelate may be of assistance in better understanding this complex situation. The three issues indicated at the top of the figure, relating to accountability, mainstreaming philosophy, and fiscal responsibility for special education, might be viewed as somewhat different from the other ten. Decisions relating to these three are more likely to be made on a political or philosophical basis and might be made with only limited influence on the other ten. The other ten issues are highly interrelated, as you will see in reviewing them.

In some instances, settlement of one issue in one particular direction "settles" other issues. (For example, if learning disabilities, behavior disorders, and mental retardation are not specific handicaps, issues relating to certification or instruction by category are meaningless.) With respect to the issue of local, state, and federal fiscal responsibility, resolution in the direction of less, or no, federal involvement in the financing of programs for handicapped students would certainly lead to greater variation in how other issues might be settled, but it would be difficult to predict the final result.

In total, the representation of issues provided in figure 12-1 is a fitting way to conclude this text. The concept represented by the figure could be seen as one of uncertainty, confusion, or lack of direction. It could be interpreted to mean that educators of learning disabled, mentally retarded, and behavior disordered students are moving in circles with very limited hope for the future. However, we do not view the situation in that way. There are many questions and unresolved issues; that is a certainty. There is much left to research, much more that we must learn. When we attempt to deal with human learning, we are attempting to deal with what is perhaps the most complex issue confronting humankind. But that is the challenge—that is why the professional field of education of the disabled and handicapped must attract the best minds and the highest levels of motivation and dedication in the field of education. And that is why we have written this book.

What is the proper "mix" of fiscal responsibility of local, state, and federal agencies?

How does cognitive learning take place in non-handicapped students?

How does the concept of normal development stages apply to each of the handi-capping/disabling conditions?

Can "learning styles" be identified which have consistent value in guiding instructional planning decisions?

How does and/or should the concept of cost-efficiency apply to education of the handicapped and/or disabled?

What is the proper balance in advocating "mainstreaming" for the sake of potential values in involvement with nonhandicapped students and in advocating a "special environment" for the sake of specific academic skills?

The issues, questions, and concerns reflected in this figure are highly interrelated. Almost without exception, each has an effect on the rest. In some instances, a major change in just one would result in changes in all of the rest. In most instances, these are not questions or issues which are likely to be "solved" with any certainty in the near future. **The Answers to These Issues, Questions, and Concerns (which May Be Based on Hypotheses, or Dictated by Monetary or Political Pressures) Will Determine Future Trends in Special Education.**

What instructional groupings and other service delivery variables are most effective for the different levels of learning disabilities, behavior disorders, and mental retardation?

How should the concept of accountability as sometimes applied to non-special education be applied to special education?

Are learning disabilities, behavior disorders, and mental retardation discrete, specific handicaps or disabilities?

What are the most reliable, programmatically feasible assessment and identification techniques which apply to these handicaps/disabilities?

What are the influences of cultural differences and cultural deprivation on learning disabilities, behavior disorders, and mental retardation?

How should special education teachers be trained and certified; by category, by degree of disability, or other criteria?

What percentage of the total pupil population should be considered disabled/handicapped? What variations may be expected or predicted with respect to geographical areas, poverty/affluence, and similar factors?

FIGURE 12-1 The Interrelated Nature of Major Issues, Questions, and Concerns in Special Education

SUMMARY

As with any professional field, special education is beset with many issues, concerns, and controversies. Some relate to factors over which we have little or no control and to questions which we may not answer in the next hundred years—or ever. For example, owing to the complexity of what we sometimes call the human mind, we may never fully understand how children learn. We will expand our knowledge in this arena, but such expansion will likely be slow, and our knowledge will remain incomplete. Therefore, as we attempt to develop better strategies to teach students whose learning is atypical, we will do so based on hypotheses and partial information.

In other arenas, such as the question of who should support the financial cost of special education, our solutions will continue to be dominated by political and philosophical considerations. Answers will be "right" or "wrong" depending on the philosophical belief system of the perceiver, on political realities relating to reelection, or on the trade-offs required for passage of some legislative package that may have absolutely nothing to do with special education. Questions relating to "mainstreaming" are also political but have sufficient researchable potential that some resolution, based on hard data, may be achieved. However, decisions about individual students will still be based on clinical (subjective) judgment, which is influenced by philosophy and bias.

Technological advance is with us, and it should lead to more effective instructional efforts with students. With proper guidance from educators who are willing to try new approaches with an open mind, the results of this trend should be very positive. Funding problems will slow some potentially valuable programs and possibly inhibit research, but the eventual result should be good.

A majority of the major issues in special education that relate to education of the learning disabled, the mentally retarded, and students with behavior disorders are highly interrelated. This interrelationship was discussed in this chapter, and a chart illustrating these relationships was provided. As special educators attempt to resolve these issues, it is imperative that the manner in which each of these issues affects the others be carefully considered so that maximum benefit may be achieved from our efforts.

REFERENCES

ANDERSON, D. Microcomputers in education. *Journal of Learning Disabilities* 15 (1982), 368–69.

ARCHER, A. Study skills. In D. Carnine and J. Silbert, *Direct Instruction: Reading*. Columbus, Ohio: Charles E. Merrill Publishing Co., 1979.

CHANDLER, H. Retention: Edspeak for flunk. *Journal of Learning Disabilities* 17 (1984), 60–61.

FISHER, F. Spelling by speech synthesis: A new technology for an old problem. *Journal of Learning Disabilities* 16 (1983), 368–69.

FLAVELL, J.   Metacognition and cognitive monitoring: A new area of cognitive developmental inquiry. *American Psychologist* 34 (1979), 906–11.

GEARHEART, B.   *Learning Disabilities: Educational Strategies.* St. Louis: C. V. Mosby, 1973.

GILLESPIE, E., AND L. LIEBERMAN.   Individualizing minimum competency testing for learning disabled students. *Journal of Learning Disabilities* 16 (1983), 565–66.

HARTMAN, N., AND R. HARTMAN.   Perceptual handicap or reading disability? *Reading Teacher* 26 (1973), 684–95.

HOFMEISTER, A.   Technological tools for rural special education. *Exceptional Children* 50 (1984), 344–49.

MEICHENBAUM, D.   Cognitive behavior modification with exceptional children: A promise yet unfulfilled. *Exceptional Education Quarterly* 1 (1980), 83–86.

SHEINKER, J., AND A. SHEINKER.   *Study Strategies: A Metacognitive Approach.* (Teacher's/trainer's manual.) Rock Springs, Wyo.: White Mountain Publishing Co., 1983.

YSSELDYKE, J., AND B. ALGOZZINE.   *Critical Issues in Special and Remedial Education.* Boston: Houghton Mifflin Co., 1982.

Glossary of Selected Terms

Accountability (in education) The concept that educators must be accountable; that is, there must be measurable evidence that students are being effectively educated. The demand for accountability has received wide attention in recent years with respect to minimum-competency tests that students must pass to be eligible for graduation from high school with a standard diploma.

Adaptive Behavior Reflects adaptation to the environment; is recognized as being difficult to measure and, to some extent, vague. The American Association on Mental Deficiency considers such factors as independent functioning, communication, physical abilities, and economic ability in attempting to assess adaptive behavior. Some might say that social ability, adaptability, and "street behavior" (how well a person can function on the street) are major components in adaptive behavior. Adaptive behavior is an important *concept* in that present definitions of mental retardation require that to be considered mentally retarded, individuals must be retarded in both intellectual measures and adaptive behavior.

ADAPT Method ADAPT is an acronym for the five steps in the "develop-it" method. This method for assisting students to develop needed learning strategies (explained in detail in chapter 3) involves *A*ssessment, *D*isequilibrium, *A*lternatives, *P*ractice, and *T*ransfer: ADAPT.

Alternative Assignments May mean either: (1) assignments planned for the handicapped student that are parallel to the regular assignments but adjusted to the student's special needs; or (2) assignments planned by the special teacher (for the handicapped student) that take into account the fact that the student may require more or less work, at a simpler or a more complex level.

Antisocial Behaviors Behaviors such as hostility, anger, and aggression, which tend to disrupt interpersonal behaviors and thus increase social distance.

Assessment Involves the gathering of valid, reliable, relevant information that may become the basis for decision making. Assessment includes test administration, but it must include much more than test scores to be of maximum value in educational planning and should be an active, ongoing process.

Back-up Reinforcer   The "power" behind token reinforcers. For example, the free time, extra time at the microcomputer, or the candy bar for which token reinforcers may be exchanged. (See *token reinforcers* and *reinforcement* for further discussion.)

Behavior Modification   A technique used to change behavior through the use of reinforcement. Related techniques include operant conditioning, behavior management, contingency management or contracting, behavioral modeling. All are based on the belief that learning occurs as a result of the consequences of behavior.

Blockages   Restrictions or conditions (sometimes imposed deliberately by the teacher) that tend to lead to the student's stopping the problem-solving process. Imposing blockages may force the student to stop and reconsider the process he or she is following.

Brain Damage (or brain injury)   Actual damage of brain tissue. This is a medical diagnosis and cannot be properly made by educators or psychologists. Though it specifies actual damage, at times it may be diagnosed on the basis of a variety of inferential information.

Brain Dysfunction   Indicates suspected malfunctioning of the brain. It is a term of questionable value; but, in fact, a brain or neurological-system dysfunction is inferred when the term *learning disabilities* is used. It *does not* mean that actual damage has taken place, and thus there is the hope that "proper" or "normal" functioning can be restored.

Classification (a)   As applied in special education, means the official decision made by a designated, multidisciplinary committee (often called a staffing committee) that, according to guidelines in existing regulations, a student is learning disabled or mentally retarded or has whatever handicapping condition is diagnosed. At present, classification is a prerequisite to provision of special education services and the state and federal funding that accompanies such services.

Classification (b)   The ability to accurately group objects according to various defined characteristics (i.e., color, shape, size, function). The ability to classify requires an understanding of relationships.

Clinical Interview Technique   A technique developed by Piaget through which teachers may discover how students are arriving at answers or solutions to problems so as to know how to assist them to develop correct processes and meaningful concepts. (A way to determine a student's cognitive structures.)

Closed Search   Involves selecting from among a number of established strategies, based on the knowledge that one of these strategies will work. (See *open search* for contrast.)

Cognition   The process of knowing; the understanding of information. This term is more often used as in "cognitive activity" or "cognitive development," meaning those attempts made by humans to learn, to understand, to relate new experiences to previously developed knowledge.

Columbo Method   A strategy in imitation of the television detective Columbo, who feigned ignorance, acted confused, presented fallacies, and often carried the criminal's explanations to logical, but obviously inapplicable or ridiculous, conclusions. (A method to encourage disequilibrium.)

Constructivist   A term sometimes applied to those (such as Piaget) who believe that cognitive structures are "constructed" upon earlier cognitive structures and that new developmental stages integrate with, and transform, previous knowledge. It may be seen as essentially synonymous with *developmentalist*.

Contingency Contracting   Establishing, through a written contract, that certain events will follow specific behaviors. The "contingency" is the relationship between the behavior and the event that follows. This is a type of behavior modification.

Countersuggestions   Part of the ADAPT technique, countersuggestions are specific suggestions provided by the teacher that *conflict* with a student's explanation of how to think about or solve a task. They are used by the teacher to determine whether a student understands the conflict between explanations.

Creative Writing   See *expressive writing.*

Cross-Categorical   A term applied to classes, programs, or services that are provided or applied "across" categories of handicaps or disabilities; that is, to groups of students who have been classified as having different handicaps or disabilities. This term is presently used in a variety of ways, but all indicate some type of crossing of categorical boundaries.

Cueing Strategies   Plans designed to assist students to develop personal awareness of how to learn, solve problems, and carry out tasks. Cueing strategies may be divided into two major types, perceptual cueing strategies and language cueing strategies. Each of these two types may be used alone, or they may be used together.

Developmentalist   One who subscribes to developmental theory. See *constructivist.*

Disequilibrium (see also *equilibration*)   A condition in which the student understands that his or her concepts and/or strategies do not match with current experience. With such understanding, it is expected that most learners will try to keep their ideas in balance with their experiences. Without disequilibrium, there is little motivation to change or learn.

Due Process   As applied in special education, refers to the various procedures required by federal regulations (related to Public Law 94-142) and state regulations, which are designed to assure fair treatment and protection of student and parent rights in provision of services to handicapped students.

Dyscalculia   A historic term for unusual disabilities in mathematics, often assumed to be related to neurological impairment.

Elaborative Strategies (or approaches)   Strategies such as drawing inferences, the use of self-questioning, utilizing open-ended questions, or developing self-generated examples, as strategies for problem solving. (For contrast, note the description of mechanical strategies or approaches.)

Empathy   The ability to share another person's emotional responses; the mediator of prosocial acts. Empathy has a cognitive component (comprehending the social situation) and an affective component (emotional responsiveness which permits "matching" another person's feelings and emotions).

Equilibration (see also *disequilibrium*)   A concept accepted by most developmental theorists based on the idea that progress through the developmental steps or stages is enhanced by a process through which the individual brings disturbing or conflicting elements in the environment into balance or equilibrium. The different theorists (for example, Freud and Piaget) would view the basic *reasons* for conflict, tension, or disequilibrium somewhat differently, but each would suggest that learning takes place as children must regularly reestablish "balance."

Error Analysis   A system through which errors are reviewed and analyzed in the belief that systematic error patterns may underlie students' performance. In mathematics (for example) this might mean the examination of computational responses and a classification of errors as the basis for making instructional decisions.

Expressive Writing   Expanding on some given theme; expressing personal feelings and interpretations; a form of writing which encourages the use of both convergent and divergent thinking (contrast with *functional writing*).

Extinction   Abruptly removing a positive reinforcer that is maintaining certain behavior. Used when inappropriate behavior is being reinforced by certain identifiable factors.

Functional Writing (sometimes called utilitarian writing)   Writing with the express purpose of conveying meaning. Requires an understanding of the target audience and usually relates to very specific objectives. (Contrast with *expressive writing*.)

Holistic Assessment   Assessment based on a developmental perspective that emphasizes consideration of the functional relationships among the wide variety of factors that may affect a student's academic and social behavior, as opposed to a more atomistic view, which is primarily concerned with discrete behaviors. This approach also emphasizes how children think and how they acquire new knowledge.

Impulsive Responding   As applied to students' responses in academic settings (for example, recognition of some word in a reading passage), this means giving an immediate response with no reflection or consideration of such information as context clues, picture clues, or phonetic clues. Impulsive responding is the opposite of reflective responding.

Individualized Education Program (IEP)   A written program plan, required by PL 94-142, which must be developed individually for any student who is determined to be handicapped and in need of special educational services. Very specific elements are required for the IEP.

Internal Language   Sometimes used interchangeably with *inner language*, this is the language of thought; the internal symbolic organization of experiences.

Language Cueing Strategies   One major type of cueing strategy, language cueing involves the use of verbal or language cues to remind students to use a strategy or the steps in a strategy. Language cueing strategies may be used along with the other major type of cueing strategy, perceptual cueing.

Learning-Strategy Instruction   Instruction in various learning skills or strategies; "learning how to learn." May include study skills such as skimming, summarizing, note taking, and outlining.

Mapping Strategies   Involves the development of a "map" of a number of associated ideas that are to be learned. This may include a "central idea," with related ideas radiating out from this center. It appears that some students have more success with mapping if the overall shape of the map relates to the content of the material under consideration. Mapping may take *many* forms.

Mechanical Strategies (or approaches)   Strategies that are related to automatic, routine performance, usually involving a set of memorized steps that may be effective in solving a problem. Students may simply select among these steps or procedures. (For contrast, note the description of *elaborative strategies, or approaches*.)

Mental-Structures Approach (to assessment)   Emphasizes attempts to identify students' thinking and level of response as they perform various tasks. (Also see *holistic assessment*.)

Minimal Brain Dysfunction (MBD)   A somewhat vague term indicating behavior signs of brain dysfunction with no specific, neurological signs. (See also *brain damage* and *brain dysfunction*.)

Minimum-Competency Tests   Usually basic skills tests, required at various grade levels throughout the K-12 school program but with emphasis on tests at the secondary level, which students must pass if they are to graduate from high school with a "standard" diploma.

Mnemonics   Systems or techniques for improving memory. Much perceptual cueing can be properly considered to be mnemonics; may include such things as the use of the word HOMES to remember the names of the Great Lakes (this is an organizing mnemonic).

Modeling   Suggested by the tendency of individuals to model, or imitate, the behavior of others. Reinforcing the modeling of others who exhibit certain desired behavior is a behavior modification technique.

Moral Autonomy (see also *moral heteronomy*)   The second stage of moral development (the first is moral heteronomy), as viewed by Jean Piaget. At this higher level of moral development, the child is aware of differing viewpoints regarding rules, understands that rules may be flexible, and that children should obey rules because they are related to mutual agreements and are based on the rights of others.

Moral Heteronomy (see also *moral autonomy*)   The first of two stages of moral development, as viewed by Jean Piaget, in which children believe that actions are either right or wrong, rules are unchangeable, what is "wrong" is what is punished, and degree of guilt is determined by the amount of damage.

Open Search   This is a problem-solving approach, which may be used when the problem solver is uncertain how to proceed. In this approach, the individual tries out various strategies, based on anything that is known about the problem, then modifies or starts the process all over again, based on results. (See *closed search* for contrast.)

Operant Conditioning   A specific type of behavior modification in which operant (voluntary) behavior is paired with (followed by) consequences designed to increase or reduce that particular behavior.

Perceptual Cueing Strategies   One major type of cueing strategy, perceptual cueing involves the presentation of visual signs or symbols to remind students to use a strategy or the steps in a strategy. Perceptual cueing strategies may often be used along with the other major cueing strategy, language cueing.

Perspective Taking   The ability to assess others' thinking and their needs, to deal with whatever situation is confronting them.

Procedural Errors   Those errors in which students do not follow the appropriate step-by-step procedure for arriving at the correct answer. The type of error frequently made in mathematics.

Procedural Safeguards   As applied to special education, the various steps indicated in both federal and state regulations that school-district officials must follow in the process of assessment, staffing, and possible identification of a student as handicapped. These steps safeguard the rights of both students and parents.

Prosocial Behaviors   Behaviors that draw people together, which assist individuals to respond appropriately to expectations and standards and to handle positive and negative emotions toward others in socially acceptable ways.

Reflective Style   An approach to new tasks in which the individual tends to "stop and think" before proceeding. This is the opposite of an impulsive style.

Reinforcement   Any event or factor that results in the maintenance of, or increase in, any particular behavior. *Primary reinforcers* include food, warmth, and sex. *Conditioned reinforcers* are events or objects that originally were essentially neutral, but have become reinforcers through frequent pairing with primary reinforcers or other strong conditioned reinforcers.

Screening   A procedure designed to identify students for consideration for further assessment, for referral to a medical doctor or optometrist, or for further review. The most commonly utilized screening procedures are applied to determine the need for further consideration with respect to possible problems in visual or auditory acuity.

Self-Instructional Approach   Any system utilized by the student in which some type of "reminder" on how to proceed is utilized. Often involves a series of steps (perhaps remembered through some acronym) that guide the student on to how to proceed. Ideally, such steps should be memorized, but in the early stages students may be guided by the teacher or by a "prompting card."

Service Delivery   The manner in which special education services are to be provided to the student. This may range from a minimal, consultative, or special-materials program to the most restrictive type of service, a twenty-four-hour, residential setting.

Shaping   The reinforcement of behaviors that approximate some desired behavior in an attempt to "move" the student closer to a desired goal. "Shaping" a student's behavior in the direction of some desired behavior is a type of behavior modification.

Social Role Taking   See *perspective taking*.

Staffing   A term used commonly and extensively in some parts of the nation and not so commonly in others. Refers to the multidisciplinary team meeting in which assessment results and all other available information are considered in attempting to determine whether there is an identifiable handicapping condition and what special educational services should be provided.

Student-Centered Environment (or classroom)   Classroom organized for a variety of *student* activities, such as individual learning areas, interest centers, and study carrels, and to facilitate movement from space to space and activity to activity. (This is the opposite of a teacher-centered classroom, which is organized primarily for lecture and a rigid structure.)

Teaching Style   The manner in which a teacher attempts to achieve major instructional goals; most teachers use a combination of styles. Descriptions such as "the discovery teacher," "the lecturer," "the entertainer," and "the role-learning teacher" have sometimes been used to describe teaching style.

Time Out   Includes placement outside the classroom, sometimes in an established time-out room. This behavior modification related procedure is based on the assumption that something in the immediate environment (as in the classroom) is reinforcing inappropriate behavior. Placement outside the environment is designed to remove that reinforcement.

Token Reinforcers   A special kind of conditioned reinforcer, often used in the classroom. (See *reinforcement* for further discussion.)

Underlining Strategies   A perceptual cueing strategy that involves underlining words that convey the main idea of a paragraph or learning unit. Research indicates this to be an effective strategy if it is specifically taught to students.

Utilitarian Writing   See *functional writing*.

Index

A

Abacus, 204
Abikoff, H., 98
Accountability in education, 318–20
Action-oriented projects, 256
ADAPT strategy, 55–73, 79
Addition, 203–6
  of decimals, 215
  of fractions, 213
Affective factors, 192
Alberto, P., 269, 280, 281, 288
Alford, N., 105
Algozzine, B., 10, 314
Allen, C., 126
Allen, R. V., 126
Alley, G., 23, 66, 106, 136, 158, 159
Alternatives, developing, 69–72
Altruistic motivation, 237
Alvarez, M. C., 147
American Association on Mental Deficiency
  (AAMD), 3, 4, 6
American Educational Research Associa-
  tion, 300
Anderson, D., 321, 322
Ankerman, R., 126
Apter, Steven J., 6, 8
Archer, A., 320
Arithmetic, 173
  assessment of needs in, 178–87
  instructional strategies for, 203–9

Arithmetical properties, 173–74
Aronfreed, J., 237
Assessment, 28–48
  in develop-it method, 56–65
  holistic, 41–47
  of mathematical performance, 178–87
  needs-based model for, 32–41
  and perceptual cueing strategies, 78–79
  purposes of, 30–33
  of reading strategies, 118–21
  tools and techniques for, 315–16
Assisted reading, 132
Associative property, 173
Atkinson, R. C., 88
Attention, cueing for, 80–82
Axelrod, S., 273, 280

B

Bachor, D. G., 180, 181
Back-up reinforcers, 274
Bailey, J., 283
Bandura, A., 275
Barenbaum, E., 149
Behavior, language cueing and, 104–6
Behavior management techniques, 264–89
  case studies in application of, 284–88
  to increase existing desirable behaviors,
    271–79
  limited effectiveness of, 288

Behavior management techniques (*cont.*)
to reduce undesirable behaviors, 280–84
terminology of, 268–71
theoretical perspectives on, 267–68
Behavior modification, definition of,
268–69
Belch, Peter J., 13
Bellezza, F. S., 84, 86
Biehler, R., 14, 19, 230
Bijou, S., 303
Biological factors, 222–23
Birch, H., 222
Blackwell, S. L., 80, 81
Blanchet, A., 110
Blau, H., 94
Bley, N. S., 189
Boder, E., 163
Bootzin, R., 283
Bornstein, P. H., 98
Borthwick, S., 5
Bos, C. S., 132–33
Bovet, M. C., 66, 77, 78
Bower, E. M., 7
Brain injury, 9
Brain patterns, 91
Briggs, L. J., 175
Brown, A. L., 77, 138–39
Brown, D., 130
Brown, R. T., 105
Bruner, J. S., 176
Bryan, T., 241, 242
Burns, M., 200, 202
Burris, N. A., 153
Buzan, T., 91, 150

C

Calkins, L. M., 153
CAPE strategy, 87–88
Capelli, C. A., 137, 138
Capitalization, 162
Capps, L. R., 173, 177
Cardinal numbers, 196–98
Carlson, J., 200, 203
Cawley, J., 173, 184–85, 200, 202, 203
Chandler, H., 319
Change, planning for, 301–2
Chess, S., 222
Chomsky, C., 145
Clarizo, Harvey F., 12
Clark, F. L., 139
Class dialogues, 255–56
Classification, 188
Clay, M. M., 145
Clinical interview techniques, 181–87
Closed search, 110, 111
Cognitive behavior modification (CBM), 23,
257–60
language cueing in, 104–6

Cognitive behavioral strategy, 207–8
Cognitive development:
clinical interview techniques and, 181–87
empathy and, 237–38
mathematics and, 176–78, 187–89
moral development and, 233, 237, 238
social development and, 228
theory of, 16–19
Cognitive modeling, 53
Cognitive-processing factors, 189–92
Cognitive-strategies approach, 22–23
Cohen, S. B., 148, 149
Columbo method, 66–68, 71, 182–84
Communication, 308–11
Commutative property, 173, 203–4
Competence, social, 240–42
Composition strategies, 158–59
Comprehension, cueing for, 89–94
Computational strategies, 203–9
for decimals, 215
for fractions, 213–14
Computer Based Resource Units (CBRU),
321
Computers, 321–22
Concrete-operational period, 176
Conditioned reinforcers, 273
Conditioning, 15, 269
Conflict resolution, 252–54
Conoley, Jane C., 6, 8
Conservation, 189
Constitution, U. S., Fourteenth Amend-
ment to, 4
Constructive-fairness approach, 254
Constructivist approach, 19–22
Context strategy, 107
Contingencies, 269–70
Contracts, 277–79
Copeland, R. W., 176
Coping statements, 54
Counting, 196
Covert self-guidance, 53
Craig, P., 12
Craighead, W. E., 258, 270, 275, 276
Crain, William C., 19, 230
Creative projects, 256
Crisis intervention, 246
Criterion-referenced tests, 178, 179
Cross-categorical programs, 12–14
Cueing strategies, 75–94
assessment and, 78–79
for attention, 80–82
for comprehension, 89–94
for memory, 84–89
for motor performance, 83–84
for perception, 82–83
theoretical perspective on, 76–78
See also Language cueing
Cultural-group membership, 223–25
Curriculum presentation,
modifications in, 304–5